The Working Class in American History

Editorial Advisors
David Brody
Alice Kessler-Harris
David Montgomery
Sean Wilentz

D0887093

A list of books in the series appears at the end of this volume.

Men, Women, and Work

Men, Women, and Work

Class, Gender, and Protest in
the New England Shoe Industry,
1780–1910

MARY H. BLEWETT

University of Illinois Press
Urbana and Chicago

Illini Books edition, 1990
© 1988 by the Board of Trustees of the University of Illinois
Manufactured in the United States of America
1 2 3 4 5 C P 5 4 3 2 1

This book is printed on acid-free paper.

Library of Congress Cataloging-in-Publication Data
Blewett, Mary H.
    Men, women, and work.
    (The Working class in American history)
    Bibliography: p.
    Includes index.
    1. Shoe industry—New England—Employees—History—
19th century. 2. Shoe industry—New England—History—
19th century. 3. New England—Economic conditions.
I. Title. II. Series.
HD8039.B72U63   1988   338.4´768531´00974   87-19039
ISBN 0-252-01484-7 (cloth : alk. paper)
ISBN 0-252-06142-X (paper : alk. paper)

I dedicate this book with love and gratitude
to the memory of my father,
Leslie Robert Hedge.

Contents

Acknowledgments

I have many people to thank for their support, interest, and help in the preparation of this book. The long-term support and encouragement of Milton Cantor and Tom Dublin were especially important in sustaining my commitment to this study. I thank Irwin Yellowitz, Linda Henry, Susan Hartmann, Susan Reverby, Helena Wright, Paul Faler, Carole Turbin, Ava Baron, Gary Gerstle, Bruce Laurie, Mari Jo Buhle, Alice Kessler-Harris, and David Montgomery for their useful suggestions and helpful criticism. Student researcher Kristin Szylvian sampled the 1910 Lynn federal census of population for me when my energy flagged. University of Lowell librarians Jill Ellowitz, Susan Klingberg, Joan Ellis, Mary Parlee, Rosanna Kowalewski, Martha Mayo, and Ann Robinson responded to my requests with gracious attention, imagination, and efficiency. The Andrew W. Mellon Foundation, the Wellesley College Center for Research on Women, and the National Endowment for the Humanities gave me crucial financial support during the period of research, and the University of Lowell granted me a sabbatical leave for the period of writing and revision. The timely gift of a word processor from my mother, Eunice V. Hedge, aided immeasurably in the preparation of the manuscript. I also thank my editor, the sharp-eyed and diligent Carol Saller, for her help and courtesy.

The librarians and archivists of Essex County were invaluable in my search for the elusive record of women's involvement in the shoe industry, especially prior to the development of the factory system. I thank the incomparable Irene Norton of the Essex Institute, Kathe Landergan of the Lynn Public Library, Faith McGoon and Janet Lane of the Lynn Historical Society, Richard Trask of the Danvers Archival Center, Mark Simpson of Old Sturbridge Village,

Paul Hudon of the Museum of American Textile History, Howard Curtis and Gregory Laing of the Haverhill Public Library, Mary Barnard of Baker Library, and Harry Miller of the Wisconsin State Historical Society.

I also wish to acknowledge the collections of other institutions whose records on the shoe industry in the nineteenth century were important to this work: the Beverly Historical Society, the Stoneham Historical Society, the Stoneham Public Library, the West Newbury Historical Society, the Middleton Historical Society, the Andover Historical Society, Baker Library, Harvard University, the American Antiquarian Society of Worcester, Old Sturbridge Village, the New Hampshire Historical Society, the Massachusetts State Archives, the Boston Public Library, the Federal Records Center, Waltham, Massachusetts, the New York Public Library, and the Library of Congress. I especially wish to thank Mrs. C. Nelson Bishop of the Reading Historical Society for her assistance and for access to her private collection.

I am grateful to my husband Peter for teaching me much about writing, for sharing the research as well as the joys and sorrows of this project, and for giving me his love and loyalty.

Introduction

This book is a study of the interrelationships among men and women workers as the industrial revolution transformed the New England shoe industry in the nineteenth century. It encompasses the full scope of the slow and uneven process of industrial change from the early national period when shoes were made by hand in kitchens and small shops to early twentieth-century work in electrified shoe factories with minute divisions of fully mechanized labor. Attempts by New England capitalists to dominate the national market for boots and shoes led to this fundamental reorganization of work, while acts of collective resistance by men and women shoeworkers represent one of the most vital traditions in the American labor movement.

Labor historians have neglected the role of these women workers in labor protest and the process of industrialization, but the richness and variety of the evidence disclose a diverse and lively female experience. Hardy, opinionated New England women with strong ideas contended throughout the nineteenth century with each other and with working men over issues of work, family, and protest. During the 1860 strike, shoe stitcher Clara Brown exclaimed to her sister workers: "Oh for God's sake, don't act like a pack of fools!" and her sisters replied vigorously to her in kind. Their angry voices are fully human despite the confines of true womanhood and separate spheres.

But women's place in industrial work must not be seen as simply separate and different but as connected in a systematic and integral way with the male experience of work, family, and labor protest. Historians need to integrate the studies of men and women workers rather than write discrete histories of their experiences and politics.[1] When they do so, a genuinely inclusive history of the making of the American working class can be written.

The experiences of men and women in the New England shoe industry must also be appreciated as a link between the activities of workers in their communities and their role in the regional and national activities of the American labor movement. Beginning with the rebellious artisans in their shops, this labor protest included early forms of female resistance in the 1830s, the unprecedented regional strike of 1860, and efforts to build regional and national forms of organization in the late nineteenth century. This study of gender relations and the regional and national politics of New England shoeworkers is intended to deepen and widen the meaning of class and community.[2]

The historiography of the New England shoe industry has powerfully shaped research and thinking about American labor history. John R. Commons's important 1909 essay on the nineteenth-century patterns of shoe production used labor economics to formulate the early outlines of a new historical field. His students, Blanche Hazard and Don Lescohier, and later John Philip Hall, utilized Commons's conception of the stages of industrial development and focused on the circumstances and responses of Massachusetts shoeworkers. Early historians of women's work Edith Abbott, Augusta Galster, and Helen Sumner began to explore the experience of women involved in the national shoe industry.[3] The influence in the 1970s of British labor historians, especially Edward P. Thompson, on American labor history produced three important studies of the nineteenth-century community life of the shoemakers of Lynn, Massachusetts, by Alan Dawley, Paul Faler, and John Cumbler. These studies in the new labor history emphasized the ideology, social values, politics, religions, and recreational activities of male artisans in preindustrial society, their transformation, and their legacy for industrial workers.

The decade of the 1970s was also a period of rapid development of another field in social history, the study of women's experience, and the introduction of the category of gender into historical analysis. Much of the new labor history assumed that an examination of male culture could stand for the experience of all workers or that evidence on other social groups was sketchy or lost. David Montgomery touched on gender analysis while analyzing the autonomy and manly behavior of late nineteenth-century skilled workers, including shoeworkers, but most historians have ignored the process and implications of gender formation and the sexual division of labor.[4] The use of gender analysis in studying the culture, ideology, and politics of workers is essential in order to understand fully the meaning of the social experience of the American working class. A study of the social and political relationships of the men and women shoeworkers of Essex County, Massachusetts, provides an opportunity to demonstrate the power of gender analysis to enrich the meaning of that experience. While *Men, Women, and Work* concentrates on the changing patterns of production, gender, and protest, it does not attempt to address systematically the responsibilities of women for the work of social reproduction: child rearing and household labor. It follows the admonition to labor historians made by David Brody in 1979 to study "men and women *at work*."[5]

The focus of the new labor history on community life and cultural experience has produced a series of studies of Lynn, New York City, Newark, Philadelphia, and other cities. A community focus, however, neglects regional labor markets and regional systems of production in both preindustrial outwork and in country factories subsidiary to urban industrial centers. Efforts by shoeworkers, male and female, to organize and confront New England capitalists in powerful regional coalitions are lost in a focus on a single community. Also lost are the political relationships of shoeworkers to national movements, such as the National Labor Union, the Knights of Labor, and the American Federation of Labor. To understand and appreciate fully the nineteenth-century response of shoeworkers to shoe manufacturers' attempts to reorganize production, a regional approach is imperative.

The scope of this project rests on the firm groundwork laid by the historians who have examined the experience of male work and culture, but I owe a special debt to the research of Edith Abbott, Helen Sumner, and Augusta Galster as an inspiration to uncover new evidence on the work and cultural experience of women workers. My sources have included diaries, account books, reminiscences, government documents, local histories, statistics of manufacture, vital records, newspapers, and the federal manuscript census of population records for Lynn from 1860 to 1910. In many of these sources, the researcher is fortunate to hear the articulate voice of the New England woman worker, a reflection of her excellent public school education and her expectations of social status and respectful treatment. The culture of New England females enabled them to leave a record so that historians do not have to rely, in Leslie Tentler's words, "on middle-class pens" for information on working-class life.[6]

The trade journals of the industry are a very important source for the changing process of work in shoe factories and for capitalist perceptions of the changing national market. These perceptions led to major decisions to alter the process of production and to develop a vigorous defense of those decisions with an ideology based on the primacy of market forces. Yet significant gaps exist in the primary source material. There are no business records or payrolls for the shoe manufacturers of Essex County. The official records and membership lists of major women's labor organizations such as the Daughters of St. Crispin and the stitchers' assemblies in the Knights of Labor have been lost. Newspaper accounts, convention proceedings, and legislative and arbitration hearings remain as the only surviving record of the important activities of these women's organizations.

The introduction of the sexual division of labor into shoe work late in the eighteenth century in Essex County reshaped the work experiences of men and women. This division of labor survived the transformation of production from the domestic system into factory operations and remained a fundamental social category of work until the early twentieth century. Men and women shoeworkers accepted and defended this division of labor that eliminated competition between them. The nearly total monopoly that women had on stitching shoe uppers in factories led to the development of a hierarchy of skills that gave some women access to the work of vamping, foxing, and other fine stitching processes. The division of labor rewarded the skill and experience of some female industrial workers, which they used to control the work process. Women workers also effectively utilized the monopoly that they had over part of the process of shoemaking for collective resistance. They borrowed cultural resources from gender experience to create justifying ideologies for their labor protest. They organized separately as women, but cooperated with the labor organizations of men.

Female workers in Massachusetts shoe production received the highest wages paid to women industrial workers in the late nineteenth century. They engaged in sustained and persistent labor protest on the community, regional, and national level, developing organizations to represent their interests and arguments to justify their actions. A significant portion of these women workers were geographically mobile, and many were native-born daughters of New England families who represented a continuation after the Civil War of the involvement of Yankee females in industrial work.

Gender experience provided strength in labor protest for women shoeworkers, but also revealed the vulnerabilities in the social position of being female. After the Civil War, shoe manufacturers attempted to alter the division of labor in factory production by introducing women to undercut the wages and skilled work of men. Men and women fought these efforts successfully, but a differential stitching wage for a few male workers remained as an irritating issue for self-supporting women workers.

Efforts of manufacturers to recruit New England women to work in the Essex County industry during the busy seasons of production meant that part of the female work force was mobile and essentially transient. These women were vulnerable to public fears that rootless or homeless females represented a moral danger to community life in ways that were not shared by transient male workers. As women, they faced the need to develop the defensive status of "lady stitcher" to protect their respectability as moral if mobile female workers.

The work experience and labor protest of both men and women shoeworkers were caught up in the changes that reorganized production in the nineteenth century. The strategy of Lynn manufacturers to dominate the post–Civil War national market transformed the nature of work. They justified their actions and the new relations between employer and employee by evoking the impersonal forces of supply and demand in the marketplace. To oppose these arguments, shoeworkers called on the equal rights tradition that defended workers' rights and their control over work. Equal rights had, however, different meanings for men and women and different implications for active involvement in political life. Gender experience shaped both the ideology and politics of labor protest.

Gender experience also had different meanings to various groups of women workers. The distinct social roles of men and women in family life, especially the different contributions of men and women to the family economy, caused serious divisions among women shoeworkers. Women outworkers were often divided and isolated from each other and submerged in family life. Women who continued to work at home after the introduction of mechanization and the factory system identified their interests with those of the family rather than with the young women who stitched on machines in factories. Unmarried or widowed women and female heads of families who worked in post–Civil War shoe factories needed to support themselves and often supported dependents. They saw themselves in conflict with the wives and daughters in male-headed families with whom they competed for work. Marital status and differing roles in the family economy fractured the unity of women shoeworkers. Nineteenth-century categories of gender shaped the class experience of workers in powerful ways: most importantly by the division of labor in production, in the family economy, and in the strategies, ideology, and politics of labor protest.

The organization of this book follows the outlines of the involvement of women in shoe production, beginning with the implications of the introduction of a sexual division of labor into the craft of shoemaking. Chapter 1 explores the ways in which gender formation and the shoemaking craft were preserved as artisan families recruited their women into household production as contributors to the family labor economy. Chapter 2 analyzes the movement of women's work out of the family labor system onto the wage labor market and the circumstances that prompted and defeated early labor protest in the 1830s by women outworkers in Essex County. Chapter 3 investigates the outwork system in the late 1830s and 1840s and the ways in which women's responsibilities in the family shaped their domestic ideology and their lives as outworkers. Chapter 4 considers the ideological, political, and economic positions of women workers in the context of important labor protest by male artisans in the 1840s. Chapter 5 represents an analysis of the early factory and the controversial role of women shoeworkers in the regional shoe strike of 1860, the most significant expression of collective protest by American workers before the Civil War and an open challenge to the development of the factory system.

Differences in gender experience continued to shape the work, culture, and protest of shoeworkers in the late nineteenth century. Chapter 6 discusses the rapid industrialization of shoe production in the post–Civil War years and the response of men and women shoeworkers as Knights and Daughters of St. Crispin to attempts by manufacturers to alter the sexual division of labor and change the relationships between capitalist and worker. Chapter 7 analyzes the defeat of the Crispins during the depression of 1873 and the ideological, political, and social divisions among women shoeworkers that underlay the decline of women's involvement in Crispinism. Chapter 8 reveals the significant role of men and women shoeworkers in the district and national organizations of the Knights of Labor and the transformation of a defensive ideology based on the assumed status of lady stitcher into a means to unite and empower women workers. Chapter 9 explores the involvement of men and women in two important shoe strikes in 1895 and 1903, the first of which led to the organization of the national Boot and Shoe Workers' Union and the second of which signaled the abandonment of the new union by the shoeworkers of Essex County. The association of the BSWU leadership with the American Federation of Labor and an association with the Women's Trade Union League in 1903, important for women workers, led to a divergence between the militant traditions of women shoeworkers in Essex County and attempts to organize women into the AFL. This separation meant the loss of a valuable legacy of female labor protest to twentieth-century women in organized labor.

This reconstruction of the labor protest traditions of the many self-supporting women shoeworkers in the late nineteenth century restores to the increasing numbers of working female heads of families in the late twentieth century their rightful, historic heritage. Furthermore, the late nineteenth-century labor activism of New England women shoeworkers provides a link between the gender-conscious militancy of pre–Civil War textile operatives and the labor activity of female workers in the garment trades in the early twentieth century. This link suggests the existence of a distinctly female pattern of protest within the nineteenth-century American labor movement.

How have historians studied women workers? Women's involvement in work and labor protest has consciously or unconsciously been interpreted in the context of a male model of work and labor activism. Patricia Branca criticized this approach as ignoring the different experiences of working women that prompted different responses in situations of conflict with employers.[7] The distinct work culture of women has been explored by Susan Benson, Barbara Melosh, Leslie Tentler, and others, while Thomas Dublin analyzed the relationship of the work and cultural experience of early nineteenth-century women textile operatives to the traditions of New England labor protest.[8] A study of the shoeworkers of Essex County can reveal how those distinct work cultures were handled by men and women workers in the same industry.

Many labor historians see the family as the basic social unit of class structure, arguing, for example, that family unity is the foundation of class solidarity in strikes or that nineteenth-century labor protest rested on the shoulders of the male householder.[9] Family, class, and culture have been the organizing categories of many studies of working-class women, prompting detailed analysis of the family economy or the family wage.[10] Other categories that historians have used to define the culture of class experience, e.g., community, household, kin, ethnicity, and status, provide a context for but do not specify the experience of working women.[11] A focus on these categories tends to obscure the differential experience of women as family members, as a gender, as workers, and the politics and ideology of those experiences. Men and women shared the work in the nineteenth-century shoe industry, but they experienced it differently. None of these categories adequately illuminates the differences in these experiences or the tensions among working men and women over gender consciousness or family loyalty as the basis of female labor protest, a persistent theme for nineteenth-century shoeworkers.

Socialist feminists such as Heidi Hartmann and Rayna Rapp see the dynamics of family relations as one crucial half of an equation that defines class experience. Theorists like Hartmann see the sexual division of labor and the family wage as phenomena explainable only through an examination of the interplay of gender relations in the family within the economic development of capitalism. One exceptional model is Sarah Eisenstein's study of the gender and class experience of late nineteenth- and early twentieth-century working women. Eisenstein's exploration of the meaning of womanhood in the experience of working-class women avoids both a focus on the family and the dominance of middle-class ideology. Mari Jo Buhle effectively used class and gender politics to reconstruct the role of women in American socialism. Jackie West has raised crucial questions about the meaning of class for women, especially for married women. Iris Young has advocated the substitution of the gender division of labor for the sex-blind category of class in order to build a single theory for feminist historical materialism.[12] The study of women at work reflects the current theoretical and historical debates over how to convey most effectively women's experience as workers and as family members.

The experience of men and women shoeworkers in the nineteenth century cannot be understood through the traditional concept of family as the social basis of class. The invasive nature of industrialization transformed women's work while it still remained within the household and family. The sexual division of labor separated and distinguished the work cultures of men and women within a preindustrial family setting. The concept of the family has served to obscure the differential impact of industrialization on men and women workers and the penetration of family life by economic change. Gender analysis can reveal the political, economic, and social connections between men and women within the family without mystifying the family.

The divisions within the female work force between women inside and outside of the family economy during the transition to the factory system and during the late nineteenth century illustrate that the economic and political roles of women in the family and society were the subject of debate and disagreement among shoeworkers themselves. Marital status and relationship to family appear as potentially divisive for working-class women as skill, ethnicity, or race. Gender analysis not only permits an examination of the work cultures of men and women, but it also provides a way to analyze the politics of the division of labor and the meaning of the family wage to both men and women as well as the historical alternatives offered by feminist labor protest. An integrated approach encourages an understanding of the changing meaning of the social roles of men and women during industrialization and the ways these distinct roles shaped the politics and ideology of labor protest. Gender analysis not only adds a new dimension of working-class experience to labor history, but it also challenges the way that male gender has unconsciously been made the measure of human experience.

In 1904 Nora Beatrice Drinkard Dykeman lost her young husband to an attack of acute appendicitis and faced life as a young widow with an infant child in a small rural town in central Missouri. After a period of confusion, she left her daughter with her father, who worked a small farm, and went to the capital of the state, Jefferson City, to work in the country factory of the International Shoe Company of St. Louis. She learned the work quickly and became a skilled machine vamper. When her daughter, Eunice, was sixteen, she joined her mother in the shoe factory, working during the summers as a backstayer and as a sample maker while she prepared to be a schoolteacher. Beatrice Dykeman, who was my grandmother, often told me that she refused to join the union at the factory, but would have joined if they had had one that to her mind, "amounted to something." I wrote off her attitudes as the antiunion views of a genteel but powerful woman whose bourgeois manners and bearing I often observed as a child, fascinated especially by her habit of extending her little finger as she drank from a cup. After concluding this study, I have come to appreciate her attitudes as those of a hard-pressed, self-supporting woman whose work in a shoe factory provided her with a reasonable income, but required her to develop protective pretensions and carefully scrutinize those who would claim to represent her interests. Many nineteenth-century women workers in the Essex County shoe industry shared her dilemmas and her attitudes.

Men, Women, and Work

CHAPTER ONE

The Origins of the Sexual Division of Labor, 1750–1810

[Binding sealskin boots] was a dirty disagreeable job; only love for my uncle, and a desire to promote his interest could have induced its undertaking.

—Sarah Smith Emery,
Reminiscences of a
Nonagenarian (1879)

In the late eighteenth century, the shoemakers of Essex County began to recruit the women of their families to work on shoes. In doing so, they introduced a sexual division of labor into an artisan craft of male workers. The implications of this division of labor shaped the social dimensions of shoemaking throughout the nineteenth century as production moved from preindustrial to industrial organization. The world of gender influenced economic change in important and persistent ways.

Sarah Smith, who lived on a farm in Newbury, Massachusetts, just south of Newburyport, was one of the women who came to share the work of shoemakers. As a young girl, she had observed and participated in the strenuous, daily labors of her mother and aunts for their families and households. They prepared food, performed housework and child care, made cheeses from the milk of ten cows, and sold them along with butter, eggs, vegetables, and fruit to augment the family income. They also spun and wove woolen and linen cloth and made the family's clothing and stockings. For Sarah Smith, their contributions of labor to the family economy were familiar and part of being female.

In 1794 a mill for spinning cotton opened in Newbury, and a factory in nearby Byfield began to manufacture woolen cloth. These factory-made textiles relieved Sarah's relatives from overwork and provided opportunities for young women like her to earn wages. Sarah, however, preferred homework, braiding straw bonnets for a general store in Haverhill. She also sewed the upper parts of shoes and boots for her two uncles, Joe and Ben Little, who operated a shoe shop in the neighboring town of New Rowley with another shoemaker and several apprentices. Her uncles hired other local shoemakers to work for them, exchanging goods from their general store for finished shoes. Living as bachelors assisted by the house-keeping of their partner's sister, Ben and Joe Little often brought shoes to their niece Sarah to sew. In an emergency, she was the family resource to which they turned.

In her reminiscences, Sarah Smith Emery recalled one such emergency that illustrated the shoemaker's ability to enlist the labor of female relatives in the family's economic interest. Uncle Joe arrived at the Newbury farm one afternoon when Sarah was in her early twenties with a lot of one hundred pairs of sealskin boots that had to be finished in five days. Sarah insisted that she could not complete the work in time, but "yielding to his ardent solicitation," she agreed to try. "It was a dirty disagreeable job; only love for my uncle, and a desire to promote his interest could have induced its undertaking."[1]

She stitched for five days and just finished on the last. As Uncle Joe claimed the work, Sarah's fiancé, David Emery, walked in to find her exhausted and covered with dirty sealskin oil. He tossed the last boot at her uncle and warned him not to impose again on Sarah's good nature. After that, Sarah worked only on clean leather for her uncles and only in emergencies. Her account of the incident mentions no wages paid to her for the work. Sarah Smith's efforts on behalf of her male relatives occurred within the context of the contribution of Essex County women to eighteenth-century household production.

Essex County, Massachusetts, stretches along the Atlantic coastline north of Boston from the salt marshes of Saugus on Massachusetts Bay around the tip of Cape Ann to the tidal basin of the Merrimack River. Turning inland at New Hampshire's southern border, the county's boundary follows the state line westward paralleling the

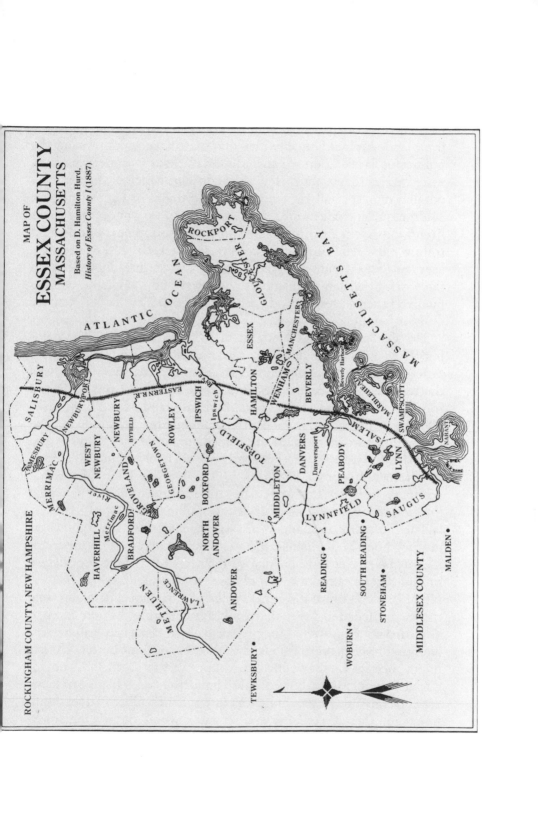

MAP OF
ESSEX COUNTY
MASSACHUSETTS

Based on D. Hamilton Hurd.
History of Essex County I (1887)

ROCKINGHAM COUNTY, NEW HAMPSHIRE

ATLANTIC OCEAN

MASSACHUSETTS BAY

ROCKPORT

GLOUCESTER

ESSEX

MANCHESTER

WENHAM

BEVERLY

Beverly Harbor

SALISBURY

NEWBURYPORT

HAMILTON

EASTERN R.R.

IPSWICH

Ipswich

SALEM

MARBLEHEAD

NAHANT

AMESBURY

NEWBURY

BYFIELD

ROWLEY

TOPSFIELD

DANVERS

Danversport

PEABODY

LYNN

SWAMPSCOTT

MERRIMAC

WEST
NEWBURY

GEORGETOWN

BOXFORD

MIDDLETON

LYNNFIELD

SAUGUS

RIVER

GROVELAND

Merrimac

BRADFORD

NORTH
ANDOVER

READING

SOUTH READING

HAVERHILL

METHUEN

LAWRENCE

ANDOVER

STONEHAM

MALDEN

TEWKSBURY

WOBURN

MIDDLESEX COUNTY

bends in the river to Tewksbury. Plunging southeasterly, the county line rejoins the ocean at Saugus. In the eighteenth century, the commercial seaports of Salem and Newburyport with their maritime trade and shipbuilding activities dominated the economy and the politics of Essex County. Smaller coastal towns with deep harbors were centers for Atlantic fishing expeditions. Much of the county's population, especially in the villages and towns of Lynn, Danvers, Middleton, and Haverhill, were farm families who earned their livelihoods from the often thin and rocky soil, piney woods, and rolling hills.[2] The rural household in seventeenth- and eighteenth-century Essex County operated as a joint venture dependent on the work of all family members. As wives and daughters, women involved themselves in productive work crucial to the subsistence of their families.

The general patterns of work in the rural household of colonial New England divided the activities of men and women into different yet interlocking endeavors. The colonial wife processed the raw material that her husband brought in from the fields and forests.[3] Along with housework, child care, and agricultural tasks adjacent to the house, women also commonly worked at the domestic manufacture of items for the immediate use of their families and in bountiful seasons for exchange with their neighbors. Women's involvement in household production in the New England colonial economy provides the setting for the introduction of the sexual division of labor into the craft of shoemaking.

The income or exchange from women's work in the eighteenth-century household enabled their families to obtain the services of a shoemaker, but did not involve them directly in the production of shoes. The account book of Deacon David Marsh of Haverhill (1721–37) illustrates the dealings of a custom shoemaker who made and mended shoes and took agricultural produce, lumber, and cordwood, as well as the products of women's labor, in barter.[4] Debits for shoes were balanced with exchanges of butter, cheese, honey, beeswax, tallow, and cider. One entry in April 1725 noted: "Your daughter with us for 5 days" indicating an exchange of labor for shoes by one of the daughters of widow Elizabeth Page.[5] Spinning shoe thread, combing and spinning wool, and dyeing stockings represented other services commonly performed by women and credited to their families in the Deacon Marsh accounts. His son, David, who made shoes to order until the early nineteenth century, also accepted women's labor. He made and mended shoes for the widow Sarah Black and her daughter Hannah between 1791 and 1801. In return Sarah and Hannah Black combed flax and wool, spun linen thread, husked corn, and harvested onions in Marsh's fields. Widows in Haverhill also paid Marsh in hides and cash or appealed as indigents to the town to pay for their shoes.[6] But other than the spinning of shoe thread, these exchanges of work did not involve women in the work of making shoes.

Little is known about the activities of shoemaking in Essex County before 1750. Although reference to an occasional female shoemaker appears in the advertisements of colonial newspapers, shoemaking was the work of men and boys. Many boots and shoes used by New England farm families were crudely fashioned by the men of the household who had no actual training in shoemaking, but who did have a ready supply of hides from their own livestock or nearby woods and access to a local tannery. Family members who wore these rough foot covers for protection against the New England winters welcomed the prospect of more comfort in shoes made by an itinerant cobbler who earned little, sometimes only board.[7] When these journeymen shoemakers settled in towns and villages, they anticipated higher earnings by providing the leather from which the custom-made shoe was worked. In Essex County, the itinerant and the settled stages of custom work overlapped each other, depending on the locality, density of population, and proximity to seaports and commerce.

English shoemakers arrived in Essex County early in the seventeenth century to offer their services to the local market. Phillip Kertland and Edmund Bridges came to Lynn in 1635. Andrew Greeley began the craft in Haverhill in 1646, and in Danvers (then Salem Village) both the Porter and the Putnam families were among the earliest settlers in 1638. These men trained a very limited number of apprentices, probably only their sons and nephews, and combined shoemaking with many other forms of work. For example, James Brown of Newbury combined making and mending shoes with his other activities as farmer, carter, and glazier. His account book (1759–89) indicates steady periods of work on custom shoes for local families. In exchange he accepted corn, oats, rye, hides, a little cash, and a silk handkerchief. He carefully noted when the customer provided leather, thread, and heels for the shoes, which reduced the price for making them. The production of these shoemakers was limited to local demand and showed little evidence of growth before the 1780s.[8] While established early in Essex County towns, shoemaking was no more widespread or important to the local economy before 1750 than blacksmithing.

Lynn was the first town in Essex County to move from the handicraft or order stage to the production of shoes for sale. Historians have attributed this increase in production after 1750 to the geographical location of the town. Lynn did not have a suitable harbor for the maritime trade, but was close enough to Salem and Boston to import raw materials for shoemaking purposes: hides and hemlock and oak bark for tanning. Although only three Lynn shoemakers had enough demand for their work to employ journeymen in 1750, they were making shoes for sale in the local market as well as on order. Blanche Hazard suggested that the workings of the order system created this change. Custom-made shoes rejected for unsatisfactory work or fit had to be sold elsewhere or the shoemaker faced a loss of material and labor. Apprentices and journeymen had to be fed whether customers ordered shoes or not. Idle hands were put to work making average sizes at lower cost than custom work. These were sold at the local general store or sent out of town to other markets.[9] The dispatch of locally made shoes to other towns brought Lynn products into competition with English-made shoes.

Growing markets stimulated shoe production in Lynn and elsewhere in Essex County. The mercantile policies of the British Empire encouraged trade in raw materials, but tried to discourage the production of finished goods by American colonists. Nonetheless, Lynn shoemakers reorganized their work to meet the much higher English standards. John Adam Daygr, a Welsh cordwainer, arrived in Lynn in 1750, and some historians have credited him with redirecting the course of shoemaking in Essex County. Before 1750 the artisan system in Lynn consisted of custom shoemakers who worked as individuals in their homes. Only a very few employed journeymen in addition to apprentices. Daygr's activities in Lynn reshaped the craft by setting higher standards for work and expanding production. Shoemakers analyzed and copied English methods and styles in women's shoes and imported higher quality leathers.

Production increased in the 1780s, and Lynn became dotted with artisan shops called "ten footers," a reference to the dimensions of the small wooden structures. By 1784 there were 150 ten footers in Lynn, and five years later at least 400 artisan masters, journeymen, and apprentices.[10] The craft of shoemaking in Essex County, planted in the early seventeenth century and kept alive by the limited and relatively crude demands of a scant agricultural population, flourished after 1750 in pursuit of new markets.

Political resistance to British trade regulations through nonimportation agreements after 1765 helped to expand the domestic market for Lynn shoemakers. Colonial protests against parliamentary policy involved women in collective political action, especially the boycotting of English imports. The Daughters of Liberty spun, wove, and wore their own cloth, and as herbal teas replaced the English import, the domestic functions of colonial women assumed a new political importance. It is possible that the women of Boston and Philadelphia who wore homespun and drank a patriotic brew thought twice before purchasing a pair of English slippers. The products of Lynn shoemakers may have found market opportunities in the newly awakened political sensibilities of patriot women. Furthermore, after the war of the American Revolution had been won, the political importance of female domesticity took a republican direction. Responsibility in the home for rearing children to be citizens of the young Republic, new interest in female education, and the reevaluation of the role of women in society discouraged ostentatious English styles of dress.[11] New political attitudes may have helped the shoemakers of Lynn survive the reopening of competition with English imports, but in 1789, merchant-capitalists obtained the more certain barrier of a protective tariff.

In the late eighteenth century, production of women's shoes came to dominate Lynn shoemaking. Historians have argued that in addition to Daygr's success in copying English styles for a growing domestic market, the surplus female population of coastal Essex County in the decades 1790 to 1810 determined the direction of shoemaking. As the argument goes, these women sewed shoes the year around while their fathers and brothers went to sea as sailors and fishermen. When the men returned, they busied themselves during the winter months, finishing up the work that their womenfolk had begun.[12] Yet the sexual division of labor in shoe production was not introduced into the seafaring households of Essex County, but into the families of shoemaking artisans. The surplus of females in Essex County would be tapped for shoe work, but not until after the shoemaking family ceased to be the locus of production. The availability of local female labor helped to expand production in Essex County, but did not determine its direction.

Historians have also concluded that the needle skills of the women of Essex County, which were best utilized on the light leathers of women's shoes, determined the direction of shoe production.[13] Women workers, however, commonly used waxed threads attached to hog bristles to work on the coarse leather of men's boots and shoes in Essex County and in central and southern Massachusetts.[14] Sewing tough leather was not a barrier to women's participation in domestic production. A careful analysis of how and where women were recruited to work on shoes in the late eighteenth century demonstrates that the social context of an artisan craft and the interest of merchant-capitalists in expanding production shaped the creation of this new work for women.

Women had no direct role in shoemaking in colonial New England, but their relationships to shoemaking husbands or fathers had encouraged them to contribute services to the craft. Women in shoemaking families spun flax into the linen thread used by shoemakers to sew the shoe together. If their husbands employed journeymen, additional places at the table were required and often sleeping spaces as well. The boarding of apprentices made greater demands on the females of the household, who looked after their behavior and moral training as well as their domestic needs. Some wives shared space and cooking facilities with journeymen and their relatives. In 1785 Jonathan Porter of Danvers set up as a shoemaker in his cousin Zerubbabel Porter's tanning shop and boarded with him for a year. Jonathan then rented a room in Zerubbabel's house and brought his sister Mehitable to live with him as a housekeeper and share his cousin's kitchen. In 1788 he took an apprentice, and sister Hitty looked after him. The following year, Jonathan married his second cousin, Lydia, and the young couple lived with the Porters for another year.[15] This integration of kin and apprentices into the living space of the shoemaking household required the cooperation of female members of the family.

Apprentices, journeymen, and artisan masters performed all

work on shoes prior to the expansion of production in the 1780s. One of the first skills acquired by a shoemaker's apprentice after he had learned to temper and point awls was the ability to sew a tight seam in the upper half of a leather shoe. When sewing uppers for his master or "working on the seam," the apprentice was called a seamster. The rest of his training involved instruction in cutting leather hides and putting together the upper and sole to size, and attaching the sole to the heel. Before the 1780s these lessons took place within the shoemaker's house, often in the kitchen, in an ell, or in an attached shed. Work was performed in a domestic setting where shared family work might have evolved as in hosiery-making or spinning and weaving in England. However, the refinement of artisan methods based on higher standards and the demands for increased production required a new work space to accommodate several journeymen and boys. The artisan shop or ten footer provided this work space for men where the craft and its social relationships could be taught and practiced.[16] Many wives must have been pleased to rid their households of the clutter, dirt, and smell of the shoemaker's paraphernalia.

Three changes of fundamental importance were altering shoe production in Essex County in the late eighteenth century. A new group of merchants, who supplied the industry's need for capital, provided leather in large quantities to shoemakers and sought out markets for the finished shoes, especially south of New England. Control over raw materials meant control of profits, as all shoemakers knew, and artisan masters borrowed money if they could to purchase their own leather.[17] This control over raw materials would become more formal and direct in the early nineteenth century as cutting operations were organized into central shops, thus separating the capitalist or shoe boss, sometimes a former artisan master, from the journeymen in the shoe shops.

Merchant-capitalists like Moses Gale of Haverhill and Zerubbabel Porter of Danvers responded to the new market opportunities created by the activities of Ebenezer Breed of Lynn, who led the fight to establish the protective tariff on shoes in 1789. Storekeeper Gale began to make dry hides available to local shoemakers in 1795, either for cash sale or on long-term credit, in exchange for shoes. After 1810 other storekeepers followed his example, and shoes and slippers made in Haverhill began to be shipped to southern markets. In Danvers, Porter organized the local shoemakers in 1779 to work on leather supplied by his tannery and marketed the finished shoes in his general store. By 1789, he made his first sale of brogans or rough, unlined work shoes made especially for slaves in the South and the West Indies and became the marketing agent for most of the brogans made in Danvers. Men like Breed, Gale, and Porter, who provided the capital and marketed the product, stood between the shoemaker and his customer. Merchant-capitalist control of profits as a result of the ownership of leather and the direction of sales was changing the role of shoemaker from artisan to wage earner.[18] As the custom shoemaker had profited over the itinerant cobbler by having the chance to work on leather that he owned, so the merchant-capitalist profited from the control of raw materials and access to markets. These changes also created new demands for increased production.

The growth in the number of Essex County shoe shops in the 1780s created a new locus for artisan life and a new social setting for the training of apprentices. Men's work left the home, if only for the short walk to the ten footer.[19] This group experience of training, work, and its traditions of mutual obligations and loyalties defined artisan culture. The "mechanic ideology," analyzed by Paul Faler, expressed the virtues of an artisan culture that rested on the labor theory of value and a republican political heritage from the American Revolution. The apprentice system provided an orientation to the male world of the artisan and to its work, rituals, ideology, and hierarchy of subordination and dominance. The apprentices not only learned the craft, its traditions, and its social customs, but they also served the master and the journeymen in various ways. They ran errands, obtained rum, filled in at various jobs when needed, lit and tended the fire in the shop, got more leather stock from the storekeeper and sometimes delivered the shoes, changed the dirty water used to soak the leather, prepared the paste and wax, and turned the grindstone to sharpen the knives. Apprentices had few rights, and unruly or stubborn ones were disciplined, ridiculed, and occasionally physically punished in the shop, but they were also treated to clam chowder parties at nearby beaches in Nahant that included games, wrestling, singing, and drinking with their shop mates. These apprentices soon became journeymen who aspired to be masters themselves.[20]

Old-time Shoemaker's Shop. Courtesy of Lynn Historical Society.

This combination of work and leisure in the preindustrial phase of shoe production in New England was a golden age for artisan life. Decentralized production allowed groups of male artisans to exercise significant control over the work process and fostered a proud tradition that Alan Dawley has called "Equal Rights," a political heritage that remained central to collective resistance by shoemakers for most of the nineteenth century.[21]

Demands for increased production in the late eighteenth century drew the female members of shoemaking families into work on shoes, but women workers remained on the periphery of the social and political life of artisans in the ten footers. The introduction of the sexual division of labor into the craft was a response to the needs felt by both artisan-shoemaker and merchant-capitalist for increased production. Storekeepers, however, had no control over the assignment of work in the shoe shop or within the artisan family. Facing the loss of profits made from providing raw materials or finished shoes directly to the trade, the artisan found an economic motive to encourage family members uninvolved in shoe work to join the men of the family in production. The introduction of women into shoe work was an accommodation by the artisan to the changes in the system of production, an accommodation that left artisanal control of work relatively undisturbed. It promised additional income to the shoemaking family by dividing up work in the shop and recruiting the labor of more of its members. Shoe production increased sharply in Lynn between 1768 and 1783 with little commensurate increase in the town's population,[22] evidence of the recruitment of female family members to new work. The merchant-capitalist welcomed the increased potential for production, but paid no wages directly to women workers. The lowered costs of labor involved in using women to sew shoes remained hidden within the family economy. Together, the capitalist and the artisan created a major change in the preindustrial mode of production.

The influence of the reorganization of production redefined work in the shoe shop and gave part of it new social meanings. Most of the work on shoe uppers was removed from the group activity of men in the shop, leaving the shoemakers to concentrate on the processes of lasting (the shaping of the upper and the inner sole to size) and bottoming (the final step of fastening together the sole, heel, and upper). Apprentices continued to be trained to make the entire shoe. Shoemakers also cut out shoe parts from leather stock, but by the early nineteenth century this process, for which skill, judgment, and economy were crucial to protect profits, was performed under the watchful eye of the capitalist.

Female family members adapted their needle skills to handsew the leather uppers of low-cut slippers and shoes for women and brogans and boots for men. This new work was performed in the kitchens of shoemaking households alongside domestic duties and child care; this setting made the work seem appropriate for females. "Shoebinding," a new word that was introduced with the sexual division of labor, became a commonplace category of women's work in early nineteenth-century New England. Apprentices who sewed uppers had been called seamsters, and if elderly shoemakers with stiffening fingers bound shoes for others, they were not often called binders. A new tool, the shoe clamp, appeared exclusively for women's work. A binder did not straddle a shoemaker's bench, but used a long, flexible wooden clamp, usually fashioned from barrel staves, which rested on the floor and which she held tightly between her knees, freeing her hands to use her awl and needle. Shoe clamps would later be sold by employers as tools of the trade. After making holes in the leather upper with the awl, the shoebinder sewed up the back, front or side seams, put in the lining, bound the top edges, and sometimes added handworked eyelets or designs.[23]

Why didn't the apprentices do the sewing of uppers to meet the needs of expanded production? They certainly had learned the skill as part of their apprenticeship and worked occasionally on uppers when they were needed in the shop. If they had specialized only in sewing uppers, the apprentice system as craft training and as an orientation to the male world of artisan culture would have been disrupted. Sewing uppers on a continuous basis would have interrupted the services they performed for the master and journeymen and the lessons they were learning about hierarchy in the craft.[24] Furthermore, to use apprentices would not have solved the long-term need for expanded production; in a few years they became "jours" and were no longer available to sew seams. Some more dependable source of new labor was required, one that the capitalist would accept in the interests of expanded production yet

Shoebinder. Drawing by Frank L. Wyman.

would not have to supervise or pay. The utilization of women in shoemaking families was a solution that met the needs of both artisan and capitalist and threatened no change in the traditional patterns of gender formation. The introduction of this division of labor into shoemaking was carefully controlled by artisans, guaranteeing the subordinate role of women by separating the work of shoebinding from any knowledge of the other skills of the craft and by maintaining separate work places for women and men.[25] These patterns survived the transformation of the shoe industry into the factory system at mid-century and constituted a fundamental social dimension of work.

According to late eighteenth-century account books, binders in shoemaking families earned no wages before 1810, but they did contribute their labor to family production and to the wage it commanded. The emergence of shoebinding testified to the adaptability and persistence of women's labor in household production. At this time, women in Essex County had few alternatives to hard, seasonal agricultural work or barter to add income to their families. The first shoebinder might have been the daughter of a Lynn shoemaker who had observed her father making shoes in her mother's kitchen and for whom the first shoe clamp was devised to accommodate her long skirt and apron. By working on leather in her mother's kitchen, she could assist her father's work and contribute her labor to the family's income.[26] Robert Gilman, traveling through Essex County in 1797, observed the general involvement of women in shoemaking: "In our way to Salem we passed through a number of pretty little villages one of which, Lynn, is scarcely inhabited by any but shoemakers. This little town supplies even the Southern States with women['s] shoes for exportation. The women work also and we scarcely passed a house where the trade was not carried on."[27]

Although shoebinders worked in their kitchens where domestic tasks and child care continued, the demands of the artisan shop for sewn uppers intruded. When the shoemaker brought home the leather stock from the merchant-capitalist, the work of the master, journeymen, and apprentices could not begin until the shoemaker's wife or daughter had sewn a few uppers. The prototypical description of the role of the shoebinder in the family labor economy is found in David Newhall Johnson's *Sketches of Lynn* (1880).

As the wife and daughters "bound" the shoes made by the workmen of the family, the "uppers," all ready to "bind" with the needful silk, cotton and thread, and sometimes beeswax, made part of the load carried home in the "little cart," or in some other way, from the boss' shop. Then there would be a little delay, perhaps, until a shoe was bound, with which to start off the new lot.

But, generally, before the "jour" got his "stock" seasoned, one or two "uppers" were ready, and enough were usually bound ahead to keep all hands at work. And so, now and then, the order would be heard—"Come John, go and see if your mother has got a shoe bound: I'm all ready to last it." [28]

As the shoebinder sewed in her kitchen, the demands of the artisan shop shaped her work. Since she had to keep ahead of the requirements of all of the workers in the shop with a ready supply of sewn uppers, shoebinding combined both task labor, in the form of domestic chores, and timed labor, in the erratic but compelling need to keep up with the men in the shop. [29] The kitchen was transformed into a workplace where external demands from the ten footer shaped both time and tasks.

Binding shoes was not considered skilled work; shoebinders were not taught to make an entire shoe. Learning to bind shoes did not provide the shoemaker's daughter with a trade, but trained her in household work of little more immediate importance than the efficient feeding and boarding of apprentices or the spinning of shoe thread. The low wages paid to binders after 1810 reflected this lack of craft status. [30] There was no reason for women to enter the ten footer; someone, a son or apprentice, collected the uppers from the binder and took them to the shoemakers. Neither did shoebinders share in the political or religious discussions in the shop, in the good times at the Nahant beaches, or in the gatherings of the militia and fire companies. [31] The group nature of men's work and their social and recreational activities supported a tradition of resistance to the reorganization of production, but this tradition did not mirror the experience of women workers. They were disciplined by the work, but were not a part of the craft.

The primary responsibilities of women in shoemaking families for domestic work in their households, however, limited their capacities to complete work on uppers needed by shoemakers. Sarah Smith's strenuous efforts to complete the hundred pairs of sealskin boots in five days for her Uncle Joe would have been impossible for a wife with small children and many pressing domestic chores. The domestic setting of the work of shoebinding for the family labor system contradicted increasing demands for production. Account books in the late eighteenth century list two to five pairs of shoes as a lot or unit of work for shoemakers. By 1800 a lot consisted of ten to fourteen pairs, and within two decades, fifty, sixty, and seventy pairs per lot were common. The larger the lot of work, the more pressure was placed on the shoebinder to finish uppers so that the shoemakers in the shop could finish up the lot and settle accounts with the storekeeper. A shoemaker might try to recruit the wife or daughter of a neighbor to increase the available supply of sewn uppers, but this would require some kind of a payment for their labor. Gradually after 1810, shoebinding, while still performed in the home, became work paid in goods or wages, hired and supervised by merchant-capitalists.[32] As it moved onto the wage labor market, this new work for women became increasingly separate from the shoemaking family as a center of coordinated production.

CHAPTER TWO

The Rise of Early Labor Protest, 1810–37

[T]here appears to be somewhere a manifest *error*, a want of justice, and reasonable compensation to the females; which calls imperiously for redress. While the prices of *their* labour have been reduced, the business of their *employers* has appeared to be improving, and prosperous, enabling them to increase in wealth. These *things ought not so to be!*

—Preamble, Constitution of the Female Society of Lynn and Vicinity for the promotion and protection of Female Industry, 1834

In March 1809 Israel Buffum, a shoemaker and small entrepreneur of Lynn, paid Eben Keney for a year's work of shoebinding done by Keney's wife, Abigail. She had bound 409 pairs of shoes for Buffum at prices ranging between three and five cents a pair. The wages earned by Abigail Keney appear to be the earliest evidence in Lynn of a shoebinder taking work directly from an employer for wages rather than contributing her labor to the income earned by joint family effort.[1]

The shift of shoebinding out of a family labor context and into a wage relationship in which an employer supplied work from outside the home signaled an important change in women's employment in shoe production after 1810. Market forces had invaded the home and family to alter the conditions of women's work. The expansion of the system of domestic manufacture involved many additional Essex County women in work that became separate from production in artisan shops. The family wage economy in which wages earned by individuals working at home were pooled in the family's economic interest replaced the family labor system.[2] These changes in the coordination and control of work and the direct payment of wages in goods and in cash represented new material conditions for women workers and a new relationship to production. In the early 1830s, shoebinders responded by protesting their grievances in incidents of collective action. Changing conditions of work prompted expressions of a new consciousness among female outworkers in the shoe towns of eastern Massachusetts.

Between 1810 and 1840 the economy of southern New England shifted rapidly from subsistence farming and the commercial and maritime activities of seacoast towns to the development of a series of factory centers and mill villages. Spinning cotton and woolen yarn was mechanized first in southern Massachusetts and Rhode Island, and later the Waltham system of integrated manufacture of all cotton textile processes created the factory system, which flourished at Lowell in Middlesex County. In Essex County, small factories for textile production sprang up in Andover, Newbury, Amesbury, and other towns. Factory centers like Waltham and Lowell drew population to them and created markets for commercial agriculture. The availability of the cheap machine-made cloth that they produced brought significant change to the family economy of the New England farmer: the decay of household industries, especially the production of homespun cloth. The shift to factory calicos eased the burdens of hardworking farm women, but the need for cash to buy these coveted textiles encouraged rural people to find new employment for farmers' wives and daughters or face the prospect of paying out money to clothe "idle" females.[3]

The problem of unemployed female hands and the ensuing danger to rural society became a subject of speculation for progressive agricultural opinion in the early 1830s. Correspondents with the *New England Farmer and Horticultural Register* discussed the impact on household budgets and mortgages of unproductive daughters who chose a genteel way of life over a contribution of labor to the farm family. One farmer's daughter explained her refusal to card and spin wool to knit the family's stockings or make butter and cheeses as her mother and grandmother did in terms that reflected significant changes in attitudes toward traditional forms of women's work during early industrialization. "Why, father! no young lady does that; and besides, it is so much easier to send [the wool] to the mill and have it carded there. . . . [M]other never taught me how to knit, because she said it would interfere with my lessons; and then, if I knew how, it would take a great deal of time, and be much cheaper to buy the stockings at the store." The anxiety of farm families over the lack of employment for daughters and the need for cash to purchase market-produced goods was resolved in the 1820s and 1830s by the departure of many young women to work in textile factories, in schools, or as domestic servants. Others stayed at home and worked at new occupations as outworkers. This new work included the sewing of men's garments, making palm-leaf and straw hats, and binding shoes.[4] Employers often paid their homeworkers in factory-made textiles along with staple goods and foodstuffs rather than in cash wages.

By the 1810s the labor of female members of shoemaking families proved insufficient to meet the demands of expanding markets in the South and in the West Indies. Storekeepers and the owners of central shops recruited women outside of shoemaking families and gave out work directly to shoebinders who returned the sewn uppers to their employers. These bound uppers were then given out to the shoemakers. The family labor system in which both binding and making were performed for the same employer coexisted with the new system of divided work, but the control over the assignment and coordination of work was passing into the hands of the employer. The surviving account books of storekeepers and shoe bosses who owned central shops in Essex and neighboring Middlesex Counties illustrate the slow development of the separate employment of shoebinders.[5]

In the account books from the late eighteenth and early nineteenth centuries, one price or wage paid for shoemaking per pair signified that either the shoemaker or the family labor system produced the entire shoe for the employer. After 1810, as shoebinding moved onto the labor market, additional prices for binding separate from making begin to appear in the accounts. The entries for 1811 in the accounts of John Goodwin of Reading in eastern Middlesex County included three categories of prices for shoe work: twenty to twenty-five cents per pair depending on style for making, thirty cents per pair for making and binding, and five cents per pair for binding.[6] Goodwin supplied leather to local shoemakers and marketed the shoes both in Reading and in Boston. He employed several shoebinders as individuals in 1811, including his eighteen-year-old niece, Lydda Batts, at prices that ranged from three and one-half to five cents per pair. Lydda's father, Samuel Batts, was a shoemaker who also worked for Goodwin, but Lydda did not bind the same kind of shoes that her father made. They worked on separate lots for individual wages. Because the earnings of wives were credited to their husbands' accounts, Goodwin kept accounts only for unmarried binders. Some wives of shoemakers worked on the same shoes that their husbands made, but other shoemakers arranged to have the cut uppers bound by women in neighboring families and paid them for it.

Goodwin also employed two young unmarried women of Reading and Woburn as shoemakers. The rare employment of women to make shoes represented the survival of the eighteenth-century custom whereby a father's trade was carried on by a daughter or a husband's trade by a widow.[7] Emely (Emily) Farrington of Woburn made a few pairs of shoes for Goodwin in 1810, probably having learned how from her father. She made a few more pairs in 1812 in exchange for calico and gingham goods kept by Goodwin. Farrington's work was only occasional, and when she married in 1813, she ceased working for Goodwin. Nineteen-year-old Lucinda Baley (Bailey) of Reading worked for six months as a maker for Goodwin in 1828–29. Both young women received the same price for shoemaking as the men whom Goodwin employed, but female shoemakers were anomalous. One, however, was the vigorous mother of shoemaker Joseph Lye, Jr., of Lynn.

Historians have used the journals of Joseph Lye, Jr., to illustrate the control that artisan shoemakers exercised over their time and work and the patterns by which the shoemaking family functioned as a center of training and production.[8] Fathers trained sons, and mothers trained daughters, but Anna Heart Lye worked as a shoemaker as did her sons and received her training from male members of her family. Joseph Lye, Jr., was one of nine children born to Joseph and Anna Lye. The father died in 1807 at the age of forty-eight, but he had succeeded in partially training his eldest son, Joseph Jr., and he in turn trained his brothers. Lye and his activities were representative of the early nineteenth-century artisan who worked on shoes in a ten footer, but frequently put the craft aside for fishing, sailing, and farm work. The activities of his mother were much less typical of women in preindustrial shoemaking. When her husband died, Anna Lye was left with eight children to support. Her sons, Joseph, Burrill, John, and Robert, ranged in age between fifteen and four.[9] Her efforts to support her family included working as a shoemaker for storekeeper Samuel Bacheller of Lynn.

At the age of fifty-two Anna Lye worked from March to December 1819, earning $78.83, while her son John earned $54.93 making shoes for Bacheller from February 1819 to January 1820. The Bacheller accounts also show many dealings with shoebinders in Lynn at a common price of five cents a pair, paid both in cash and in goods. John probably recruited his mother to work for his shoe boss, encouraged by the higher wage she could earn as a maker rather than as a binder. In comparison, Irena Lewis, a twenty-two-year-old single woman of Lynn, worked steadily all of 1819 for Bacheller as a shoebinder and earned only $47.90 in cash. Anna Lye may have also bound or made shoes for other storekeepers in Lynn in 1819. As a practicing shoemaker, she probably had some unacknowledged role in training her sons or they in training her.[10] She died in 1848 at eighty-one, outliving all of her children but one, a remarkable relic of the family labor system.

In another surviving but anonymous account book of Lynn between 1825 and 1827, Mrs. Sally Farrington, a widow with grown children, worked steadily for two years as a shoemaker, but she received only store goods as wages. The work of Emely Farrington, Lucinda Baley, Anna Lye, and Sally Farrington was atypical of women's involvement in shoe production in Essex County. As daughters and widows of shoemakers, they had acquired some craft training from their families and received wages considerably higher for their work than shoebinders, but their sex excluded them from group work with men other than their immediate relatives. When shoemaking became centered in ten footers occupied by teams of male workers, most women, like widow Sally Whittaker of Haverhill, did shoebinding at low wages for several bosses or shoemakers while exchanging other goods and services with neighbors.[11]

The practice of giving out work to shoebinders who returned it to the central shop before the sewn uppers were given out to shoemakers made the shoe boss responsible for coordinating the process of work. Often shoemakers were forced to wait at the central shop for bound uppers to be returned by women workers. The Joseph Lye, Jr., journals, which begin in 1819, indicate that on many occasions he "[w]aited most of the day for work." [12] Sometimes he had to close up or sew the side seams of uppers himself in order to proceed with his work, but the low price for binding discouraged shoemakers from binding for themselves if they could avoid it. As women's work, shoebinding lowered labor costs to shoe bosses, and the low prices for binding convinced men like Lye not to waste their time sewing uppers. It was no longer acceptable work for artisans. Even if her husband made or "bottomed" shoes, a term that reflected the separation of work on uppers and bottoms, a shoebinder who worked for the same shoe boss frequently sewed different styles of shoes and did not often pass her work on to her husband, but returned it to the central shop. The shoe boss decided to which shoemaker these sewn uppers might go. A bound upper could be transported long distances without damage, but lasting and bottoming operations, by which the shoe was shaped to size and soled, had to be done in one place. [13] The central shop coordinated women's work in the home with that of the craftsmen in the shops and thus began to exert more control over the work performed by shoemakers.

The separation of shoebinding from shoemaking, which developed after 1810 and appeared in almost all of the surviving account books of shoe bosses in Essex County, not only shifted the direction of women's work into the control of the central shop, but reduced the wage that the family labor system commanded. Two early examples of this diminished earning capacity are found in the account books of Jonathan Boyce of Lynn (1793–1813). [14] Benjamin Willson, an unmarried shoemaker of eighteen, fresh from his apprenticeship, worked for Boyce in 1810 and 1811. Willson's account in Boyce's ledger credits him with making seventeen lots of shoes at twenty-six cents per pair for a total of $97.02. On the debit side of the accounts appeared a variety of items: sundries, tea, flour, rice, sugar, coffee, payments to third parties, and some cash. Also entered on the left column of the account are debits for shoebinding at an average of six cents a pair at the amount of seventy pairs of uppers or $4.20. Apparently Willson had contracted with Boyce for shoebinding that was not directly related to his own work as a maker, possibly counting on his mother, his two unmarried sisters, or women outside of his family to do the binding, but wages for shoebinding were not subsequently credited to his account. The debits can be explained as work separated from Willson's shoemaking, for which the amount of leather stock and the price for binding was listed as a debit on Willson's account, but for which the labor was not performed in his family. This young unmarried journeyman may have found it difficult to persuade the women of his own family to do the work and instead operated as a middleman to locate binders for his employer.

The account of James Ston, who also worked for Jonathan Boyce, showed more sizable debits for shoebinding between 1811 and 1812. After his first wife died in 1809, Ston remarried in 1810 at the age of twenty-six, and his second wife, Eunice, bore him two children in 1811 and in 1813. In early 1811, Ston's account was credited with making thirteen lots or approximately 314 pairs of shoes for a total of $94.20, while he was debited for the binding of 65 pairs of uppers, which totaled $2.95. In the period from June to November 1811, Ston made 271 pairs of shoes and was so credited, but was debited for the binding of 77 pairs. Other debits for binding appeared in Ston's account in later 1811 and in 1812. This period coincided with the birth of his two children and the debits in his accounts represent work for which he had contracted with shoebinders outside of his immediate family. Whatever the family circumstances that explain the lack of credits for binding in Ston's accounts, his earnings as the head of a rapidly growing family were reduced by this amount. Other shoemakers in the Boyce accounts were also debited for shoebinding, but none for so large an amount as Ston. The accounts of other shoemakers showed a steady stream of credits for shoebinding, indicating work performed for the shoe boss by female members of their families. However, most of the transactions in the Boyce accounts of Lynn represent entries for shoemaking only and do not list binding as either a credit or a debit. The Boyce accounts represent a transitional phase in the reorganization of shoe work with evidence both of the family labor system of production and of the separation of binding and making.

The family labor system of the late eighteenth and early nineteenth centuries had led shoemakers to expect that their female family members or relatives would contribute their work on binding uppers to the family economy. Low wages for sewing uppers in comparison with making also encouraged husbands and fathers to try to persuade their wives and daughters to do the work. Some, like Benjamin Willson, James Ston, and Isaac W. Merrill of Haverhill, faced limits that their wives and sisters put on the abilities of their husbands and brothers to act as agents for the storekeeper or shoe boss in the putting-out system.

The diary that Isaac Merrill kept between 1828 and 1878 provides evidence of the dynamics of this relationship with his wife.[15] Merrill's diary also gives historians an overview of the changes of five decades experienced by one New England journeyman in the shoe trade. By 1820, storekeepers and shoe bosses in Haverhill had begun to specialize in light shoes and slippers, obtaining leather from tanneries located in Danvers and following the example of Lynn shoe bosses by marketing their product in the South. Isaac Merrill made shoes in his shop located in the North Parish of Haverhill and began to keep his diary in September 1828, when he was twenty-six years old. He took cut leather from a variety of small shoe bosses in neighboring Bradford, crossing the Merrimack River to return his finished shoes and pick up more stock. He occasionally took apprentices, and once he moved into a neighbor's ten footer, only to leave hurriedly because the shop owner disliked Merrill's smoking and Merrill in turn objected to his use of strong language. During the years before his marriage in 1831, an event for which he yearned impatiently, Merrill usually worked on shoes for Bradford bosses who could supply him with bound uppers. Occasionally, however, he used an apprentice to sew uppers, hired a neighbor, Mrs. Brickett, to bind the uppers for him, or if he was forced to accept a lot with unbound uppers, he set to work sewing them himself. Marriage and a willing wife could resolve these difficulties for him.

In October 1831, after a lengthy courtship, Isaac Merrill married twenty-two-year-old Lois M. Chase. On November 5 he confided to his diary that the "delicate disorder" that was taxing Lois's health was "the falling of the womb." Isaac did not rush to ask his ailing bride to help him with his work, and on November 30 he was hard at work sewing shoe uppers himself. On December 15, however, he recorded that he made eight pairs that day and that Lois was earning 25 cents a day binding shoes. Her work as a binder did not continue long; on December 29 Isaac commented that "[o]n account of having no shoes bound I made only five pair." The next day he wrote, "[M]ade five pair. Lois has a sore finger." In February 1832 Isaac made five pairs a day, fewer than the eight pairs that having his wife's sewn uppers permitted him to finish in December. His comments on his wife's poor health continued for the next several months, and in April he sent for a doctor who told him that "her illness is owing to hard work and taking cold which occasions a weakness in her back." By May, Lois had begun to improve, but she apparently was not asked to do shoebinding again by her husband. When Merrill could not obtain sewn uppers from his shoe boss, he used an apprentice to bind them or did it himself.[16] An energetic and cheerful man, Merrill accepted the limits that his wife's troublesome health placed on the family economy and pushed himself harder, increasing his daily stint to ten pairs, working steadily throughout 1832, and frequently exhausting himself.

By the early 1830s the separation of making and binding and the shift in the coordination of work performed in the home and in the ten footer to the central shop characterized much of shoe production in the rapidly growing shoe towns of Lynn, Danvers, and Haverhill. The stock book for 1830–31 of an unidentified Lynn shoe manufacturer exemplifies these changes.[17] This stock book kept a tally on the numbers of pairs of cut leather stock given out by the central shop to be made and bound, the names of the shoemaker and the shoebinder to whom the stock was entrusted, and the date given out. The book carried no notation of wages paid or the date when the work was returned, but was used simply to identify and coordinate the assignment of work. I selected the months of March 1830 and 1831 to calculate the quantity of shoebinding performed separately from shoemaking for this large Lynn shoe boss. In March 1830 a total of 2,692 pairs of cut stock were given out to shoeworkers. Of that number, only 256 pairs or 10 percent were bound and made by a family labor system or by a wife and husband, father and daughter, or brother and sister identified as such by the same last name. Ninety percent appeared to have been made and bound by persons working as individuals for the shoe boss. In March 1831, monthly production had doubled to 6,174 pairs of shoes distributed to shoeworkers, of which 1,205 pairs or

20 percent were bound and made in a family labor context, while 80 percent of the stock was given out to individuals. Whether the rise in the use of the family labor system to increase production between 1830 and 1831 is significant is not clear. The evidence in this stock book illustrates the extent of the separation between making and binding processes for one large Lynn manufacturer in the early 1830s. Similarly, the John and Charles P. Preston central shop in North Danvers, which put out brogans, women's boots, and children's shoes, began to keep separate account books for making and for binding in 1833.[18] The Binders' Books that the Prestons used until 1845 indicated the degree to which binding and making had been separated and removed from the family system.

By the early 1830s, shoe manufacturers in Lynn and Haverhill had begun to develop in eastern Massachusetts towns networks of shoemakers and shoebinders that stretched north across the Massachusetts state line into Rockingham County, New Hampshire, and York County, Maine.[19] Central shop owners in Danvers also recruited shoebinders in the rural towns and villages of Massachusetts. Anna Rea of Topsfield worked as a shoebinder for a Danvers boss between 1819 and 1832.[20] Her personal accounts after 1820 illustrate the marginal nature of the work and the low level of earnings that shoebinders with dependents could expect working for central shops. Her father died of consumption in 1821, leaving his widow a one-third interest in the family farm and a very small annuity. His sons inherited most of the family property, while Anna and her unmarried sister, Rosamond, each received $200.

Faced with the need to support themselves, Anna, her sister, and her mother attempted to run the farm and earn additional income. When Rosamond married in 1827, Anna was left to support herself and her mother, but was unable to earn more than a total of $40.40 for almost nine years of intermittent work at binding shoes while performing farm and household chores. The prices for binding had risen slightly between 1820 and 1829, but her earnings represented only a marginal contribution to her support. After 1829 Anna Rea combined her work on shoes with employment as an agent who coordinated outwork on woolen cloth for small mills in North Andover. Occasionally, she put out shoe uppers to local women as well, probably for her former shoe boss. Her work as an agent in the outwork system in Topsfield improved her economic situation.[21]

Between 1832 and 1840 her chief source of income came from her work in putting out wool to be spun and woven in Topsfield by homeworkers, while shoebinding disappeared from her accounts. For Anna Rea the wages earned in binding shoes proved inadequate even as a supplement for a self-supporting farm woman with a dependent mother.

An analysis of the surviving account books of storekeepers and central shop owners in Essex and eastern Middlesex Counties indicates that the wages paid for shoebinding remained relatively steady from 1810 to 1830. Prices ranged between two and six cents a pair, depending on the style of the shoe. Complicated sewing on fine leather or extra work on straps or on the long legs of boots brought the highest wages. The shoebinder earned the least for unlined work shoes and for children's sizes. The account book of William Richardson of Stoneham (1811–39) provides the clearest examples of the differences in styles and their corresponding prices.[22] Between 1824 and 1826 Richardson organized a network of men and women shoeworkers in Essex and Middlesex Counties and in southern New Hampshire. He paid two cents for binding unlined brogans, two and one-half to three and one-half cents for children's laced boots, three cents for youth's laced boots, four cents for strapped boots and women's shoes, and five cents for laced slippers or fancy satin shoes. Laced shoes required the binder to work the holes for the lacings.

In Lynn and in Haverhill much of the work involved binding women's kidskin or morocco shoes and boots. For five cents a pair, the binder sewed or "closed up" two long side seams and a heel seam in a high-cut kidskin boot with a doubled linen or silk thread. Then she turned and pressed down the inside seams, seamed up the linings, and "fitted" the lining and the kid upper together. The top edges were "bound" with a leather strip that was turned down and stitched to the lining.[23] From each step of the binding process came the terms—closing, fitting, and binding—that represented a division of labor within shoebinding. Each step had a different price, which varied with the style of the shoe. According to the surviving account books, John Burrill of Lynn and Caleb Eames of Wilmington paid the highest price of six cents a pair for binding ladies' boots. This represents the highest wage earned by shoebinders in

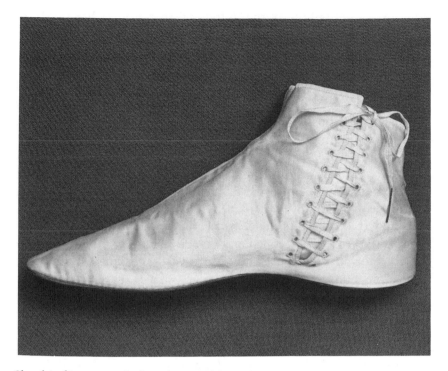

Shoebinding on satin bootine, wedding slipper of Emily Alden Davis, c. 1840, courtesy of Lynn Historical Society.

eastern Massachusetts before the late 1840s. The lowest prices were offered by Samuel Bacheller of Lynn, who offered one-half cent per pair for trimming shoes with rosettes or making bows and two cents for children's shoes in 1826. Essex County shoe bosses paid higher wages for shoebinding than did shoe bosses in other areas. Of the twelve occupations listed for females in New Hampshire in the McLane Report of 1832, shoebinding ranked among the lowest paid women's work along with domestic service and palm-leaf hatmaking.

The prices paid for shoebinding tell little about the daily, weekly, or annual wages earned by women workers, which are difficult to reconstruct. Most accounts were settled over a period ranging from several weeks to over a year, occurring when the shoebinder or a member of her family got to the village or town where the shoe boss was located to settle up. The account books do not make clear how long it actually took the individual to complete her work on a lot of uppers, and no diaries of shoebinders before the 1840s have survived.[24] It is likely that shoebinders did other kinds of work such as domestic service, teaching school, or other kinds of outwork. The accounts of shoebinders' employers, unlike the personal records kept by Anna Rea, do not indicate their total earnings as workers. Shoe bosses made binding available to women workers irregularly, and it was performed within a context of the interruptions of home life. Production varied with personal circumstances and generally was part-time and intermittent. The part-time nature of this homework, however, encouraged the women of the first Missionary Society of Stoneham in 1828 and the Female Benevolent Society of Danvers in 1835 to bind uppers to raise funds for their activities.[25] The Stoneham women averaged three pairs per member for an occasional afternoon's work, earnings so low that they soon abandoned their efforts.

Surviving accounts do not support Edith Abbott's contention that in the early nineteenth century many women in eastern Massachusetts who took work from bosses in shoe towns became "in a measure self-supporting."[26] Reminiscences of shoemakers in Haverhill indicate that a shoebinder might work steadily all day to produce ten pairs of sewn uppers at three to five cents per pair, but that she was required to furnish needles, thread, and sometimes lining material for the work, the costs of which reduced her earnings. Philip Swett of Haverhill recalled sewing uppers himself as an apprentice in the 1840s and remembered that the work required strong hands and tough fingers.[27] He estimated that the maximum earnings for any binder who worked many hours was fifty cents a day. The periodic and irregular nature of production conducted in the home encouraged the shoe boss to develop extensive networks of shoebinders along the freight lines and turnpikes in neighboring towns, rather than attempt to recruit male workers or get intensified production from binders by raising the price per pair. Using men or boys would have more than doubled the costs of labor. During the booming times for shoe production before the depression of 1837, Isaac Merrill of Haverhill actually paid his apprentice David Parker twelve cents a pair to sew uppers for shoes on which Merrill was making forty cents. He noted on March 26, 1836: "Shoemaking is real prime," and his Bradford bosses often picked up his finished shoes and delivered more stock rather than wait for him to come to town.[28] No shoebinder ever earned as much as twelve cents to bind uppers in the 1830s.

Prices for shoebinding did not rise in the flourishing shoe market before 1837, but other changes affected wages. In the 1810s most shoe bosses paid their binders only in store goods and made no cash available at all. Others paid largely in goods except for a tiny percentage of the total earnings that was paid off in cash to settle the account. After 1820, storekeepers who previously paid only in goods made some cash available on a regular basis.[29] In the 1820s and 1830s many shoemakers and shoebinders complained about the order system, which compelled them to accept their wages largely in goods rather than in cash. The order system was profitable to the central shop and to the storekeeper who could benefit from wholesale prices for goods and avoid the obligation of having ready cash for wages. If the central shop kept no goods, they issued orders on a local general store, and the storekeepers often discounted the orders as a service charge. Lynn shoe manufacturers organized special stores in the late 1820s to provide goods to their workers instead of cash. James H. Turner, reminiscing in 1896 about early nineteenth-century shoemaking in Haverhill, recalled that storekeeper Ezekiel Hale owed his father forty dollars at one time and forced him to take his choice of an equivalent value in "out of fashion white linen pants and vests or in yards of red flannel." Feeling cheated, Turner's father took the flannel, sold it at auction, and accepted the meager cash proceeds.[30] In response to the protests in the early 1830s of Essex County shoebinders against the order system, the sympathetic *Marblehead Gazette* reported that in 1834 one Lynn binder had received only two dollars in actual cash for three years of work, and the editor, labor activist Peter Dixey, Jr., demanded "an increase in remuneration and cash pay, instead of buckram and staytape."[31]

The separation of shoebinding and shoemaking characteristic of early nineteenth-century shoe production encouraged binders to organize themselves in order to protest low wages and the order system. Two outbreaks of collective resistance occurred in eastern Massachusetts in the early 1830s over the low prices offered by shoe bosses for binding despite a rising market for shoes. Although shoebinders sought and received the support of organized artisans, especially in Lynn, they created separate societies to represent their interests. They also attempted to utilize artisan ideology to justify their protest. In doing so, they began to argue for new rights for women. Their status as individual wage earners in the putting-out system and the sense of connection that some of their leaders had with factory operatives helped to create a new consciousness for them as working women.

The shoebinders of Reading and surrounding towns in Essex and eastern Middlesex Counties formed a Society of Shoebinders in the summer of 1831 to protest low wages and to obtain a uniform wage scale for binding various types of work. The *Lynn Mirror* of August 6, 1831, described an advertisement by the Reading society published in a Boston newspaper that had been signed by "two or three hundred names" representing shoebinders in the towns of Reading, South Reading, Stoneham, Malden, Lynn, and Woburn. The objective of the society was to encourage binders to cooperate in resisting individual wage bargains with the shoe boss, so that inexperienced women would not "work for nothing and find [furnish] themselves," that is, provide the shoe boss with free labor. The *Lynn Mirror* commented that the wage scale that the Reading society sought was the same as that commonly paid in Lynn.[32]

Five shoe bosses from Reading and neighboring towns replied to the protesting shoebinders on August 10 in the pages of the *New England Christian Herald*, a Methodist newspaper published briefly in Boston. The bosses rejected the demand for an increase in wages, which they claimed they had paid customarily for ten years. They attempted to undermine the binders' society by insisting that its membership was much smaller than represented and that few men supported the binders' cause. The shoe manufacturers maintained that "we are unacquainted with this new mode of doing business, and firmly protest against it, but are willing to employ them [the members of the Reading society] on fair and honorable terms as heretofore."[33] The August 12 issue of the *New England Christian Herald* contained a long letter to the editor from the Reading society, challenging the figures used by the shoe bosses to defend prevailing wages and charging that employers had refused to give work to any binder who sought higher wages. The letter also criticized the payment of wages in goods rather than in cash. The society insisted that it represented 227 shoebinders and that only eight women had withdrawn from the organization, several under pressure from their employers. The letter claimed that hundreds of local men supported their demands.[34] Although nothing more has survived about the activities of the Reading society, these shoebinders in 1831 were conscious of the vulnerability of the individual female who worked outside the family labor system. Drawing on their identification with the dignity and independence of artisan life, they expected fairness and good treatment from the shoe bosses and were critical of the unwillingness of their employers to share the profits of a rising shoe market. Perhaps the most striking achievement of this early example of collective resistance by working women was the establishment of an organization that represented a network of shoebinders working at home and living in different towns.

Two years later the shoebinders of Lynn and Saugus organized a second protest. By 1833 there were about 1,500 women in Lynn who earned wages as shoebinders. A wage cut prompted over half of them to organize the "Female Society of Lynn and Vicinity for the protection and promotion of Female Industry." In their public statements the shoebinders voiced the mechanic ideology of artisan shoemakers, blending it with an expression of their grievances as women wage earners and using it as a defense of the worth of their labor as female members of artisan families. As important, however, was their claim to new political and economic rights— the right to public action as women and the right to earn enough to make a significant contribution as wives to their families and as daughters or widows to earn enough for their own support.

The Lynn binders who organized the Female Society met at the Friends' Meetinghouse on December 30, 1833, where, as the *Lynn Record* noted, women could speak freely in public. About 1,000 women attended the meeting, the largest convention of females to meet together in New England, according to the *Record*. They were joined a few days later by 125 binders who met at the Methodist Church in neighboring Saugus and who adopted the same objectives, ideology, and constitution. In the preamble to the Lynn society's constitution, the binders accused their employers of "a manifest *error,* a want of justice, and reasonable compensation to the females; which calls imperiously for redress. While the prices of *their* labour have been reduced, the business of their *employers* has appeared to be improving, and prosperous, enabling them to increase in wealth. These *things ought not so to be!*" [35]

The demand of the Lynn binders for higher wages was based on the labor theory of value. In an address to the first meeting of the society, printed in the *Lynn Record* and signed by Chairman Mary Russell and Secretary Elizabeth K. Keene, the leadership of the society argued for a wage increase on the grounds

> that all individuals in the community should receive something like a corresponding remuneration for their exertions. It is highly reasonable, that those who perform a considerable portion of the labor, should receive a considerable portion of the recompense. Neither those who bind the shoes nor those who make them, and who, of course, perform the greater part of the labor, receive so much as those who cause them to be made, is evident from the fact that manufacturers frequently become wealthy, while the more laboring portion of the community, are obliged to struggle hard for a competence, and are frequently distressed. [36]

As workers, they believed they were not earning a just compensation, which threatened their independence and respectability. Furthermore, this economic injustice enriched the shoe boss; as such it represented a violation of the dignity of their labor and a moral outrage.

To redress their grievances, the shoebinders of Lynn demanded an increase in wages and an extension of the equal rights doctrine of the artisan tradition. "Equal rights should be extended to all—to the weaker sex as well as the stronger." Many of the women who attended the society's first meeting on December 30, the preamble claimed, supported either themselves or their families on their earnings as binders and had become dependent on wage labor. The disadvantages that women experienced "by nature and custom" should not be aggravated by "unnecessary and unjust" treatment as workers. The preamble expressed the belief that "women as well as men, have certain inalienable rights, among which is the right at all times, of 'peaceably assembling to consult upon the common good.'" [37] In this, the Lynn binders were responding to criticism that they were forming a combination against the manufacturers, which endangered the town's prosperity. They replied that the shoe bosses themselves combined to hold down wages and to pay the binders in store orders. The women in the Lynn society demanded the right to political action and equated their interests as workers with the interest of the community, regarding the welfare of the town as consisting "not in the aggrandizement of a few individuals, but in the general prosperity and welfare of the industrious and laboring classes."[38]

The recent reduction in wages, the preamble went on, prevented the shoebinders from obtaining "a comfortable support." The use of this seventeenth-century concept of the appropriate contribution of women to the family economy represented a preindustrial argument for a just wage, a feminine version of the competency sought by artisans.[39] However, in calculating their comfortable support, the shoebinders used as a measure not their work in production, but their duties and responsibilities as female members of artisan families. The shoebinders used their roles as wives, daughters, and widows of New England mechanics to insist upon a wage level that would confer dignity and independence on them. They calculated the price of the household services that a wife performed as seamstress, washwoman, nurse, and maid and demanded a wage high enough to cover these expenses.

> The poor man who employs help, must pay as much as the rich man. For the servant girl he must pay one dollar, or one dollar and a quarter per day besides her board. For the seampstress [*sic*] he must pay fifty cents per day. For the wash woman, he must pay seventy-five cents, and in some cases, one dollar per day. For the nurse he must pay two or three dollars per week besides her board. And these expenses are all that the rich man is required to pay for the same services. It is therefore evidently reasonable, that the wife of the mechanic, should receive a sufficient remuneration for her services, in order that she may assist her husband to defray their expenses, and to provide for their children.[40]

For a daughter, wages should be high enough to cover her expenses: board and personal upkeep, so as not to constitute a drain on her father's income or force her to leave home.

> Again, the mechanic may have daughters grown up, and in that case they should pay him at least, one dollar and twenty-five cents a week for their board. . . . But the mechanic is induced to board his daughters for one dollar per week because he knows that they cannot earn enough to pay more and at the same time provide themselves with

suitable clothing. He is therefore at a continual loss on their account. . . . All this inconvenience might however be easily remedied, by such a reasonable increase in wages, as would enable young ladies to pay a suitable price for their board, and to support themselves respectably and independently. . . . Yet more, it is well known that in factories young ladies receive a high price for their services; and unless our females receive nearly an equal amount, they may be induced to seek employment in the factory, the printing office, or some other place.[41]

As for a mechanic's widow with dependents, her wage level should ensure a subsistence without the necessity and degradation of applying to the town for poor relief:

Many families in this town consist of widows and orphans, who depend entirely on their own exertions for their support. If their means of subsistence are stinted, they are under a constant liability of calling upon the town, or upon their friends, for relief; and this is a source of unhappiness, in addition to the continual grief and affliction, which must rise in their hearts and surround them at every step, from a sense of destitution, . . . To allow such a just compensation, for their industry is an [act] of right and benevolence, which affords the means of supporting themselves respectably, and without a sense of dependence.[42]

The society particularly condemned the practice of paying widows who worked as shoebinders in store orders rather than in cash. As a society, the shoebinders of Lynn demanded "a reasonable compensation for our labor, as shall enable us to defray our expenses and ensure us that freedom from want, which is the natural right of the honest and industrious."[43] The activist shoebinders in 1834 recognized the new demands and opportunities that wage-earning represented for women in the early nineteenth century and sought to integrate wage work into their lives within a context of justice and morality. They linked morality to political action, which they saw as appropriate and necessary for female labor protest.

To be effective, the Lynn shoebinders' society had to organize all working women in the local industry whatever their attachment to the mechanic's family and artisan culture. The ideology that the society's leadership borrowed from artisan tradition and reshaped to their experiences of gender within the family betrayed, however, a contradiction between their demand for equal rights and the domestic basis on which their claim to a just wage for women rested. Equal rights for women as workers suggested the primacy of their paid work; women's wages calculated on the expense of household services indicated that domestic duties were primary. For the Lynn shoebinders, their role in the artisan family transformed the labor theory of value into a measure not of their work in production, but of their domestic duties. Rebellious shoebinders justified their protest by invoking artisan ideology, which, however, emphasized their gender role as family members rather than their class position as workers.

The artisan shoemakers of Lynn promptly offered their support to the Female Society in 1834 by voting to refuse work from any manufacturer not agreeing to the wages demanded by the binders. Earlier, when the Lynn shoemakers had organized a Society of Journeymen Cordwainers in 1830 to defend their wages and the privileges of the craft, they regarded the low wages paid for shoebinding as an injury to themselves. "Look and see how they [the shoe bosses] have depressed the price of female labor, and reduced it down to almost nothing! This has an effect on us as husbands, as fathers, and as brothers." [44] They saw the binders' grievances as a problem not for women but for artisan families. Although the leadership of the shoebinders' and cordwainers' societies did not represent an association of kin, the two groups worked together closely in 1834, and William Phillips of the cordwainers' society and a sympathetic manufacturer, Israel Buffum, served as the Female Society's delegates to a meeting of the Boston Trade Union in March. [45]

The mechanics and the wives, daughters, and widows of mechanics found cooperation easy enough in 1834 based on the sharing of preindustrial cultural traditions in the family, but the demand of the binders for a wage sufficient to make a reasonable contribution to family income and their use of the mechanic ideology to justify their public action were explicit claims to new rights for women. The leadership of the Female Society claimed a new moral role for women involving them in public activity on behalf of new rights. Some of the society's leaders would continue this activity on behalf of public morality in the Lynn Female Anti-Slavery Society in 1836. [46] The shift of women's work out of the family labor system and onto the wage labor market carried with it implications for changes in the consciousness of women and in the social relations of the sexes. In the typology of traditionalist, loyalist, and rebel developed for Lynn shoemakers by Alan Dawley and Paul Faler, the organized shoebinders of Lynn and Saugus in 1834 were early rebels.[47] They saw their interests as workers opposed to those of their employers and regarded collective action as the only means to secure accustomed living standards and a measure of independence. While their arguments for a just wage betrayed the special problems of homebound females engaged in wage work, they added the important dimensions of female gender and feminism to their expressions of class consciousness.

While the leaders of the binders' society spoke in rebellious terms, the rank and file wavered. By the late spring of 1834 the Female Society was divided and in trouble. Three-fourths of its members were either working for wages below the society's scale or had not paid their dues.[48] In an effort to overcome the divisions and disunity within the Lynn society, Mary Russell addressed a meeting of its members on June 9, urging the lagging membership to become "a band of sisters, each considering the welfare of the society as her own particular interest." In what appeared to be a reference to the turnouts in February 1834 by the female textile operatives in Lowell against a wage cut, Russell insisted, "We cannot see the propriety of denying the shoebinders that liberty which other females have, that of setting their own prices upon their own work; and we have but little doubt in saying, that if all members of the society were to be firm and determined that it would be but a short time ere they might be equally free from oppression."[49] Russell warned the society's members that disunity and failure would convince the public that their opponents rightly regarded them as fickle-minded and vain females. She urged the members of the society to be alive to their interests and their honor and not disappoint their supporters. Plans to start a cooperative central shop and to divide work and share wages during slow seasons or dull times, and exhortations to "think seriously, make exertions, be not discouraged" produced little response. The Lynn society fell apart; the last notice of the society's quarterly meeting appeared in early December 1834.

The development of a sense of common sisterhood among women reflected changes in gender definition in the early nine-

teenth century. As production left the household during early industrialization, middle-class women came to experience their domestic sphere as a female vocation. A cult of domesticity defined this
sphere and encouraged the development of a group consciousness
with a positive social role expressed as sisterhood. This sense of
sisterhood was a precondition for early nineteenth-century feminism.[50] Working women in New England shoe production also
experienced gender consciousness as a sense of sisterhood. With
the assignment of new work for women in the home and its separation from the family labor system, shoebinders turned to each
other to organize resistance against their employers. The sexual
division of labor reinforced the idea of a separate sphere for women
and provided an economic basis for the cult of domesticity among
women homeworkers. The artisan tradition promoted the domestic
locus of women's work, but by the 1830s the family labor system
had given way to the employment of women directly by the shoe
boss. The wage labor market had invaded the home and reshaped
the conditions of women's work. Sharing the bonds of womanhood both in work and in their domestic sphere, the leaders of
the shoebinders society in 1834 saw themselves as a female community organized for self-improvement and for the improvement
of society. Mary Russell actively sought to extend the idea of sisterhood as an organizing principle, but the shoebinders of Lynn
and Saugus could only respond hesitantly. The objective conditions
under which many shoebinders labored—isolated from each other
in private families outside a group labor system and combining
wage work with domestic responsibilities—discouraged collective
activity. The tension between their relationship as workers to the
equal rights tradition and their subordinate role as females in the
artisan family was exposed by their arguments for a just wage
based on the value of their domestic duties. Neither the social relations of the artisan family nor the realities of working for a shoe
boss encouraged the average shoebinder of Lynn to identify with
her working sister in the Lowell textile mills or to conceive of herself as a worker capable of self-support who could unite with her
peers to protest mistreatment.

Textile operatives in pre–Civil War Lowell demonstrated that
women workers could organize collective protest without a preindustrial craft tradition. Despite a temporary commitment to work,

Lowell women organized turnouts in the early 1830s drawing on the relationships created by group life at work and in the mill corporations' boardinghouses. They also utilized an ideology based on a revolutionary republican tradition similar to the equal rights arguments of artisan shoemakers. They saw wage cuts as an affront to their dignity as the daughters of freemen, the freehold farmers of New England. Their sense of sisterhood operated for them as craft solidarity did for skilled male artisans.[51] Although Essex County shoebinders shared with the Lowell textile workers a similar justification for protest and a similar view of their status as New England women, they remained immersed in family life in their communities and isolated from a group experience of work. The domestic setting of the lives and work of Essex County shoebinders contradicted their efforts to gain new rights or confront their employers. Decentralized homework separated the shoebinder from the wider experience of the textile operative. Although changing material conditions had created a new consciousness among some Essex County women working in shoe production, their role in family life and the objective conditions of their work presented them with unresolvable problems of organization and ideology.

The efforts of the Lynn Female Society had little success in 1834, but the booming market for shoes in the early 1830s brought some changes to the terms of wage payments for shoeworkers. Shoe manufacturers, eager to increase production, shifted from store orders to cash wages, which satisfied the demands of shoeworkers until 1836.[52] A brisk market for shoes also encouraged the bosses to become more active in coordinating the work by picking up the sewn uppers and finished shoes from the homes and shops of the workers. Bosses paid cash to those who demanded it, and the Lynn Female Society had a share of success in this, but wages for shoebinding remained steady in the booming market and never approached even the declining wages offered in the late 1830s and 1840s to women workers in textile mills.

The depression of 1837 hit shoeworkers hard. James Turner of Haverhill was ten years old that year, and he witnessed the dull times and remembered the general distress. Hundreds of shoemakers were unemployed, and families like the Turners, who had supplemented their income with the work of wives and daughters who bound shoes, lost the extra wages that had provided them with clothing and household furnishings. Turner recalled: "Fitting shoes by hand . . . was not confined to one class, but the high and the lowly with hardly an exception, did something of the work, so that the distress was more or less general." [53] The impact of the loss of work and wages hit hardest those vulnerable, wage-dependent women whom the leaders of the Lynn Female Society sought but failed to represent. In the reviving markets after the depression of 1837, the bosses in eastern Massachusetts shoe towns reorganized shoebinding into a more geographically extensive system that recruited women in distant villages and towns and on farms. This new rural outwork system gave capitalists the ability to ignore the demands of women shoeworkers in traditional centers of production. As a result, the labor protest of shoebinders who lived in the shoe towns of Essex County and who had fought against wage cuts in the early 1830s ceased.

CHAPTER THREE

The Social Relations of Production
in the Rural Outwork System,
1838–45

For years it was as common to see the
stitching clamp in the kitchen of a
Massachusetts farm house as the churn,
and more so than the cheese press.

—Letter from "Cordwainer,"
Shoe and Leather Reporter,
August 17, 1876

In February 1847 Ann Swett wrote to her sister Sarah from Manchester, New Hampshire, where she worked knitting loom harnesses in a textile factory. To be a boarder with free time, she wrote, was "grand." She had just pocketed four dollars for her first two weeks of work and was figuring out her potential as a wage earner. Her letter expressed newly discovered feelings of economic independence, and she assured her sister that she would never again bind shoes as an outworker in her Haverhill, Massachusetts, home. Her prospects were now brighter: "By and by when I get to knit real fast then I shall pay my board and after all that shall have twice as much as though I were binding shoes. I guess you [won't] catch me to do that little thing again, not I! You cannot think how funny it seems to have some money."[1]

Other mill operatives, such as Harriet Farley, who became the editor of the *Lowell Offering*, had chosen factory work over outwork. Farley was born in Claremont, New Hampshire, and beginning at the age of fourteen, she made palm-leaf hats, sewed garments, and bound shoes. However, when she left home determined to make her own living, she came to Lowell, where as a mill operative she earned good wages and saved her money. The possibilities of an independent life and relatively high wages for female workers in the textile factories of New England contrasted sharply with the experience of women in outwork shoe production. Working as isolated individuals in their rural homes, women who bound shoe uppers in the putting-out system in pre–Civil War New England were offered low wages and erratic employment. Those who could leave their homes, like Ann Swett and Harriet Farley, eagerly abandoned outwork for factory work. The conditions of the outwork system in shoe production, palm-leaf hatmaking, and garment work encouraged the decisions of the young New England women who went by the thousands into textile factories before 1850.[2]

As a system of production, outwork in New England contrasted sharply but coexisted with the early textile factories. Instead of shifting work outside of the home and leaving women in the family separated from production and wage-earning, outwork introduced new paid employment into the home. The outwork experience was widespread; more women participated in outwork in Massachusetts prior to 1850 than worked in textile factories. Industrial production of textiles, however, provided economic motives for women to bind shoes or make palm-leaf hats in order to obtain factory-made cloth. This in turn encouraged merchant-capitalists to develop the outwork system of shoebinding to increase production without centralizing work, adopting mechanization, or raising wages. In New England, this system was referred to as domestic production or as the given-out or commission system. It involved the production of consumer goods for a mass market by workers who earned wages by laboring in their own households on materials furnished to them by merchant-capitalists.[3] In early nineteenth-century America, both the factory system and outwork were reshaping women's work in the home.

The extension of the outwork system in Essex County marked a transition for women workers from the family labor economy characteristic of premodern work to the family wage system. In the late eighteenth and early nineteenth centuries, shoebinders worked in a system of joint family effort coordinated by the male head, but increasing demands for production put limits on the abilities of women to bind quantities of shoe uppers while also fulfilling their other household duties. When the family labor system proved inadequate to meet the needs of production, shoe bosses hired other women from nonshoemaking families and coordinated their work. Part of the work performed on shoes moved out of the control of artisans and into the hands of shoe bosses. Outwork on shoes by women living at home dominated female employment in Essex County in the early nineteenth century. By 1845, 80 percent of the total number of women earning wages in the county worked as shoebinders.[4] The successful organization of the labor power of women into the outwork system was one important factor in the rapid development of shoe production in Essex County and its growing dominance in southern markets.[5]

For many rural women, money earned by shoebinding represented the first cash wages that they contributed to family income other than by working as agricultural laborers and domestic servants or selling home-produced commodities. This wage work brought them into direct contact with an employer outside of the family and into the relations of the marketplace. These connections with a new economic world encouraged women to make a distinction between wage work and domestic tasks, a separation that contrasted with the blending of household production into the steady routine of domestic work in the eighteenth-century family economy. For most women, however, the wages that they could earn in shoebinding were only an intermittent supplement to the family's economic well-being. The primary contribution of married women remained domestic work and child care. Only unmarried daughters or wives and mothers driven by severe economic need worked steadily sewing shoe uppers. In separating wage work from domestic work and keeping domestic concerns primary, rural homeworkers began to distinguish between work and domesticity in ways that resemble the experience of middle-class women in the early nineteenth century.[6] This distinction marked the development of new attitudes toward work and life even for women who took work into their homes.

During the first two decades of the nineteenth century, merchant-capitalists began to recruit women workers outside of shoemaking families to work in the putting-out system for wages. By the early 1830s, Essex County shoe bosses had created extensive rural networks of shoebinders in eastern Massachusetts and southern New Hampshire. The inability of many homebound women to work steadily for shoe bosses encouraged the extension of these networks of part-time, casual workers into neighboring areas. In addition, labor protest by shoebinders in the Essex County towns of Reading, Lynn, and Saugus in the early 1830s provided another motive for bosses to develop a new labor supply. Work in the form of cut leather stock was delivered by team, by stage, or by cart, if the binder lived in the vicinity. Shoemakers often acted as agents in the putting-out system, recruiting women in their villages to bind shoes for the boss. Masters and journeymen sometimes assigned the sewing of uppers to apprentices, but only when wholesale prices were high and the shoe boss could afford in effect to pay double for binding. Some shoemakers, out of necessity or desperation, bound uppers for their own work, but on the whole the sexual division of labor continued to categorize shoebinding as women's work at low wages.

The account books of shoe bosses John and Charles P. Preston (1811–45) of Danvers, Massachusetts, provide one example of the development and operation of the rural outwork system in Essex County.[7] Surviving account books documenting the outwork system in shoe production are rare. While the Preston operation has the most complete records, it was small and may not be representative. However, when its accounts with outworkers are linked to vital records and census manuscripts in the towns into which the Prestons' network reached, a unique picture emerges of the process of production that European historians call protoindustrial. These historians have examined the impact of outwork on rural people in the early modern period, especially the influence of wages from outwork on population growth before the industrial revolution.[8] The Preston accounts supply information on one form of outwork in New England in the early nineteenth century, but also provide an opportunity to examine the patterns of work and life for women outworkers.

Protoindustrialization in Western Europe and in England has been studied from the perspectives of the family and of the demographic changes created by early industrial capitalism. Outwork as a new source of wage income for landless rural families lowered the age of marriage and contributed to population growth before the development of the factory system. Historians see the family interacting with the outwork system in a complex fashion that reinforced the family as a social structure but altered its internal dynamics. In some ways, the outwork system in shoe production in Essex County conformed to the European pattern. An underemployed group in terms of wage work was recruited to outwork on shoes: females residing in rural households. However, their families were not landless, but likely to be small farmers. The recruitment of this new source of labor to shoe production was the result of the development of markets by merchant-capitalists. But there is an important difference between the outwork system in Danvers, Massachusetts, and the protoindustrial systems of production in Shepstead, Leicestershire, the canton of Zurich, or Saxony. The sexual division of labor and the separation of binding and making that developed after 1810 altered the family basis of work, and young children were not commonly employed in shoe production except as apprentices. Rather than share work as a family team in the same physical location, shoemakers and shoebinders increasingly worked in separate places on different lots of work and for different bosses. The erosion of the family labor system in shoemaking produced a distinct form of outwork in New England. As Thomas Dublin has pointed out, the outwork system in New England appeared simultaneously with the factory system, rather than as a prelude.[9]

The rural outwork system in Danvers promoted the sexual division of labor and the separate work roles of men and women in ways that did not appear to support early marriage, at least for the women who earned very low wages as shoebinders. In other ways, however, the Preston accounts and local sources indicate similarities with the European protoindustrial system. Outwork replaced seasonal agricultural labor and domestic work for the older sons and daughters of local families. In addition, the limits that household duties placed on the productivity of shoebinders suggest that once family subsistence needs were met, it was difficult for shoe bosses to persuade women workers to increase their productivity. The Prestons came to rely for over half of their shoebinding on a very small proportion of their outworkers who kept production going out of economic necessity and personal circumstance. In fact, the Prestons were dependent on a small number of steady, productive workers within a larger network of casual workers with lower productivity. In many respects, the Preston accounts resemble the putting-out system in England: hard work and low wages, little disciplinary control by the capitalist over the work force, and low productivity by the outworkers. However, the difficult social and economic circumstances of the lives of the few steady shoebinders on whom the Prestons depended shaped their capacity and willingness to produce large quantities of work.

Danvers, located in Essex County just north and inland of Salem, had a population of over 4,000 in 1830. South Danvers (now Peabody) dominated the town's economy with its tanneries and small manufactories that turned out tinware, bricks, axes, nails, and glue. North Danvers was agricultural. The farmers of North Danvers typically produced two kinds of marketable goods before 1830: onions in the summer for the wholesale produce market in Boston and in the winter the crude, unlined work brogans worn by agricultural workers. Because of long-term credit arrangements with southern wholesalers, the shoe bosses who put out leather to the farmer-shoemakers of Danvers had little access to cash and preferred as much as possible to pay their workers in goods that they stocked themselves. Farm families made do with the staples and goods that the boss offered or they obtained an order on his credit with a local store. Shoe bosses rarely paid cash for such work.[10] The onions that also brought income to the farm family were harvested in the fall, then bunched and braided by the daughters of local farmers. Aside from onion-bunching, there was little wage labor available to the women of Danvers. The only other employment for women in the town was in two small factories that made carpets and stockings. Sons of small farmers worked for larger farmers, and their sisters sought work as hired girls.[11]

In the early 1830s John Preston's brother Samuel and other young men began to expand and diversify shoe manufacture in North Danvers. Samuel Preston obtained a patent in 1833 on a simple, hand-operated shoe-pegging device, which made the joining together of the sole and the sewn upper by small wooden pegs a faster and cheaper, if less durable, operation than if sewn by a shoemaker. The Prestons in Danvers began to produce a better grade of men's shoes in addition to brogans, which were also pegged, as well as women's and children's shoes. They sold these shoes, as did many Danvers shoe manufacturers, in the developing wholesale market in Boston rather than on long-term credit to southern merchants. The Prestons obtained cash and leather stock in return and were willing to pay wages in cash rather than in goods.

The availability of cash wages for outwork changed the prospects of the sons and daughters of farm families in Danvers. First, the wages paid for making and binding prompted many of them to abandon agricultural labor. Daughters of small farmers no longer braided onion tops with shoe thread borrowed from their fathers. Shoe boss Edwin Mudge recalled that "[t]he shoe business wrought a great and happy change in many families in town." Once the children of small farmers had to leave their homes to seek agricultural work and live with others. Now "they could all remain at home, and work upon shoes," to the profit of the local shoe bosses.[12] This expansion of production did not separate work from the home, but extended the putting-out system in Danvers to new workers. As a result, onion-growing farmers had to recruit men and women from other areas of rural New England to fill jobs in seasonal agricultural labor. The new system of outwork on better grades of shoes for cash wages increased rapidly in Danvers and the surrounding rural towns in Essex County; from 1837 to 1845, the number of shoemakers and shoebinders more than doubled in Danvers and in neighboring Middleton.

One of these new shoe bosses was John Preston, who operated a partnership with his son Charles between 1832 and 1845. He built a central shop on a farm near the Middleton town line that held the simple machinery for rolling and splitting leather and the tools and space for cutting and preparing the stock. Here he dispensed cut leather and pegging devices under his brother's patent and took in, finished, and inspected shoes for marketing. To this central shop came the local shoemakers and shoebinders to pick up stock for men's, women's, and children's shoes of various styles: brogans, buskins, ties, pumps, and slippers.

The Preston business was probably more typical of the outwork system in rural Essex County than the system of production conducted in the shoe centers of Lynn and Haverhill. Output was relatively limited, and the records of its operation appear simple. The transactions were conducted on a face-to-face basis between the boss and the worker, but the shoemaker often operated as a middleman between females in his family or his village and the shoe boss. Ledgers served the most basic needs of bookkeeping with debits and credits representing the stock entrusted to the maker or the binder, the prices paid, and the wages earned.[13] The early John Preston accounts cited all work under the names of shoemakers, but by 1833 the existence of separate ledgers for shoebinding, called Binders' Books, demonstrates the scale to which binding had become separate from making operations.

The Prestons paid their workers in cash and also in an array of goods that they kept in the central shop, including cotton textiles, illuminating oil, corn, potatoes, and oats. A typical account of shoemaker Charles R. Fisher from April to November 1835 revealed credits of $235.59 earned by making children's boots and debits for shoemaker's findings (lasts, thread, and pegs, which were available by the quart and the bushel), plus $160.37 in cash, leaving a balance carried forward to the next account (see Appendix A). Other debits included a pegging apparatus, brushes, awls, and aprons. In April 1836, just before his marriage to Sophronia Guilford, who worked as a shoebinder for the Prestons, Fisher bought his bride-to-be a new pair of shoe clamps. Her labor on shoes would be credited to his account after their wedding.

Additional items available from the Preston central shop were skins and hides, whole or cut, hammers, lampblack, twine, money to borrow at interest, and a horse and carriage for hire. Charles Fisher's account listed debits for shoes and slippers, indicating a purchase of leather goods that he did not make himself. One of the primary characteristics of the putting-out system was a division of labor that separated the shoemaker from the finished product marketed by the shoe boss. Although shoemakers took part of their wages in leather stock, many of them also acquired shoes, boots, and slippers. Fisher's account also listed debits for orders on the Jonas Warren store, a popular and reliable source of staple and dry goods for the farmers of North Danvers. The Prestons also arranged payments to third parties and checks drawn on the Village Bank.

An analysis of the patterns of work for both shoemakers and shoebinders indicates that although the Prestons employed about 300 men and women between 1833 and 1845, they depended for most of the outwork production on a small group of steady workers. The geographical area of the Preston network was extensive given rudimentary transportation over rough and muddy roads, although the area was crossed by both the Essex and the Newburyport Turnpikes and there was a regular freight service to Boston. Nearly half of the shoemakers in the Preston accounts lived in Danvers, while a quarter lived in neighboring Middleton. The remainder lived in towns to the north and west of Danvers, as far away as Newburyport, about fifteen miles. The network of shoebinders was more narrowly confined to Danvers, which represented the residence of two-thirds of them; one-quarter lived in Middleton.

Of the 133 shoebinders employed by the Prestons, only twelve worked steadily for two years or more, but they produced over half of the total production of sewn uppers between 1833 and 1845. Sixty-five percent of the total number of women employed were married, and their husbands were shoemakers, farmers, traders, carpenters, and laborers. The rest of the binders (35 percent) were single or widows. The occupations of many fathers and husbands of shoebinders were not identifiable even when linked to the 1850 census.[14] Their ages ranged from sixteen to seventy. One-quarter of the accounts in the Binders' Books were held in the names of a husband or father, but three-quarters were in the name of the shoebinder herself, indicating a direct relationship with the shoe boss.

Wages for shoebinding before 1845 varied only with the style of the boot or shoe and the type of sewing it required, according to the account of one of the steady workers, Mrs. William Hutchinson of Middleton who worked for the Prestons for nine years. In 1843 Mrs. Hutchinson earned three cents per pair for binding and closing children's boots, the same price paid to her in 1835. The lowest price was two cents a pair for closing the unlined brogan upper, but some binders seamed linings at one-quarter of a cent per pair. New styles introduced by the Prestons in 1842 paid better wages—six cents a pair for closing and binding women's buskins and calfskin boots—but closing brogans dominated Mrs. Hutchinson's work after 1838, cutting her former earnings by half.

Earnings also varied with the ability of the shoebinder to work steadily. Mrs. Hannah McIntire of Middleton, a busy farmer's wife with two small children, took eleven months to finish binding four lots of shoes or about 240 pairs. This work earned her $7.45, which she took in cash ($2.10), in store orders, and in binding thread. In contrast, Miss Nancy Putnam of Danvers, who was in her early twenties, worked for five months from August 1837 to February 1838 and bound twenty-six lots of shoe uppers or about 1,560 pairs. She earned $40.35 in cash.

The evidence in the Preston accounts does not support the estimates of shoebinders' wages in traditional sources, which ranged from twenty-five to forty cents a day or $1.50 to $2.40 a week, wages nearly comparable to the earnings of textile operatives.[15] Even the hardest working Preston binder averaged only about seventeen cents a day over a three-year period, and as a group the twelve steadiest workers earned between fifty cents and $1.50 a week. Shoebinders who worked for a year or more for the Prestons, about a third of the work force, earned an average wage of $42.72 a year or eighty-two cents a week, although they may have worked for other shoe bosses as well. These earnings meant access to cash.

Cash wages induced many people in Danvers and Middleton to work for shoe bosses, and the accounts of shoebinders reflect this interest. Married women took their credits in both cash and store orders, but only one-quarter took store orders for staple goods exclusively. One-third of the wives took both orders and cash, and nearly half worked only for cash wages. Half of the unmarried or widowed shoebinders worked exclusively for cash, while only about 10 percent worked solely for store orders. The rest took their wages in both cash and orders, indicating that some daughters might have shared a part of their earnings with their families.

Table 1. Wages paid to shoebinders in the Preston Binder's Books

	Wives	Single and widowed women
Orders only	24%	13%
Orders and cash	31%	37%
Cash only	40%	49%
Total	95%*	99%*

* 5% of the wives and 1% of the single and widowed binders returned the work unfinished and received no payment.

The Prestons made cash wages available to three-quarters of their binders, representing for many women, especially those living in rural Middleton, the first money they had ever earned.[16]

Many of the shoebinders who worked for the Prestons sewed uppers for a period of six months or less. Although their production was minimal, their work habits and apparent motivations are revealing. Five of the Preston brothers, their wives, and their daughters joined forces as kin to supply initial labor as John Preston's business expanded in the early 1830s. For example, John Preston's wife, Clarissa, bound shoes for two years from 1836 to 1838, often finishing up odd lots. None became steady workers, and most abandoned this helpful role after 1837.

Shoemakers sometimes arranged for their wives to work as binders to pay off debts that they owed to the Prestons or to third parties. Nancy Peaseley Putnam of Danvers married shoemaker Truman B. Clifford in 1835 and worked as a shoebinder from December 1843 to August 1845, paying off her husband's debt to the Prestons and earning an additional $10.00 in cash. In most cases, the shoebinder had no previous record as a wage earner for the Prestons, but worked hard for a period of time simply to clear her family of debt.

Some wives worked as binders to supplement family income under what appeared to be singular and difficult conditions. The wife of Sylvester Eveleth of Danvers put in two months of very hard work, turning out eight lots of shoes in exchange for $18.00 in store orders while caring for five children under the age of thirteen. This feat of binding sixty pairs of shoes a week over a period of eight weeks probably represented a family financial emergency. It was the only work that Mrs. Eveleth ever did for the Prestons. Hannah Moore Perkins of Middleton produced four lots of uppers in four months in 1841 for $7.78 in store orders. She was the mother of four children and gave birth to her fifth child one month after turning in her work. Her advanced pregnancy must have made the manipulation of the binding clamp awkward, and her exchange of work for store orders suggests family need. It was the only occasion when she worked for the Prestons.

Some shoebinders appeared to work for the Prestons for a definite and limited objective, such as a wedding outfit. Mrs. Betsey Fisher became a shoebinder in 1844 specifically, it appeared from her account, to buy a new cooking stove through the Prestons. She worked an additional year, earning $65.47, most of which she took in store orders. A few binders were members of whole families who worked for the Preston operation, but the majority were employed as individuals. Their reasons for participating as casual workers in the putting-out system largely concerned their families: loyalty to a family business, the repayment of debts, or the supplementing of family income in emergencies. Harriet Beecher Stowe used the character of Hepsey Lawson in her novel *Oldtown Folks* (1869) to explore the situation of a rural New England wife who did outwork on both shoe uppers and garments to supplement her family's income. Hepsey was "a gnarly, compact, efficient, little pepper-box of a woman" who supported her six children, mostly on her own exertions. Her husband, Sam, was a storyteller, sometime tinker and blacksmith, and the "village do-nothing."[17] Stowe based these characters on her observations of her husband Calvin's hometown of Natick, Massachusetts, a center of shoe production for Middlesex County. Hepsey's experience portrays a rural wife's intensive efforts as an outworker, which sometimes provided a source of income crucial to family survival.

Twelve steady workers produced over half of the total production of bound uppers for the Preston operation between 1833 and 1845. Their characteristics raise questions about the prototype of the shoebinder in traditional sources. David N. Johnson's *Sketches of Lynn* (1880) described the shoebinder in Lynn as the wife of a shoemaker who found time to bind enough uppers to keep all the journeymen in her husband's shop busy as well as care for her children and complete domestic tasks.[18] In contrast, five of the twelve steadiest workers in the Preston accounts were unmarried, one was an elderly bachelor, and six were the wives of farmers, some of whom also worked on shoes. Few of these binders worked in a family labor context, and the most steady production of quantities of sewn uppers was possible only for those single women relatively free of domestic work and child care. For example, Ruth McIntire of Middleton was unmarried and thirty-three years old in 1837 when she began working for the Prestons. She worked steadily for five years and earned an average annual wage of $52.00, taking 56 percent of her earnings in cash and the balance in shoes, binding thread, and store orders.

The one male outworker in the Binders' Books was sixty-three-year-old Jonathan Prince, who lived in Danvers, boarding with an unrelated family. His only sister was married and living in nearby

Boxford. Prince, an elderly shoemaker, eked out a small living binding brogan uppers, which required less strength from his aging fingers than shoemaking. He earned an average annual wage of $40.04 between 1834 and 1837; Preston shoemakers who worked steadily averaged $255.90 a year. Prince may have been increasingly crippled in his hands, as his production diminished considerably during his last months of work for the Prestons. In 1837 he moved to Boxford, where he lived with his widowed sister until his death in 1847. His presence in the Binders' Books represents the necessity of one aging shoemaker to find employment in the outwork system and the decline in status and earning capacity that went with binding shoes.

Two steady Preston binders provide evidence of the impact of marriage and childbearing on their capacity to sew uppers. Lucinda Wyatt of Danvers began working for the Prestons in 1833 at the age of twenty-three. She worked for five years, averaging an annual wage of $40.61, of which she took 73 percent in cash and the balance in shoes, binding thread, cotton cloth, store orders, and a payment for pew rent in a local church. In 1840 she married Daniel White, a shoemaker who also worked for the Prestons. As Lucinda Wyatt White, she worked on four lots for the Prestons that were credited to her husband's account in early 1842. Later the same year she had a daughter, who died as an infant. Daniel did not make shoes for the Prestons after 1842, and Lucinda completed only two additional lots in 1844 for store orders. Once married, she severely curtailed her work for her former employers.

The case of Sarah Towne of Danvers, who started out working for the Prestons in 1834 when she was twenty-four, provides another example of the limitations that marriage seemed to place on the work capacity of shoebinders. She returned her first sixty pairs of morocco slippers unfinished, but in 1835 she began a nine-year period of shoebinding for the Prestons. Her marriage in 1838, however, produced a sharp decline in her work for them. Sarah Towne was the most prodigious worker in the Binders' Books. She averaged a production of sixty lots of uppers or 3,600 pairs every six months for three years, 1835–38. This represents twice the number of pairs estimated as the daily potential of the steadiest binder. As a consequence she earned the highest annual wage of $115.00, close to that of a textile operative, and took 72 percent of her earnings in cash. Whether her spur was poverty or ambition is not known. In December 1837 she bore a child, according to the Danvers town records, and married Eben Payson Colcord, a Preston shoemaker, in August 1838. Her first child, whom she apparently had to support by her own efforts, scarcely deterred her exertions as a binder, but when she married, her work for the Prestons fell off markedly.

Eben Colcord continued working for the Prestons, making coarse brogans almost exclusively during the depression of 1837, but Sarah Colcord did not bind them for him. While bearing three more children between 1839 and 1842, Sarah did fit and bind eight lots of women's shoes credited to her husband's account. She may have been able to obtain other work on a better grade of shoes from another shoe boss in Danvers. Sarah returned to steady binding as a widow after Eben died of a fever in 1852 on an expedition to the California goldfields, but her steadiest work for another Danvers shoe boss, James P. Hutchinson, hardly rivalled her arduous efforts before her marriage.[19] Her average annual earnings as a widow in 1856–58 were, nonetheless, a respectable $50.00 a year.

The steady shoebinders who were wives with many children and heavy domestic duties found their ability to produce work limited. Their annual wages were half of those earned by single women: $26.20 for wives and $57.73 for unmarried steady binders. Married binders, however, worked for longer periods for the Prestons, averaging eight years to the four-year average of single binders. This pattern suggests a contradiction between the assignment of production in the rural outwork system to homebound, married women and the limits that their domestic duties for the family placed on their ability to work steadily. However, the accounts of the six steady binders who were wives reveal glimpses of their strenuous activities.

Betsey Evens of Danvers was fifty-seven years old in 1834 when both she and her youngest daughter, Susan, worked as binders for the Prestons. Betsey Evens had worked intermittently for John Preston's uncle beginning in 1815, and her husband Eliab was a classic farmer-shoemaker, applying himself to each kind of work according to the season. Susan ended her account in 1835, but her mother worked on. Mrs. Evens averaged $23.30 a year for ten years until her death from consumption in March 1845, when she was sixty-eight. Incredibly, the month before she died, her account listed a payment for closing sixty pairs of brogans. Sophia Wilkins married Samuel Russell of Middleton in 1823. Her work for the Prestons paralleled burdensome responsibilities at home. She began in 1836 with six children under the age of eleven, working hardest during the period 1838 to 1842. In 1838 and 1839, while closing very large numbers of brogans and taking her wages almost exclusively in store orders (suggesting financial straits), she bore and buried her seventh child. Mrs. William Hutchinson of Middleton began working in 1834 at twenty-eight and worked steadily for nine years, closing brogans. She earned the highest annual wage of all of the married shoebinders ($39.47), added income for her family of three small children and farmer husband.

European historians of protoindustrialization have argued that access to wages for families in the putting-out system that included the labor of women lowered the age of marriage by providing a means of support other than land inheritance for young couples. The limited evidence obtained from the Preston accounts, especially on the marital age of single binders who worked for the Prestons for more than six months, does not support this argument for New England. The sexual division of labor in shoemaking and the subsequent separation of making and binding undercut the ability of families to function as work units. Of the five unmarried steady binders who earned the highest wages and therefore could bring this earning capacity into marriage, the vital records do not record any marriages for three before 1850, and the other two married relatively late at twenty-eight and thirty. The average age of first marriage for single women both in Danvers and Middleton between 1830 and 1849 was twenty-three.[20]

An additional six single women worked for the Prestons for a period over six months. Two appeared not to have married at all, and of the remaining four, three married later than the average age of their peers. Only one, Fanny Bradstreet of Topsfield, who married a shoemaker when she was twenty-one, conformed to the European pattern.[21] These examples of eleven single shoebinders who demonstrated a commitment to work for their employers for over six months does not suggest that wages for binding encouraged them to marry earlier than their peers or to choose husbands with whom they could work in family units. Put together with evidence on the low productivity and slender earnings of the many married shoebinders who appear in the Preston accounts, involvement in the rural outwork system in New England shoe production did not seem to offer the same economic encouragement to early marriage that family involvement in protoindustrial work did in European countries.

As the Prestons reached into their extensive network of relatives in Danvers to provide makers and binders for the initial expansion of their business operation in the 1830s, the shoemakers who worked for the Prestons recruited women in their own families and in those of relatives and neighbors to sew uppers. In effect, the shoemaker was acting as a middleman to locate binders for the shoe boss. The outwork system required many agents to find and coordinate the female labor force. Evidence of debits for shoebinding appears in the Preston shoemakers' accounts beginning in the 1820s and continues until 1845. These debits designated the cut upper stock and wages for binding provided to the shoemaker by the shoe boss and listed in the shoemaker's account as a debit or a deduction along with other cash payments and store goods. The money and the upper stock represented the capital of the shoe boss entrusted to the shoemaker in order to locate and pay for shoebinding. Whether the shoemaker received any remuneration or consideration from the shoe boss for his services as a middleman is not clear from the Preston shoemakers' accounts. Binding done by female members of his own family was credited to the shoemaker's account along with his own work on making.[22] No debits ever appear for shoemaking, and there were none for binding in the Binders' Books. Debiting for binding uppers in shoemakers' accounts began to appear in Essex County as early as the 1810s and marks the transition of women's work on shoes out of the shoemaker's family and onto the local labor market.

The debiting for binders' work in the accounts of shoemakers represents their attempts to resolve the difficulties of getting shoe uppers sewn by female domestic workers. Low productivity of individual binders had encouraged the shoe bosses to separate binding from making and expand the network of the putting-out system by whatever means they could. The availability of prepared uppers was essential to shoemaking, but few shoemakers spent their time sewing uppers for two to six cents a pair when they could make shoes. These low wages encouraged shoemakers to seek out shoe-binders, whether in their own families or in the families of neighbors, or rely on the shoe boss to furnish sewn uppers for their work.

The ninety-one casual shoemakers who worked for the Prestons for less than two years produced a total of 741 lots of shoes between 1835 and 1842. The female members of their families bound the uppers on only 25 percent (192 lots) of the total number of shoes these shoemakers made. Their accounts were debited for binding another 17 percent (127 lots) of their total work. But the shoe boss had to provide over half of the sewn uppers on which these shoemakers depended for their work.

The efforts of the twenty-two steady shoemakers who worked for the Prestons for over two years to recruit binders were even less successful. As a group, the steady shoemakers produced 1,881 lots of shoes between 1835 and 1842, while their family members bound only 13 percent (240 lots) of their work. On the debit side of these accounts appears an additional 13 percent (251 lots) of the shoemakers' work, totaling, however, only 26 percent of the total production of the steady male workers.

Table 2. Binding undertaken by shoemakers, 1835–42, in the Preston Binders' Books

Lots of shoes	Casual shoemakers	Steady shoemakers
Bound by family members	192 (25%)	240 (13%)
Bound by nonfamily members	127 (17%)	251 (13%)
Provided by shoe boss	422 (58%)	1,390 (74%)
Total lots	741 (100%)	1,881 (100%)

The shoe bosses provided abut three-quarters of the sewn uppers for their most productive shoemakers, and this increased the makers' dependence on the central shop. Two-thirds of all of the shoebinding for the approximately 2,600 lots of shoes made for the Prestons between 1834 and 1842 was done by shoebinders listed in the Binders' Books. Although one-quarter of these accounts were listed in the names of husbands and fathers who had recruited family members for the shoe boss, most of the sewn uppers came from the hands of women workers employed directly by the shoe boss.

An analysis of the accounts of the shoemakers who worked steadily for the Prestons for two years or more shows a wide disparity in the capacity of wives and daughters to bind uppers for their families. Although marriage and childbearing limited the ability of most shoebinders to engage in outwork, some wives continued to bind uppers for their shoemaker husbands. But even the hardest-working wife produced less than half the number of lots made by the male head of the family. Sophronia Guilford Fisher of Danvers had been a shoebinder for the Prestons before she married her husband, Charles, in 1836. She had no children until 1845, which may explain her ability to produce the quantities of sewn uppers listed as credits in her husband's account. Her work, however, amounted to less than half of her husband's total number of lots of work.

Some accounts suggest that female family members did not work on the tiring and unremunerative work of closing brogans. The early work record of Mary Demsey of Danvers is impressive. With seven children under the age of fifteen in 1835, Mary and her husband, Isaac, worked together binding and making children's and women's boots, work that paid them relatively good wages. By late 1837 and as a consequence of hard times, Isaac shifted to low-paid brogan-making and depended less and less on Mary to bind brogans for his work, which continued for the Prestons until 1842. Clarissa Rounday of Danvers, who was a young wife with a two-year-old son in 1835, seemed willing enough to bind children's soft boots for her husband, Cornelius. When he became a brogan-maker in 1836, he depended on the Prestons to supply him with bound uppers. If some wives and daughters did not or would not bind brogan uppers, the Prestons depended on four steady binders: Mrs. Samuel Russell, Mrs. Betsey Evens, Mrs. George Thomas, and the elderly Jonathan Prince, who concentrated their efforts on the always abundant work sewing coarse cowhide uppers for small wages.

Shoebinders and shoemakers who worked for the Prestons between 1833 and 1845 may have also worked for other shoe bosses in Danvers. A single set of account books can provide no parallel evidence on the relationships of outworkers with shoe bosses whose records have not survived. In addition, some binders may have worked on shoes in the winter and garments or palm-leaf hats in the summer. The accounts of James P. Hutchinson, which begin in 1846 and continue until 1860, extend the chronology of shoe production in Danvers after the Preston accounts end. Hutchinson was one of thirty-five shoe bosses operating in the town in the 1850s who employed makers and binders. The social relations of production in the Hutchinson accounts are similar to those characteristic of the Preston operation and suggest that before the mechanization of sewing and the introduction of the factory system in the late 1850s, outwork in rural areas changed little. Hutchinson employed sixty-two shoebinders between 1846 and 1860, but only fourteen (23 percent) were steady workers who earned an annual income of forty-five dollars for two years or more. The rest were casual workers whose experience as outworkers was characterized by low earnings and limited productivity. However, as the Hutchinson operation was located in the town center, these binders had more access to other shoe bosses than those who worked for the Prestons in rural North Danvers. About the same percentage of wives worked steadily for Hutchinson as had worked for the Prestons a decade earlier. Likewise, over half of the fourteen steadiest workers for Hutchinson were members of families not headed by shoemakers. However, wages for shoebinding rose slightly after 1845: three cents was the standard price for binding children's boots for the Prestons, while the Hutchinson accounts list three and a half to four cents for the same work.[23] Similar increases appear for women's boots, but these wage increases disappeared after 1852 with the mechanization of shoebinding.

In many respects, the Preston and Hutchinson accounts confirm for rural Essex County Duncan Bythell's picture of the putting-out system in England. Shoebinders who worked for the Prestons typify the casual nature of the work for the majority of binders. But the Preston account books also disclose a small minority of steady workers who were either single women living with their families or hard-pressed farmers' wives motivated by severe family need. Nonetheless, if the Preston accounts are typical of the rural outwork system in New England, the work of most wives did not represent a steady source of supplemental income in the 1830s and 1840s. Indeed, marriage and childbearing do not associate closely with the steadiest work in the Preston accounts. Casual work for the nearly three-quarters of wives, mothers, and daughters who worked for less than one year for the Prestons yielded such low returns as to seem negligible. Of these casual workers, two-thirds were married. For some wives, shoebinding was a welcome but temporary source of income in family emergencies. Yet there is evidence of the avoidance by some women workers of the most rough and low-paid work on brogans. This suggests that wives and daughters could impose limits on their contributions to family income in outwork. These limits may represent what historian Hans Medick has identified in the European protoindustrial system as self-regulation of work by the family, which opposed higher levels of production once subsistence needs had been met, a mark of preindustrial social behavior that represented resistance to wage incentives and contradicted the maximization of profit by the capitalist.[24] Some shoemakers' wives may also have been conscious of the growing degradation of the craft and refused to sew tough cowhide for next to nothing.

By the 1830s more and more shoebinding was taking place outside of the shoemaker's family. As the shoe boss became increasingly important to the coordination of production and the recruitment of women to bind shoes, the relationship between the shoemaker and his employer changed. The shoemaker was regarded less and less as an agent or middleman in the recruitment of labor for the shoe boss, who now ran the central shop and directed the work of both binder and maker. As the locus of shoebinding shifted out of the shoemaker's family, pressures on the level of family income produced some of the tensions between shoemakers and shoe bosses. In the early 1830s, organized shoemakers in Lynn had complained about the "injury" to their families of low wages paid to shoebinders. This change in the relationship of shoemaker and shoe boss, plus the pressure on the family economy as a result of the shift of shoebinding out of the shoemaking family, may be underlying reasons for the outbursts of labor protest by Essex County shoemakers in the 1840s.

The typical workers in the English outwork system were female, but little is known about their lives. In England the labor market for outwork was full of highly competitive cheap labor, which kept outwork wages low and encouraged the persistence of the system. In contrast, the Preston and Hutchinson operations relied primarily on a very small number of steady workers. In Essex County shoe towns, the low status and low wages of shoebinding were associated with a sexual division of labor that assigned binding as women's work with no apprentice training and little access to alternative homework. As production expanded and female members of shoemaking families failed to produce enough work, binding passed out of family control onto an extensive labor market of rural female homeworkers whose only real option was seasonal agricultural labor. As binding moved out of the family labor system, shoemakers, save for those in difficult situations, avoided binding uppers for their own work. Wages for binding remained low.

Essex County shoe bosses who operated networks of female outworkers and produced better grades of women's shoes came to depend in the 1840s on the skill and energy of certain shoebinders, such as Sarah Towne Colcord of Danvers. According to one Lynn observer writing retrospectively in 1859, some bosses enjoyed a near monopoly on the best quality of sewing by shoebinders and were willing to wait for the work even if it took six months.[25] The low productivity and difficulties of coordinating outwork led many shoe bosses, especially in Lynn, to regard the adaptation in 1852 of the Singer sewing machine to stitch light leather as a solution to their problems of obtaining sewn uppers. By the late 1850s, centralized production on machines, powered by foot and later by steam, would transform shoebinding into full-time factory work for women.

The female outworker both in England and in rural New England seemed incapable of self-defense against the hard conditions of the system. A look at the structure of outwork in Essex County can clarify this point. Shoebinding had become increasingly dissociated from work conducted in a family unit. Even while the head of the family coordinated the work, shoebinders labored in their kitchens isolated from group life in the shoe shop and the work culture on which the vigorous tradition of artisan resistance rested. Early labor protest in the 1830s by shoebinders in the shoe towns of Essex County was undercut by the isolation of women workers in their homes and by their submersion in family life. The response of shoe bosses to their demands for higher wages was to push the outwork system into rural areas of eastern Massachusetts, New Hampshire, and Maine. Women workers entered and left the outwork system in tune with the primary demands placed on them by their families and their domestic responsibilities. The more produc-

tive unmarried outworkers living at home still experienced isolation and a domestic context for their work. Although the outwork
system in shoe production made cash wages available to them, the
wages earned by these single women never approached the level of
wages available to women working in the textile factories of the
Merrimack Valley. There is little evidence in the Preston accounts
that access to cash wages stimulated early marriage. Shoebinding
did not pay a high enough level of wages to permit single women
or widows to support themselves or their families, except at the
cost of unusually arduous labor.[26] For the unmarried daughter, this
new work in the home kept her tied to the dual authority of her
parents and her employment.

In contrast, the nature of outwork in the shoe towns of Essex
County was probably less grim. The situation for binders who lived
in Lynn, Haverhill, or Marblehead was easier: better wages for
higher quality work, a chance to escape the isolation and drudgery
of farm life, and the ability to purchase more goods in the market.
Still, there was no comparison for the shoebinder to the possibilities of personal independence and relatively high wages common
for women in the textile factories of New England. Ann Swett recognized this when she wrote to her sister from Manchester, New
Hampshire, in 1847. After a chance to compare factory work with
outwork, she declared that she would no longer do "that little
thing."

For working women in Essex County, the outwork system and
factory employment characteristic of early industrial capitalism
provided a context for a changing domestic ideology that defined
the work role of early nineteenth-century women. Republican
motherhood and domesticity became the primary middle-class
model of correct female work. This was the case even for women
who worked in early factories, as their involvement in production
was not intended to provide the means for economic self-support.
Industrialization and capitalism emphasized the economic dependency of women within the gender hierarchy of the family and
encouraged the withdrawal of wives from the labor force.[27] Ann
Swett might relish her independence as a factory worker in contrast
to her drudgery as a shoebinder, but she doubtless looked forward
to an experience of marriage and motherhood that did not involve
wage-earning except for unforeseen family emergencies. In devel-

oping and living a dual model of working girl and homebound wife, working-class women actively helped to shape a sense of proper gender relationships within the new economic system.

In Essex County, early industrial capitalism provided new work for women both in textile factories and at home as outworkers. Unmarried young women either left their homes for factory work or labored intensively as homeworkers. Both kinds of work were temporary. Once married, a woman's work was defined by her primary obligation to housework and child care. Forced by family circumstances or drawn by the consumer power of wage-earning, the shoebinders who sewed for the Prestons provide unique evidence to assess both the motives and the limits with which women outworkers confronted the new world of industrial production. Working as identifiable individuals who earned cash wages, they lived at home combining wage-earning with domesticity. Most wives limited involvement in production to a supplemental or infrequent but occasionally significant contribution to family income. Their experiences helped to develop the dual model of women's work: temporary, full-time work for single women and occasional wage-earning for married women. Working-class women shared with middle-class women the primary definition of their womanhood as mothers and housewives, but their economic circumstances often forced them to integrate wage-earning into their lives. In contributing to the dual model of female work, these women redefined the domestic ideology of nineteenth-century gender in accordance with their class experience.

In 1842, representatives of shoe manufacturers in Massachusetts met in Boston as a convention to lobby for the extension of the tariff on boots and shoes. In their defense of tariff protection for their industry, the leadership of the convention cited the impact of falling prices on women workers in shoe production and described their work and their lives. However disastrous the results of lowering the tariff would be for shoemakers in Massachusetts, they argued, the shoebinders would face a "calamity": a sharp decline in wages for a group "heretofore not overpaid for their services" and perhaps even a total disappearance of demand for shoebinding.[28] Men, according to the convention report, could find other employment in other locations. The 15,000 women in Massachusetts who bound shoes did not have these possibilities; they were described as dependent, helpless, and homebound. The convention leaders in 1842 recognized the vulnerability and isolation of shoebinders and utilized it for political purposes. They predicted general distress and suffering for female shoeworkers if Congress lowered the tariff. They succeeded in maintaining protection for the industry, but as outworkers, shoebinders remained dependent and isolated.

As production expanded in the early 1840s and an extensive outwork system penetrated into rural Essex County and reached northward into New Hampshire and Maine, the position of most shoebinders became even more isolated and vulnerable to low wages. As shoe manufacturers tried to assure a steady supply of sewn uppers for their central shops by recruiting the cheap labor of rural women, they created an outwork system characterized by inefficiency and low productivity, but a system that seemed an unlikely source of collective protest against low wages.

CHAPTER FOUR

Women and the Artisan Tradition

Thank heaven our movement is not a political one. If it
were, it would not be warmed into life by the bright
sunshine of woman's smiles, nor enriched by the
priceless dower of her pure affections. But as it is
strictly a moral enterprise, it opens to her willing heart
a wide field of usefulness.

—"Woman," *The Awl*,
December 21, 1844

In the early 1840s, shoe bosses in Essex County towns who were
attempting to reorganize production encountered strong resistance
from shoemakers in their artisan shops, which quickly spread into
a regional movement for labor reform. The male experience of
group work and artisan training shaped the ideology and structure
of this labor protest. Their labor paper, the *Awl*, also reflected the
conviction of the journeymen cordwainers of Lynn that a recognition of the virtues of mechanic life by the middle class could
provide part of the basis on which to achieve social harmony. In
one moral tale published on September 4, 1844, "Frank Russell or
The Village Blacksmith" marries the beautiful and accomplished
daughter of a wealthy merchant, thus defying the restrictions of
genteel society. Frank achieves this destiny through his training as
a mechanic, which has taught him "the principles of noble action"
and how to be "useful and happy," virtues that embellish his good
looks and personal grace with a devotion to duty and to "manly
and open conduct." These attributes have swept his bride off her
feet and won the approval of her father to the astonishment of
their circle of wealthy friends. Their marriage proves a success,
and "Frank Russell and his happy wife stand as ornamental pillars

of their village where they are loved and honored." The growing social divisions among classes in Lynn as a result of early industrialization could be bridged by a demonstration of mechanic virtue and by the willingness of the middle class to recognize it.

Feminine virtue was also part of the mechanic way of life and essential to a harmonious social order. Protesting shoemakers tried to enlist women into their organization, but their leaders saw women primarily as moral beings and family members rather than as workers in production. In contrast to the separate organization and self-direction of the shoebinder societies in the early 1830s and their reliance on the social bonds of working women as a basis for protest, artisan perceptions of the role of females in society limited the involvement of women shoeworkers in the labor activism of the 1840s. Protesting shoebinders in the 1830s had seen political action and new rights as essential to their pursuit of justice as women workers. In the 1840s, artisan leaders emphasized the moral rather than the political role of women in labor reform. Some female members of shoemaking families shared this view of women's participation in shoemaker protest despite the subordinated position it offered them. As a basis for organization and as an ideology, artisan tradition failed to encompass the experience of women workers or offer them solutions for their isolation and vulnerability as outworkers.

By 1837, Essex County led all other counties in Massachusetts in shoe production and in the employment of women workers in the industry. Although shoebinders also commonly labored in Norfolk, Worcester, and Plymouth Counties where men's shoes and boots were made, shoe bosses in Essex and Middlesex Counties who specialized in light work employed almost twice as many females as the other counties. Furthermore, the shoe bosses in the towns of Lynn, Haverhill, Marblehead, and Danvers accounted for a total of 4,790 female workers, or 68 percent of all women involved in boot and shoe production in Essex County. Many of these shoebinders actually lived in the rural areas and small villages that surrounded the shoe towns. This extensive network of rural outworkers developed rapidly between 1837 and 1845, and the number of female workers in Essex County increased by 28 percent. The annual output of shoebinders in Lynn between 1831 and 1860 dropped from

941 pairs per binder in 1831 to 689 pairs in 1850.[1] This decline represented the recruitment of essentially part-time rural workers by the shoe bosses. The central shops located in the four major shoe towns of Essex County had centralized their direction of shoe production by organizing the rural population into an extensive outwork system.

In 1837 the 15,366 Massachusetts women involved in shoe production at home outnumbered the female work force of 14,759 in cotton textile factories. While other female employment included work in woolen textiles (3,485), paper (605), and hats (304), shoebinding represented 45 percent of women employed in industrial production. This large-scale employment of women as outworkers for the shoe industry grew rapidly between 1837 and 1855 and touched the lives of more women in Massachusetts than full-time factory employment. By 1845, shoebinders working for Massachusetts shoe bosses numbered 18,678 compared with 14,407 female operatives in textile mills; and in 1855 nearly 10,000 more women worked in shoe production than in the cotton and woolen mills.

Furthermore, the recruitment of women living at home to work on shoes dominated female employment in Essex County in the early nineteenth century. In 1845, other industries, such as cotton and woolen textiles, palm-leaf hatmaking, cloth printing, and the hosiery, yarn, and thread mills, claimed 1,830 women workers. This represented only 20 percent of the total number of women earning wages in Essex County; the remainder were shoebinders.[2] By 1855 almost 20,000 women worked for Essex County shoe manufacturers. In the mid-nineteenth century, these manufacturers were producing half of all shoes and one-third of all boots made in Massachusetts. This represented one-third of the total value of product in boots and shoes for the state. The successful organization of the labor power of rural women into the outwork system stimulated the rapid growth of shoe production in Massachusetts.

The expansion of the outwork system and the recruitment of rural workers by central shops in shoe towns was part of the effort to rationalize shoemaking in the late 1830s and early 1840s. Without centralizing production, adopting machines, or raising wages, the shoe bosses sought a more pivotal role in directing work. This was done by setting new standards and by increasing the available labor supply by pushing the network of shoeworkers into distant rural areas. The shoe manufacturer's desire for greater production of better quality shoes, however, conflicted with the social realities of the lives of both men and women workers. In the mid-1830s William Richardson of Stoneham, Massachusetts, manufactured women's and children's shoes and sold them to retail stores in Manchester and Portsmouth, New Hampshire; in the Massachusetts towns of Ipswich, Gloucester, Beverly, and Reading; and in Boston, New York City, Baltimore, and Cincinnati. He also acted as a commission agent for Haverhill manufacturers. His correspondence with retail store owners and with outworkers indicates some of the pressures that led shoe bosses to try to control the process of production more closely.[3]

One of Richardson's customers in New York from whom he received many orders was the retail firm of Crawford and Reece. Letters from this New York store carried constant complaints about the quality of the children's shoes made by Richardson's firm, specifically complaints concerning unstable dyes in the leather, poor assortments of sizes, bad work, and high prices for inferior quality shoes. Nonetheless, Crawford and Reece continued to reorder from Richardson, but urged him to obtain better work. Another consistent retail outlet for Richardson's shoes was storekeeper Samuel Dike of Beverly, who ordered shoes between 1828 and 1837. Dike specified the qualities that he wanted in children's shoes: "I want the kid soft & nice fit for little feet," and he urged Richardson to obtain "a good sew-round & stiffen the heel well." Dike often complained about delays and difficulties in getting Richardson to fill his orders. "I received a small lot of you the other day, most of which, I like, but I thought you cut some rather near." Two letters to Richardson in 1835 and 1836 expressed Dike's exasperation over unfilled orders and included his injunctions to "please see that they are sewed well."[4] In order to mollify his retailers, Richardson had to obtain better work and more prompt delivery from his network of outworkers in Essex and Middlesex Counties and in the towns of southern New Hampshire.

Richardson's correspondence with some of his outworkers indicated that production was often slow and halting. In 1826 shoemaker Benjamin Hosmer of Chelmsford in Middlesex County apologized for disappointing him by not completing several lots of shoes in the time expected. Delays were familiar, and Hosmer continued to make shoes for Richardson.[5] A letter from William K. Cooke, a shoemaker of Bedford also in Middlesex County, who cut leather and recruited men and women workers for Richardson, detailed why he had been delayed in sending his work to Stoneham by stage.

> July 17, 1835
>
> Sir, I send you 48 pr leather Boots and 30 pr A [ankle] ties which is all I have got done. I have cut two lots more and they are part made. I am verry much troubled to get them bound. Mr. Webber's wife have bound all he has made as yet except those that came bound. If you can bring up some that are bound you help me along verry much.

Cooke's problems, especially in recruiting shoebinders, meant constant delays in production.

Another set of letters to Richardson from Jesse Reed of New Ipswich, New Hampshire, in 1838 detailed the difficulties of transporting cut leather stock and finished shoes by stage and team, distributing work to the outworkers, locating shoebinders, and settling accounts as well as dealing with the general human frailties involved in this system of domestic production.

> November 21, 1838
>
> Sir I shall have 2 Lots of your shoes done next week & shall send them in Saturday if it comes right for the teamers to be there that day. I wish you to have some stock ready for them to take back. . . . I am verry much in want of a little *money* say *ten dollars* for this is a cold country. I should like you to send one Lot of the shoes bound on part of A lot for I have but one binder Bacon's. . . . have but hard work to get them bound.

> December 24, 1838
>
> Dear Sir I shall send you 2 lots of shoes next Saturday I should had them all done but for want of getting them bound. I should like to have you get some ready with part of them bound, say one pair in three & then I can get along. . . . I have promised part of the money the first of January I wish you to send me twenty dollars. that will establish my credit till the first of May. . . . My respects to all your good folks tell them to rite to me for I feel rather lonesome in this wooden country.

Jesse Reed did not live to complete Richardson's work, but died of consumption in early January 1839. A neighbor returned the lot of shoes on which Reed had been working; only part of it had been completed.[6] Richardson's correspondence indicated that his greatest problem as a shoe boss in the 1830s was the need to coordinate and improve the pace and standard of work done by shoemakers and to recruit shoebinders to sew uppers. Shoe manufacturers in Essex County who faced similar problems in the 1830s and 1840s began to assume a more central position in the work process, especially in the recruitment of shoebinders. To seek changes in the direction of work in the artisan shoe shop was, however, to court trouble with the cordwainers.

The shoemakers of Lynn, Danvers, Marblehead, and Salem who worked in groups in their ten footers resisted the attempts by shoe bosses to control or discipline the work process. Many stories from the folklore of shoemaking in the 1830s and 1840s attest to the tensions felt by worker and boss over efforts to alter work patterns. These recollections and reminiscences demonstrate the limits of the employer's power to change work procedures in the artisan shop. After an apprentice had learned his trade, he went "a bossing," or sought work from a shoe boss. After finishing his first lot of shoes, the young shoemaker faced the inspection of his work with some trepidation. The rooms of the central shop were, however, arranged so that the inspection of the work would be carried out in private. The cutting of the uppers and soles and the giving out of the work to makers and binders was done on the first floor, and the boss usually gave his opinion of the workmanship on the second floor. Typically, according to the stories, the shoe boss accepted the work with only a suggestion of criticism, e.g., to "put another stitch to the inch in the next lot" as some of the shoes "grinned a little too much."[7] The shoemaker then picked up another lot of work. If the shoe boss rejected the work, it was customarily done with courtesy as well as in privacy: "I guess I won't have any more of that kind made."[8] Employers paid cutters who worked in the central shops more often in cash than the shoemakers and also treated them with careful respect. For example, one employer found that his cutters were wasting leather remnants that could be used for piecing together into heels. Shoe boss Moses Putnam of Danvers, who himself worked the extra odds and ends into heel stock, questioned his cutters mildly. "Oh, but are not these pieces a little large to go down cellar?"[9]

Occasional hard judgments by shoe bosses and resistance by shoemakers appear in many reminiscences. Christopher Robinson of Lynn paid his workers entirely in cash, but had the reputation among shoemakers in the 1840s of being very hard to please. Robinson had regulations printed and passed out to his makers and binders in an attempt to get his workers to conform to his standards of order, cleanliness, and promptness. He required his shoemakers to place their stitches a certain distance from the edge with a specific number of stitches sewn to the inch.[10] One of the best shoemakers in Lynn worked for Robinson for several years before he was told that his shoes finally met the high standards. He reacted with artisan independence. "One day he carried in a lot that was satisfactory, and the workman said, since he had finally succeeded in suiting [Robinson,] he wouldn't take any more work."[11]

Another issue between shoe bosses and shoemakers involved surplus leather and shoe thread that along with uppers, cut or already sewn, stiffeners, and linings were routinely given out to the shoemaker. According to custom, any surplus materials belonged to the shoemaker, and the "embezzlement" or "cabbaging" of leather by shoemakers had encouraged the initial centralization of all cutting operations under the watchful eye of the shoe boss in the central shop. Extra thread often ended up as kite string for the shoemaker's boy or, in the case of Danvers shoemakers, was used by their daughters to braid and bunch onions when they worked as seasonal agricultural laborers. Shoe bosses tried to limit the waste of their materials without, however, risking a confrontation in the ten footer. "One of our prominent bosses called on one of his workmen in Marblehead and the big drawer [in the shoemaker's shop] being open far enough to reveal several balls of surplus thread in the back part, he [the boss] said nothing, but came home and gave orders to reduce his supply of thread in the future."[12]

Custom limited the inspection of shoes to the central shop, and those bosses who attempted to judge work prematurely faced rebukes. William Stone of Lynn recalled such an incident in the 1850s. "One evening a boss came into my father's shop, and approaching one of his workmen said, as he took a shoe from the nail to examine it, 'I wish you would be more particular in the future, as the last lot you brought in looked like a lot of fried mackerel.' The workman responded, as he took the shoe from him, by telling him to let the shoes alone till they were brought in. It ended in a laugh and the boss left the shop."[13] The ability of artisan shoemakers to resist changes in the supervision of work in the 1830s and 1840s rested on the group nature of their work, their successful articulation of the mechanic ideology, and the dependence of the shoe manufacturer on the system of decentralized production.

In the 1840s, shoemakers in Lynn organized protests on behalf of a common standard of wages to be paid in cash by the shoe bosses. They extended these activities to other shoemakers in Essex County and throughout Massachusetts, while joining with workers in other industries through the New England Workingmen's Association, which held regional conventions in 1844 and 1845. Increasing demand for shoes during the recovery from the 1837 depression stimulated journeymen to organize as they had in the early 1830s. They utilized the mechanic ideology and pressed their employers to respond to their grievances concerning low wages and payment in goods.[14] Their efforts to organize shoemakers both in the shoe towns and in the rural outwork system indicated that to some extent the common male experience of group work and craft tradition enabled them to transcend the limits of residence and community. New England labor protest in the 1840s was spirited and widespread, but it yielded limited results. Labor protest in this decade represented the defensive activities of preindustrial workers who depended on the traditions and ideology of an earlier system of production to curtail the power of a growing capitalist order.[15] Furthermore, the organization and ideology of this labor protest offered little chance for women to involve themselves as shoeworkers in these collective activities, despite their heritage of protest in the early 1830s.

To convey their message of protest, the Lynn shoemakers who formed the Mutual Benefit Society of Journeymen Cordwainers in early 1844 established a labor reform newspaper, the *Awl*. This paper, published between July 1844 and October 1845, became their most successful endeavor. It reached a large circulation, claiming to have a subscription of 1,200, which represented most of the shoemakers in Lynn and others in the shoe towns of Essex and Middlesex Counties.[16] The editors hoped to promote class harmony, but believed it likely that conflict would result from the concentration of wealth in the hands of the few. They feared that economic privilege imperiled the tradition of equal rights that was their political heritage from the American Revolution.[17]

While the 1840s represented a high point of labor activism among the cordwainers of Essex County, there is little evidence of the involvement of shoebinders in the strategy, policies, or membership of the journeymen's society or in the workingmen's association. In the first issue of the *Awl* published on July 17, 1844, the editors identified a constituency and a set of objectives that relegated shoebinders to an auxiliary role in the society. The circumscribed position for women in this protest movement offered most shoebinders no ideological or strategic position with which to associate themselves as workers with the cordwainers' society. Shoemakers welcomed women to their cause as female members of shoemaking families, but the society offered little to those who actually worked on shoes. The editors of the *Awl* vigorously sought the support of shoebinders throughout the year and a half of publication, but they strictly limited the terms on which women might participate in the activities of the organization.

The first issue of the *Awl* carried the clearest statement of the aims of the society in a draft circular to "all brothers of the craft" throughout New England. The organization sought uniform wages for shoemaking in all New England shoe towns and villages in order to restore the economic and social status of shoemakers in a society that the editors perceived as rapidly developing invidious class distinctions. The denial of a competency, a reasonable income that would support an artisan's family comfortably and supply savings for old age, threatened the equality and rights that freemen had won in the American Revolution. The society of cordwainers was especially sensitive to the declining status of those whose only wealth lay in the useful pursuit of a trade. The *Awl* championed the fundamental values of manly labor and linked the interests of cordwainers with all mechanics and artisans, as well as with the female operatives in the textile factories of Lowell and other mill towns and with all working people, male or female, free or slave, who could not live decently and respectably in the economy of the 1840s.

At the first meeting of the cordwainers' society on June 29, the members agreed to urge "the ladies" to give their support to the organization. Membership in the society was, however, defined by craft. The sexual division of labor in shoemaking prevented almost all women from joining the organization, although the society did accept as members three women trained as cordwainers: Mrs. Eliza Tuttle, the wife of a shoemaker, and her two female apprentices. Tuttle's membership was immediately advertised in the pages of the *Awl* as an example of female courage to the more reluctant male shoemakers of Lynn to get them to join the society.[18] The editors urged other women, including shoebinders, to act as an informal auxiliary to the men's society rather than form their own organization as they had in the early 1830s. The ladies to whom the *Awl* directed its appeal seemed to be female members of families headed by shoemakers, women who were not necessarily shoebinders. This distinction, however, did not mean that the cordwainers' society recognized the implications for women workers of the dissociation of binding from the shoemaking family. An appeal for the presence of women at the society's meetings became a persistent theme in the *Awl*. The cordwainers' society frequently used the participation of ladies, like the membership of Tuttle, for their exemplary and moral significance. The appeals for women to attend the society's meetings every Saturday night at the Town Hall were predicated not on their status as wage earners or their work as shoebinders, but on their abilities as wives, mothers, and sweethearts to persuade other shoemakers in Lynn to join the organization.

The *Awl* printed several direct appeals for female support of its activities in the fall of 1844 that made the grounds on which women were invited to participate very clear. Women, especially young women, would be able to attract prospective suitors to the meetings where these men would then be persuaded to join the society. "Then ladies, continue to give us your presence. You have influence, and can do much. Your attendance, of course, will cause a larger attendance of the young men, who, when they visit your houses, and find by your mothers that 'you are out,' and at the Town Hall, where they ought to be, and that you are attending to your immediate interests, this will nerve them to action, and they will eventually act."[19] The *Awl* invited local women to sing cordwainers' songs, to make speeches "if the men wont," and if they regarded speaking in public as inappropriate, to publish their sentiments in the paper.[20] Memories of the vigorous nature of the pronouncements by the Female Society in 1834 apparently had not faded, but very little material from women subsequently appeared in the newspaper.

Some women supporters of the cordwainers' society accepted this definition of their activities as moral auxiliaries. In the September 11 issue a letter from "Girtrude," who identified herself as "a friend of humanity," rather than as a shoebinder, urged all women in Lynn to join in the "moral combat of mercy" on behalf of equal rights. She appealed to mothers and daughters to oppose "oppression," which she defined as an injury to family life, including the interruption of the education of children by poverty resulting from low wages.[21] Girtrude and other women assumed that the interests of most women in the objectives of the cordwainers' society were familial, that is, by bettering the wages of the shoemakers, be they husbands, fathers, or sons, women's own economic interests would be served.

As the cordwainers' society planned social activities for its membership, the leaders made a special appeal for the ladies to organize temperance tea parties. At a December meeting of the society in 1844, women voted for the only time as participants in the society's activities on the question of arrangements for the parties, which began in late December. A toast made at one event held on December 26 expressed in extravagant and morally dubious terms the ways in which some members of the society hoped to utilize the power of females to recruit support: "May the enemies of the working classes be embargo'd from your embraces—cursed with a perpetual non-intercourse, and blockaded from all ports of matrimony."[22] The editors, however, made a different appeal for female support, published under the title "Woman," which illustrated how they viewed the nature of women and the limits that these views put on women's involvement in the activities of the society: "Thank heaven, our movement is not a political one. If it were, it would not be warmed into life by the bright sunshine of woman's smiles, nor enriched by the priceless dower of her pure affections. But as it is strictly a moral enterprise, it opens to her willing heart a wide field of usefulness."[23]

The editors saw women as essentially moral beings and called upon them to "hallow and ennoble" the objectives of the society. Although they addressed every woman in Lynn, "especially every laboring woman," the editors appealed less to their interests as workers than to their natural capacities for self-sacrifice and morality. Earlier, the *Awl* had reassured women that it was as moral for them to meet with the cordwainers every Saturday night as to attend church on Sundays.[24] Indeed, the presence of women at these meetings would guarantee their propriety. The leaders of the shoemakers' society viewed women's power and influence as moral, unselfish, and spiritual, not as material, self-interested, or political. The contrast with the words and deeds of the Lynn Female Society in 1834 is sharp.[25]

A new industrial morality developed in early nineteenth-century Lynn as a result of attempts by moral reformers to alter social behavior and attitudes and undermine the relaxed morality of traditional eighteenth-century customs by imposing discipline on practices such as bundling, on activities at public celebrations and festivals, on school-yard behavior, and on sexual and social conduct in general.[26] Cordwainers who were involved in collective resistance in the 1830s and 1840s utilized the new social virtues of hard work, sobriety, and morality to check the prerogatives claimed by shoe manufacturers. Whether this new industrial morality that the Lynn rebels accepted and used also resulted in the transformation of working-class attitudes on the nature of women into purified, moral beings is an interesting question for historians concerned with the social relations of working-class life.[27]

The concept of women as moral agents in society was crucial to the public activities of middle-class women involved in religious and reform organizations and central to the changing role of women in American society in the early nineteenth century.[28] In a similar way, the Lynn Female Society in 1834 justified its public protests over low wages for shoebinding by advocating a new moral role for working-class women in society, but also by demanding new political rights. In 1837 a few of the society's leaders found a home in the moral politics of the Lynn Female Anti-Slavery Society. From 1841 to 1843, women's activism in Essex County towns turned to female temperance groups. Members of shoemaking families joined other women to form separate women's societies that demonstrated their fervent dedication to the total abstinence cause of the Washingtonian societies. Temperance women were particularly active in the Woodend section of Lynn, the home of a large portion of Lynn's journeymen.[29] The activities of these women may have also reflected their economic dependence on their families as a result of low wages for both shoebinding and shoe-making in the early 1840s as well as their concern over the impact of intemperance on family well-being. In 1843 the Lynn Female Society of Washingtonians merged its activities with the men's society, and this organization provided a model for the involve-ment of women in artisan protest. The Washingtonians of Lynn were close to the cordwainers' society and emphasized the special moral role of females and their dedication to family interests.

The *Awl*'s attempts to utilize women as moral agents in sup-port of working-class objectives suggests that the artisans of Lynn had adopted new attitudes on the fundamental nature of women in addition to their views on work and sobriety. These new attitudes created tension between the different roles of men and women in labor protest. By the 1840s the concept of women as moral beings seemed to blind the leaders of the cordwainers' society to the politi-cal legacy of shoebinder protest in the 1830s and to the realities of their uniquely vulnerable and isolated position in the process of shoe production.

The appeals of the editors of the *Awl* for female participation in the cordwainers' society on the grounds of their inherent moral capacity betrayed, however, some ambivalence among working-class men over changing gender roles in early industrialization. If women were essentially moral and spiritual, characteristics that suggest gentility and the pious private virtues of middle-class life in the early nineteenth century that Barbara Welter identified as the cult of true womanhood, then the cordwainers' society rejected these values as a threat to artisan life.[30] This element of shoemakers' attitudes toward women revealed a fear that genteel social behavior in females within their own families would make them unfit for the useful life of a mechanic's wife. But the leadership of the cord-wainers' society also hoped to heal class divisions by insisting that the middle class recognize the merits and values of artisan life as fundamental to a democratic social order. Feminine virtue in arti-san families became one element essential to social harmony, and in two moral tales published in the *Awl*, the willingness of women

to bind shoes and their rejection of genteel values defined the virtuous life of a useful woman. One of these stories, reprinted from
the periodical *Family Visitor*, appeared on the front page of the
September 11, 1844, issue and demonstrated the triumph of a shoebinder over the "demon" of gentility.

> "But there is certainly a mistake. Your master did not intend to
> send a message of this import to me," said Mrs. Burchstead to an
> errand boy at the door.
>
> "He told me to go to Mrs. Burchstead's, marm."
>
> "What were you to say?"
>
> "Leave the shoes with her, he said, and tell her to bind them as
> soon as she can, for I want them; tell her when she cross-backs to be
> careful of her stitch, for the morocco is tender."
>
> "It is a mistake. Run home and tell Mr. Goodrich I will call and
> see what he means;" and mortified and angry she closed the door.

Mary Burchstead is the niece of Mr. Goodrich, a shoemaker who
had rescued her from childhood poverty by teaching her to "maintain" herself by binding shoes. Since her marriage to a sea captain,
Mrs. Burchstead had fallen victim to gentility, altering at great expense the house that her husband had bought her and acquiring
fine, new furniture, which placed him deeply in debt. As Mary
Burchstead puzzles over why her uncle sent her—a lady—shoes to
bind, she feels ashamed over her ingratitude and her neglect of her
relatives.

> "But," she argued, "If a captain's wife bound shoes, what would
> people think?"

As she glances into her mirror, she finds that displeasure and
anxiety have marred the beauty that the serenity found in binding
shoes had once placed on her face.

> "Mercy!" cried Mrs. Burchstead, "I look like a fright! . . . I must
> dress and call on uncle Goodrich, and expostulate, or, he will send a
> bundle of *cowhide brogans* next. I do wish the old man could know
> a little of gentility, or what belongs to it."

Stung by the incivility of her relatives, Mary visits her uncle and
aunt. She is told that her husband has mortgaged their house to

pay for the alterations and the new furniture and that because of a general business depression the voyage he is on may bankrupt him. Mary blames herself.

> "I persuaded him to alter the house: it was to please me that he extravagantly furnished it. But, thank Heaven, I can work, and will work too, to show him that he has not spoiled his wife, though he has let her ruin him.—Now, uncle, give me the shoes, I will take them home and begin at once."

Mary sets to work, spurns the visitors who look down their noses at her occupation, rents the house, and sells the furniture. Her husband returns, overjoyed at his wife's change of heart and her decisions, which have cleared him of debt. In admiration of Mary's determination, his employer, a junior partner in the trading firm, says to him:

> "Now you may congratulate yourself, not only for being in good circumstances, but for having a wife who has dared to sacrifice herself, as I may say, for she has defied gentility by binding shoes."

The editors of the *Awl* chose this story for its criticism of the false social values that Mary Burchstead had chosen over the virtues of hard work and plain living inherent in artisan life. Her gentility, demonstrated by her rejection of shoebinding as unfitting for a captain's wife, was symptomatic of the growing class divisions in American life and a betrayal of the equal rights tradition of Lynn mechanics. Mary Burchstead's story typified the contradictory attitudes of Lynn mechanics toward women's work on shoes. On the one hand, shoebinding was represented in the *Awl* as exploited work, both exhausting and poorly paid, but shoebinding was also seen as an appropriate and even chastening alternative to genteel pretensions. Her willingness to bind shoes became a measure of the virtue of a woman's life and a bridge to social harmony.

In the February 22, 1845, issue the editors made their views more explicit by publishing an original story, "Charles Do-Well," written by one of the *Awl*'s frequent contributors, "Noggs." "Charles Do-Well" is another moral tale set in Lynn about the contest between the social virtues of mechanics and the false values of the merchant class. The story begins as a young woman tries to decide whom she should marry.

It is no use talking mother[,] said the pert though somewhat hand-some Eliza D—, as I am determined I will never no *never* marry a *mechanic*.

Eliza's dead father was a merchant, and she believes that it is a daughter's responsibility to "keep up the dignity of [her] father's house," by marrying in the same class. Her inclination to marry a merchant is encouraged not by her kindly, sensible mother, but by the snobbish Sarah Amelia Sudora Norton, who objects to her friend Eliza's visits with shoebinders and rejects Charles Do-Well, the shoemaker, because "he smells of wax so." On the other hand, Eliza thinks, as she ponders her decision, that Charles is handsome, well-informed, and very interesting, even "if he does make shoes." Her other suitor is Mr. Cheatem, a merchant who is received in all of the best houses, but who has a reputation among working people as a liar and a "tricky trader." She wonders:

> But somehow or other it seems strange to me that a man because he sells tape and buckram, small beer and gingerbread should be any more respectable than he who makes shoes . . . !

Charles has opened Eliza's eyes to the changing prospects of the mechanics of Lynn. He has told her that

> [the] times were fast altering, that things were beginning to be called by their right names; he says the common people are better informed than they used to be, now, and that it is beginning to be considered no disgrace to get a living honestly.

Thrillingly, this vision of change seems to include Eliza.

> Women too, he says, are beginning to be acknowledged as responsible creatures, as beings who have souls as well as hearts, who were born equal with the man, and who by every right, human and divine, are entitled to a voice in our councils, and are deserving of an equal recompense for their labors.

In contrast, Eliza reflects on Cheatem's social philosophy:

> that some people were born to be drawers of water, and hewers of wood, and for his part he didn't see what the reformers wanted to make such a d——d fuss about the "niggers" and the poor folks for.

She is awakened from her reveries by her mother, and Eliza an-nounces that she is done with girlish dreaming and that she is determined, henceforth, to be a woman, and see if I can't do something for a living. I will go immediately and join the "shoebinders society of mutual improvement," and what is more I mean to bind shoes myself, for I have come to the conclusion that if we would be good members of society we must be useful.

Sarah Amelia is horrified to find Eliza binding shoes and drops her socially, remarking that she never did "keep company with the working class." But Charles Do-Well is enchanted to find Eliza binding shoes and dares to hope that his influence has produced her reformation. He always thought that underneath her surface vanity and frivolity was "strong good sense." Some day, he believed, "she would dare to be herself, a sensible, intelligent, *useful* woman." Eliza marries Charles and Sarah Amelia marries Cheatem. "Six months after," Sarah Amelia is a deserted wife with a child, left in poverty by her unscrupulous husband. She is wretched when Eliza calls on her, but much chastened by her disastrous fate.

> She [Sarah Amelia] was not now ashamed herself, to bind shoes, aye was thankful, that there was so respectable and easy [a] way for a poor stricken widow [or deserted wife] to support herself and her child.

"Noggs" used Eliza's story as a vehicle for the social criticism implicit in the mechanic ideology, but when Charles explains to her the new conception of woman as an equal partner in the moral struggle against the merchant class, it becomes clear that the new fields opening to females are designed to permit them only to be sensible, intelligent, moral and, most of all, useful: the paradigm of a mechanic's wife. Ignoring the objective conditions of shoebinders, whose work if respectable was never easy, the writer, himself a shoemaker, regarded binding shoes as appropriate and morally virtuous work for women. The useful woman represented a continuation of the preindustrial role of women's work in household production, but this image also involved the sexual division of labor in shoemaking and the low wages and status of shoebinding.[31] The useful woman was a much more flattering vision than the images of the shallow, materialistic women of the genteel class, but as a political device in artisan protest it did not represent the interests of women workers nor did it spring from their own aspirations or dilemmas.

In contrast to its moral tales, the *Awl* published constant laments over the lack of response to its energetic appeals for female participation in the society's activities. However, the explanation for this lack of response may lie less in the editors' ambivalence over woman's nature or their fear of genteel values lurking among female family members and more in the failure of the cordwainers to recognize and offer a solution for the vulnerable position of the shoebinder in the structure of shoe manufacturing. The society addressed its invitations to all women in Lynn, but also tried to offer ways in which the shoebinders could help themselves in association with the organization. The kind of help that the society offered ignored the isolation and vulnerability of the individual shoebinder, which contrasted sharply with the group nature of men's work.

In an early appeal for female participation in the September 11, 1844, issue, the editors exhorted shoebinders to come to the society's meetings and identify any shoe boss in Lynn who had cheated women as a result of the order system. Widows with dependents were urged to point out the manufacturers who discounted their wages by 10 percent if they insisted on cash in payment. Name the boss, the appeal went on, so that the world will know him. This strategy of public humiliation did not, however, persuade any shoebinders to come forward and offer evidence of mistreatment. Months later in the January 4, 1845, issue the editors made another general appeal for the "Needle" to join the "Awl," urging shoebinders to spend a hard-earned dollar, representing— the editors admitted—three to four days' hard work, and subscribe to the paper. They declared an advanced position on women's rights including equal compensation with men for their labor and an absolute equality of rights, especially the right to subscribe to a free press. The editors detailed the strategy of focusing the moral power of indignant women on their oppressors. "We assure you, sister Needle, that the oppressor dreads your point more than the point of the bayonet. . . . He'll threaten to break the thread of your existence if you look favorably on the Awl—and will try to make you sew (sue) for mercy. He will call his brother bosses to prove that his tyranny is all imaginery. If so, appeal to the *Bench*! Nay appeal to the *Awl*—and that will end the matter."

In addition to these appeals, one of the editors, E. C. Darlin, located a Lynn binder whose account book he personally examined and who, he charged, had been cheated by a shoe manufacturer.[32] The case of Mrs. Jane Atherton illustrated the uselessness of the *Awl*'s strategy for helping the shoebinders confront their employers. The identity of the writer, the boss, and the binder quickly became public knowledge as charges were made and denied. Atherton had allowed Darlin to look at her binder's book, but otherwise played no direct role in the controversy. Versions of her views came from Darlin and from the employer, Nathan D. Chase, one of the largest manufacturers in Lynn, as well as from his brother and their associate, Asa L. Breed, the sexton of the Friends' Society. Darlin charged that Atherton had been defrauded by Chase when he did not make it clear to her when she began binding shoes for his firm in 1840 that wages were four cents in cash or five cents in store orders. Reportedly when she was informed of the terms of payment, Atherton felt surprised and disappointed at the differential between cash and goods, but worked for the next three years for Chase. In February 1844 she told Asa Breed that she thought the terms rather "hard." The Chase brothers and Breed insisted, however, that Atherton told each of them that she never said she had been defrauded and that she wished the issue had not been made public. Darlin's reply to the manufacturers' account appeared in the February 22 issue, where he pointed out the injustice of the differential between goods and cash whether Atherton had agreed to it or not. He also wrote that Atherton had not known the wage terms until after she had begun to work. He alluded to her "weakness" in relation to the shoe bosses, but failed to analyze how her vulnerability as a worker influenced her behavior during the controversy.[33]

The choice of her wage record by Darlin as the issue with which the *Awl* proceeded to attack the Lynn shoe manufacturers probably horrified Jane Atherton. Her chances for work as a binder were contingent on the goodwill of the shoe bosses, whom she placated with reticence and meekness in the interviews that they reported having with her. With her husband away from Lynn during the controversy over her wages, she probably felt acutely alone. It is interesting that as the controversy over the treatment of Atherton developed in the January and February issues, shoebinders at last began to contribute innocuous letters and poetry to the *Awl*, but none of them even alluded to the Atherton case.[34] On the whole, the cordwainers' society of Lynn received little support from shoe-binders. Its ideology and organizational structure implied a re-stricted role for women. Its attempts to threaten the shoe bosses with public shame made shoebinders, like Jane Atherton, even less likely to make an issue of mistreatment, fearing a strategy that would focus the combined anger of Lynn shoe manufacturers on them as individuals and deprive them of work.

Despite an inability to analyze or resolve the dilemmas of shoe-binders, the editors of the *Awl* deplored the general plight of female workers in the 1840s by publishing poems and articles advocat-ing women's rights and equal pay for female schoolteachers. Sarah Bagley and the Lowell Female Labor Reform Association, which represented female workers in New England textile mills, used the pages of the paper to publish their notices, make arguments for the ten-hour day, and criticize the *Lowell Offering* for its profac-tory bias. In the 1840s the Lowell textile operatives engaged in continuous agitation against exploitative changes in the work pro-cess. They formed a permanent labor organization that extended to other textile centers in the Merrimack Valley. Led by women such as Bagley, Huldah Stone, and Mehitable Eastman, they participated in political action by petitioning the state legislature for a ten-hour day, testifying on its behalf at legislative hearings, and persuad-ing male voters to oppose the reelection of those who blocked the ten-hour bill.[35] As labor activists, female textile workers left their sisters, the shoebinders of Essex County, far behind.

The editors of the *Awl* vigorously defended both the factory girls of Lowell and the seamstresses of Boston against low wages and mistreatment. The June 7, 1845, issue promoted the *Voice of In-dustry*, a labor paper representing the interests of New England textile workers, which began publication in May with Bagley as one of the editors, yet nothing on shoebinders appeared in the *Voice*. The leadership of the cordwainers' society in the mid-1840s saw women shoeworkers as persons whose lives were defined pri-marily by morality and family. These views made it difficult for artisans to regard shoebinders as fellow workers outside of family relationships or to include them as equals in the ideology and poli-tics built on artisan life. The involvement of women in the cordwainers' society in the 1840s appears to have been similar to the role of English women in the Chartist movement. Their activities did not reflect an engagement in paid work, but were limited to relatively anonymous support of the movement as family members and as symbols of community and artisan values.[36]

The number of women employed as shoebinders in Lynn doubled between 1845 and 1850, and the standard prices for the work rose slightly. The general scale of wages for binding in 1850 paid two to five cents per pair for children's shoes, three to nine cents for ladies' shoes, and as high as twelve cents a pair for gaiter boots. Some of the increases in the number of binders represented female members of whole families who migrated to Lynn. Women workers living in Lynn could earn higher wages than those in surrounding towns and villages or those living on farms. A report of the Lynn Board of Health in 1850 estimated weekly wages for binding as three to five dollars, depending on "inclination, ability, and time employed." [37] Females paid out $1.25 to $1.75 per week in board, while shoe-makers in Lynn earned double the wages, but paid twice as much to eat. By 1850 a regional labor market fed Lynn with migrants from rural New England; the migration pattern for women seemed to be one of the movement of whole families, while the patterns for men appeared in the 1850s to represent migration by individuals.[38] As neither the 1850 federal census of population nor the 1855 state census provides occupational data on women, it is impossible to say how many women might have been boarding and working as individuals in Lynn, a pattern more typical of the factory system in pre–Civil War Lowell and later in Essex County shoe cities. In addition to binders who came to Lynn with their families, shoe bosses also recruited additional numbers of women workers who lived in rural areas and in nearby coastal towns, such as Beverly and Marblehead. The *Lynn News* estimated in 1849 that at least one-third of the shoebinders who worked for central shops in Lynn lived out of town.[39] Their wages were lower than those of workers in the shoe towns and their connections with labor protest and the artisan tradition in Lynn were much more tenuous.

One of those shoebinders who lived in a neighboring coastal town and worked as an outworker for a Lynn central shop was twenty-one-year-old Sarah E. Trask of Beverly, Massachusetts, a seafaring town just north of Salem. She kept a diary of her experiences between 1849 and 1851, one of the rare surviving personal documents of a working woman prior to the Civil War.[40] In her diary Sarah Trask described a female network of support to which she often turned for advice, solace, and help in her work. The experience of these women contrasted with the group training and traditions of artisan cordwainers that empowered the protest activities of the Lynn shoemakers in the mid-1840s. The friends of Sarah Trask were young women tied together primarily by their social and emotional attachments and less by their work as binders. Like the networks of middle-class women who emerge in the diaries analyzed by Nancy Cott and Carroll Smith-Rosenberg, Sarah Trask's female friendships underlay and enlivened a separate sphere of womanhood.[41] For Trask and her friends, common work in domestic manufacture provided an additional bond of womanhood. As working women, they had, however, little connection with artisan shoemakers, even in Beverly. For them the artisan tradition represented a separate world of gender and work.

Sarah Trask began her diary in 1849 prompted by an acute sense of personal uncertainty. To be a diarist in the nineteenth century required both literacy and leisure, but a feeling of uncertainty was often a primary motive to begin writing.[42] Sarah Trask had little leisure and noted with hope at the beginning: "May I improve in written before I get though this Book." The central concern of her diary was her emotional dependence on Luther Woodberry, a sailor whose voyages in 1849 and 1850 placed her future at risk. Sarah's anxieties were multiplied by her inability to act or to influence events critical to her prospects. Her task was to endure this dilemma between 1849 and 1851, and her diary is an account of her anguish. Working as a shoebinder offered her only a distraction from her troubled loneliness and the means to earn a little money while she waited for Luther to return from his voyages.

Sarah Trask's father, a laborer, had died of consumption in 1848. She shared a small rented house with her widowed mother and an unmarried brother Joshua near Beverly Harbor, where she could watch the sails of ships tacking into Salem and Boston.[43] Her sisters, Catherine and Elizabeth, had married shoemakers and brother Joshua was a shoemaker, but her diary contains no evidence of contact between artisans and shoebinders. Sarah did not bind shoes for

Joshua and does not mention his work. Her friends and acquaintances were young wives or women engaged to mariners or laborers; their fathers were either artisans or other working-class men. She recorded her sister Lizzy's marriage at nineteen in 1849, and Sarah herself expected to marry when Luther Woodberry returned from a voyage on which he sailed in January 1849 from Boston to ports in the Mediterranean. Woodberry's father and brothers also were seamen in this trade carried on by the shipping interests of Salem and Boston prior to the Civil War.[44] The route of the ship on which Luther sailed risked fierce Atlantic storms, making the length of his voyage unpredictable and intensifying Sarah's worries. At the time of Luther's departure she began her diary, in which she expressed her feelings and fears, scrutinized her conduct, and tried to improve her writing and her spelling.

As Sarah waited for Luther to return, she worked at binding shoes for central shops in Beverly and in Lynn, like "poor lone Hannah," the woman portrayed in Lucy Larcom's popular nineteenth-century poem.

> Poor lone Hannah
> Sitting at the window, binding shoes:
> Faded, wrinkled,
> Sitting, stitching, in a mournful muse.
> Bright-eyed beauty once was she,
> When the bloom was on the tree:
> Spring and winter,
> Hannah's at the window, binding shoes. . . .
>
> Twenty winters
> Bleach and tear the ragged shore she views,
> Twenty seasons:—
> Never one had brought her any news.
> Still her dim eyes silently
> Chase the white sails o'er the sea:
> Hopeless, faithful,
> Hannah's at the window, binding shoes.[45]

Like Sarah Trask, Hannah had chosen a seafaring man and waited for his return while binding shoes, but the work brought her no solace and little income. Sarah Trask's diary exposes the grim reality of anxiety, fortitude, and tedium that underlay the pathetic image of Hannah in Larcom's poem.

Sarah and her friends, the daughters of laborers, carpenters, mariners, and shoemakers, had chosen shoebinding in preference to making coats as outworkers or doing domestic work because the wages for binding seemed better. At one point Sarah wrote that four cents a pair and "thread found" struck her as "very good" for a particular style of shoe. On February 20, 1849, and with some grim irony, she had counted 719 stitches in one shoe upper for which she earned two cents. "Just for fun I counted the stiches in a shoe, the size was fives, 719 in the whole, 250 on the top, 173 in the filling, 120 on the side seams or 65 in one side, 69 in the closing or 23 on a seam, 58 in the lining, or 29 on a side, 99 on the surgeing." [46] The price varied with the style of the shoe, but binding did not pay Sarah a wage on which she could support herself even when she worked on gaiter boots at twenty cents a pair for a Lynn shoe boss. Her goal seemed to be to earn one dollar a week, but she was often unable to work as steadily as she would have liked or obtain work when she wanted it. Her time spent at work was also diminished by her duties helping her mother in the kitchen and doing housework. "At home today, finishing my week['s] work eight pairs of boots one dollar; how smart, beside my housework, and last tuesday I work for [sister] Lizzy, so there the duty of the week. I almost think I shall make my fortune soon." Like Larcom's Hannah, Sarah was poor, unable to support herself on her earnings, and lonely in the absence of her prospective male provider. Her future lay with Luther Woodberry, hostage to the dangers of seafaring.

Yet many of the entries in Sarah's diary testify to her deep ambivalence about marriage as her destiny and that of her friends. In Sarah's view, a wife accepted her husband's decisions, but bore the greater share of life's cares and trials. She recorded the marriage dates of many acquaintances and reflected on their chances for success. She watched as almost the entire work force of shoebinders, who for three years had taken work from the same Beverly central shop, disappeared into wedlock. As an active member of the Daughters of Temperance in Beverly, Sarah worried about the impact of drunken husbands on the marriages of friends. Embarking on marriage appeared to be as dangerous as setting forth on a Mediterranean voyage in January. Her diary reflected Sarah's basic recognition of her own lack of control over her life and of the uselessness and even evil of complaint against her situation. "No news from L. W. yet, and I am almost discourage, it seems as though I have look for news a year; I think some times I will not think of it, but I cannot help it, it will come up in my mind, But this will never do for me, and so I will not write my ugly thoughts, always complaining, if things are not just so, oh what a wicked girl I am." She felt sinful to be angry and impatient and begged God to make her submit to His will so that she could be happy. She struggled to subdue anger and desire and sought to develop the values of submission and piety, the values of a true and moral woman. Her many disappointments at the failure to hear news of Luther's voyage or of his return were based on the unrealistic expectations that she formed from the one letter that he sent her. Nonetheless, she believed that her devotion and her willingness to suffer daily disappointment would act as a talisman to bring Luther safely home to her. This faith insulated her from the well-meaning but often cruel skepticism of her more seasoned Beverly neighbors who had often waited out long voyages by family members.

Sarah's circumstances were common to the young women of the New England seacoast, and she shared her experiences with a network of close friends like Lydia Burnham, whose lover Samuel Foster had sailed on the same ship as Luther, and with other young women who bound shoes, made coats, did domestic work, and waited for the return of their young men from the sea. These female friends supported each other in their work and their waiting. They went together to the central shops and helped each other learn how to bind the various styles of shoes correctly. By occasionally stitching in groups, they shared the tedium of binding. They cooperated to help finish up one friend's lot of uppers to return them to the central shop. They also helped each other endure the anguish of waiting and united as a group against any masculine inclinations toward alcohol, "tobacto," or the lure of the California goldfields.

Sarah and her friends, however, did not seem to be able to translate their moral position as young women into social power or even personal influence. Sarah's involvement with the Daughters of Temperance contributed to her sense of moral duty as a woman. She and her network of friends joined together to censor male social behavior and to try to prevent decisions that would take their young men to California. The Trask diary supports Carl Degler's argument that middle-class values of the cult of true womanhood penetrated the behavior of working-class women, although Sarah's struggle to realize the values of true womanhood cost her much pain.[46] If she came to expect a relationship with Luther Woodberry close to the mutual emotional dependency of middle-class marriage, he apparently did not. Neither did he seem to acknowledge Sarah's moral superiority or show any sign of responding to her emotional dependency. Sarah's hold on Luther was uncertain. She referred to him in her diary as both "friend" and "lover," and it is clear that Luther evaded Sarah's advice and her emotional demands, choosing instead freedom of action. The moral woman expected to wield power in society, but Sarah Trask could not even translate her moral position into personal influence. The evidence in her diary also suggests that Sarah's friends had similar experiences with the working men they intended to marry.

While she and her friends waited, Sarah felt that the whole town of Beverly was watching her, testing her reactions and teasing her about her fears. The community expected the wife of a seafaring man to be brave and stoical, not moral and dependent. Powerless to speak her mind for fear of ridicule or to argue her preference for Luther's future, Sarah recorded in her diary her secret fears and angers and her strong opposition to any suggestion from her Beverly friends that Luther might profitably seek his fortune in California with the forty-niners. For her and her young women friends, as perhaps for many New England women in 1849 and 1850, the word California represented a specter of dread and potential loss. Yet when Luther returned from the Mediterranean in the fall of 1849, Sarah was unable to change his decision to try his luck in California. Her future rested with a man who was not yet her husband, one whose decisions she had no wifely right to protest. Indeed to protest would prove her unworthiness to be a Beverly mariner's bride. She felt herself to be "doom to disapointment and discourage, I dare not speak my thoughts to anny one." Again she waited after Luther's departure for California in the spring of 1850. After a year during which she kept no diary, she received word that following an illness of six months Luther had died on board ship during his passage back from California. He was buried at sea.

After the report of Luther's death reached her, Sarah self-consciously joined the community of bereaved women in Beverly. She briefly kept a second diary as a memorial to Luther and to her sister Lizzy, who had died in childbirth. Soon, however, she put aside both her writing and her shoebinding, and retreating into her family, she moved in with her married sister Catherine and helped her with her boarders. She remained a domestic servant in her sister's house until she retired to live alone in various small rented houses in Beverly. She died of consumption in 1892. Sarah Trask had been defeated by her lack of alternatives and by the loss of her one chance to marry. Her work offered her a distraction from her worries and a community of friends with whom to share her anxieties while she waited, but offered her no way to support herself or gain a sense of personal independence. The virtues that she sought to cultivate as a moral woman—submission, piety, trust in God, and hopefulness—brought her little solace when her worst fears materialized.

The life of Sarah Trask provides one example of the experience of moral womanhood for a shoebinder who worked in Essex County in late 1840s. Her life also provides a test of the potential of female morality as a basis for labor protest. Neither the artisan tradition nor equal rights shaped her work or its social and ideological context. Shoebinding did not assume a central place in her life. What group experience she had as a worker was a means of acting out gender expectations among other young women waiting for marriage. Part of this group experience involved a sense of common agreement to try to control and censor male social behavior. Although Sarah Trask became involved in local temperance activities, her sense of being a moral woman did not lead her or other Beverly shoebinders to political action as workers. To be a moral woman for Trask meant to submit to her work, to God, and to her fate. Her painful struggle to put aside anger and disappointment left her submissive and powerless. Her ordeal of waiting produced only individual defeat.

Labor protest among shoeworkers during early industrialization reflected the development of new meanings for gender and class, especially for women workers. The leaders of the Reading, Lynn, and Saugus shoebinders' societies in 1831 and 1834 had justified their activities by drawing on but redefining their relationship as women to the artisan tradition of equal rights. Separately organized and self-directed, they claimed new rights to political activism based on the objective of their cause: the terms of women's work must be just and fair in a moral society. They demanded an extension of the equal rights ideology to include them as females and to defend their public pursuit of better treatment. They drew on preindustrial culture to argue that they possessed a right to contribute a comfortable support to their families in the new system of capitalist production. Their use of the bonds of sisterhood as a collective basis for working women provided some initial support for their activities, which were, however, undercut by the objective conditions of outwork. Rebellious shoebinders in the 1830s understood that their position in production was directed by the marketplace, but when they justified their demands for higher wages with the value of their domestic work, they faced the limits that their role within the artisan family placed on their demands for equal rights and public action. Tensions within the artisan tradition in labor protest over the meaning of changes in women's work remained unresolved.

Labor protest led by artisan shoemakers in the 1840s also demanded that the terms of work must be fair and just in a moral social order, but limited the role that women could play in their movement. They perceived women as both useful and moral, but in order for women to be virtuous, they had to submit to work as defined by the sexual division of labor. The artisan tradition, however, did not include either group work or craft status for shoebinders, but relied instead on the moral capacity of women as a defense against their employers and as a link to labor protest. These activities did not require an extension of political rights for women and implied only a limited form of public action contained within their role in the family. Artisan protest failed to address the essential problems of female outworkers: that work conducted for wages within the home was still exploited by the hard terms and low wages of the market.

Women outworkers faced serious difficulties in organizing resistance to low wages in an expanding system of decentralized production that included rural women in areas distant from shoe towns. Neither a separate female organization in the 1830s nor cooperation with male workers in the 1840s adequately addressed these problems. The energies of potential leaders who could articulate the special problems of shoebinders seemed to be drawn off in pursuit of new moral responsibilities in the antislavery movement and in temperance activities. Unlike the shoebinder societies of the 1830s, these activist women, like Sarah Trask of Beverly, dissociated their moral concerns from their political interests as workers. The tensions that early industrialization brought to work and to social relationships in artisan families shaped the participation of men and women in labor protest in the 1830s and 1840s. These tensions continued as shoe production became partly mechanized in the early 1850s and moved into factories. In addition to debates over social harmony and a just economic order, pre–Civil War labor protest among shoeworkers also concerned new meanings of public action and morality for women.

CHAPTER FIVE

The Early Factory System
and the New England Shoe Strike
of 1860

Girls of Lynn, . . . strike at once. . . . Don't work your
machines; let them lie still until we get all we ask.

—Clara Brown, shop girl,
New York Times, February 29, 1860

But what of the poor bottomers? If we go to work
before the bottomers obtain their objects, the men's
work will be sent out of town, and our husbands and
brothers left to starve. . . . [O]ur work is not done.

—Mrs. Mary A. Damon, homeworker,
New York Herald, March 19, 1860

During the decade of the 1850s, changes in the process of work
began to transform the shoe industry of Essex County. The conver-
sion of the Singer sewing machine to stitch light leather mechanized
shoebinding and sharply reversed the proportion of female and
male workers employed in shoe production. More and more shoe
bosses expanded the operations of their central shops, which began
to function like factories. New divisions of work on machines powered by steam engines came under the direction of shoe manufacturers. A slow evolution toward the factory system had begun, but
would not be complete until 1865 when the McKay stitcher and
steam power to run it had mechanized the work of shoemakers.
The gradual and incremental nature of centralization and mechanization encouraged the transfer of the sexual division of labor into
the early shoe factory in Essex County. Yet while certain work processes were mechanized and centralized, most shoeworkers before
1860 continued to labor in the outwork system of hand production.

Many of them worked in towns located in southern New Hampshire and Maine, where Massachusetts bosses had organized central shops. The growing numbers of shoemakers, especially in central Massachusetts, included rural migrants and Irish and German immigrants. These shoeworkers faced falling wage levels caused by the reorganization of production and hard times.

Competition in domestic markets began to alter the process of shoe production in Essex County in the early 1850s. In an effort to reduce labor costs in a market in which leather stock prices remained high while the domestic demand for shoes slumped, shoe manufacturers in Lynn recruited additional cheap male outworkers in rural areas, especially bottomers, whose work involved shaping the sewn upper to size around a wooden last and attaching the sole. Shoe bosses in Lynn used the railroad system and hired additional express wagons to distribute this work. The number of male workers employed by Lynn manufacturers rose by 51 percent between 1850 and 1860, and by 1855 outworkers in the countryside made well over half the shoes that Lynn bosses sold.[1]

In addition to the massive recruitment of rural shoemakers, bosses experimented with centralizing and further dividing their work. By 1850 some central shops in Lynn had separated cutting operations into two rooms, one for cutting and storing the light leather for uppers and the other for preparing and keeping the heavier sole leather. This separation of cutting into light and heavy work probably reflected advances in pattern-making and the introduction in the 1850s of different shapes for left and right feet. Sets of cut uppers and soles were numbered and packed into different boxes to be sent out to the binders and the bottomers.[2]

In Haverhill, shoe boss Moses How reorganized some of his making operations into his central shop in 1855 when he moved into more spacious quarters on the town's main street. In his new location, which offered room to hire additional workers, he later recalled how he experimented with centralizing and dividing men's work before mechanization: "I brought together 25 or 30 hands [journeymen], in one room, making goods ahead and piling them up. The workmen labored three hundred days in the year, there being no divisions of the business into seasons as now [1888]. The work at the new shop was on hand-sewn goods, in addition to the work that was being done in the country, and in the new place each man had a different part."[3]

Moses How acknowledged that his shoemakers resisted centralization and division of labor. "Shoemakers were a different class of mechanics from those of other trades. You couldn't bring together a large number of men, as their work at that time was necessarily single-handed."[4] Steady work, wages paid in cash (less common in Haverhill than in Lynn), and the ability of the shoe boss to scrutinize the work process resulted in a standard product that pleased How. "I secured more uniform goods than under the old system." His advantage also lay in quality work on the finest leather, producing what he claimed were the best ladies' shoes made in Haverhill and sold in New York City. How maintained this system of shoe production, partly centralized and partly country outwork, until the invention of the McKay stitching machine, which mechanized the bottoming process. He then purchased one of the first nine machines that were built for sale and centralized all of his making operations, but had to wait until 1870 to obtain a factory equipped with steam power. By 1860 another Haverhill shoe operation, the E. T. and R. M. Ingalls Company, also located on Merrimack Street, had mechanized and centralized work by means of a pegging machine that they ran with a five-horsepower steam engine. The machine cut its own pegs out of wood strips and drove them into the soles at a rate of fourteen per second. The work was divided into various rooms in the four-story central shop, which was in effect a factory.[5] In Haverhill, the process of reorganizing men's work was slow and discontinuous, combining hand production with centralized operations on machines run by foot and by steam power.

After 1855 a change in shoe styles increased the demand for shoes with heels higher than the relatively flat ones that shoemakers had previously attached to soles. Heeling operations also became organized into central shops, and bottomers who had attached heels to soles objected to the impact on their wages of this new division of labor. In Haverhill and Natick, heelers and other shop workers earned higher wages than bottomers, which led to tensions between the two groups.[6] The first manufacturer in Lynn to employ heelers in centralized production was John Wooldredge, who also led in the application of steam power to heeling in 1858. In some central shops, workmen ran foot-powered pegging machines, while others finished off the shoes, working as buffers and greasers. Unlike bottomers, the men who worked in centralized production were not required to furnish tools or materials such as paste and blacking, which increased their net income. In their desire to expand production at reduced labor costs, some shoe manufacturers in key shoe towns in Essex County divided and centralized the work process long before mechanization had transformed the work itself. Blanche Hazard described this process as "the almost unnoticed drift toward factory-like supervision of labor," achieving both a standard product and reducing costs in labor and in expensive leather stock.[7] After 1855 David Johnson of Lynn observed workmen leaving their little shops for work in the early factories. The ten footers, formerly the locus of artisan protest, began to be converted into henhouses and coal bins, disappearing gradually from the city after the Civil War.[8]

Shoe manufacturers also mechanized and centralized women's work in the 1850s, but a portion of the work of sewing shoe uppers remained in the home. Even before mechanization, some young women had begun to work in the trimming rooms of central shops in Lynn, sewing rosettes and bows on completed shoes by hand and pasting on decorations. Edith Abbott noted a 5 percent increase in the number of women employed in Lynn between 1845 and 1855.[9] Wages for shoebinding in Essex County appear to have risen in the years just prior to mechanization. One example of the rising prices for shoebinding is the work record of Maria Poor of Georgetown, the wife of a country shoemaker. Georgetown was one of the rural villages in Essex County where outworkers labored for shoe bosses in Lynn, Haverhill, and Danvers; in 1845 there were 419 men and 237 women residents working on shoes. After she married Edward Poor, Maria bound the uppers for the shoes that her husband made in the 1830s, but increasingly in the 1840s, she worked on uppers provided to her directly by local shoe bosses, Little & Noyes and Little & Moulton. Although her total work diminished during her childbearing years, the wages she received as a rural outworker rose as high as seven cents per pair for women's boots between 1848 and 1852. In the late 1840s and early 1850s James Hutchinson of North Danvers paid his shoebinders as much as five and one-half cents per pair for women's shoes, six and one-half cents for men's shoes, and eight cents for custom work. Rising prices for shoebinding in the early 1850s also affected the training of apprentices. In the decade prior to 1860, masters and journeymen insisted that for the first five years novices work exclusively sewing seams in uppers, a practice that increased the availability of sewn uppers but that also broke down the apprentice system.[10]

After the adaptation of the sewing machine to stitch uppers in 1852, Maria Poor's wages for handwork fell. In the mid-1850s, she produced only two and one-half lots of uppers annually for prices that had fallen by late 1858 to two cents per pair for women's shoes. Another shoe boss in the nearby town of Topsfield, Andrew Gould, employed twenty-three shoebinders between 1859 and 1860 and paid them prices reminiscent of the early 1830s: between two and three and one-half cents for children's and women's shoes. Although Gould paid his binders entirely in cash, his prices in 1859 were lower than for similar work performed in the 1840s.[11] The wage record of Maria Poor, as represented in her husband's account book, reflected the impact of mechanization on shoebinding. Wages sank, and handwork became less available. The shoebinders of Essex County faced an uncertain future, working more intensively if they could obtain work and at a severe wage reduction. The adaptation of the sewing machine to work on shoe uppers did not, however, immediately separate home and work for shoebinders or create a large-scale factory system before 1860.[12] The process of shoe production evolved slowly between 1852 and 1865 toward the steam-powered factory, and the work retained many preindustrial elements, notably the sexual division of labor.

In 1851 a former Lynn shoe cutter, John Brooke Nichols, purchased machines for sewing cloth from the machine shop of the I. M. Singer Company located in Cambridge, Massachusetts, and organized a stitching room in Boston that employed eight women to make men's clothing. While manufacturing clothing, Nichols also worked for Singer and in early 1852 succeeded in converting the sewing machine to stitch light leather by using a smaller needle and more resilient thread. He then went to Lynn in the employ of Singer, who had sold exclusive rights to lease and sell his new shoe-stitching machine in Essex County to three Lynn manufacturers: John Wooldredge, A. S. Moore, and George W. Keene. Nichols organized stitching rooms for these bosses on the model of his garment operation in Boston and instructed young women in the use of the machines. Hannah Harris, the eighteen-year-old daughter of a cutter who worked for Wooldredge, was the first machine girl in Lynn. By November 1852 twenty stitching machines run by hand cranks were in operation in the shops of Wooldredge, Moore, and Keene. Lyman R. Blake, who later invented a stitching machine for bottoming operations, also trained female operators in the use of the Singer sewing machine.[13]

Nichols later set up his own stitching shop in Lynn to subcontract work on shoe uppers, and he also manufactured sewing machines as Nichols & Bliss under Elias Howe's patent after Howe had won his battle with Singer over infringement of his patent rights to the sewing machine for cloth. By 1855 two other sewing machine companies, Grover & Baker and Wheeler & Wilson, were producing machines for leather uppers under licenses from Howe. After 1855 the machines were simplified, increased in speed, and fitted with a number of attachments, including a treadle to replace the hand crank.[14] By 1860 most of the leading shoe manufacturers in Lynn had mechanized the production of sewn uppers.

In the shoe centers of Lynn and Haverhill the shoebinders organized protests to resist the introduction of the sewing machine. A. S. Moore, one of Singer's agents for Essex County and the employer of machine operatives in Lynn, faced a committee of angry binders in 1852 who tried to pressure him and his female employees to abandon their machines. In Haverhill, shoebinders and shoemakers voiced bitter resentment at Isaac R. Harding when he brought the first stitching machine into town in 1853. Some of the women shook their fists in the face of Daniel Goodrich, Harding's partner, and the firm locked its doors against both the incensed workers and curious onlookers. These binders were convinced that the new machines would destroy their work. Many must have realized that centralized machine operations would force them to choose between their domestic duties and their ability to earn wages as homeworkers. Contributing to the distress of these shoebinders was their unfamiliarity with the sewing machine for cloth. The early marketing strategy of the sewing machine companies concentrated on the use of the machines for the manufacture of garments and shoes, ignoring the potential they would later realize in the home market for family sewing.[15]

Moses How of Haverhill eagerly acquired the Singer machine, but had to persuade a machine operator from Lynn to come to Haverhill to run it for him. Pleased with the success of his first machine, How ordered a second and installed both female stitchers in the same room of the central shop as his male workers. He clearly recognized the significance of this move: "We were able, for the first time, to complete a shoe in the factory and without sending it out of the building." [16] Following his purchase of stitching machines, How further centralized his making operations.

Isaac Harding had some difficulty integrating the stitching machine into his operations located close to How's establishment on Merrimack Street; his first stitcher was a man. Other manufacturers in Haverhill ordered sewing machines, but their use in production was delayed by the unfamiliarity of women workers with the operation of any kind of machinery. Several experienced shoebinders who worked for the firm of Sawyer & Wheeler tried to run the sewing machine without success and gave up "in despair." A young employee, Alfred Ordway, was the first to master the operations of the machine for the firm. After studying and working the mechanism, he stitched three pairs of uppers satisfactorily, and his jubilant employer ran into the cutting room, shouting: "The boy has done it!" [17] Ordway then instructed female workers, who later gained considerable skill and speed, especially after the hand crank had been replaced by a treadle, freeing both hands to guide the leather. The training of female operatives in the use of the stitching machine increased the control of shoe manufacturers over the process of preparing uppers and provided a reason for them to continue to employ women.

Although shoebinders correctly feared mechanization, the system of household production continued after the introduction of the stitching machine. The changes brought to women's work in the 1850s were neither immediate nor widespread, and not all work on uppers was mechanized. For eight years after the machines were introduced in Haverhill in 1853, all linings for women's shoes continued to be sewn by hand. [18] Only with the appearance of a folding attachment in the 1860s was the entire upper produced by a machine operator. Suspicions of manufacturers about customer acceptance of machine-stitched work somewhat retarded mechanization, but if handwork was still available for domestic production, the wages for shoebinding fell rapidly as the productivity of machine work rose and labor costs declined.

By 1860, although the piece rate for machine sewing was one-quarter of the price of handwork, the machine stitcher in a factory earned nearly three times as much as the binder working by hand at home. In 1850 the scale of binders' wages in Lynn varied from two to five cents a pair for children's shoes and from six to twelve cents a pair for gaiter boots. Most binders earned between three and four dollars a week. By 1860, handwork on Congress boots had fallen to two cents a pair, and the wages of Lynn shoebinders had declined by half. Even the shoe manufacturers of Haverhill admitted in 1860 that shoebinders' wages were "outrageously low," ranging from one-third of a cent to one cent per pair for linings and, if the work was available, one to three cents per pair for stitching and lining women's shoes. Haverhill shoebinders, who provided thread and lining material out of their wages, worked very hard to earn one to two dollars a week, while shop girls working on machines earned between five and eight dollars a week, according to local estimates. Low prices for binding in the 1850s after mechanization prompted some women to borrow practices from artisan tradition. The larger manufacturers in Lynn furnished silk and cotton thread to their workers, and binders adopted the craft custom of "cabbaging" leftover materials, regarding it as compensation for the "miserably low" prices paid for their work. One Lynn manufacturer received a note in 1870 from an otherwise unrepentant shoebinder who had worked for him fifteen years earlier. Enclosed in the letter was two dollars as a repayment for her expropriation of thread.[19]

By 1855, shoe manufacturers involved in the process of adopting mechanization in Lynn, Haverhill, Marblehead, and Danvers employed 86 percent of all women working in shoe production in Essex County. Some binders in Lynn rented or purchased leather stitching machines for use at home. Estimates differ on the extent of the home use of sewing machines. The machines were expensive; in the mid-1850s the prices varied from seventy-five dollars to one hundred twenty-five dollars. The most widespread use of machines in the home occurred in Lynn, where shoe manufacturers rented machines.[20] By renting machines, the Lynn shoe bosses may have responded to the anger of local shoebinders over mechanization or they might have been simply attempting to create a larger supply of sewn uppers closer at hand. In doing so, they began to reverse the geographical extent of the outwork system and draw more heavily on the female population of the city for homeworkers. Home use of a machine allowed women workers to continue to combine their domestic duties with wage-earning. Lynn men recalled that as boys they had turned the hand cranks of sewing machines after school, while their mothers stitched shoe uppers. However, these homeworkers, like handworkers, faced the custom of furnishing: providing materials and thread for their work in addition to paying rent on machines. One home machine operator in Lynn estimated that furnishing and machine rental cost her $3.50 a week out of a six dollars weekly wage. While hand-cranked machines provided homework for women in Lynn, Salem, and Marblehead, manufacturers in other shoe towns did not offer this arrangement.[21]

Some shoe manufacturers centralized stitching operations by adding a story to their central shops. For a while Moses How of Haverhill put his stitchers in the same room as his shoemakers, but others had two-story buildings constructed to contain the operations of the central shop on the first floor and the stitching room on the second floor. Stitching was also frequently subcontracted by the central shop owner to "machine bosses" who ran shops like those of Nichols and Blake. The preindustrial separation of the work of men and women was thereby maintained despite mechanization and centralization. The work force in these shops of thirty to fifty workers were "girls," unmarried young women who had left their homes to work all day at stitching shoes by machine. The *Lynn News* estimated in 1855 that there were 1,500 to 1,800 sewing machines in operation and that most of them were run in central shops by young women who earned an average weekly wage of about six dollars. Many of these women who worked in Lynn and Haverhill were members of local families, but by 1860 a sizable proportion of them represented migrants who had left their homes in the towns of eastern Massachusetts, New Hampshire, Maine, and the Maritime Provinces of Canada to board in the shoe towns and work for the attractive wages earned in the shoe shops.[22] Centralization and mechanization drew female workers to Essex County and began to undermine the rural outwork system. Like the young New England women who had worked in the cotton mill towns of the Merrimack Valley before the 1850s, these female operatives represented a source of labor for new industrial work.

Essex County shoe bosses offered relatively high wages to per-

suade young women who lived in the shoe towns and in the surrounding region to work a ten-hour day on stitching machines in
centralized production. Factory girls were generally paid by piece
rates, although a few worked for weekly wages and not all women
who worked in centralized production ran machines. Some were
trimmers and pasters, and others worked in the shops sewing linings by hand until changes in sewing machine technology eliminated this work. By 1860 the piece rates in Lynn allowed most
stitchers to earn five dollars a week with a typical expense of two
dollars for board. Newspaper estimates for Haverhill and Marblehead indicate a range of weekly wages between three and seven
dollars a week, depending on the effort and skill of the operative, the piece rate, and the quality of the shoe. These piece rates
reflected new divisions of labor for stitching in factories. By 1860,
rates had been set on stitching various parts of the shoe: the foxing
(stitching on an extra ornamental overlay of leather), the goring
or elastic side of Congress boots, and stitching on the front, back,
heel, and tip of the upper. All of the prices varied with the style
and quality of the shoe.[23] Wages in the cotton textile industry,
the other major industrial employer of women in New England,
declined in the 1850s. In Lowell there were at least three cuts in
piece rates between 1850 and 1857. Native-born Yankee women
were leaving the industry, and speedups became common. A strike
in 1859 among Irish women spinners demonstrated the shift from
native-born to immigrant workers in the Lowell mills and exposed
divisions between ethnic groups in the work force.[24] For young,
unmarried Yankee women, the wages paid for work in the shoe
shops of Essex County in the 1850s made stitching shoes seem an
attractive form of industrial work.

Twenty-eight-year-old Martha Osbourne Barrett, who lived in
Salem with her widowed mother, responded to the high wages
offered to shoe stitchers and commuted by train to nearby Danversport in 1855 to work in the stitching shop of David Mead. She
complained frequently in her diary about the exhausting nature of
the work, but concluded that stitching shoes was her best chance
to earn money. "It is absolutely necessary for me to do something
to earn *money* and this work seems to be the most available just
now. So I am steadily at work."[25] When railroad service was suspended in 1856, she had to board in Danversport, a situation that

Interior of a stitching room. From *Frank Leslie's Illustrated Magazine*, March 17, 1860, courtesy of Lynn Historical Society.

she disliked. After two months and despite her continued expressions of interest in earning high wages in factory work, Martha Barrett settled for a job in a millinery shop in Salem and residence with her mother.[26] Eliza A. Bartlett, who was seventeen in 1860, learned machine work while employed at the Keene factory, stitching uppers for Congress boots and earning three dollars a week as a novice. She and her family had moved to Lynn from Portsmouth, New Hampshire, after her father died, and she was forced to find work at an early age. As she became more skilled at stitching, Eliza Bartlett turned out three to four lots of sixty pairs each day and probably earned the average wage of five dollars a week for Lynn shop girls. But the long hours involved in factory work persuaded her to rent a sewing machine and stitch at home, where she was working during the 1860 strike.[27]

Stitchers in the early shoe factories of Lynn objected to the long hours of work rather than to low wages. The *New England Mechanic*, a labor reform paper published in Lynn and edited by Alonzo B. Draper, chairman of the Lynn Mechanics' Association, criticized the long hours of work for female stitchers at their hand-cranked or treadled machines. The February 26, 1859, issue carried an editorial on machine girls that denounced the "cruel inroads" that "the present wretched [factory] system" made on their physical strength. Long hours sitting at their machines and the consequent lack of exercise injured female health, leaving them "pale, weak and emasciated." The editor also criticized the wages earned by female operatives, claiming that "they are paid the poorest and work the hardest of any class in Essex County." Drawing on evidence from the wage book of an unidentified machine girl, the editorial denounced a decline in wages of 50 percent between 1854 and 1858 as "inhumane" and "unchristian." Piece rates on machine work did decline in the 1850s, but were offset by mechanical improvements and rising levels of productivity.

Wages were not a major grievance for female factory workers in the 1850s, according to one Lynn operative who responded to Draper's editorial. She argued that the introduction of the sewing machine had produced benefits for the woman worker as well as evils, but questioned the long, tiring, ten-hour day. Defending the factory system as worthy of reform, this stitcher called on the shoe manufacturers of Lynn to reduce the workday to eight hours. This reform, she insisted, would not diminish profits to the employers nor the wages of workers. By increasing productivity during a limited workday, the stitchers would be relieved in part of the "very exhaustive" labor of running a machine by treadle. Unconsciously echoing the complaints of the female textile operatives involved in the ten-hour movement of the 1840s, she noted that long hours interrupted mealtimes and caused dyspepsia and ill health. More free time would allow the female worker a chance for "moral and intellectual" development, impossible for her when overworked.[28]

This Lynn stitcher also criticized a change in the method of paying wages to female factory workers that she argued made it difficult for a worker to meet her boarding expenses on a regular basis. For several years after the introduction of machine work, the shoe bosses had paid the operatives at the end of each week or every two weeks. Prompt payment of good wages had attracted female workers to Lynn shoe factories. But recently, the stitcher complained, some employers had begun to pay their workers only once a month, making it impossible for the operative to pay her boardinghouse keeper on a weekly basis. The result was an increase in boarding charges to offset the expenses to the boarding establishment of purchasing provisions on credit, "and credit [she noted], every businessman knows, must be paid for." The stitcher pointed out that many of those who boarded factory workers in Lynn depended on this weekly income to support their families. The worker had to bear the additional cost of board, while the manufacturer had the use of his money. She called on the shoe bosses to pay their female workers on a weekly basis as they paid off the shoemakers when the finished shoes were delivered to the central shop.

This stitcher disagreed with the total condemnation of the situation of machine girls by the editor of the *New England Mechanic* in 1859, a divergence of opinion that indicated differences between the shoemakers of Lynn and the new machine girls over the factory system. She raised no objections to the level of wages paid to shop girls and appealed not to her fellow workers, but to her employers to institute reform. The attitudes expressed by this factory stitcher indicated an interest in changing the hours and conditions of wage payments in the early shoe factory, but an acceptance of centralized machine work and the wage system. Many factory stitchers in

Haverhill who earned between five and eight dollars a week admitted in 1860 that they had to work very hard, but that they had no complaint about wages.[29] Homeworkers, however, were dissatisfied with the sharp decline in their wages and the burden placed on their incomes by the custom of furnishing materials. Two wage levels developed in the 1850s as a result of the mechanization of women's work: one for factory work on machines and another for homeworkers, who stitched uppers both by hand and by machine. These two wage levels pointed to a dual system of production: local outwork on rented machines and centralized machine production. Before 1860 the numerical majority of women in the industry worked at home; only a minority worked in factories. The dual system of production reflected community resistance to factory discipline among local working men and women, but the strike of 1860 and the disruptions of the Civil War would end widespread homework in Lynn.

Mechanization of women's work did not alter the sexual division of labor in shoe production. Manufacturers who trained young women to use the machines in factories and rented machines to homeworkers saw mechanization as a solution to the low productivity of women outworkers. They were also willing to pay attractive wages to recruit female workers throughout eastern New England for centralized production.[30] Growing competitive pressures in the industry in the 1850s provide a context for the mechanization of binding. In a letter to the *New England Mechanic* in March 1859, one small shoe boss in Lynn condemned the drive by the larger manufacturers to gain a competitive edge over the smaller manufacturers in the preparation of shoe uppers.[31] Before the introduction of the sewing machine, he argued, the owners of the smaller central shops in Lynn had a monopoly on the best quality of shoebinding, which gave them a decided advantage over larger manufacturers despite the latter's greater access to capital and credit. This control over the work of the more skilled shoebinders had been the result of the careful development of networks of part-time outworkers over the years. The sewing machine destroyed the control that the small shoe boss had had over skilled work by producing a mechanical stitch of "mathematical regularity and beauty" that few handworkers could match. The advantage now lay with capital, which could both buy machines and hire operatives. Mechanization had destroyed the value of skillful binding. Even more astonishing to this Lynn observer was the rapidity of machine operations, which enabled the factory owner to produce 1,000 pairs of sewn uppers in less time than it had taken to produce two to three dozen before 1852. In the outwork system, the uppers remained in the hands of the shoebinders anywhere from a week to six months, and it would take the manufacturer four to five weeks to finish a hundred pairs to fill an order. After mechanization, 1,000 pairs could be stitched in two days, and the order filled in three. The letter ended with expressions of pessimism for the future of small shoe bosses and journeymen alike.

Although some Lynn shoe bosses may have resented the larger manufacturers with greater access to capital, three relatively small manufacturers made the initial decision to mechanize, while establishing a monopoly in 1852 over the sales of Singer sewing machines in Essex County. In 1850 the John Wooldredge Company was capitalized at only $4,000; George W. Keene's operation had assets of $8,000. Neither appeared among the ranks of the thirteen largest manufacturers capitalized that year at $10,000 or over. A. S. Moore, the third firm to initiate mechanization, was not listed in the federal census of manufacture in 1850. By 1860 the three firms had greatly expanded their operations: Wooldredge reported assets of $20,000, while Moore and Keene had $15,000 each. The three were among the thirty-seven largest firms in Lynn out of 131 in 1860 capitalized at over $10,000, and these largest firms had grown from 11 percent of the total number of shoe manufacturers in 1850 to 28 percent in 1860. The three small firms pioneered the mechanization that once proven worthwhile, was adopted by the larger manufacturers to their advantage. In addition to the growth in capital assets, the largest firms in 1860 employed 57 percent of the total work force in Lynn as compared to 31 percent in 1850. Once mechanization had been initiated by Wooldredge, Moore, and Keene in 1852, the largest firms grew in number, size, capital assets, and total work force to dominate shoe production in Lynn.

In addition to stimulating growth among the larger shoe manufacturers of Lynn, the mechanization of women's work had a profound impact on the composition of the work force. By 1860 the productivity of machine girls in shoe shops sharply reversed the preindustrial proportions of women to men in shoe work and greatly reduced the number of female workers in the industry (see Table 3). Mechanization stimulated the demand for bottoming, while reducing the demand for binding. One factory girl working full-time at her stitching machine could supply enough work for twenty bottomers, while replacing eleven shoebinders.[32] The proportions of men and women workers in shoe production in Lynn gradually shifted from two-thirds female and one-third male in 1850, to half female and half male in 1855, to 40 percent female and 60 percent male workers in 1860.[33]

Table 3. Sex ratio of Lynn shoeworkers, 1850 and 1860

	No. of firms	Work force	Male workers (%)	Female workers (%)
1850	112	10,165	3,742 (37%)	6,423 (63%)
1860	131	9,467	5,664 (60%)	3,803 (40%)
Change	+19	−698	+1,922 (+51%)	−2,620 (−41%)

Average monthly wage for male workers rose 10.2% from 1850 to 1860.
Average monthly wage for female workers rose 46% from 1850 to 1860.
SOURCE: U. S. Census of Manufacture, Manuscripts for 1850 and 1860. The column in the census: "Kinds of Motive Power, Machinery, Structure, or Buildings" listed no data other than "Steam" and "Hand."

An examination of the percentage of men and women employed by the three firms that initiated mechanization in Lynn shows an even sharper reversal of the sex ratio in the work force.

Table 4. Percentage of women and men employed by the Wooldredge, Keene, and Moore firms, 1850 and 1860

	1850		1860	
Employer	Women	Men	Women	Men
Wooldredge	69%	31%	29%	71%
Keene	64%	36%	33%	67%
Moore	(no data)	(no data)	36%	64%

Estimates of the average monthly wages in Lynn indicate that although the number of women workers in Lynn declined by 41 percent, women's wages rose 46 percent between 1850 and 1860. The number of male workers increased by half, but their wages rose only by 10 percent. The increase in men's wages occurred during the prosperous early years of the decade, but after 1857 wages fell sharply. Increased wages for women went to machine operators in factories, while female homeworkers who continued to sew by hand faced severe reductions. The total number of women employed in shoe production dropped off steadily in the 1850s, and mechanization, far from resolving the difficulties inherent in the outwork system, intensified the increasingly harsh conditions of labor for most men and women outworkers in Essex County.[34]

The productivity of sewing machines in the 1850s in Essex County plus the introduction of a waxed thread sewing machine to stitch the heavy leather uppers of men's shoes and boots made in central and southern Massachusetts shoe towns prompted manufacturers throughout the state to recruit additional bottomers. This increasing demand drew on various new sources of labor. Rural migrants from other New England states showed up in large enough numbers in Haverhill by 1853 that the local *Essex Banner* warned the town of the potential threat of disorder, and its editor began a successful campaign to establish a Young Men's Christian Association in 1855 to control the behavior of young, unmarried male shoeworkers. The *Lynn Reporter* expressed similar fears in 1860 about an uncontrollable "floating population" of young male workers. By 1860, male shoeworkers born in other New England states constituted 13 percent of the work force in Lynn.[35]

Irish immigrants in the 1850s laid aside the pick and shovel of manual labor and learned how to bottom shoes for better wages. In 1860, Irish-born immigrants represented 12 percent of the work force of shoemakers in Lynn, and Irish-born women in small numbers began to stitch shoes. German immigrants also worked as bottomers in Worcester County shoe towns.[36] Many of these men were new to the industry and represented workers with little association with apprenticeships or with the artisan traditions of the New England craft. Their presence in large numbers in the shoe towns of Massachusetts created a downward pressure on wages.

Outworkers located in country towns in southern and central New Hampshire were an additional source of male labor recruited in the 1850s as a response to mechanization and severe competition among manufacturers. By 1858, Lynn and Haverhill shoe bosses had organized a system of outwork for bottomers in Northwood and the surrounding towns and villages in central New Hampshire. The outwork system in the Northwood area depended on five express teaming operations, which carried thousands of boxes of sewn uppers, soles, and other materials back and forth for fifty cents a box each way. The high costs of transportation lowered the wages paid to Northwood area bottomers. Natick manufacturers sent shoes and brogans by railroad to be made up in Dover and neighboring towns near the New Hampshire seacoast. Part of this labor system involved the use of untrained boys from twelve to eighteen years of age on the simpler procedures. They received lower wages than bottomers. The country bottomers and their boy workers were relatively untrained in shoemaking in comparison with most of the shoemakers in Essex County. Country outworkers were often blamed for the alleged prevalence of cheap, shoddy work that drove wholesale prices down.[37]

Sharp competition among shoe manufacturers, the recruitment of large numbers of male outworkers, new arrivals in shoe towns, persistent high prices for leather stock, and the collapse of demand for shoes, especially in western markets with the economic depression of 1857, brought a crisis to the shoe industry of Essex County. Wages fell, inventories remained full, and privation and uncertainty spread. The conservative press in eastern Massachusetts and the *Shoe and Leather Reporter*, the first trade journal of the industry, defined the basic problem as overproduction and low demand, which could be remedied only when shoeworkers submitted to the market forces of supply and demand and reduced their numbers. Even editors of newspapers sympathetic to shoeworkers, like the *Natick Observer*, wrote of the "inexorable law of supply and demand" that controlled wages and that despite combinations by labor, would ultimately achieve equilibrium in the market. Manufacturer as well as shoemaker would bow before this "prime law of Nature." Many editors targeted the rural migrants and the Irish immigrant for removal from the overabundant labor supply and for westward migration or a return to heavy physical labor. They dismissed these newcomers to shoe production as loungers in the streets who "turned up" their trousers and smoked bad cigars. The removal of these elements from shoe towns would also, in the view of many conservative editors, result in a welcome decline in appetites for alcohol, tobacco, and gambling and lift the burden of low wages from the backs of local family men.[38] The potential for hostility and division among the various groups of Massachusetts bottomers was enormous during the depression years of the late 1850s. The reassertion of the moral and political values of the artisan tradition during the strike of 1860 countered the threat of these divisions and met the challenge of the supply and demand arguments of the shoe manufacturers and their supporters.

The transition to the early factory system and the depression of 1857 created a crisis among shoeworkers in Essex County. In 1860, men and women joined together in a great regional strike that opposed the fundamental changes taking place in the industry. Shoe bosses justified the low wages of the late 1850s with arguments based on the primacy of market forces and the economic laws of supply and demand. In reaction, the strikers in 1860 drew on their traditional sources of artisan resistance: the mechanic ideology and the forms of collective action utilized in the 1840s. They organized on an unprecedented scale, summoning support from within their communities and from the shoe towns of Essex, Middlesex, and Worcester Counties, and from Rockingham and Strafford Counties in New Hampshire. Rather than directly confront the challenge of the factory system, the Essex County strikers, led by the strike committee in Lynn, fought to maintain decentralized production and to improve wages. The male leaders of the Lynn strike committee rejected a potentially important alliance between women outworkers and the new female machine operators in factories. Instead, they concentrated on defending the family wage system. The strike of 1860 was a remarkable demonstration of the power of artisan tradition to command a unified response from the shoeworkers of New England, but the sources of traditional resistance proved inadequate. The 1860 strike represented the final moment of artisan protest in Essex County.

The shoemakers of Essex and Middlesex Counties who led the 1860 strike asserted the preindustrial values of the artisan tradition in ways that rejected the capitalist analysis of the source of troubles in the industry. They used artisan values to justify their actions and to rally the bottomers—rural migrants, Irish and German immigrants, and journeymen in the shoe towns and in the country—to the common cause of the regional strike. Their emphasis on the brotherhood of the craft with its close association of work and manhood did not permit distinctions or dissension among the various groups of bottomers or divisions within the ranks of striking shoemakers. The target of the strike was the emerging factory system and the changes that threatened the economic survival of shoeworkers outside of centralized production.

By 1860 the effects of mechanization and competition had created widespread fear and anger. The old ways were giving ground to powerful new forces. The family wage economy based on the availability of work to men and women outside factory walls was in jeopardy. The new factory workers—the machine girls, the heelers, and the small number of journeymen who had left their little shops for factory work—seemed an alien group.[39] Those who remained outside the factory reaffirmed family, community, and craft solidarity. Their hostility became focused on the expressmen who each day loaded their wagons with hundreds of boxes of shoes to be made by workers living outside Lynn, Haverhill, and Natick. For the strikers in 1860, the sense of crisis extended beyond the problems of overproduction and low wages to a conviction that fundamental changes were being made in the system of production, changes beyond the control of local communities, changes that bound workers in Essex County together with workers in Middlesex County, in New Hampshire, and throughout New England. It was this common sense of crisis that underlay the regional nature of the strike.

The growing identity of interests among shoeworkers in New England led the leadership of the separate strike committees in Lynn, Haverhill, and Natick to try to organize the country bottomers of eastern Massachusetts and southern New Hampshire to refuse work from manufacturers in Massachusetts shoe towns, while they simultaneously halted production in the urban central shops. A regional strike represented a practical strategy for shoeworkers as well as a reflection of common values and fears. The bottomers of Natick adopted a resolution that reflected this strategy the day before they struck on February 11, 1860. "That in order to secure good prices for any length of time for making shoes, it is necessary for all the larger towns, *both* in this state and New Hampshire, to demand prices equal with ours, so that our town may not be overrun with shoemakers from abroad."[40] Uniform wages for New England shoemakers would defeat the pull of market forces on the regional supply of labor, forces that undermined the position of workers in Massachusetts shoe towns.

After months of planning and advice from shoemakers in the South Shore towns of Massachusetts who had conducted a successful strike in 1858, journeymen in Lynn and Marblehead struck on February 22, 1860, using a mass parade through the streets on George Washington's birthday to link the strike with the political traditions of the American Revolution. Haverhill journeymen joined the strike on February 23, followed by country shoemakers in Dover, Farmington, Rochester, and other New Hampshire towns. In each town the strikers insisted that shoe manufacturers accept a "bill of prices," or wage list, which increased the wages of bottomers. In Lynn the strikers demanded increases of 10 to 25 percent, depending on the quality of work.[41] Despite the efforts of the Lynn strike committee to control the reactions of striking workers, hostile confrontations broke out on the streets of Lynn between some strikers and the expressmen. To these strikers, preventing the expressmen from carrying work out of town on the morning of February 23 seemed a quicker and surer way of disrupting production than activities to organize the country shoemakers. Significantly, the first serious conflict in the Lynn strike involved express teams that carried bottom stock and uppers, machine-stitched by female factory workers employed by John Wooldredge and A. S. Moore, to bottomers in Marblehead, Salem, and Danvers.[42] Both had pioneered mechanization and centralization in Lynn, and Wooldredge had introduced steam power into his factory in 1858. These firms symbolized the emerging factory system.

The confrontation between the expressmen and some of the Lynn strikers, which involved verbal harrassment, attempts to intimidate drivers, and a few punches, indicated the danger involved in letting the control of events slip out of the direction of the Lynn strike committee, which was headed by Alonzo Draper of the Lynn Mechanics' Association. Lynn police, under orders from the city marshal to protect the property of shoe manufacturers from the crowds in the streets, also came under attack by strikers. The city marshal himself was quick-marched to and fro inside a crowd of strikers, and someone cut off his coattails. Sensing a potentially disastrous shift in the strike after the successful parade the previous day, members of the executive committee immediately went into the streets to halt any further violence and regain control of the situation. Draper argued heatedly that there was no need to stop expressmen, because the organization of shoemakers outside of Lynn would disrupt production more effectively. Other members of the executive committee warned the strikers that any more violence would destroy the "moral force" of the strike and alienate sympathizers in Lynn and in other communities. Lewis Josselyn, editor of the Lynn *Bay State* and an adviser to the strike leadership, personally cautioned the strikers that any appearance of lawlessness would undermine the morality of their efforts.[43]

All New England watched the events in Lynn. Special detachments of police from South Danvers and Boston arrived to restore order, a development that outraged many Lynn citizens and underscored the sense of a situation out of local control. The Boston police were harrassed and stoned as they arrested strikers on February 24. Militia units were called up, and Massachusetts Attorney General Stephen H. Phillips conferred with local authorities. In neighboring shoe towns where sympathy and support for the strike were crucial to its success, editorials bemoaned Lynn as a town disgraced by riotous activities in its streets. The editor of the *Salem Register* deplored the events in Lynn. "The civil officers were assaulted and interfered with while discharging their legitimate duties; expressmen were obstructed in the transportation of merchandize; manufacturers were hooted at and threatened with violence; tumultuous crowds thronged the streets; and listened to exciting haranges; and a degree of disorder prevailed which no law and order abiding community could consistently tolerate." The more sympathetic *Salem Gazette* observed that "the lawlessness of a portion of the strikers has deprived the whole movement of a great part of its moral force and turned public sympathies against it." Newspapers more hostile to the strike suggested that the situation in Lynn resulted from the violent and intemperate behavior of Irish shoemakers. Some reporters for the Boston press characterized the striking journeymen as starving, riotous, and reckless. Most significant, on February 24 the shoemakers of Marblehead listened as the leaders of their local strike committee denounced the violence in Lynn.[44]

The executive committee moved swiftly to restore order to the Lynn strike and refurbish its moral symbolism. Strike leaders spoke of the values of the artisan tradition based on mutual and inter-dependent interests between workers and employers. They rejected the manufacturers' use of the laws of supply and demand to jus-tify wage cuts and explain hard times. The mutuality of artisan relations implied a set of community values opposed to the forces of the impersonal market, values that economic change threatened to both violate and destroy. Strikers and their sympathizers spoke in 1860 in terms of morality, justice, and truths, rather than of natural or economic laws. As one striker in Natick put it when he refuted the supply and demand argument: "[T]here are moral as well as money relations between different classes of society. . . . It is not hostility to capital nor to Employers, but an assertion of self-respect which justifies [the present] strike." Furthermore, he cautioned his fellow strikers in Natick to think and talk about the abuses of power by the manufacturers and their effect on morality. Another striker dismissed supply and demand arguments as "an old shoe boss idea" and simply the product of greed among manu-facturers. A striker in Dover, New Hampshire, insisted that all of the shoes made in Dover during the past season had already been contracted for in advance at reasonable prices by wholesalers, and the manufacturers' attempt to cut wages was therefore the result of an unjust combination among the wholesalers and the large manufacturers. The sympathetic editor of the *Dover Gazette and Strafford Advertiser* predicted that the allegedly impersonal laws of supply and demand could be influenced by political action. The editor of the *Marblehead Ledger* argued that "competition, that spirit among men to outdo his neighbor, . . . is the main cause of the depression among shoe manufacturers." He encouraged the shoe bosses to combine to raise their prices to consumers, prices that would reflect the "full worth" of the shoes and pay the worker a "fair price."[45]

Alonzo Draper had suspended publication of the *New England Mechanic* during the 1860 strike, and the *Bay State*, edited by Lewis Josselyn, became the voice of the strike committee in Lynn. Even before the strike, Josselyn had expressed fears of the economic and moral consequences of sending work out of town, depriving local workers and merchants of their right to a greater share of the wealth produced by the shoe industry. He wrote many editorials about the mutual interests between capital and labor. "The true interests of capital and labor, enterprise and skill when fully understood, will be found to be one and the same. . . . [W]hen labor suffers, capital must suffer. . . . These truths are self-evident."[46]

Many of the men and women strikers in 1860 shared these views and felt unjustly degraded by changes to their position in the industry. They carried banners in the strike parades that read: "American ladies will not be slaves" and that bore lines exhorting the rights and duties of manhood:

> Now by your children's cradles
> Now by your fathers' graves,
> Be men today cordwainers,
> Or be forever slaves.[47]

The rapidly collapsing moral stature of the Lynn strike preoccupied a worried Alonzo Draper as he addressed a meeting of strikers at Lyceum Hall on the evening of the first day of street violence. He insisted that the morality of their efforts was the most powerful weapon that the strikers possessed. Draper went on to announce that at that very moment the shoebinders and machine stitchers of Lynn were gathered together at a mass meeting at another public hall. He reported them to be as ready to strike on behalf of the men and as ready to prove their devotion to the cause as were "the Mothers of the Revolution in the cause of liberty."[48] An alliance with the women of Lynn that would involve them in public action on behalf of the strike offered new hope for the successful resolution of their efforts, Draper promised, if all violence ceased.

The Lynn strike leaders promoted the participation of local women in the strike to erase its images of violence and disorder and redeem its moral eminence. The active support of women would emphasize the nature of the strike as a defense of traditional values and the New England family, rather than a movement that involved foreigners or an uncontrollable population of rural migrants. As one shoemaker in Beverly saw it, the journeymen were on strike "not as citizens and men merely but as heads of families."[49] This attempt by Draper to enlist the moral stature of women and use their standing as family members on behalf of the 1860 strike represents a link with the attempts of cordwainers in the 1840s to utilize the moral role of women in society to promote their objectives. The artisan view of women as moral agents and as family members limited the participation of women in the 1860 strike as it had limited the relationship of women to labor activity in the 1840s. The interests of women shoeworkers, whether they worked in the new factories or at home, remained secondary to their role as female family members who by their very presence in strike activities could restore morality to the shoemakers' cause.

Draper and the executive committee had carefully considered their decision to involve the women of Lynn in the 1860 strike. Draper first mentioned including women in the strike to the executive committee on February 21. He had learned the day before of a successful strike for higher wages by female factory stitchers against the Joseph Harris shop in Marblehead. Draper proposed that a meeting of the women workers in Lynn support the strike by refusing to take any work from bosses who were unwilling to pay the bottomers an increase in wages. He also personally urged the Haverhill strike committee to organize their women. But the executive committee did not act on Draper's recommendation until after the outbreak of violence in the streets and in the context of widespread criticism of the Lynn strike in the New England press. Later, during a dispute involving the members of the executive committee, John R. Parrott recalled, "There was not a word said [against] . . . the running of machines, or of the women striking, for some time after we struck."[50]

Although Draper had urged the crowds of strikers on the afternoon of February 23 to send their wives and sweethearts to a meeting that evening at Liberty Hall to boycott the work of "scab bosses," factory girls dominated the first women's meeting and unexpectedly organized their own strike to increase the wages of women shoeworkers. Draper called the meeting to order and appointed two women, Mrs. Elvira Hall and Mrs. Willard F. Oliver, as chair and secretary. Hall's husband was a shoemaker, and Oliver's was a politically active watchmaker who had served as the chief marshal of the mass parade on February 22 and represented widespread community support for the strike. As Draper addressed the several hundred assembled women, the striking journeymen waited for him at Lyceum Hall for word of the women's decision to support the strike. "Will you strike?" he asked, and a hundred voices answered "Yes!" "Remember ladies," Draper went on, "especially, you young and blooming ones, that if you want husbands, wages must go up, for no one can get married at present prices." Cries of "Shame! Shame!" greeted his remark.[51] Draper went on, speaking of the economic interests of women as identical to the interests of their husbands, brothers, and sweethearts. One voice from the audience interrupted him with the comment, "We don't have any sweethearts." Unwilling to stay any longer and eager to tell the waiting journeymen the news of the women's decision, Draper quickly left the meeting after gaining a unanimous strike vote.

After his departure the women remained in Liberty Hall, where in the presence of two Boston reporters they debated at length their own grievances over wages and ways in which to organize support for their own strike. Old and young women, shoebinders and machine girls, they poured out angry stories of wrongs that overwhelmed more orderly procedures and filled the hall with noise. Heated criticism of the manufacturers led to proposals to tar and feather certain shoe bosses, but despite the noisy tumult, the meeting produced several decisions: to strike to raise the wages of women shoeworkers, to appoint committees to canvass for additional local support and draw up a list of wage demands, and to organize other women shoeworkers in the shoe towns of Essex County: Marblehead, Newburyport, and Danvers.[52] Draper's move to marshal women workers in support of the men's strike had released a new set of energies in Lynn.

The voices that had interrupted Draper during the meeting belied his assumption that all working women in Lynn had connections, marital or familial, with local shoeworkers and testified to the presence in the early factories of young, migratory, single women who were boarding and working in the city.[53] Of the small number of factory stitchers (371) enumerated in the 1860 federal census of population, half (52 percent) boarded in Lynn with unrelated families. Of these boarding stitchers, nearly one-third were natives of states other than Massachusetts, principally Maine and New Hampshire. Nineteen percent were foreign-born women from either Ireland or Nova Scotia. The remaining half were natives of other cities and towns in Massachusetts who were living with Lynn families as boarders. Female workers who boarded in Lynn, however, may have formed attachments to working men and, therefore, identified with their interests, but a search for the names of these women in the Massachusetts marriage records indicates that only

15 percent of them married in Lynn between 1860 and 1865 and might be said to have had "sweethearts" during the 1860 strike. Another 8 percent married in Lynn after 1865. Three-quarters of the factory girls listed as boarders in the households of unrelated families in the 1860 census did not subsequently marry in Lynn. These young women working in centralized production had relatively little association with the community or its artisan values. They formed a new and distinct set of interests in the 1860 strike, which emerged at the first meeting of the women strikers, and they subsequently challenged the Lynn strike committee over who should speak for the interests of working women.

On February 27, four days after the first meeting, 1,500 to 2,000 women packed into Liberty Hall for the second meeting of women strikers. Willard F. Oliver, representing the men's strike committee, chaired the meeting, but the enthusiasm of the assembled women and the vigorous debate on the question of the wage list for stitching uppers overrode his attempts to maintain order.[54] A public meeting of hundreds of women, drawn together for the first time by their work, gave many of them the heady sense of power that others had experienced at the previous meeting. Vulnerable and isolated homeworkers called for justice. One elderly shoebinder spoke of burdens imposed by the shoe bosses, who insisted that she furnish nearly everything for the work including beeswax and still expected her to do the work cheaply. This, she protested, was unjust and not the way things used to be, "but the bosses took their last farthing to *grandize* their houses with." She predicted: "[T]here was to be an awful shaking of things, and the bosses would feel it."[55]

When the women's committee reported its recommendations on the wage list, a struggle began between the factory girls and some of the homeworkers who identified their interests with the male strikers. This conflict, which continued during all three women's meetings over a period of five days, ultimately clarified the difference between the two groups of women workers, who had different relationships to centralized work and to the family in Lynn. Their debate illuminated a fundamental disagreement over the meaning of the 1860 strike for Lynn workers: was it a strike for higher wages for working men and working women or a strike to defend the family wage by raising men's wages and maintaining homework for women?

Miss Clara H. Brown of the women's executive committee read

the proposed price list to the assembled women. She was a twenty-one-year-old shop girl and a native of Medford, Massachusetts, who boarded in Lynn with a shoemaker's family. Brown dominated the debate during the meeting of February 27, arguing in support of the committee's recommendations to increase the wages of factory workers and homeworkers with machines as well as raising the piece rates for binding by hand. She developed a strategy during the women's meetings similar to that used by the brothers of the craft to rally support throughout New England for their strike. Brown proposed an alliance between women who worked at home and women who worked in the early factories, an alliance based on gender and on their common work in production. The *Shoe and Leather Reporter* commented with wonder on this female alliance: "We believe we have never heard before of hand labor raising a 'striking' combination with machinery."[56] Clara Brown's strategy may have been a response to the situation of the twenty-three-year-old wife of cordwainer Addison Young, with whom she and another shop girl boarded. With a five-month-old child, Mary Young would have no choice but to take in boarders or accept homework with its lower wages and furnishing costs.

The power of Brown's proposal lay in the strategic position of the machine girls in factories whose productivity in centralized shops offered the potential of shutting down the large bosses, like Wooldredge, Moore, and Keene. Without sewn uppers, the express teams could not leave Lynn, and the country workers would have no choice but to stop their work. Unity as women would protect the wages of the married and the unmarried, the homeworker and the shop girl, and would in addition powerfully benefit the shoemakers' strike. This unity would link the advancement of the cause of working women in Lynn to the new sources of wages and power in centralized production in the factories. Clara Brown and the factory girls were beginning to advocate an alternative to the family wage for working women. An alliance based on gender would protect working women whatever their marital status and wherever the location of their work and offered them a vital and powerful connection with female workers in the new factory system. For the factory girls, raising the wages of working women was fully as important an objective in the 1860 strike as increasing the wages of working men.

Homeworkers, however, immediately raised objections to Brown's proposals during the second women's meeting on February 27. Mrs. Mary A. Damon, the wife of a Lynn shoemaker, who herself worked at home but as a seamstress, and Mrs. William Graham, a home machine operator, spoke for the homeworkers' position. The heated debate swirled around the issue of the wage list prepared by the women's executive committee, which recommended an increase in all categories of women's work. Some at the meeting warned, "Don't set the prices too high," while others scoffed, "Don't be bluffed or faint-hearted; we shall get our prices." Unwelcome comments provoked cries of "Put her out!" or "Dry up!" Brown and Graham debated the price of handwork for binding and eyeletting. Brown denied Graham's contention that higher prices for binding were impossible to get. She argued that "only Lynn girls can bind shoes as they should be bound" and predicted that out-of-town competition would prove of no worth to the bosses.[57] One married homeworker, repeating an earlier statement by an elderly shoebinder, complained of paying out all but fifty cents of her six-dollar weekly wage in board, machine rent, and furnishing. Addressing the needs of homeworkers, the striking women voted to set the price of closing gaiter boots at twenty cents higher for homework than in the shops. The difference was intended to offset the costs of furnishing by homeworkers. This resulting "high wage" list raised wages for both home and shop work.

For supporters of the men's strike like Mary Damon and Willard Oliver, the central issue of the 1860 strike was increasing the wages of the bottomers. They rejected the arguments of shop girls like Clara Brown and became alarmed when after lengthy debate and the adoption of amendments on certain piece rates, a large majority of the women at the February 27 meeting voted for the high wage list. Oliver, who had lost control of the meeting and disagreed with the vote on the wage list, then announced a proposal by the men's strike committee for the women to join the bottomers in a great show of unity by marching in a mass parade through the streets of Lynn on March 7. After many expressions of concern from women in the audience over the propriety of females parading and its effect on the morality of the strike, the women voted by a small majority to join the procession. However, after this second women's meeting, Oliver, Damon, and the men's strike committee insisted that the issue of women's wages be reconsidered at an additional meeting the following night.

For the third women's meeting, on the night of February 28, Lyceum Hall, the largest public hall in Lynn, held almost 2,000 participants, and representatives and supporters of the men's strike committee tried again to defeat the high wage list promoted by Clara Brown and the shop girls. Oliver, wishing to join the debate on wages, temporarily reinstalled Elvira Hall as chair. Alonzo Draper, who had first called the women together on February 23, addressed the meeting and spoke of the widespread support for the bottomers' strike in fourteen other shoe towns. Then he criticized the women's high wage list, pointing out that it was much more important for their husbands to get wage increases than it was for the ladies. A factory girl provoked laughter from the audience by interrupting with: "Sposing we ain't got any husbands." [58] After urging the women to cooperate with the men's strike by supporting the bottomers' demands for higher wages, Draper turned the meeting over to Oliver.

Oliver opened the debate on the reconsideration of the high wage bill by admonishing the assembled women to be modest and ladylike. "Speak in a judicious and womanly manner," he insisted, warning the women that their influence could produce both "evil and good." He criticized the newspaper reporters from the out-of-town press, especially Boston and New York, for printing accounts of the women's meetings that emphasized, he argued, the divisive and frivolous. Oliver claimed that the committee of women who had prepared the high wage list did not represent the women of Lynn. He then produced another wage list prepared by the homeworkers close to the men's strike, read both lists quickly to the audience, and called for comment from the floor. Again the debate reflected the conflict between Clara Brown for the shop girls and Mary Damon for the homeworkers. Damon argued that the machine bosses like Nichols and Blake who subcontracted machine stitching for manufacturers would not pay the higher wages and warned that in retaliation they would remove all machine work from the home. [59] The potential impact of the elimination of homework on women with domestic responsibilities or who objected to the long hours of factory work was obvious. Mary Damon had raised the crucial question: who spoke for the working women of Lynn?

The Third Women's Strike Meeting, February 28, 1860. From *Frank Leslie's Illustrated Magazine*, March 17, 1860, courtesy of Lynn Historical Society.

Clara Brown vigorously countered by pointing out to the meeting that the factory girls would not strike "for nothing." The low wage list prepared by the homeworkers, she noted, actually cut piece rates on shop work. She spoke angrily about the situation of a friend of hers who sewed linings by hand in a shop for very low wages. "Girls of Lynn, Girls of Lynn, do you hear that and will you stand it? Never, Never, NEVER. Strike then—strike at once; Demand 8 1/2 cents [per pair] for your work when the binding isn't closed, and you will get it. Don't let them make niggers [slaves] of you. . . . keep still; don't work your machines; let them lie still till we get all we ask." [60] Brown was reiterating her vision of an alliance of working women involved in production in the factory and in the home, an alliance that could raise women's wages throughout the industry. Her eloquence and enthusiasm swept through the meeting, and a large majority of the women strikers once again voted to support the high wage list.

After the vote on the high wage list had been reconfirmed, the chair ordered it to be printed and circulated among the strikers for their signatures. A disgruntled Oliver, irritated at his inability to control the meeting and at the defeat of the low wage list, announced that he had changed his mind and now opposed the participation of the women in the March 7 parade. After additional debate punctuated by fervent speeches from Lynn residents who desperately wanted to join the line of march with their fathers, husbands, and brothers, the women at the meeting again rejected Oliver's advice and voted unanimously to march.

Oliver, Damon, and the bottomers' strike committee still did not give up their efforts to control and redirect the objectives and energies of the striking women in Lynn. Instead of having the high wage list printed, members of the homeworkers' faction took over the committee responsible for circulating the wage list. Ignoring the votes at both women's meetings, they substituted the low wage list for the high and had it printed up and circulated as the official list by the canvassing committee. Outraged, the shop girls led by Brown confronted Damon, Oliver, and their allies at a tumultuous fourth meeting on the night of March 2. One of the members of the canvassing committee informed the reporter for the *New York Times* that she hoped he could attend the meeting, "for they were going to have a high old time, and if Clara B—— dared to open her head, she was to be kicked downstairs." [61]

After it had become common knowledge that Oliver had personally altered the figures on the wage list, he could not chair the meeting on March 2. Instead James Dillon, the vice president of the Lynn Mechanics' Association, presided at this fourth women's meeting, but he also supported the low wage list. Dillon opened the meeting with an appeal to the assembled women to be reasonable in their wage demands and to support the men. He emphasized the role of females as nurturing and supportive of their families. "[W]e rest on you; you, who suckle us in our infancy, who court us in our prime, who succor, support and comfort us in our old age and declining powers, we rest on *you* to help us *here,* now, at *this* time; give us, journeymen shoemakers, your encouragement and cooperation, and we'll go on, on, on, e'en to Death's grim door."[62] Dillon was challenging the women at the meeting to deny that support of their families was their primary and appropriate role in the strike.

Ignoring the successful efforts of the women strikers to organize other women workers in neighboring shoe towns, Dillon warned that the machine bosses would hire out-of-town girls to do their work. "If a man has a hundred machines in Salem or Marblehead, and he can find girls willing to run these machines well, at $5 per week, and the Lynn operatives strike for $5.50, will not the owner be justified in taking the work from Lynn, and have it done on his machines for the Lynn manufacturers for $5 per week[?]"[63] After defending the search for cheap female labor as justifiable for machine bosses, Dillon told the women at the meeting that if they continued to demand an "unfair" increase, their strike would be crushed in three weeks. He then sidestepped the issue of the wage list by suggesting the formation of a committee of women to negotiate homework prices with the machine bosses. Mary Damon quickly seconded the idea of such a committee as preferable to a debate in a public forum, and Oliver added truculently that wage decisions should be made by "sober and discreet women," and not by "laughing" and "thoughtless girls."[64]

Many homeworkers regarded Clara Brown as a member of a group of "smart girls" who earned high wages in factory work and who as single, young women had no family responsibilities or direct connections with family life in Lynn. One of the homeworkers described her as "one of a few smart girls who could earn higher wages than the majority of the shop girls and regardless of the general welfare was stirring up the working women to strike for higher pay than the bosses would be willing to pay, other than to such as she." In this view, the smart girls represented irresponsible young women who were motivated by selfish individualism and ignored the common interests of the working women of Lynn, while interesting themselves only in earning wages to spend on lavish dress. One factory operative, while urging harmony and unity among women workers, defended the reputation of the shop girls from extravagance, but insisted that they had "just as good a right to switch a long-tailed skirt as the proudest lady in the land."[65] But according to many homeworkers, shop girls had interests antithetical to theirs that threatened the family wage economy and the effectiveness of the Lynn strike.

At last Clara Brown got the attention of the audience and raised the central question of the fourth meeting: who had dared to change the wage list? When she received no reply, she began to address the women strikers. Trying to heal the divisions within the women's strike and rally the supporters of the high wage list, Clara Brown again emphasized the power of the shop girls as industrial workers who could obtain the higher wage list for all women workers. "For God's sake, don't act like a pack of fools. We've got the bosses where we can do as we please with 'em. If we won't work our machines, and the out-of-town girls won't take the work, what can the bosses do?"[66] Her appeal was greeted with cheers, hisses, and cries of "Shame" and "Hoe her out." To prevent Brown from igniting the crowd of women again, Oliver took over the chair from Dillon, denounced the "wranglin'," and boasted defiantly: "Them pencil marks [that altered the wage list] is right!" Brown interrupted him with: "Mr. Oliver, I say if we are going to strike for anything, let's strike for something worth having."[67] Damon quickly came to Oliver's aid: "We must have the machine men with us; we can't get along without them, can we ladies?" The issue of the high wage list had become a test of loyalties: to the family wage system in Lynn or to the possibilities of an alliance among women shoeworkers.

Oliver cut off debate on the wage issue and abruptly called for a vote on the high wage list. Swayed by pressure from the homeworkers and torn by the emotional appeals for family loyalty made to them by the strike leaders, the majority of women at the fourth meeting reversed their vote on the wage issue and rejected the high wage list. Over 1,700 women signed the low wage list after the meeting and accepted the idea of a special committee to negotiate an agreement on homework with the machine bosses.[68] It was never clear how many of these, if any, were shop girls, but the female factory workers as a group played no further public role in the Lynn strike. At the conclusion of the meeting, the now triumphant Oliver was elected the chief marshal of the March 7 procession of striking women. The executive committee of the striking bottomers and the homeworkers had won; the cause of the family wage and decentralized production prevailed. The Great Procession of March 7 was their day of glory. On the day before the strike, Oliver instructed the women how to conduct themselves. "Come, he said, without your silks, your satins, or your furbelo riggin'; come in modest attire, and the great God above you will be on your side; your bosses will give you your rates, and your beaux will be pleased."[69] Those not marching, he directed, should not stand about in the streets.

The day of the legendary parade of Lynn women was stormy. A late winter northeaster pelted sleet, rain, and snow on the muddy streets. In defiance of the dismal weather, 800 women marched, led by Chief Marshal Oliver and Mary Damon. An artist for *Frank Leslie's Illustrated Newspaper* captured the stirring scene. Lewis Josselyn recruited Leslie himself to cover the event and publish accounts of the strike and illustrations of the procession of women and their other activities.[70] The sketch of the women's march of March 7 has epitomized for historians the involvement of women in the Lynn strike, but it obscures the battle that took place among the strikers over the relationship of the women workers of Lynn to the strike. The procession of women five abreast stretches on into the distance. In the front line, flanked by four women strikers, walks Chief Marshal Oliver, wearing a severe dark suit, top hat, and carrying a beribboned baton. The women marchers wear crinoline-stiffened dresses, ruffled and lace-trimmed bonnets, and carry parasols against the falling snow.[71] Despite Oliver's advice, the women had turned out in style and in contrast to the plain dress they wore in *Leslie's* other sketches of their meetings and marches. Behind the front line of marchers a banner is borne along, carrying the homeworkers' inscription: "American ladies will not

The Women's Procession on March 7, 1860. Detail from *Frank Leslie's Illustrated Magazine*, March 17, 1860, courtesy of Lynn Historical Society.

be slaves. Give us a fair compensation and we will labour cheerfully." Onlookers smile with approval, and one man decorously waves his handkerchief. The procession was self-consciously dignified, and it created a sensation in the regional press. The *Bay State* proudly described the day as a demonstration "to prove the purity of their motives, the justice of their cause and the determination to accomplish their objects."[72] Many newspapers noted that there was no trouble for the police, no arrests, no violence, only good order. With the appearance of the marching women, the Lynn strike had regained its moral force. The political stance of the women marchers that day was most clearly represented on one of the many banners that they carried: "Weak in physical strength but strong in moral courage we dare to battle for the right, shoulder to shoulder with our fathers, husbands and brothers."[73] With the women's parade in early March, the 1860 strike hit its peak of support in the region. An estimated 10,000 male shoeworkers were on strike, including 4,100 in Lynn, 1,100 in Marblehead, 1,500 in New Hampshire towns, 1,500 in Natick, and 600 in Haverhill. Among the women on strike were the nearly 2,000 in Lynn, with 600 out in Marblehead and Newburyport and 450 in Haverhill.[74]

In other shoe towns, the involvement of women in the 1860 strike was far less dramatic than in Lynn. Alonzo Draper had gone to Haverhill on February 26 to encourage the local bottomers and women workers to coordinate efforts with their Lynn brothers and sisters. But all machine operations on shoe uppers had been centralized in small factories, and the only work available to women at home in Haverhill was binding and sewing linings by hand for very low wages. Without machine work for homeworkers, there was no direct link between home and factory work and less possibility for the development of a sense of common interests for women stitchers. Two hundred attended the first meeting of Haverhill women, held on March 8, but fewer than twenty were machine stitchers. Most were poorly paid shoebinders who sewed by hand. The twenty sympathetic machine stitchers expressed concern for their hard-worked sisters and promised to canvass the 300 machine girls who worked in Haverhill's central shops for their support of the strike. They found little interest in the strike among the factory girls and general contentment with the wage scale paid for stitching. On March 13 the twenty stitchers reported that unless at least two-thirds of the factory girls agreed to stop work, there would be little point to a strike at all. The men's strike committee in Haverhill expected all women shoeworkers would strike "for the sake of their husbands and brothers" and that the machine girls would join with the shoebinders out of sympathy and indignation. A few did, but the great majority continued to work at their machines. At the next meeting of the Haverhill women, 464 women formally joined the Haverhill strike.[75] Among them were the twenty sympathetic stitchers, and most of these factory workers were natives of Haverhill who lived with their families. One local observer surmised that "[t]he reason why so few of the stitchers sympathize in the strike is that most of them are non-residents. Having no relatives, husbands or brothers among the strikers, though some have lovers among them, and such are ready to come out in their aid."[76] On March 22 a disappointingly small turnout for a procession of strikers that included only 100 women marked the collapse of the strike of 1860 in Haverhill.[77] The possibility of an alliance among women workers in the factory and at home was unique to Lynn during the strike.

Women strikers in Lynn had made efforts to contact women workers in other Essex County shoe towns to build regional support for their cause. One Lynn factory stitcher, a native of Newburyport, returned home to organize 300 women who met in the local Methodist Church. On March 17 half of them were still on strike. Women workers were reportedly out on strike in Beverly and Salem and in rural Groveland, but there was little activity among women in nearby Stoneham or Danvers. The shoe towns in central Massachusetts and New Hampshire generally employed men to stitch uppers on waxed thread machines, but the women of Natick who supported the striking journeymen helped canvass their neighbors for support and pressured reluctant bottomers to halt their work. These women also marched in parades with members of their families.[78]

While the Lynn strikers planned clambakes, taffy pulls, and additional activities in March, the women's committee negotiated a new wage scale with the machine bosses for homework and presented the list to the striking women for their approval. At their meeting on March 15 with Mary Damon presiding, Willard Oliver read the list of proposed increases to nearly 1,000 homeworkers, but he argued that the women should not even think of resuming work for the machine bosses until the manufacturers raised the wages of the striking journeymen. Mary Damon spoke with great emotion of the obligation of the women to sustain the bottomers' strike. "But what of the poor bottomers? If we go to work before the bottomers obtain their objects, the men's work will be sent out of town, and our husbands and brothers left to starve. . . . [O]ur work is not done."[79]

Three machine bosses from Lynn and Salem who attended the meeting warned the women strikers to go back to work immediately or the bosses would not sign the wage agreement that they had just negotiated with them. One Salem boss noted that there were "plenty of girls" within twenty miles of Lynn who could be recruited to run machines, and the two Lynn bosses pointedly advised the homeworkers to resume their work. Despite this direct threat to eliminate homework in Lynn—the very issue that had defeated Clara Brown and the high wage list on March 2—the majority of striking women refused to abandon the bottomers and voted to continue their strike even at the risk of alienating the machine bosses. They emphasized their steadfast support by parading that afternoon with women strikers from neighboring Swampscott and Marblehead. The banners carried during the parade underscored the importance that the male strikers attached to female loyalty.

Union is a powerful weapon in the hands of the fair sex.

Many daughters have done virtuously, but thou excellest them all.

Woman—a friend in need.[80]

The machine bosses of Lynn and Salem unwisely called another meeting of homeworkers for March 17 from which they attempted to exclude Oliver and the supporters of the bottomers' strike. Striking journeymen infiltrated the meeting, and the women again voted to reject the bosses' demand that they return to work. On March 28 a group of 250 striking Lynn women marched five miles under escort to Marblehead where they were cheered and fed by sympathizers.[81] However, the machine girls who worked in Marblehead shops and had struck successfully for higher wages just before the great strike had begun on February 22 were not active in the Marblehead protest.

In mid-March, the bottomers' strike was still holding firm throughout the region, especially in Lynn. The *Shoe and Leather Reporter* noted the beneficial effect the general work stoppage was having on excess inventories. Reduced stocks had raised the wholesale price of shoes, and the editor facetiously advised the manufacturers to contribute to the strike fund to keep it going.[82] These brighter prospects in the market encouraged shoe bosses in eastern Massachusetts to raise wages slightly for bottoming, but as a group they resisted signing any wage bill with the strikers. Gradually, and despite the refusal of most of the shoe bosses to sign an agreement with the bottomers, the strikers began to go back to work at higher wages in late March. In doing so, New England shoeworkers were implicitly accepting the discipline of market forces on wages, and the strike slowly fell apart in the region. Some manufacturers, like Moses How of Haverhill, had been willing to advance wages early in the strike, and on April 10 twenty-seven small manufacturers in Lynn agreed to a 10 percent increase in wages, but only for about 500 bottomers.[83] The editor of the *Lynn Reporter* saw the disintegration of the strike as a confirmation of the laws of supply and demand and denied that the women's strike had had any impact on production. At a meeting on March 31 Willard Oliver shocked the women strikers in Lynn by recommending that they return to work without insisting that the manufacturers or the machine bosses sign wage agreements. Still convinced of the rightness of their cause, the women angrily forced him to resign, but by the time Mary Damon organized a Ladies' Association of Stitchers and Binders on April 10 with 300 members, the great shoe strike of 1860 was over.[84]

The New England shoe strike revealed the rapid changes taking place in an industry that had been characterized for almost a century by decentralized hand production, a system that had nevertheless made Essex County and eastern Massachusetts the center of the American shoe industry. The slow evolution toward centralization and mechanization had begun in the early 1850s with the transformation of shoebinding into machine stitching. By 1860 significant portions of women's work were performed in steam-powered factories. Shoe bosses in the 1850s also divided and centralized parts of men's work, while the productivity of women working on stitching machines expanded and altered the nature of the male outwork force. The McKay stitcher, invented in 1862, would represent only the final stage in the reorganization of production into steam-powered factory work.[85] By 1860 an important part of the work force in the Essex County shoe industry was already at work in early factories.

The preindustrial system of work had supported a strong tradition of collective resistance and the development of an ideology of equal rights concerned with the moral and political relations between workers and employers that justified and sustained the strike in 1860. The support that artisan values and traditions summoned from local communities and throughout the region indicated that the laws of supply and demand cited by shoe manufacturers and their spokesmen in the press did not satisfactorily explain or justify economic conditions for many elements of New England society in 1860. In addition, the emphasis in preindustrial ideology on the close connection between manhood and work for shoemakers sustained unity among the various groups of bottomers in the strike and provided a standard to which native, migrant, immigrant, rural, and urban workers could and did rally. Male shoeworkers stood on the threshold of the factory and fought the forces that were impelling them through the door.

The struggle over who would speak for the women workers of Lynn in the 1860 strike also pointed to the emergence of industrial conflict. The factory girls most closely approached the mentality of modern industrial workers with their sense of the possibilities of advancing the interests of all women workers through the power of those in centralized production. These shop girls offered their gender alliance as a bridge between preindustrial patterns of homework for women and the factory system. The impact of industrialization on European women in the nineteenth century has produced a lively debate among historians on the consequences of wage-earning for females, especially relating to high rates of fertility and illegitimacy.[86] In Lynn, popular attitudes toward young, unmarried factory girls from other towns created divisions among the strikers. Factory girls who possessed discretionary income from wage-earning and who boarded in Lynn as migratory workers seemed to violate the community values of the local shoeworkers. However, the strategy proposed by Clara Brown and the shop girls actually represented an effort to build labor protest on prefactory experience. They accepted the sexual division of labor and tried to link their interests with those of other women despite the centralization and mechanization of their work.

Most shop girls in Lynn, Haverhill, and Marblehead accepted factory work and the wage system, but in 1860 they tried to increase their wages in Lynn and Marblehead and maintain them in Haverhill. The factory symbolized new opportunities for higher wages and group work for women, a sharp contrast with the low wages and isolation of their outwork experience. Female factory workers in Lynn responded to the strike by drawing on their sense of connection with other working women and by attempting to construct an alliance that would link women workers in the home to those in centralized production. The high wage list addressed both the requirements of homeworkers to offset the costs of furnishing and the demands of shop girls for wage increases. After lengthy debates, a majority of striking women, both homeworkers and shop girls, voted for this high wage list on two separate occasions. These votes prompted the men's strike committee and its supporters to undermine this female alliance by subterfuge and appeals based on the family wage. While the culture and ideology of artisan life created solidarity among the work force of homeworkers and bottomers, it did not incorporate the interests of the female factory workers who represented the new world of work. The failure of the gender alliance among women shoeworkers meant a continuation of the patterns of the family wage system in which women homeworkers were subordinated to male wage earners and disconnected from female industrial workers. The defeat of the factory girls confirms the strike of 1860 as the last defensive action by Essex County shoeworkers to hang on to decentralized production and to the vestiges of artisan culture.[87] Divisions between early factory workers and outworkers crippled labor protest in Lynn during the most important strike conducted by American workers before the Civil War.

Since the 1780s, homework for women on shoes operated as an economic basis for domesticity that maintained the sexual division of labor and the secondary status of women's work in the craft, while prescribing physical isolation and low wages for women working in shoe production. Mechanization and centralization, which drew women into factory work in the 1850s, maintained the division of labor, but meant access to higher wages for growing numbers of female workers and an end to working in isolation at home. These changes, however, reduced the total number of women involved in shoe production and eliminated married women from the newly centralized work. An alliance between homeworkers and those young women who stitched shoe uppers in factories represented a real chance in 1860 for married or single women working at home to make a valuable connection with female industrial workers, a chance to erase the artificial distinctions between home life and early industrialization.[88] In return, the young, female factory workers could anticipate that when they married, they too could work at home on shoes for decent wages. Common work rather than marital status or family attachment would unite them. The alignment of many of the homeworkers with the brothers of the craft during the strike offered working women only the subordinated position inherent for them within the family wage system. Late in the events of the strike, the bottomers and their supporters demonstrated their willingness to risk the continuation of homework itself and its supplementary contribution to the family wage in order to win wage increases for men. Homeworkers who battled machine bosses and manufacturers side by side with the bottomers fought as working-class women for their families' interests and to maintain the economic basis of their domestic role. These homeworkers embraced the cult of domesticity and the family wage and accepted the moral and familial role of women as the primary basis of their contribution to the strike. The submersion of their interests as workers within the family wage system and artisan tradition made an alliance with the factory girls unachievable. In contrast, the shop girls rejected the cult of domesticity by making a connection between the interests of women working at home and those working in the factory through collective, public action.

Marxist feminists have debated whether the family wage served the interests of patriarchy or served the ability of working-class families to resist exploitation. Heidi Hartmann has argued that paid work outside the home for women threatened patriarchal control in the family as well as men's wages and jobs. She regarded the sexual division of labor and the family wage as a means of containing and controlling wage work for women and keeping them in a subordinate position in the family and in society. In contrast, Jane

Humphries argued that working-class families pooled their labor and their wages from work as a survival strategy to defend their standard of living. By focusing on the importance of a high wage for the male head of the family, working-class people best served the economic interests of the family and contributed to the ability of the family to resist exploitation of all its members.[89]

Both the Hartmann and the Humphries models appear to have operated in Lynn in 1860 as the conflict among the strikers over the appropriate relationship of women to their efforts ultimately pitted female homeworkers against shop girls. As a strike objective, the family wage meant that homeworkers defended an increase in men's wages as more important than an increase in women's wages and worked to preserve women's work in the home in the interests of supplementing family income. They accepted the definition of women's role in the strike by the bottomers' strike committee. The factory girls led by Clara Brown seemed unconsciously to challenge patriarchal control in the family by contesting with the strike leadership over who spoke for the interests of women workers and by offering an alliance with homeworkers based on the sexual division of labor. The factory girls proposed that women act together in their own interests to raise women's wages and protect homework. The actions and rhetoric of the striking bottomers defeated this gender alliance. Homeworkers rallied to the ideology of artisan life, and they outnumbered the factory workers in 1860. The family wage and artisan values dominated the shoe strike in Lynn, but at the cost of losing valuable allies among the female factory workers.

The roots of this ideology of work and gender reached deep into the experience of shoeworkers in Essex County. Contradictions between perceptions of the proper gender role for women in the family and their consciousness as workers in production marked labor protest in the 1830s and 1840s. Women shoeworkers negotiated the tension inherent in these contradictions within the value system of artisan ideology. In doing so, they built limits into their perception of themselves as workers and into their ability to act together as women to defend their interests or claim new rights, the political heritage of their own labor protest in the early 1830s. Artisan ideology defined the role of women primarily as family members and as moral agents in society. This ideology in the hands of the Lynn strike committee and its women supporters cut off the new female factory workers from contributing significantly to labor protest in 1860. The perceptions that shoemaking artisans had developed of work and gender made it difficult for them to regard women as fellow workers outside of the family, to include them as equals in the ideology and politics built on artisan life, or to see in the experience of the shop girls what awaited all workers as capitalism in shoe production moved toward the factory system.

CHAPTER SIX

Crispin Protest in the
Post–Civil War Shoe Factory

When walking on the crowded street,
  A lovely lass attracts your eye,
and while you gaze your glances meet,
  You smile—alas! you soon will sigh
For Cupid from her beaming eyes,
  His shining arrows thickly hurls;
And hard indeed must be the heart—
  That can withstand the stitching girls.

  The stitching girls, the witching girls—
  The jaunty, dainty, stitching girls
  With Cupid's dart they pierce the heart—
  The pleasing, teasing stitching girls.

—"The Stitching Girls" by
Joseph A. Batchelder
Lynn Transcript, June 26, 1869

For seven years after the conclusion of the Civil War, the shoe industry of Essex County grew, changed, and prospered. The pacesetter of these activities was Lynn, whose large manufacturers spearheaded the drive toward a new system of production based on the centralization of work in new factories and the utilization of new divisions of labor and steam-powered machinery. A desire to dominate their segment of the growing and fiercely competitive postwar national market led shoe manufacturers in Essex County to alter the process of work, experiment with the sexual division of labor in the industry, and defend these actions by developing new rationales that justified changes in the relationship between labor and capital. Shoeworkers resisted these changes as the Knights and Daughters of St. Crispin.

The beginning of the war in 1861 had cut the shoe industry in Essex County off from its richest market, the South, and forced shoe manufacturers to alter their system of finance and rethink their operations. The loss of the southern market with its substantial investments of long-term credits was aggravated by the effects of wartime inflation, which drove up prices and cut off Lynn and Marblehead manufacturers from a lucrative trade in Canada, Cuba, and South America, where they had competed successfully in the 1850s with British and continental manufacturers.[1] Government contracts for Union army shoes stimulated production primarily in Massachusetts shoe towns outside of Essex County and in Pennsylvania, but this demand for production also encouraged the development and utilization of the McKay stitching machine.[2] The McKay stitcher was a sewing machine mounted above a movable horn over which the upper, inner sole, and outer sole were placed after lasting. Its curved needle penetrated and firmly sewed together all the layers of leather. The machine was introduced in 1862 and was subsequently developed by the McKay Association organized in 1866, which operated a machine shop in Lawrence, Massachusetts, and counted among its members many of the large manufacturers in Lynn. By 1873, factories in Lynn and Haverhill were running more McKay machines (227) than those in New York City and Philadelphia combined (184).[3]

The shoe manufacturers of Lynn took the lead in Essex County in reorganizing production to incorporate the new machines and steam power. The first McKay stitchers in the city were acquired in early 1862 by three of the largest manufacturers, including John Wooldredge and George W. Keene, who had bought the first available Singer machines a decade earlier. By the end of 1862, nine machines were in operation in Lynn (two in the Wooldredge factory), while Philadelphia had five. As the war ended, the use of McKay machines had extended to Marblehead, to cities in New York State, and to England, but one-third of all the work produced on the machine was done in Lynn.[4] In 1866 the McKay Association began to lease the machines for thirty years rather than sell them outright, collecting royalties on each pair sewed. The leasing system promoted further technical developments in the McKay machine, and part of the proceeds was invested in the development of machinery for other parts of the work process. In 1868 the association marketed the American Beating-out Machine, which leveled out the bottom of the sole after the shoe had been stitched together on the McKay. Economies of scale on a volume of production meant larger manufacturers could afford to pay the costs of leasing, which in turn financed the development of more and better machines.[5]

Essex County manufacturers produced fewer shoes during the early years of the war, but made important decisions for postwar production. Some Lynn manufacturers decided to specialize in a new style of ladies' shoes: the high-cut polish or side-opening button boot.[6] The upper of this high-buttoned shoe was made of imported serge cloth, a durable worsted wool less costly than kidskin or morocco leather, which allowed the shoes to be sold at retail for about two dollars. By 1872 there were hundreds of thousands of customers for this shoe.[7] Women moved into public activity and paid work during the postwar years, and Lynn manufacturers supplied this new market of teachers, retail clerks, clerical and industrial workers, and middle-class reformers and clubwomen. Serge shoes came to replace leather shoes for house wear and for warm weather in the North and made the spring season for this light trade from January to May the busiest season in Lynn. The fall trade of thick work with double soles and waterproofed uppers was produced in the late summer and early fall.[8] This style of medium-grade, high-buttoned ladies' shoe, sewn on a McKay machine powered by steam, became the staple product of Lynn factories by 1870.

Despite some persistent customer preference for the hand-sewn upper in ladies' shoes, the sewing machine run both by foot and by steam power was in general use throughout Essex County by 1865. Shops that specialized in stitching uppers required only a small capital investment and served as subcontractors to large factories. By 1867 the shoe factories and stitching shops in Lynn ran 5,000 to 6,000 machines, while changes made in their stitching capacities increased by one-third the number of stitches per inch and required more skill from the operative and better tanned leather or more flexible upper cloth.[9] Stitchers experienced eyestrain working at night on black leather and complained about overwork during the busy season. During the postwar years, women supervisors began to oversee stitching operations in factories and shops, while a machine to eyelet the uppers of front-laced shoes and boots (bal-morals) indicated the possibilities of further mechanization of work on uppers.[10]

Civil War casualties and an imbalance in the sex ratio in Essex County shoe towns seemed to guarantee a supply of young women to work in the shoe factories in the postwar years. In 1865 the Massachusetts state census reported 18,000 shoeworkers in the four principal Essex County shoe towns: Lynn, Haverhill, Danvers, and Marblehead. Forty-two percent of the work force employed by the 146 factories and shops in Lynn were women.[11] The state census of population in 1865 also examined the impact of the Civil War on the distribution of the population by sex and age and noted a surplus of females to males, especially in the marriageable age group of twenty to thirty years old. This surplus, swollen by the availability of work for young, unmarried women in shoe factories and subcontract shops, was larger in Lynn than in any other shoe center. In 1865 the percentage of females in the state population was 52.48; in Lynn the percentage of females was 52.96 and in the group aged twenty to thirty years, the percentage was 56.67.[12] By 1865 more women stitched shoes in Lynn than worked in the textile mills of Lawrence, and more women worked for the shoe industry in Essex County than worked in the total of all other industries, principally textiles and clothing. Essex County women shoeworkers (7,044) also outnumbered the women (3,992) working in the cotton and woolen textile industry in Middlesex County. The numbers of women who worked on shoes in Essex County represented 63 percent of all of those female workers involved in boot and shoe production in Massachusetts in 1865. Women shoeworkers ranked third, following garment and cotton textile workers, in the total number of females involved in all kinds of manufacturing in Massachusetts. The value of the boots and shoes produced in Essex County ($18,011,197) was more than half of the combined total value of product ($33,179,105) of the four other principal counties in the state where boots and shoes were made: Worcester, Plymouth, Norfolk, and Middlesex. Most of this production occurred in large factories powered by steam.

By 1870 half of Lynn's factories had steam engines or bought power from those who did. Seventy manufacturers owned capital assets of over $10,000, which reflected investments in steam-powered mechanization. Comparatively, the other shoe towns in the county were being left behind. The shoe manufacturers of Haverhill subcontracted most of their making operations to eighty shops, and only 6 percent of all these firms had access to steam power. Moses How, who had reorganized and centralized some of his operations in the late 1850s, ran both the McKay stitcher and the sewing machine for uppers by foot power until he moved to a new location in late 1870. Only 15 percent of the manufacturers of Danvers had steam power and McKay machines, but 66 percent had sewing machines for uppers. Marblehead manufacturers made shoes or stitched uppers as subcontractors for Lynn factories. Only thirteen of these companies had assets of $10,000, and only one factory in Marblehead, Joseph Harris and Sons, had steam power. McKay machines were used by one-quarter of the firms, but nearly 90 percent ran upper-stitching machines.[13]

The five largest manufacturers in Lynn in 1870 had capital assets of between $90,000 and $125,000. They employed 16 percent of all of the shoeworkers in the city, averaging 217 workers per firm, and all had steam power and machines for stitching uppers and for the process of making. They produced 12 percent of the total annual product in Lynn. Sixty-five of the next largest companies, which were capitalized at between $10,000 and $90,000, employed 73 percent of the shoeworkers of Lynn in 1870, averaging seventy-eight workers per firm. Sixty-two percent had steam power, three-quarters had upper-stitching machines (although some of them were stitching subcontractors), and 38 percent used the McKay method. Their share of total annual production in Lynn was 79 percent. The combined numbers of the seventy largest manufacturers indicated the extent of the shift away from hand methods and small shops toward centralization and mechanization by 1870. Eighty-nine percent of all Lynn shoeworkers labored in these largest factories and produced 91 percent of the total annual production.

The movement of the larger shoe manufacturers of Essex County toward centralization and mechanization represented an attempt to exert control over production and its costs in order to obtain an advantage in the highly competitive postwar market for ladies' shoes.[14] Shoe manufacturers perceived this market as greatly tempting, but highly dangerous. The completion of the transcontinental railroad opened the national market to New England manufacturers, but might also create opportunities in eastern markets for western competitors. In the minds of Massachusetts capitalists, any shoe factory built beyond the Hudson River represented western competition. The threat of this competition would be met by cutting costs and increasing the speed of production.[15] Machinery and an intensified division of labor would allow the recruitment of unskilled labor, keep wages low, and undercut any attempt by older, skilled workers to interrupt production or resist these changes.

Large shoe manufacturers regarded labor as a commodity to be purchased at the lowest possible cost. Market forces would set the price of labor by the law of supply and demand that governed the price of everything, according to the *Lynn Reporter*, "from a government bond to a pound of cheese."[16] The demands and temptations of the national market swept away pre–Civil War expressions of harmony and mutual interests between worker and employer. The increased speed of production created by dividing work and using steam-powered machines gave the shoe manufacturer the ability to complete work in weeks rather than in months, saving labor costs.[17] Large manufacturers with the capacity for speedy fulfillment of orders could purchase leather stock at judicious intervals, obtaining the lowest price. The reduction in the time spent in production also permitted the manufacturer to make closer judgments about the prospects of the market: "The greater rapidity of the machine enables him to wait until the news as to the crops in the West and South and other incidents of the year can give a basis for estimates as to the probable amounts of orders, and then hurry through his production accordingly."[18] This policy, which attempted to fit the supply of shoes manufactured to the market demand, set up the conditions of the alternately busy and dull seasons of production. As a strategy for profits and control of the market, it was initially unsuccessful, but as a general approach it guided industrial production in the postwar era.

In the late spring of 1867, agricultural prospects had looked bright to the shoe manufacturers of Essex County, who accordingly produced a large volume for the fall trade. The markets of the West and the South, however, did not absorb even the spring trade. By November it was clear that crop prospects in May were not a reliable guide to the demand for shoes. Moreover, the dullness in the market created by overproduction in 1867 lingered through mid-1868. After their mistaken judgment of 1867, the larger manufacturers in Lynn began to organize a new system of marketing that would allow them to tailor production during the busy season more closely to demand.

One of the features of these new arrangements was a more intensive specialization in certain lines of goods. In 1868, Lynn made ladies' serge boots of medium grade in huge quantities. Haverhill specialized in the turned shoe for slippers and low-cut shoes, many of them still hand-sewn by outworkers. Marblehead concentrated on children's shoes, while outside of Essex County, the shoe towns of Natick and Milford made boots for the western trade, abandoning the russet brogans, which Southern freedmen refused to wear, regarding them as a symbol of servitude. Some towns on the South Shore of Massachusetts specialized in a trade for a particular regional market, e.g., the various towns of Abington, Bridgewater, Randolph, and Weymouth made shoes and boots for the California and New Orleans markets. This specialization gave manufacturers in each town a chance to forecast demand in their particular line and keep a closer watch on competitors.[19]

Between 1868 and 1872 the second feature of the new marketing system became a general practice in Lynn: the production of shoes only for orders placed by buyers in advance. The pre–Civil War system of marketing shoes to buyers through offices and warehouses located in Boston close to the leather district had been replaced by the development of commission houses where on Wednesdays and Saturdays the shoe manufacturers made themselves available to buyers. The manufacturers tried to figure out the demand for shoes by examining the price of leather and calculating the responses of the buyers. The wholesale dealers and jobbers then bought the shoes by the case, usually sixty pairs, which were packed into paper boxes and cartons instead of the crude trunks used before the war. The common practice was to make up the cases of shoes before the buyers arrived in Boston in early January and again in early July. Buyers, however, shopped around for the lowest prices and the best quality, and the manufacturer, bearing the costs of goods already produced, remained at a disadvantage.[20] Most Haverhill manufacturers sold their shoes only from their local warehouses, forcing buyers to take the train to examine their goods. One local observer mused that a well-aimed cannon loaded with grapeshot could mow down every manufacturer in town as they lined up eagerly awaiting the Boston train every morning during the start of the buying season.[21]

When the 1872 busy season in Lynn began, the new system of marketing shoes to advance orders was in place. In November and December of 1871 the large manufacturers of women's light goods, who represented a new generation of young businessmen, such as the sons and nephews of shoe manufacturers George W. Keene and L. M. Bubier, had sent out commercial agents to both wholesalers and retailers in the West and the South with cases of sample shoes. Furthermore, these traveling sales agents had succeeded in persuading the buyers to place orders with Lynn manufacturers before the Christmas holidays. No longer would the opening of the season rest on "the tedious waiting upon the dilatory buyers," wrote the editor of the *Shoe and Leather Record* of Boston. Drumming the trade with traveling salesmen and cases of sample shoes was "the new order of things."[22] The advantages of determining the quantities and costs of shoes to be produced by steam-powered machines offered a chance to balance supply and demand in the market. Guaranteed, speedy production of goods ordered in advance would stave off competitors eager to fill orders canceled or delayed in Lynn by production difficulties or trouble with workers. The shoe cities of Essex County could continue to dominate the national market for ladies' and women's shoes. By 1873 the practice of producing shoes only to fill advance orders was the general rule in Lynn factories.[23]

While setting in motion the new system of traveling drummers who obtained advance orders, the large manufacturers of Lynn made changes in the organization of production. These changes reshaped the architecture and interiors of the new red brick factories that by 1870 had begun to alter the look of the manufacturing center of Lynn. In this congested district of factories and shops encircling the Union Depot of the Eastern Railroad, blocks of buildings that housed several factories were common, such as those built by Samuel Bubier between 1868 and 1872. In 1868 Bubier enlarged his factory on Oxford Street and built a new engine house with a commanding eighty-seven-foot chimney. The forty-horsepower steam engine, coal-fired, decorated in maroon and gold and enclosed by a brass railing, furnished power and heat to Bubier's factory, which was expanded to accomodate nearly 400 workers.[24] By 1872 Bubier completed additional structures and rebuilt Frazier's and Bubier's Block, which had been destroyed with Lyceum Hall in a fire in late 1868. On Market Street, the central commercial thoroughfare of the industrial district, the new Frazier's and Bubier's Block contained both retail shops on the ground floor and factories above. These factories were powered by a single steam engine built into an engine house at the rear of the block. Bubier's New Block on adjacent Oxford Street, completed in 1871, contained four factories powered by a new steam engine of 125 horsepower, which had replaced the one installed in 1868. This engine supplied power and heat to Bubier's own factory and nineteen others by shafting that ran through an archway 367 feet long midway between Oxford and Market Street.[25] The size of Bubier's factories, the extent of his real-estate holdings, and his control over the steam power utilized in many other shops made him a dominating force in Lynn. Other manufacturers like Brown Brothers, the Charles D. Pecker Company, and Keene Brothers also built factory blocks and shared power from common engine houses.[26] By 1872 the Keene company had begun to build a new factory on the corner of Oxford and Washington Streets and acquired their own seventy-five-horsepower engine, which they named the "John Adam Daygr."[27] These factory blocks were peculiar to Lynn and Haverhill in the 1870s. The Joseph Harris factory in Marblehead, rebuilt in 1868 after a fire, the E. & A. Mudge factory in Danvers in 1872, and the J. D. Pike Company of Newburyport each stood alone as the largest factory in its town, self-contained and furnished with its own steam capacity.[28]

The organization of the space inside these factories reflected the divisions in the work process, each division placed on a separate floor, with the heaviest machinery for preparing sole leather located in the basement. Cutting and stitching operations, which usually occupied the top floors, were either on separate floors or divided off from each other by partitions. Some factories provided separate entrances for men and women workers. Work tables for cutters and stitchers were placed under large windows set in the outside walls, and gas jets were installed next to sewing machines for night work during the short daylight hours of the busy season for the spring trade. In the center of the room, additional tables provided an area for workers to baste and glue the cut uppers and linings for stitching. Pipes carried steam heat throughout the building, and each room in these modern factories had separate washrooms, dressing areas, and water closets. The work of putting the upper and sole together was done in the bottoming room, where groups of men worked together as teams, lasting the sewn upper to the sole, sewing the parts together on a McKay stitcher, beating out or leveling the sewn shoe, and putting on the heel and finish.[29] In Lynn and Marblehead this work was done by a three-man "string team" that received its work from the laster, while in Haverhill factories, such as the Moses How Company, the finisher led a five-man team that included the laster. The pay that these teams received as a group from their employers conformed to a customary wage and work stint of a certain number of pairs each day.[30] All of the floors in the new factories were connected by elevators that moved the work up and down between floors and by speaking tubes for directions to foremen.

During the immediate postwar years the large manufacturers of Lynn also began to experiment with changes in the sexual division of labor in shoe production. As early as 1868, women were at work as lasters in the bottoming rooms of several manufacturers, the first change in the nineteenth-century division of labor in the trade.[31] The work of these female lasters was, however, restricted to the cloth uppers of serge boots and rarely extended to work on leather. In the bottoming room of the Benjamin Dore factory on Washington Street, a group of female lasters worked with pincers and hammers, their mouths filled with tacks as they drew the sewn cloth uppers over the last and tacked them to the inner soles. Women were also assigned work that preceded the lasting process, e.g., pasting and tacking together the taps and soles of ladies' boots. One young woman, responding to a wager between two manufacturers, finished twenty cases of sixty pairs (with four pieces to a pair) in ten hours, tacking together eight taps and soles each minute or a total of 4,800 pieces in ten hours. The exhausted woman allegedly received half the bet.[32] In addition, a process was developed in late 1870 to last shoes with thread instead of tacks, a procedure that would employ women's needle skills rather than require them to work with the traditional tools of lasters. The process was designed to use a head block or jack rather than a wooden last and the sewing was done by using a palm thimble to force the 4 1/2-inch needle through the cloth and leather. Once lasted with thread, the outer soles could be laid on by machine. The *Shoe and Leather Reporter* predicted savings of 20 to 40 percent in labor costs.[33] Several large manufacturers tried out the new method in early 1871. One of them was Samuel Bubier, in whose lasting room men and women workers used both tacks and thread to last ladies' serge boots, the only goods that Bubier was manufacturing.[34]

Manufacturers also attempted to realize savings in labor costs from the assignment of women and machines to parts of the work process traditionally performed by men as cutters. In 1874, machines operated by women in the Mudge factory in Danvers, for example, cut into the leather uppers after they had been removed from the cutters' hands. Machines to cut scallops in edges and to punch holes for eyelets were operated in cutting rooms by women, while other female handworkers skived or beveled the edges of leather pieces with sharp knives against blocks of glass or marble. Some of the work to prepare the uppers for stitching could be performed outside or even inside of the cutting room by women at considerable savings in labor costs. Changes in the sexual division of labor in the shoe industry also occurred in the stitching rooms, where the number of male stitchers who worked at sewing machines increased during the postwar period to 3 percent of the work force. These men received a differential wage of about a dollar more a day on the average than female stitchers.[35] The general pattern of these experiments with the division of labor, however, was to save labor costs by incorporating women and machines into the work process.

Other attempts to divide labor involved the bottoming process and the introduction of new machines to replace handwork at lower costs. In the early 1870s, Lynn bottomers faced mechanization of trimming, edge-setting, heeling, buffing, burnishing, and finishing. As each machine was introduced, the manufacturers reduced the piece rate on the work. The result was lower wages, fewer workers required for the work, longer dull seasons when the factories were idle, and more exhaustingly intensive work during the two short busy seasons. The impact of mechanization on shoeworkers was especially galling to the teams of bottomers, who were the last group to feel the discipline of centralized and divided work as individuals. Capitalist perceptions of ways to survive and dominate the national market were shaping the busy season and its rigors.

Before the rise of modern business operations with multiple units and hierarchies of salaried managers, market forces regulated the activities of most small, personally owned and managed companies of the late nineteenth century. However after 1865 Lynn manufacturers made serious attempts to gain an advantage in the competitive market and maintain control over a significant share of the national wholesale trade. Reacting to the growth of domestic consumer demand and to the development of railroads and telegraphs, these small-scale capitalist enterprises sought to shape and dominate market forces and shackle them to the interests of Essex County shoe producers. In doing so, they made decisions that changed the work process, tied it to short seasons of intensive production, and transformed the relationships of capital and labor in the New England shoe industry. Mechanization of hand production, centralization, and the division of labor provided what Alfred Chandler has called the "economies of speed" that lowered the costs of distribution to a mass market.[36] A marketing revolution in the boot and shoe industry set new terms for work in shoe factories just as many workers were entering the doors.

Changes in shoe production after the Civil War transformed Lynn, its citizens, and the work they did. The city, which still contained sizable acreage under the plow in 1865, faced a future of rapid physical and economic growth. In the center of the city, contractors tore down wooden frame structures, and the whole business district was rebuilt in brick.[37] The chimneys of steam engines outreached the spires of churches. A new City Hall with a stylish mansard roof and an Italianate tower was finished in 1867. The local Republican party, which had come to power during the Civil War, dominated municipal politics and created an armed, uniformed police force to keep order in the rapidly changing city.[38]

Many observers feared that rapid change would hurtle local society out of the control of its residents. The editor of the *Lynn Transcript* voiced these fears in its first issues in 1868. The *Transcript* noted that of the 311 couples who were married in Lynn in 1867, 65 percent were natives of other towns and other states, while one-quarter were foreign-born. The smallest group were Lynn natives.[39] In three editorials on the future of Lynn in 1868, the editor faced the implications of the emerging factory system.[40] Mechanization was destroying the old values of artisan life and reducing the need for skill among the workmen. Mechanics were becoming "mere operatives." This meant lower wages and a shorter work season. Capital was becoming concentrated in the hands of the few. Wide gaps would develop among classes. The tenement house had already begun to crowd out the homestead, and Lynn would soon resemble the squalid factory towns of England. Where labor was regarded as a commodity subject to the laws of supply and demand in a fiercely competitive market, workmen could expect "no just share in the earnings of machinery."[41] Nonetheless the editor of the *Transcript* concluded on February 29 with a note of false optimism, trusting that the mutual benefits of cooperation by workers and manufacturers for the general good would sustain harmonious relations in Lynn. He advised workmen to cultivate practical education and moral culture, while young men should act like capitalists and invest their leisure time during the dull seasons in the improvement of machinery. Although the editor of the *Transcript* continued to worry over the level of wages in relationship to the cost of living, the brief period of overproduction and idleness in 1867 gave way to a prosperous fall season in 1868. Workers crowded into Lynn tenements and jammed the horse-drawn omnibuses that carried them each day from Saugus, Marblehead, Swampscott, and Salem.[42] The sustained prosperity after 1867 stimulated a rise in real-estate values in the city from $10 million in 1860 to $21 million in 1870, largely as a result of the construction of new factories and residences and the rising price of undeveloped land.[43]

The *Lynn Reporter*, the other major newspaper representing local manufacturing and real-estate interests, had fewer doubts about the benefits of centralization and mechanization to the community. For years the editor had applauded the demise of decentralized work in neighboring towns and villages as good for the residents of Lynn. In January 1872 he celebrated the beginning of the busy season as if the industry epitomized the vital forces of life and nature, as if it possessed magical qualities that stimulated the whole city into animation. The musical hum of machinery and the flood tide of activity prompted appropriate feelings: "We feel like taking hold of work with a new zest, and really appreciate the privilege of laboring."[44] Yet the *Reporter* also printed expressions of apprehension, many by clergymen, over the state of public morality in a city crowded with tenements. In its pages a concerned public called for reading rooms, better boarding houses, and wholesome activities for the masses of factory workers as alternatives to their walking the public streets "to see and to be seen." In November 1869 the Lynn Board of Trade led by Samuel Bubier and George W. Keene committed itself to the moral welfare of Lynn as well as to its commercial and manufacturing interests; especially, in the words of Bubier, to "the multitudes of young men and women who are attracted hither from their homes by the great manufacturing interests of the place."[45]

Among these workers who came to the Lynn factories during the busy seasons were the young women who worked as stitchers. The *Reporter* took a special interest in these young women, defending them from criticism and condescension, while supporting efforts to protect their reputations. This sensitivity to the quality of life and morality among the female stitchers of Lynn reflected both the concerns of the shoe manufacturers who wished to encourage the movement of young women and men to the factories during the busy seasons and the concerns of middle-class citizens who were fearful of the social and moral consequences of mobility among a floating population of workers.[46] The community of Lynn responded to the changes that threatened to overwhelm its moral order by building protective institutions, especially for those female workers attracted to Lynn by the wages paid for stitching. A justifying and defensive ideology cloaked these otherwise rootless women workers with dignity and respectability. The community also encouraged the integration of this female industrial work force into the private family life of Lynn, where as boarders they would receive the attentions and guardianship of home life. Unlike the textile centers of Massachusetts, the manufacturers in Essex County built no corporation boardinghouses for their female workers, but relied instead on the resources of public concern and private life in the community to resolve the potential problems of a seasonally mobile work force.

In the pages of the *Reporter*, the stitching girls were described as laughing, smartly dressed young women who exemplified the bustling enterprise of the postwar years without sacrificing their status as ladies: respectable, moral, well educated, well mannered, and high-minded. The image was intended to be a credit to them and to the manufacturers who employed them. Work in the stitching rooms and shops was characterized as effortless and well remunerated. Operators ran "magic" machines, driven by steam power in groups of thirty to fifty per room. Experienced stitchers disdained to work by foot power. They were assisted by gummers and basters who prepared the work, while pressers ironed out the seams after stitching. For this skilled work, the most productive stitchers earned, according to the *Reporter*, ten to twelve dollars a week, and very few fell below six dollars a week.[47] The highest wages were probably earned by those who still stitched the fancy leather uppers of ladies' shoes, which constituted an important but declining portion of goods produced by Lynn manufacturers in the postwar years. The demand for luxurious, highly ornamented ladies' shoes with fancy stitching or embroidery persisted for a brief period between 1867 and 1873. These goods, made of kid-glove leather, were specially designed to recapture the southern market from foreign competition and combined "colors and embroidery in stitching, and little notions of foxing and a milliner's tact in trimming with bows and buckles."[48] The stitching work on the uppers of these shoes required skill and forced the manufacturers to pay a premium for the work as long as the demand for it lasted. For the spring season of 1872 the designs for these shoes reflected the extravagant taste of the post–Civil War public. Among the novelties were: "a croquet shoe . . . of black glove kid, lined entire with white kid, a rosette of black ribbon with buckle . . . , a street boot with glove tips, foxed with morrocco, square heels in imitation of gentlemen's wear, and kid facings of blue . . . , a buttoned walking shoe, of pebble goat . . . the trimming is of pink kid, button holes in scalloped edge, stitched by hand, heels finished with a row of highly finished copper tacks."[49] For several seasons the fashion of shorter dresses for street wear meant that the world would see what the Lynn manufacturers could put on ladies' feet.

In the early 1870s the manufacturing interests of Lynn developed and extolled the image of the factory stitcher as lady. In 1872 the editor of the paper angrily defended a young stitcher against criticism that it was "nonsense" for a "common machine girl" to spend her hard-earned wages on music lessons. This "young lady" who honorably worked for her own support could cultivate her talents as she pleased, and her sacrifice and dedication to music was more to be admired than the gadding and gossip of the leisured daughters of the wealthy. Music furthermore relieved the mind of "wearisome toil" and strengthened the worker for new efforts.[50] Access to relatively high wages for working women during the years of postwar prosperity meant that some stitchers could afford public acts of generosity. Such incidents were celebrated in the pages of the *Reporter*. On various occasions a group of stitchers presented their forelady or overseer with a handsome gift, often jewelry, in appreciation of a well-managed workroom.[51] These occasions provided proof of the satisfaction of the stitchers with their work and their wages. Furthermore, the *Reporter* equated the social status of stitchers with female schoolteachers and with the clerks and bookkeepers who worked in offices throughout Lynn. Stitchers could reap the benefits of their enterprise by becoming supervisors in stitching rooms, and some even set up their own stitching shops. At the end of the workday, "our working girl is the lady" who moved with social ease in any circumstances, "on the fashionable promenade, at the popular lecture, mingling with the musical associations of the day, attired in the most stylish costumes and forming an attractive feature of the social assembly."[52] But it was precisely what the factory stitcher did with her time away from work, especially on Saturday nights, that worried the clergy and the middle class in Lynn and prompted the defensive concern of the manufacturers.

Saturday night on Market Street came to represent the dangers of city life in industrial Lynn for young women and for young men. After working the official ten-hour day or longer during the rush of the busy season in mid-winter and in mid-summer, shoeworkers sought recreation and gaity on the streets of the city. Saturday meant a full day's work, 7 A.M. to 6 P.M., but Saturday night was payday, and the retail stores on Market Street stayed open late to attract customers. The post office and the Academy of Music, which staged concerts and theatricals, were located there, and the new Music Hall where many of the city's amusements, lectures, and fairs took place was on nearby Central Street. In the opinion of one shoeworker in 1871, these factory operatives preferred entertainment to lectures or self-improvement during their hours away from work, and the best time for circuses or minstrel shows in Lynn was Saturday night.[53]

One of the scenes in a serialized novel, "The Queen City! : or Life in the Shoe Factories of Lynn," published in the *Lynn Record* in 1872, depicted the excitement felt by young workers who promenaded the streets on Saturday nights, dressed up in their best clothes.[54] Multitudes flocked the streets. Girls paraded up and down, passing the corners under the gaslights where young men gathered in crowds, greeting them as they passed. Flirtation ran riot. This scene was charged with the sexual daring of young men and women, eyeing each other, far from the restraints of family and home. The hero of "Queen City!," Eben Pool, followed one flirtatious girl to her rooming house; according to the story, he was in danger of being entrapped by the "dark ways" that lurked in Lynn. Later he succumbed to the temptations of the beer shops conveniently located on every street in the industrial district. The gay thoroughfare of Market Street disturbed and excited. One observer captured the temptations, disappointments, and frustrations of the scene in a poem, "The Stitching Girls," published in the *Lynn Transcript* in 1869.

> When walking on the crowded street,
>   A lovely lass attracts your eye,
> and while you gaze your glances meet,
>   You smile—alas! you soon will sigh
> For Cupid from her beaming eyes,
>   His shining arrows thickly hurls;
> And hard indeed must be the heart—
>   That can withstand the stitching girls.
>
>   The stitching girls, the witching girls.
>   The jaunty, dainty, stitching girls
>   With Cupid's dart they pierce the heart—
>   The pleasing, teasing stitching girls.
>
> . . . Again you meet her and she plys
>   And sings and smiles for you alone,
> Charmed by her gentle, loving ways,
>   You hope to call her all your own,
> But should you kneel and tell your love,
>   With cruel scorn her lip will curl:

And you'll be left alone to sigh:
  I'm jilted by a stitching girl.
  The stitching girls, the witching girls—
  The singing, clinging stitching girls
  They break your heart and then depart
  The naughty, haughty stitching girls.[55]

In this atmosphere, the lady stitcher was transformed into a heartless tease, an elusive but fascinating symbol of rootless femininity. Many boardinghouse keepers, however, forced working girls to meet their friends and beaux on the streets of Lynn by refusing to allow any social visits. Saturday night on Market Street was filled with challenges and perils of all kinds for the promenading lady stitcher. One machine operator complained to the *Little Giant*, the Lynn Crispin paper, that tobacco-spitting young men fouled the sidewalks and ruined a dress for which she had paid a dollar a yard. Worse, when she "remonstrated," she received an insulting reply.[56]

Responding to fears about the rapidity of economic change in Lynn and its implications for the morality of local society, the middle class and the shoe manufacturers took steps to protect and defend the young women who came to work and board in the city. In September 1868 the wives and daughters of prominent manufacturers, retailers, physicians, and clergymen organized the Woman's Union for Christian Work. The organizers of the Woman's Union were conscious that several thousand young women workers were living in the city outside the protection of home life and that Lynn, unlike the textile cities of Lowell and Lawrence, provided no supervised and safe boardinghouses. A major complaint of the Woman's Union members against the boardinghouses in Lynn was that they offered only lodging and daily meals, but nothing that resembled a home or encouraged the young woman worker to stay there for the evening rather than stroll on Market Street. The union's purpose was to contact the women who came seeking work in the Lynn factories, obtain suitable places for them to board and work, and invite them to church on Sundays. For the new arrival in Lynn, it was often difficult to find out which boardinghouses customarily accepted women and which did not. The Woman's Union asked families in Lynn who wanted boarders to leave their names at the Union's reading room on Market Street. The factories and boarding places that the organization recommended and the services offered by its members were intended to bring these young women under beneficial moral and religious influences.[57]

In November 1869 the Woman's Union opened their reading room on Market Street where young ladies could avoid "undesirable places of amusement." They also began plans to construct and operate their own boardinghouse. In the Market Street reading room, which was open Monday to Saturday from 8 A.M. to 10 P.M. and on Sunday in the afternoon and evening, a young woman could seek information, use the library, obtain rest and refreshment, and meet a sympathetic and "morally correct" representative of the organization. The reading room also offered diversion: social gatherings, various classes in penmanship, drawing, sewing, and waxwork, and an occasional prayer meeting. It was supported by public contributions and by the sympathy of the local clergy and the newly organized Young Men's Christian Association, which offered similar services to transient young men and lent its rooms for the meetings of the Woman's Union.[58] One young Congregational minister new to Lynn, the Reverend Joseph Cook, gave an inspirational lecture to the members of the union in September 1870 and congratulated them on their work.[59] Cook would later draw upon the fears of middle-class residents to question the moral purity of work arrangements within the shoe factories of Lynn. Although the Woman's Union of Lynn also organized a committee on the poor and appealed to the public for financial support on the grounds of a general program of charitable activities, the commitment of most of its members was strictly limited by their class interests.

The Market Street reading room became a place where female factory workers came with their troubles. The annual reports of the organization describe the fears of deserted wives who had children to support and of homesick, confused girls from country homes. Some of these women who were not strong enough or healthy enough to stand the pace of work during the busy season left the factories for an hour or so during the day to find a cup of tea and a pillow at the reading room. The impressionable claimed that the influences of the reading room had prevented them from going "astray." Occasionally, the desperate would be provided a meal and a night's accommodation, but the attention of the Woman's Union remained with the idealized lady stitcher whose claim to social status, education, and manners attracted the concern of its members.[60]

In early 1873 the Woman's Union faced public criticism for its treatment of an unemployed woman and her thirteen-year-old daughter, who were sent by a local employment office to the reading room seeking domestic work. The homeless and ragged woman and her child were turned away by the reading room superintendent, who made them understand that the room was for the use of "nice, young ladies," who sought employment in the shoe factories. In defending her actions, the society's leaders insisted that the woman appeared to be intoxicated and degraded, but that both mother and daughter had been treated correctly and with courtesy. Nonetheless, the policy of the Woman's Union of extending its assistance to only a small portion of working women in Lynn undermined its appeal for support from a charitable public.[61] Yet even the lady stitchers who were permitted to use the services of the Woman's Union were kept at a distance by the members. The boardinghouse scheme remained only a dream, and membership and funds dwindled in 1874. Miss P. M. Merrill, who had been the superintendent of the reading room for almost five years, sadly resigned that year, citing lack of interest and funds. She commented that most members of the association refused even to meet the girls who visited the reading room and that these attitudes contradicted the aims of the organization.[62]

The typical young unmarried woman who came to Lynn seeking work as a stitcher and who faced confusing choices about a place to board represented about one-third of all of the women employed in the shoe factories in 1870. Eighty percent of all of the stitchers who boarded in Lynn lived with private families, and the remaining 20 percent, about whom the Woman's Union expressed so much distressed concern, boarded in large boardinghouses that averaged thirteen persons in an establishment managed by a resident family. In almost all of these large boardinghouses, stitchers lived with other women stitchers or family members, usually sisters. Twenty-two percent of all boarding stitchers, wherever they lived, resided with their sisters. These relationships may not have provided the restraint of home influences that the Woman's Union thought imperative to maintain morality, but living with a sister or other stitchers provided companionship and access to experienced advice. Three-quarters of these boarding stitchers were natives of New England, and one-third were natives of Massachusetts. At an average age of 25.4 years, they were as a group the oldest of all the stitchers sampled in the 1870 census of population for Lynn. Only 20 percent were foreign-born, and the vast majority of these had crossed the Bay of Funday by steamship from the Canadian Maritime Provinces of Novia Scotia, New Brunswick, and Prince Edward Island to Boston and to ports in Maine and had taken the train to Lynn. The background and nativity of these young women, their seasonal mobility, and their status as boarders and temporary workers in shoe factory towns suggest an analogy with the experience of pre–Civil War textile operatives in the cities of the Merrimack Valley.[63] Presumably driven to shoe factories by motives similar to those of textile workers before 1850, the postwar circumstances of a surplus female population in Massachusetts meant, however, that many stitchers could no longer afford to regard industrial work as a brief period in their lives before marriage.

In 1870 the shoe factories in Lynn employed nearly 3,000 women, comprising four distinct elements: boarding migrants, wives, female heads of families, and daughters of resident families. Although only 9 percent of the total work force were wives, the composition of the Lynn female work force was much more complex than that of the work force of cotton textile operatives prior to the Civil War. Nonetheless, over 40 percent of the Lynn female work force in 1870 boarded either as single or newly married young women. The average age of married women workers was a remarkably low twenty-two years. Another 21 percent of the total work force resided in families headed by their mothers, their sisters, or themselves. Many of these women appeared to be self-supporting or providing support to other family members and therefore dependent on the wages they earned, even though they lived in resident families. About 35 percent of the total work force resided in male-headed, largely nuclear families, and half of this youngest group of stitchers had gone out to work as the first child available to contribute to family income. These male-headed families with young daughters at work also had the highest percentage of foreign-born parents, largely Irish.[64]

The stitchers in the Lynn work force in 1870 had been drawn to the relatively high wages paid in shoe factories during the years before the depression of 1873. They could bring to industrial work the experience of young women in the 1860s of using a sewing machine at home to make family clothing, as Singer and other manufacturers had flooded the postwar domestic market with their machines. The scarcity of marriageable males between twenty and thirty years of age in the New England population as a result of Civil War casualties and westward migration raised questions about the duration of these young women's involvement in industrial work. Their idealized status as lady stitchers in 1870 would be threatened both by long-term industrial employment and by the efforts of shoe manufacturers to alter the sexual division of labor.

In March 1872 a worried member of the middle class wrote to the editor of the *Reporter* about the needs of factory workers in Lynn. The city streets at noontime were congested with workers hurrying to their dinners and back to work. These people, many of them part of the floating population, needed better places to board, a municipal hospital, and closer contact with the churches and the city's residents. The writer reminded the middle class of Lynn that their "flowers," their "well-clipped lawns," and their "green houses and graperies" had been provided by the labor of these people hurrying to and from their work.[65] The shoeworkers of Lynn agreed with these views. During the postwar period of rapid change and prosperity, both men and women workers organized strong unions that struggled to maintain decent wages in the face of the efforts of the manufacturers to cut labor costs.

The working men of Lynn felt the impact of the developing factory system most sharply in the immediate postwar period. To prevail in the national market, the large manufacturers had divided and mechanized the work process and concentrated the season of production. Desperately hard work was required to provide enough income to tide a family over the dull season of three to four months to the next rushed season of work. The seasonality of production was intensified by the decisions of some of the manufacturers in 1868 to produce shoes only to fill advance orders, which became a general practice in Lynn by 1873 and later the national standard. As manufacturers insisted on defining labor as just another commodity subject to the laws of supply and demand, shoeworkers came to regard the opening of the busy season with mixed fears and hopes. More and more, the cent or half cent per pair in wages that a finisher, trimmer, or laster could earn took on a crucial significance. Although there were still a number of male workers paid by the week, the piece rate on the edge-making, McKay, or other machines became the central issue for most factory workers in Lynn.

Several workmen described the pressures and grievances experienced by shoeworkers in Lynn in the *Second Annual Report* of the Massachusetts Bureau of Labor Statistics in 1871.[66] The experience of factory work meant a loss of status and skill that produced new, disturbing feelings of insecurity. Since the centralization of work in factories, there had been no steady work at all in contrast to memories of regular work in the ten footer for a period of seven to ten years, interrupted only by general hard times. The subdivision of labor and the mechanization of work had destroyed the utility of experience and training. Apprenticeships had no meaning when a farm laborer from New Hampshire could learn a job in three days. The migration of male workers from other towns crowded the labor market during the busy season with men regarded by Lynn workers as less skilled or reliable. The onset of the busy season forced the worker to work as hard as possible. "The temptation is very great for a man who has been without anything to do, week after week, to work thirteen hours a day . . . , even if by doing so he is reduced in a few weeks to a mere skeleton."[67] The workday of ten hours was regularly stretched by men trying to earn reasonable incomes by intensive effort.[68] Some shoeworkers were at the factory from 4 A.M. to 10 or 11 at night, snatching a noontime meal in fifteen minutes. The season, alternately busy or dull and based on the decisions of manufacturers to fill only advance orders, was the primary cause of their troubles.[69]

Despite their efforts, few workingmen were able to do more than meet their regular family expenses. Home ownership for a factory worker seemed to be out of the question. Rents were also high.[70] Unpredicted or unusual expenses such as illness, an emergency, or a new baby drove shoeworkers to borrow money from their employers or turn to their fellow workers in desperation. Unemployment during the dull season could mean no money for clothing or books to send the children to school. Sometimes it meant hunger. With no margin of earnings or expectations for steady work, the shoeworkers faced indebtedness and loss of self-respect. One work-man complained in 1871 that "the working men do not occupy the same relative positions as other classes in the community; that they are falling behind, that they do not get as much proportionate pay for their labor, as the manufacturers do for their capital."[71] Beneath the surface of postwar prosperity, wealth was concentrating in a few hands. This shoeworker believed that machinery and the division of labor were being utilized to undermine the fair share of labor's contribution to production, creating a population of over-worked, underpaid hirelings, not unlike the cotton mill workers of Massachusetts.[72] For these men, organization was the only way they knew to try to maintain wage rates during the rush for work in the busy season and to control, if possible, the supply of labor. Lynn shoeworkers rejected the manufacturers' view of labor as simply another commodity, but found themselves caught in a local labor market, the conditions of which had been determined not by abstract economic laws or machine technology, but by the decisions made by Lynn manufacturers to survive postwar competition and dominate the national market for ladies' shoes.

The Knights of St. Crispin (KOSC), one of the most success-ful national unions of workers in the nineteenth century, repre-sented these new factory workers in their struggle to defend their wages and use the equal rights tradition to challenge the manufac-turers' efforts to justify relations between worker and employer by using the argument of supply and demand forces. Historians of the Knights have traditionally emphasized the concerns of artisans in the national organization about the flooding of the labor market in the industry's major cities. This issue has been labeled the "green hands" problem, and it dominated the rhetoric of the publications and conventions of the organization.[73] Since the factory system and the division of labor had destroyed the apprentice system, the green hands question seemed to represent the larger problems of migra-tory labor, the threat of foreign contract labor such as the use of Chinese workers in a North Adams, Massachusetts, shoe factory in 1870,[74] and might even include resistance to the experiments by Lynn manufacturers that altered the sexual composition of jobs such as lasting. The obsession with green hands also suggests the impact of supply and demand categories on the thinking of the Crispin leaders.

Among the rank and file and in the strikes conducted by the KOSC, the major issue was wages, especially as new machines prompted manufacturers to trim piece rates. The green hands issue was related, however, to the wage issue. With labor regarded as a commodity by the manufacturers, an overcrowded labor market justified lowering wages. With much of the male work force organized into teams in the factories, the employment of green hands to the exclusion of more skilled workers chosen by their teammates depressed the wages of the work team as a group. Had skilled shoeworkers been paid as individuals, the green hands issue might have had a less immediate impact on the wages they earned. According to one Massachusetts KOSC leader: "It became evident to them [the Crispins] that the rates of wages paid to the 'green hands' fixed the rate of their own wages which became too low to enable them to support their families." [75] Factory workers who worked in teams joined others such as lasters and cutters to organize resistance to the policies of the new factory system.

Lynn manufacturers regarded the new Crispin organization with great apprehension. The editor of the *Lynn Reporter* argued in early 1869 that market forces determined the price of labor and that no organization could change the law of supply and demand. To attempt to interfere with economic laws would injure the worker and produce combinations of capital that would try to control labor. The *Shoe and Leather Reporter* reminded working men that in the strike of 1860 they had been the losers, while the manufacturers had made moderate profits.[76] As Crispinism spread in Lynn in 1869 and claimed 30,000 members in Massachusetts, conflict seemed unavoidable. However, shoe manufacturers, like George W. Keene, still believed in the advantages of cooperation between shoeworkers and employers and in the possibilities of mutual benefits to retailers, workers, and manufacturers from industrial prosperity. As vice president of the Lynn Board of Trade in 1869, Keene argued that extreme seasonality injured both workers and manufacturers and proposed that the industry attempt to stabilize work and wages.[77] He spoke for the numerous smaller manufacturers in Lynn, less able to finance rapid changes or produce huge quantities of goods for advance orders. With manufacturers like George Keene on the board of trade, the Crispins were able to arbitrate a citywide agreement on wages for two years.

In the summer of 1870 as the industry shifted from thin, single-soled work to thick, double-soled work for the fall trade, the KOSC decided to adopt a uniform price for lasting and to oppose efforts by their employers to reduce wages on tap-sole work, both processes where manufacturers were experimenting with the introduction of women workers. The lasters, who were not members of the three-man string teams common to making operations in Lynn, organized themselves into Unity Lodge in the KOSC and operated within the Crispin organization as a semi-independent group. The Crispins went out on strike in mid-July, timed to put pressure on the manufacturers just as the busy fall season was beginning. Their leaders insisted on negotiating wages with the board of trade as equals. President Samuel Bubier, hot-tempered, hostile, and the largest manufacturer in Lynn, at first refused to talk to L. C. Legrow, the head of the KOSC in Lynn, but after two weeks of idleness with the orders piling up, negotiations began and a citywide wage scale for all male shoeworkers was agreed upon for one year. George Keene apparently convinced Bubier and the board of trade to arbitrate wage rates that year. Five Crispins and five manufacturers formed a joint board of arbitration and conciliation that followed an English model (probably that of the hosiery industry in the 1860s) designed to avoid the rigors of competition on both manufacturers and workers. Despite an immediate move by several large firms to open auxiliary factories in Pittsfield, New Hampshire, the agreement in 1870 ended much of the local competition among Lynn manufacturers over labor costs and was renewed without change in the summer of 1871. Meanwhile, the Crispins involved themselves in the labor reform cause in Massachusetts state politics.[78] These two years represented the peak of their activity and power as an organization.

In late 1868 the women workers of Lynn also joined the Crispin cause. A group of young female factory workers circulated a petition among the stitchers that urged them to help organize an association along the lines of the KOSC to prevent reductions in wages. The Daughters of St. Crispin (DOSC), Central Lodge #1, was organized in Lynn on November 12, 1868, and the members chose as the "First Directeress" of its activities Miss Carrie A. Wilson, a twenty-five-year-old stitcher who boarded in Lynn and supported her widowed mother. Another young, unmarried boarding stitcher, Abbie Jacques, served as secretary.[79] Much of the leadership of the DOSC would come from young women who supported themselves and others on their earnings as workers. Additional lodges were quickly established in other shoe towns. Like the Knights, the Daughters of St. Crispin were factory workers determined to protect their wages against the manufacturers' policy of cutting labor costs.[80] For the Knights and Daughters in Lynn, a basic similarity in conditions of factory employment and the absence of serious competition between men and women over jobs meant a real chance for close identification of interests and mutual support. Like the collar workers of Troy, New York, women shoeworkers did not represent a threat to men's work or wages; the sexual division of labor in shoe production encouraged their cooperative relationship with male unionists.[81] Both organizations accepted this division of labor in the industry and tried to use their influence to insist that any female laster or male stitcher be paid the same wages as the vast majority of lasters and stitchers.

Thirty-one delegates from local lodges attended the first national convention of the Daughters of St. Crispin, which met in Lynn for three days in July 1869. A strong KOSC lodge in Danvers had encouraged the establishment of a lodge for women shoeworkers in 1868, but in Haverhill, where the Knights had also organized early that year, there was no trace of a DOSC lodge. In March 1869 a DOSC lodge formed in Stoneham, Massachusetts, a ladies' shoe town located in eastern Middlesex County, close to Lynn. The Stoneham lodge furnished a number of national leaders for the DOSC between 1869 and 1874.[82] Some of the delegates represented lodges hastily organized in Auburn, Maine, and in South Shore towns in Massachusetts. The delegates, although few in number, represented a national chain of lodges stretching from Maine to California and south to Philadelphia and Baltimore. Samuel P. Cummings of Danvers, the leader of the KOSC organization in Massachusetts, opened the convention and appointed two leaders of the Lynn DOSC lodge as temporary officers: Carrie A. Wilson and Abbie Jacques. His statement to reporters made it clear that while the KOSC backed and guided the new organization, the stitchers had organized themselves: "The order had been formed at the request of some young women workers in shoe factories, who in a petition had urged the necessity of organization in order to more effectively prevent unnecessary reduction of wages."[83]

The following morning, the DOSC convention adopted a constitution and elected national officers. Mrs. Emma A. Lane, a hardworking member of the organizing convention, was elected the First Grand Directeress. She was the wife of a Lynn shoeworker and a strong supporter of Crispinism. Martha Wallbridge, a thirty-year-old unmarried stitcher and native of New York who worked and boarded in Stoneham, was elected Second Grand Directeress. Other officers included Miss Ora Bates of Auburn, Maine, Miss Nancy Whitmore of Rochester, New York, and Miss Hattie Goodell of Danvers. Carrie Wilson became national treasurer. The national secretary was twenty-year-old Mrs. Frances R. Jones, a self-supporting and apparently childless woman who was the president of the Excelsior Lodge in Stoneham.[84] The eight officers of Excelsior Lodge represented a diverse group of women workers employed as stitchers in Stoneham factories. Half were married women, but two of the wives had no children in residence, and Mrs. Jones boarded with a local family and appeared to be either widowed or separated from her husband. Of the unmarried women leaders of Excelsior Lodge, two lived in female-headed families (one lived alone), one boarded, and only one resided with her male-headed family. Five of the eight leaders of the DOSC in Stoneham were boarders, indicating a high degree of geographical mobility among activist women. The leadership of Central and Excelsior Lodges, which provided many of the national officers of the DOSC between 1869 and 1874, represented the self-supporting boarding stitcher and the female-headed family to a greater extent than the constituency of residents living in male-headed families. The officers of the national DOSC in 1869 represented New England and New York State female factory workers, many of whom were either unmarried or self-supporting women.

Jennie Collins of Boston, a former textile worker and activist in the cause of working women and labor reform in Massachusetts, attended the Lynn convention and addressed the afternoon session on July 28. Her reminiscences of the convention emphasized the qualities and character of the delegates, which combined the "skill of the working girls, and the dignity, grace and refinement of the most fashionable ladies of the land." Collins believed that the musical accomplishments of the delegates, their genteel manners, personal charm, and beauty reflected the merits of the working population of stitchers, rather than their cultural and social backgrounds, which appeared unusual for industrial workers. But her impressions of silk dresses and exquisite poses in the *tableaux vivants* of the "Goddess of Liberty" and the "Mourning Mother" during the entertainment on the night of July 29 also conveyed some astonishment at a group of women workers unlike many with whom she had previously dealt. Collins, who also spoke at the entertainment that night, gave a fighting speech, possibly to restore a working-class tone to the proceedings, denouncing the Massachusetts State House as "a central countinghouse for the capital of the Commonwealth." She described the members of the DOSC as the "pride and joy" of their families, whom misfortune had forced into the work force, and she called on all female shoeworkers to be as independent and self-respecting.[85]

Mrs. Elizabeth L. Daniels of Boston, who with Collins and Aurora H. C. Phelps had organized the Boston Working Women's League on April 26, 1869, also spoke at the DOSC convention. She was intent on allying the Daughters of St. Crispin with the league's activities. Mrs. Daniels believed that skilled working women like the DOSC members should be recruited as leaders for the less skilled, such as the women of Boston who sewed clothing as outworkers or in sweatshops. Experienced, well-paid women, like the stitchers of Lynn and Stoneham, were better equipped to help organize and protect their "less favored sisters," than men or "ladies of refined leisure."[86] Aurora Phelps had noted the absence of women shoeworkers at the Boston convention on April 21 that had launched the league. On April 22 Daniels, Phelps, and Collins had joined Lucy Stone of the Massachusetts Woman Suffrage Association to testify at legislative hearings on the proposed ten-hour law, where they cited low wages and the homeless condition of poor working women, while arguing for the state to provide decent housing or homesteads for women as well as the ten-hour day. Only Stone supported suffrage for working women at the hearing.[87] The issue of suffrage, which the Working Women's League of Boston did not yet endorse in 1869, surfaced at the DOSC convention.

Both Elizabeth Daniels and Samuel P. Cummings of the KOSC emphasized that the right of working women to a decent wage for their labor should be more important to the DOSC than the right to vote. Daniels insisted that the Daughters should not seek the ballot, but instead a reasonable compensation for their labor. She advised the convention delegates to support their brothers in the cause of labor reform and to reverence marriage, not advocate women's rights. Cummings helped to close the long day of convention activity by stating his general support for advocates of woman suffrage, but his greater admiration for the women of the DOSC, whose first concern should be their rights as workers. He then pledged 30,000 KOSC votes in Massachusetts for the vindication of the rights of working women.[88] Despite the advice of these speakers, the apparent conflict between woman suffrage and the interests of working women remained unresolved after the Lynn convention. The meaning of women's rights for female workers became a divisive issue for the DOSC as the national leadership began to advocate the interests of women shoeworkers after 1869.

For the next twelve months the DOSC expanded its organization locally and nationally. The relationship between the Crispins, male and female, in Lynn was supportive and friendly, but aside from public demonstrations in February 1870 on behalf of a strike in Worcester by the Knights and cooperation at fund-raising and social activities, the Knights and Daughters held separate meetings and conventions and chose different newspapers in Lynn and in the national labor press for their official public statements.[89] The DOSC played no role in the successful effort by the Knights to negotiate a citywide wage agreement in July 1870. The Daughters apparently experienced no serious wage reductions or major disputes with their employers until 1871, and their wages were not included in the yearly arbitration agreements between the KOSC and the manufacturers. On the other hand, the DOSC displayed no public sympathy for the activities of the Woman's Union for Christian Work and competed for the interest and attention of the stitchers of Lynn by meeting every Monday night at Harmony Hall near the factory district and offering as entertainment a fair and a series of lectures by Jennie Collins and Elizabeth Daniels beginning in October 1869.[90] By December 22 the DOSC in Lynn had nearly 500 members, who were treated to an evening's recital of instrumental and vocal music, short dramas, and tableaux much like those presented at the convention in July. The order also grew outside of

Lynn. Twenty-four lodges were formed in just six months, fourteen of which were in Massachusetts. Rochester, New York, had the largest lodge, with 700 members. Thriving groups had organized in Natick, Boston, Marlboro, and Worcester, and in 1871 coalitions of Knights and Daughters won important strikes in Syracuse and Baltimore.[91]

In August 1869 at the annual convention of the National Labor Union in Philadelphia, the DOSC became involved in a struggle that convulsed the organization over the actions of women's rights advocates on behalf of the admission of working women to skilled trades and over the propriety of an alliance between the NLU and middle-class women reformers. At the previous convention in 1868 Susan B. Anthony and Elizabeth Cady Stanton attended as delegates, hoping to find allies in the labor movement for their newly formed Woman Suffrage Association.[92] William Sylvis, president of the NLU, supported woman suffrage, admired the work of Anthony and Stanton, and aided their cause at the 1868 convention. Anthony attended as a delegate representing a hastily formed Working Women's Association, which began with about a hundred clerks and typesetters who, despite her exertions, placed greater importance on wages and organization than suffrage.[93] Stanton also participated in the 1868 convention, although she claimed to represent only her suffrage association. When Irish-American representatives of the New York City building trades threatened to withdraw from the convention if Stanton were seated, the delegates compromised and voted to admit her, but made it clear that the organization did not thereby endorse woman suffrage.[94] The women's rights advocates made the most of their opportunities in 1868, organizing to elect women to NLU offices and gaining the convention's endorsement of equal pay for equal work and the necessity of organizing women workers. As Philip Foner has pointed out, none of these activists were working-class women.[95] A Committee on Female Labor recommended to the convention resolutions supporting the eight-hour day for women, equal pay, unions for all working women, the opening of all trades and professions to women, and the ballot. All of these recommendations but the last were adopted by the NLU in 1868, establishing a precedent of activism on behalf of the needs of working women that was continued in subsequent conventions by delegates from the DOSC. As a result, a portion of the female industrial work force made contact with the women's rights movement. However, at the next convention of the NLU in 1869, the divisive issue was not suffrage, but the sexual division of labor in the skilled trades.

In the spring of 1869, while the typographers' unions of New York City were on strike against several printing establishments, Susan B. Anthony, as she had earlier in 1868, encouraged women to seek training in the printing trades during the strike, a move that undercut the union and aided their employers.[96] Anthony's behavior, in addition to the opposition within the NLU toward woman suffrage, put her on a collision course with the trade unionists. Members of the Typographers' Union, Local #6, instructed their delegate, M. R. Walsh, to challenge the seating of Anthony at the 1869 convention because she had violated the principles of trade unionism and represented no organization of working women. Walsh had the support of Augusta Lewis, the president of a female typographers' union in New York City that the men's union, under pressure to control women in the trade, had taken under its guidance.[97] Earlier in 1869 Augusta Lewis had left Anthony's Working Women's Association in disgust over its domination by middle-class lady reformers, but her criticism of Anthony contained in a letter that Walsh read to the convention was limited to the defects of that organization.[98] Susan B. Anthony herself supplied the rest.

By advocating the economic needs of self-supporting women in her response to Walsh, Anthony developed a feminist critique of the family wage and of the exclusion of women from the skilled trades. She freely admitted on the convention floor that because of the barriers that the union of male typographers had placed against the admission of women to the trades, she had encouraged self-supporting women to get training in any way possible, including strikebreaking. She said that she worked "for a class of women that had no husbands and who were on the streets penniless, homeless and without shelter. . . . The real fact of life is that these women have to support themselves."[99] Because of the intransigence of the typographers, their choice, she claimed, was to starve or accept training from the employers. She admitted that the trade unionists would not like what she did, but argued that she was serving a cause greater than their union.[100] Anthony then challenged the unions to say how many women they had admitted to the trade. In response, Walsh insisted that the union permitted only fellow members to work, but that the typographers had recently admitted two girls. Walsh defended the exclusive control of the membership by the trade union and challenged Anthony to explain why the *Revolution*, which she and Stanton edited, was printed in a nonunion shop. The crucial fact was, however, that Augusta Lewis and the female typographers supported the male trade unionists at the convention.

The debate in 1869 pitted trade union principles against a commitment to larger reform questions including Anthony's demand for a change in the sexual division of labor to benefit working women.[101] The NLU represented a coalition of reformers and trade unionists, and the issue proved deeply divisive. Initially Anthony was seated on a 55-52 vote, but as in 1868, the New York City trade unions threatened to walk out of the organization unless she was denied a seat. The expulsion of Anthony from the NLU in 1869 has seemed to historians an unequivocal severing of feminism from the national labor movement.[102] For Susan B. Anthony and other middle-class suffrage leaders, the choice between women's rights and trade union principles was not a difficult one to make. For women shoeworkers within the labor movement, it became a dilemma that they debated for years.

Almost unnoticed in the midst of the controversy over women's rights and trade unionism, the delegates from the Knights and Daughters of St. Crispin in Massachusetts supported Anthony on both votes to seat her at the convention. Martha Wallbridge of Stoneham, Second Grand Directeress of the DOSC, stated during the debate that the working women of Massachusetts wanted Susan Anthony seated at the convention and pointed out that there were many men participating as delegates who did not actually represent worker organizations. Samuel P. Cummings of the Massachusetts KOSC seconded her statement.[103] Wallbridge represented a constituency of self-supporting women in the DOSC for whom the meaning of equal rights for women was an open question. Although Elizabeth Cady Stanton castigated the "sycophancy of NLU women to the men of their class," in the *Revolution*'s report on the convention, the *American Workman* of Boston on August 28 pointed out that the New England delegates had been unanimous in their support of Anthony and that Martha Wallbridge could not receive enough praise "for her courage, her discretion, her warm espousal of Miss Anthony's cause" and for her work on the Committee on Female Labor.[104] Stanton had this article reprinted in the *Revolution* on September 2, which drew the attention of women's rights advocates in New York to the new organization of women shoeworkers.

Martha Wallbridge chaired the Committee on Female Labor at the 1869 convention, which supported an endorsement of equal pay for equal work and, significantly after the expulsion of Anthony, the opening of all "avenues of labor" to women equally. Even delegate Walsh of the New York typographers, who had earlier distinguished Wallbridge in contrast to Anthony as a "bone fide working woman," voted for the resolutions presented to the convention by the committee. However, after the 1869 convention the NLU *Workingman's Advocate* shifted its editorial policy to an antisuffrage, anti–women's rights position.[105] An editorial on "Woman's Place in the State" on December 11, 1869, by A. C. Cameron insisted that women were properly represented in the state by the male head of the family and that even unmarried women were represented by unmarried men "in passe [*sic*] if not in esse." In her column "To the Wives of Workingmen" on February 19, 1870, Mrs. M. Wynkoop advised her readers to hear no more of women's rights and concentrate on their duties as wives and mothers.

Despite this hostility to women's rights within the NLU, Martha Wallbridge as the newly elected leader of the DOSC demanded during the Cincinnati convention in August 1870 that the NLU again endorse equal pay, the opening of all trades to women, and the welcoming of women into "just competition" with men.[106] Mrs. E. O. G. Willard of the Chicago Working Women's Union, a supporter of woman suffrage, was elected the second vice president of the NLU in 1870 and 1871.[107] The efforts of Wallbridge in 1869 and 1870 formed a link with the activities in 1868 of the embattled and tarnished suffragists. Stanton and Anthony may have severed their connections with the NLU and trade unionism, but working women had just begun to debate seriously the meaning of suffrage and women's rights. In addition, the commitment to equal pay and equal access to work in the trades as well as the necessity of organizing working women was kept alive in the NLU and later in the Knights of Labor supported by the activity and the legacy of the DOSC.

The national DOSC organization, whose leaders came largely from New England and from the shoe cities in upper New York State, represented a diverse group of women industrial workers. The demand for skilled stitchers during the postwar years of prosperity meant relatively high wages for women. A significant portion of these young working women were mobile, moving from town to town as the seasons changed, looking for good places to work and board and the highest wages for stitching. The DOSC seemed to function as a collection of local lodges with little direction from the national leadership on day-to-day matters.[108] In February 1870, in an effort to centralize operations, Emma Lane and Martha Wallbridge appeared before the Massachusetts Committee on Labor asking for a charter on behalf of its 2,000 members and numerous lodges, despite a denial in 1869 by the legislature of a similar charter for the KOSC.[109] Both women argued for the incorporation of their organization to coordinate the activities and oversee the finances of the lodges, which they described as "centers of good influence" that provided working girls places to spend their evenings. The DOSC leaders saw the role of their lodges as much like that of the Woman's Union in Lynn: to assist newcomers in finding work and to give them a place to spend their leisure time. Wallbridge emphasized that music and discussions attracted young women to the lodge meetings and that charity in time of need was also provided. She pointed out the special advantages of the chain of lodges for "girls going from one place to another." This chain of lodges was also an effective method of spreading the word about the DOSC to stitchers in other shoe towns. Wallbridge denied that the DOSC had ever refused to teach other women their trade, a charge that had been used in 1869 to defeat the KOSC petition. Emma Lane explained that although the local lodges did not have a set scale of prices for work, DOSC members refused to replace their sisters who had been fired over a wage question.[110] However, after the hearing, the Committee on Labor took no action, and the DOSC petition was withdrawn in May.

The unanimity of the testimony of Emma Lane and Martha Wallbridge belied a developing conflict among the national leaders of the DOSC over the question of suffrage and its relevance to working women's interests. Emma Lane, the wife of a Lynn Crispin, had served as a field nurse during the Civil War, and had apparently worked for a few years in the shoe factories. She was a strong supporter of the Labor Reform party in Massachusetts.[111] Her energetic activity at the founding convention of the DOSC in Lynn had encouraged the delegates to select her as their first national leader. Lane's opposition to suffrage represented the position of women shoeworkers who resided in local families and who believed that their political interests were adequately represented by the activism of their male relatives in the Crispin movement. Her strong opposition to woman suffrage in 1869 and 1870 probably cost her reelection at the DOSC convention in April 1870, where the Stoneham and New York State delegates demonstrated their growing influence. Martha Wallbridge represented those women active in the DOSC who were self-supporting as single or widowed women and who often supported dependent relatives on their wages. These self-supporting women viewed suffrage as a potentially useful right of working women who were otherwise unattached to Crispinism through their families. Their status as single, self-supporting women seemed to shape their interest in individual political rights.

Wallbridge replaced Lane as the first officer of the DOSC in 1870. She was drawing closer to the position of Jennie Collins, who openly endorsed woman suffrage in early 1870 as vital to the interests of working women. However, as Wallbridge drew closer to Collins's position, Emma Lane, who remained a national officer of the DOSC, denounced suffrage and claimed to speak for the organization's membership.[112] She announced plans for a weekly journal for working women called *Work and Wages* to be published in Boston, reputedly with an antisuffrage mission. When the journal failed to materialize, she took herself to Washington, D.C., where she sought an interview with the president on behalf of the DOSC and the working women of Massachusetts.[113] Lane appeared at rallies for the DOSC and the KOSC in 1870, but the relationship between these activities and the rest of the national DOSC leadership remains unclear.

The second convention of the DOSC at Stoneham produced an

uneasy truce over women's rights. While Wallbridge succeeded Lane, most of the women elected at the founding convention continued in office: Nancy Whitmore of Rochester, Carrie Wilson of Lynn, and Frances Jones of Stoneham. They, like Wallbridge, were self-supporting workers. Among the resolutions adopted were demands for equal pay with the tiny number of male stitchers employed in the industry. Another resolution condemned the practice of one stitcher making a commission from the wages of another stitcher whom she had recruited, a practice in shops outside New England. The issue of women's rights was smoothed over with a conservative resolution to the taste of Emma Lane and others who agreed with her. The DOSC delegates voted to reassure "our fellow-citizens that we only desire to so elevate and improve our condition as to better fit us for the discharge of those high social and moral duties which devolve upon every true woman." [114]

Despite this truce, the issue of suffrage continued to divide the DOSC in 1870 and 1871. In March 1870 the *Revolution* published part of a private letter from Jennie Collins to Susan B. Anthony that argued that factory girls in Massachusetts understood the potential power of the ballot and that anyone who denied this simply did not understand the position of working women. In a letter to the editor of the *Boston Post* on April 19, 1870, just after she had been replaced as Grand Directeress by Wallbridge, Emma Lane insisted that the DOSC members did not want the ballot. She wrote that she had put the question to a majority of the DOSC lodges, and only one member in 150 wanted the right to vote. Lane stated further that she knew that among the New York unions of cap-makers, umbrella and parasol-makers, and typographers, none wished the ballot. As head of the DOSC, she had attended a meeting at the Cooper Institute in New York City on March 10, 1870, where the Working Women's Labor Union for the State of New York was organized. Mrs. Daniels of the Boston Working Women's Association introduced the suffrage question at the meeting and after some debate was, according to Lane's recollection, ruled out of order. We speak, Lane wrote to the *Post* in April, as "bone fide" working women who support the labor reform movement and identify the interests of working women with working men. In a parting shot, she criticized the "estimable ladies" who tried to speak for working women on suffrage and advised them to go home and earn the love and respect of their male relatives.[115] In her response, also published in the *Post*, Jennie Collins dismissed both Emma Lane and her arguments as unimportant to the cause of working women.[116] The long debate within the DOSC over women's rights was not, despite what Emma Lane believed, carried on between middle-class suffragists and working women, but among working women themselves.

These divisions within the DOSC in 1870 may have made it difficult for the organization to respond effectively to a series of sensational public revelations made in Lynn in early 1871 under the auspices of labor reform concerning immorality in the city's shoe factories. An ambitious young Congregational minister, Joseph Cook, who by 1871 had been in Lynn for less than a year, took upon himself the role of moral conscience for the churches of Lynn on the question of labor reform.[117] For Cook, industrialization meant the presence in Lynn of an undisciplined army of workers, augmented by the ebb and flow of the floating population that arrived seasonally to work in the shops. The implications for immoral behavior and threats to social order were explosive and imminent. For the manufacturing interests, the clergy, the local press, and the Woman's Union, the problems of morality lay in the anonymity of the boardinghouse and the dangers that lurked on the streets of Lynn. As Cook began his immensely popular lecture series from the platform of the newly built Music Hall on January 22, 1871, he made a crucial shift in the focus of concern about the sources of immorality in Lynn. For Cook, the real danger lay not in the streets or boardinghouses, but squarely within the power of the manufacturers themselves: in the work arrangements of the shoe factories. As Cook put it mawkishly in his first lecture: "The irregulated boarding-house and the street school may strip the flesh from the peach, but the down of the peach was brushed away in the workrooms."[118]

Cook's most sensational charge, which dominated the controversy over his lectures in 1871, was an attack on the moral character of the women who boarded in Lynn and worked in the factories. He questioned the morality of both male and female members of the floating population, but the examples he used in his first lecture suggested an obsession with the moral dangers of the homeless female. Cook's criticism focused on the practice of employing both male and female workers in the same workrooms. In 1871 those rooms would have included work done by stitchers, lasters, and packers, but Cook explicitly cited a workroom that combined cutting and stitching operations and implicitly referred to rooms in which five women worked, probably as lasters, beside larger numbers of men. Cook directed public attention to the changes that the large manufacturers were making in the customary division of labor.

The danger for Cook lay in the uncertain morality of the floating population employed in these rooms and in the unknown character of their overseers. Cook stated that he had visited one workroom in Lynn where he personally witnessed the moral dangers of mixing the sexes, which he characterized as the "foul system." This workroom contained, as he described it, six or eight girls and as many men. The girls were "coarse, low, vulgar and bad-featured" and, according to the man who showed him the room, no virtuous young man could work there for any length of time without facing moral ruin, "because the girls were so bad."[119] Cook's prescription for this danger lay in the total separation of the sexes in the factories and in certifying the moral character of overseers. In contrast with the manufacturing interests who had developed an image of the lady stitcher who was welcome in Lynn if in need of protection and moral guidance, Cook's images of the female floating population included "foul mouths" and "repulsive boldness."[120] The tensions implicit in social and economic change in the community were projected by him onto the character of the transient working female.[121]

Cook's analysis and recommendations offered no basis for a resolution of shoeworkers' grievances; their chief complaint in 1871 was overwork and low earnings during the intensive work seasons. The Crispin newspaper, the *Little Giant*, applauded his attack on the large manufacturers, but did not regard him as a spokesman for labor interests. For Cook, the working class had a right only to demand a moral environment in the workrooms of the factories. The attitudes of the male shoeworkers in Lynn toward his charge of immorality in the shops were ambiguous. The *Little Giant*, referring to the controversy as "that unhappy affair," regretted Cook's charges about any specific workroom, as the workers in question, male and female, had good moral reputations.[122] The shoeworkers of Lynn could not, however, overlook the implications of the introduction of women and machinery into traditionally male work processes nor ignore the power of the manufacturers to make those changes.

Immediately after the first lecture, the largest manufacturers sought to discredit Cook. L. B. Frazier and Samuel Bubier pressured him to admit that the room to which he referred was operated by the firm of Berry and Beede in Bubier's own New Block on Oxford Street. The fourteen operatives in the workroom, both stitchers and cutters, issued a statement denouncing Cook as unjust and un-Christian. They invited the public to scrutinize their characters, asserting that their only flaw was that they had to work for a living. Among the stitchers were two residents of Lynn: Lydia D. Bates, a twenty-two-year-old single woman who supported her widowed mother, and Katie A. Farrell, the young daughter of an Irish morocco dresser and the oldest child in a household of eight that included two boarders. The pastor of St. Mary's Church, Patrick Strain, angrily defended the girl, who must have been one of his parishioners. "Soulless must be the man," he wrote to the *Lynn Reporter*, who attacked poor, honest, industrious, defenseless girls who toiled to earn an honest living for their parents, their little brothers, and themselves.[123] Cook offered no apology for his statements and reiterated his charges at subsequent lectures.

The manufacturers led by George W. Keene counterattacked in a series of lectures sponsored by the board of trade during which they defended not only the virtues of the women shoeworkers of Lynn, but their policy of altering the sexual division of labor in the factories. Keene recalled that in the 1850s the shoe bosses had seriously considered the moral implications of introducing women into the central shops to run sewing machines. However, that experience had proved a great success, and the proof was in the example of many of the early stitchers who were honored wives and mothers in Lynn. New divisions of labor, he argued, would open further opportunities for women while maintaining moral order. "With the favorable experience had in the employment of female help thus far, the manufacturers believed that many parts could be as well performed by women as by men; and wherever the circumstances are favorable, they invariably improve the condition of things around them. . . . Women are employed wherever their labor can be available, and in a large majority of factories, where they are at work with men, better order and decorum is manifest."[124] A public scandal prompted by the statements of a clergyman might convince the citizens of neighboring towns and cities that Lynn factories represented a moral danger to their daughters and their sons. Keene was obviously concerned over the impact of the Cook controversy on the recruitment of stitchers for the busy season. Speaking for the manufacturers, Keene defended the morality and character of the shopwomen of Lynn, describing them as native-born Americans who came from "good, honest Christian homes." Returning to the image of the lady stitcher, Keene invited the public to consider the behavior of the crowds that visited the fair of the Grand Army of the Republic held at the Music Hall in March 1871. Thousands of men and women intermingled during the fair's activities with no hint of impropriety and "the ladies in these gatherings were largely composed of our Lynn shopgirls."[125]

The Daughters of St. Crispin remained silent throughout the controversy. The women workers to whom Cook had alluded in his first lecture identified and defended themselves. Central Lodge #1 issued no public statement. For an organization founded to resist wage cuts by their employers, the manufacturers' defense of the morality of the female shoeworkers of Lynn as a device to break down the sexual division of labor in the factories placed the DOSC in the difficult position of having their adversaries as champions. But this public silence also reflected the peculiar situation of wage-earning women in nineteenth-century America. As Sarah Eisenstein has argued, working women were acutely sensitive to the issue of moral respectability in a Victorian society that seemed to deny propriety to wage-earning women.[126] The Woman's Union for Christian Work provided a stamp of middle-class moral approval for stitchers who boarded and worked in Lynn factories during the busy seasons. Their work retained a certain gentility as light, skilled, and relatively well paid, and the majority of female workers were native-born New Englanders; yet even the appearance of impropriety prompted fear and silence. But not for long: by September the women stitchers of Lynn had themselves appropriated the issue of morality. They used it successfully to defend their interests in a dispute with their employers over the introduction of dishonorable discharges, which cast doubt on their moral respectability and represented new attempts to control their work and cut their wages.

During the summer of 1871 the largest manufacturers in Lynn, recognizing that the Cook controversy had strengthened the sexual division of labor in the industry, abandoned their attempts to replace men with women and sought to cut labor costs through wage reductions. This decision appeared in a *Shoe and Leather Reporter* editorial that accepted the employment of male and female shoeworkers in the same building but in separate rooms as the best arrangement to preserve the morality and propriety of the people of New England and avoid "an indiscriminate mixing of the sexes." [127] The policy of wage cuts began in August 1871, initiated by the stitching subcontractors. Crispin men and women joined forces to resist these cuts.

During the busy season for the fall trade, the bosses of the subcontract shops formed an association that they called the Boot and Shoe Stitchers' Union of Lynn and Vicinity. The purpose was to prevent stitchers from moving about from shop to shop in search of better wages and conditions. The high turnover rate and free movement of stitchers, especially during the busy season, jeopardized the bosses' subcontracts with the manufacturers and created disorder, forcing them to obtain additional workers by raising wages.[128] The association also organized a committee of five to prepare a list of standard wages to end competition for labor among the subcontracting shops. The bosses concealed their intention to cut wages in a proposal to "equalize" wages among the stitchers, a change that would penalize women workers with experience and skill. One stitcher who wrote to the *Lynn Reporter* during the dispute pointed out the difference between those stitchers with a commitment to their work and the temporary operatives and compared the skilled female worker—the good workwoman—with the master workman and mechanic.

> I am a fancy stitcher; I have worked a number of years at this part of the business, trying to perfect myself as a good workwoman. Are my service of no more value to my employer than Sarah B- a young miss of fourteen who has just commenced her labors, or of Nellie C- who may have worked a year or two for pay with no interest in her work to perfect herself or no interest for her employer, only

carelessly indifferent as to whether she can do a fine job or not? Are the services of the master workman on yonder stately pile of no more value than those of the humble hod-carrier. . . ? If so, then of what use will it be for mechanics to attempt to excel in the craft? [129]

The bosses' association also insisted that all operatives give a week's notice to their employers before leaving, a notice to be guaranteed by a deposit of five dollars or the stitcher would face a "dishonorable discharge." The stitcher quoted above dismissed giving a week's notice as "absurd!" and argued that the best stitchers would "always be found where they are best appreciated." The bosses, she wrote, had "roused the lion" and could little imagine the strength they would find in opposition to their plan to be "masters of the situation." "We will not submit to being crowded; we will not be enslaved. We are free-born American women; and when they attempt to tell us what they will do, we will rise in our might, and three thousand voices will tell them what we will do!" [130] In the context of the Cook controversy and the heightened sensitivities of women workers to any charge reflecting on their morality, honor, or character, the stitchers, "feeling insulted," rebelled and went out on strike.[131] They called on the equal rights tradition of the New England labor movement as their justification.

The equal rights tradition provided an ambiguous heritage for women shoeworkers. Originally based on the moral and material rights of artisan householders who demanded the full fruits of popular sovereignty, equal rights required new meanings to serve the interests of post–Civil War industrial workers. Crispin men had used equal rights to resist the pressures of supply and demand on wages and the rigors of the busy season on factory workers. In 1871 the threat to the rights of good workwomen meant an attempt to deprive them of their freedom of movement and tie them to one employer. The shoe bosses attempted to fix wages and penalize experienced workers. They also tried to intimidate transient women workers by associating freedom of movement with impropriety and dishonor. The rebellious stitchers of Lynn acted to extend the equal rights tradition to defend their wages, their morality, and their mobility.

The stitchers who worked in the subcontract shops but had not joined the DOSC began to organize protest meetings against the actions of the bosses' association in late August. They called themselves the Workingwomen of Lynn, Known as Upper Fitters and Finishers of Boots and Shoes. A large meeting of about a thousand stitchers was held on August 31, where the angry women listened to addresses by DOSC leaders including Emma Lane and adopted a preamble and a series of resolutions. The operatives blamed one particular stitching shop for instigating the bosses' association. They knew that no stitcher would work for him if she could get a place anywhere else, because of the low wages he paid. As a result, this shop was always in trouble during the busy season. The stitchers agreed to resist the "obnoxious rules" and expose the bosses' organization as a conspiracy to cut their wages. They rejected the new regulations, which they regarded as an attempt to enslave, degrade, and deprive them of their rights as "free born women."[132]

Both the DOSC and the KOSC in Lynn rallied to the aid of the new working women's organization and made efforts to incorporate it into the Crispin movement. The KOSC lodges condemned the actions of the stitching bosses and congratulated the stitchers for resisting the "humiliating and degrading rules." While the Crispins asserted their belief in "wholesome moral regulations to be observed in the workshops of the city," they rejected any move by an employer to categorize "any employee's moral character after leaving his employment."[133] At a meeting of the DOSC in November after the strike had been won, a satire on the events and the bosses' "honorable discharge" drew a portrait of the luckless stitcher who might qualify for such an honor: "Annie Blank—a good girl. When you get her, keep her. She hath been in our employment so long a time. All kinds of abuses and deceit have been heaped upon her; thrice has she been discharged; in perils of steam, in dull times often; . . . in weariness often; in hunger, thirst and debts, hath she stuck by me. I therefore recommend her to you. Greet her in our name, and make her as profitable to you as she has been to me; and great will be your recompense."[134] Faced with the unity of the KOSC, the DOSC, and hundreds of striking stitchers, the bosses' association abandoned its new rules and its organization, and the stitchers won the strike. The ambivalence of the shoeworkers of Lynn over the Cook controversy had been resolved with their appropriation of the issue of morality in the shoe factories and the use of equal rights arguments to defend the moral and economic rights of factory workers. The stitchers would work in a shop as long as they were satisfied with the wages and the work and when they were not, they would leave without penalty. No stitcher would be disgraced by a certificate that was "beneath their dignity and degrading in every respect."[135] They had faced down their employers, not as lady stitchers but as freeborn women.

On September 21 a group called the Working Women's Associates met in Lynn to demonstrate their appreciation for the work Emma Lane had done on their behalf during the recent strike and for her advocacy of labor reform. The members of the organization appealed to the workingmen of the city to grant her some salaried office or position to repay her for her efforts on behalf of Massachusetts workers. The notice of this meeting appeared in the September 23, 1871, issue of the *Little Giant* and produced much comment, which underscored the divisions that the DOSC faced among women shoeworkers. Appreciation of Emma Lane's efforts for labor reform was not universal in Lynn. Lane's activities during the municipal elections in late 1870 had antagonized some and resulted in criticism from shoemakers that her husband worked for wages below the Crispin scale and that despite her opposition to woman suffrage, she was telling men how to vote. Critics writing to the *Little Giant* questioned the authenticity of the Working Women's Associates as a representative of stitchers in Lynn, denying that it had any connection with the DOSC members, "who have by no means taken leave of their senses." One writer asserted that the new organization was the work of Emma Lane's own "self-aggrandizement."[136] These letters particularly ridiculed the idea that the workingmen of Lynn should elect Emma Lane to any office in view of her opposition to woman suffrage and her opinion that woman's place was at home.

In response to this criticism, "Kate," who identified herself as a member of the Working Women's Associates, stated that many of the members supported woman suffrage despite Emma Lane's views, but they saw it as a secondary issue for working women.[137] She defended Lane's ambitions for public office as consistent with the activities of other antisuffrage women who had served on the Sanitary Commission during the war or who held offices in charitable societies or worked as postmistresses and clerks in the federal bureaucracy. Kate suggested without irony that the votes of workingmen could put Emma Lane on the school committee, an opportunity for women in Lynn that Lane herself had publicly opposed. Nothing more was heard of the Working Women's Associates in Lynn, and little new of the activities of Emma Lane. In January 1872 the DOSC heard a lecture by Mrs. Willard, the pro-suffrage second vice president of the NLU, followed the next week by Emma Lane, who denounced the suffrage movement's association with Victoria Woodhull and free love advocates.[138] Although the Working Women's Association did not survive, Emma Lane continued to have a loyal following who elected her president of the DOSC local in 1872. This debate between Lane and the supporters of suffrage in 1871 and 1872 demonstrated that although their immediate interests lay in organization and the protection of their wages, the DOSC and the Working Women's Association included many working women who supported woman suffrage and women's rights during the post–Civil War years.

In early 1872 the Massachusetts Bureau of Labor Statistics tallied the wages of nearly 2,000 women workers in the shoe industry, 80 percent of whom worked in Lynn and Haverhill and another 15 percent in Stoneham. The average weekly wage earned by these women was $10.38 for thirty-four weeks of work during the two busy seasons.[139] From these earnings of $352.92 a year came an average payment for board of $4.50 a week or $153, leaving an annual income of about $200. Stitching shoes in Massachusetts was slightly less remunerative than working in a printing shop, but only because the printing trade operated ten more weeks per year. The average pay for female typesetters per week in the first-class printing shops of Boston and Cambridge was $8.33, two dollars less per week than stitchers earned. The report concluded that printing work offered better pay to women because of the more regular employment, but both trades represented the highest paid industrial work available to women in Massachusetts in the early 1870s.

Efforts by manufacturers to reduce those high wages for stitching intensified in Essex County in 1871 and 1872. In Danvers the introduction of steam power by one manufacturer was accompanied by wage cuts for stitchers. Aided by a strong KOSC in town, fifty women went out on strike, joined the Crispin movement, and won a settlement. In Stoneham 300 members of the DOSC lodge struck for higher wages after a wage cut at the three largest factories in town. They stayed out for two weeks, but were replaced by new recruits. Lacking the strong support of the KOSC men because of a local dispute, they lost the strike. All but two strike leaders returned to the factories at reduced wages.[140] Attempts to cut wages for Lynn stitchers intensified with the defeat in the summer of 1872 of the KOSC citywide agreement on wages.

After the conclusion of the busy season in the late spring of 1872, some of the large manufacturers in Lynn introduced the new Hodge's trimming and edge-setting machine, subdivided the work, and cut wages for trimming and edging by one-half cent per pair. They announced the change after the unsuspecting Crispins had voted in early July to resubmit their list of wages unaltered for the third time to the annual negotiations with their employers. The KOSC did not oppose the new machinery, but feared that the cut on trimming and edging without consulting the Crispin board of arbitration was the beginning of a general attack on the level of shoeworkers' wages. Stitchers' wages were also cut by ten cents a case. In the absence of George Keene, who had retired and turned his factory over to his sons, thirty-five of the largest manufacturers, led by Samuel Bubier and backed by the Keene brothers, ended arbitration with the Crispins. They allowed the price list, which had governed wages for men in Lynn for two years, to expire on July 10 without renewal and claimed that since Crispins worked below the price list at some shops, the whole citywide agreement was unfair competition for the majority. These manufacturers with large investments in real estate and factories in Lynn refused either to move to the country or to abide by local arbitration. Their economic advantage lay in national competition, and their control of labor costs was a crucial element in signing up and delivering on advance orders. A strike by the KOSC began on July 26 to prevent a collapse of wages in Lynn, but it lasted only about a month before its defeat. The manufacturers refused to negotiate, and during the strike, the large manufacturers put together an agreement by the majority of factory owners to refuse to hire anyone calling himself a Crispin.[141]

With the defeat of the strike in late August, the coalition with the small manufacturers that the Crispin organization had used to maintain wages for two years fell into disarray. In 1872 the large manufacturers were intent on a strategy of introducing new machinery to reduce labor costs and of producing shoes only for advance orders in order to control costs in Lynn and compete advantageously in the national market. One manufacturer who had relocated to a town in southern Maine remarked to the editor of the *Reporter* that after the defeat of the Crispins, shoes were being made as cheaply in Lynn as down East.[142] Although some Crispins had begun to recognize and advocate a strategy of confrontation with the manufacturers every year just as the advance orders arrived, the shoe market was undermined by the depression of 1873.[143] But long before the panic created by the collapse of Jay Gould and Company of New York City in the fall of 1873, the shoe factories of Lynn had succeeded in cutting wages 20 to 30 percent across the board.[144] There were hard times for shoeworkers in 1872 and early 1873 and worse to come in the long depression of the 1870s.

Vast changes in the work process, experiments with the sexual division of labor, the maturation of the factory system, and the unbalanced sex ratio in the population, especially in the crucial marriage years, created confusion in expectations about work, class, and gender for shoeworkers and produced shifting images of the stitchers of Essex County after the Civil War. Observers of the industry saw women factory workers in a variety of postures: the girl laster with her mouth full of tacks who was transformed into a lady as she left the factory at night; the common machine girl who took music lessons; the confused, homesick country girl; the desperate, deserted wife; the coarse-featured, foul-mouthed moral menace; the pleasing, teasing stitching girl; the working girl in her silk dress striking poses in a theatrical moment; the young Irish Catholic girl trudging to work; the boarding stitcher who supported her widowed mother; the work woman of skill and experience; and the freeborn American who protested injustice.

The reality behind these images lay in the majority of young, single, native-born women largely of New England background who worked in the shoe factories of Essex County, many for their own support or for the support of other family members in an industry that paid high wages to female factory workers. One-third of them had left their homes to seek work, thereby postponing marriage, which because of Civil War losses and westward migration was becoming problematical for them. They, like the Lowell mill girls of a previous generation, were not a permanent industrial work force; but the social and economic circumstances of the 1860s and 1870s meant that many of them could no longer afford to regard wage-earning as only a brief period in their lives before marriage. The stitchers of Essex County were aware of the diverse nature of the female work force in shoe production. Those who were skilled, well paid, experienced, and committed to their work could afford to regard their gender as a positive attribute, whether as lady stitchers or as freeborn women. They utilized the equal rights tradition of New England shoemaking to defend their moral respectability, to justify their labor protest, and as a basis from which to debate the meaning of political rights for working women.

The Daughters of St. Crispin tried to represent this diverse group of women workers in the rapidly changing shoe industry during the years of postwar prosperity. The local lodges coordinated by the national leadership served both resident stitchers and young women of the floating population who traveled from town to town caught up in the shifting opportunities presented to them by the busy seasons in the shoe cities. These patterns of seasonal work and geographical mobility explain in part why the DOSC was the first national union organized for women. As working women, they rejected the protection and solutions offered by middle-class sympathizers and organized successful resistance to their employers. Conflicts within the DOSC reflected the postwar political debate within the female community of New England and New York over women's rights and over the relevance of suffrage to the interests of working women. Reaching out to women in other industries, they shared their grievances and experiences at the NLU and working women's conventions. Together they championed the movement of women into the industrial labor force on terms of equality with men.

CHAPTER SEVEN

Hard Times and Equal Rights
1873–80

Our brother workmen can organize, and redress their
wrongs; but for us there is no hope, and the bosses
know it just as well as we; so they snap their fingers at
us, and as each returning season comes round, they give
us an extra cut down in lieu of cutting down the men,
knowing full well there are plenty of married women,
with well-to-do husbands, and half supported girls who
stand ready to work the few short weeks in which work
is given out, at any price they can get.

—"A Stitcher,"
Lynn Record, February 1, 1879

During the long depression of the 1870s, the shoeworkers of Essex
County fought to maintain Crispinism as a defense of their wages
and their rights, while they debated the meaning of the equal
rights tradition. The Knights used equal rights arguments to try
to meet the ideological challenge of supply and demand as a justification for low wages. The Daughters of St. Crispin also used
the equal rights tradition to defend their interests, but disagree-
ments among women workers over the meaning of equal rights for
women divided and weakened their organization and their ability
to face their employers as a unified group. Crispin institutions and
ideology faced powerful and ultimately fatal opposition during the
depression years.

The hard times of the 1870s began early in Lynn. Despite the
success of the manufacturers in breaking the Crispin wage scale in
1872 and the subsequent decline in labor costs, the spring trade in
1873 was sluggish. After orders failed to materialize in January, the
salesmen for the large manufacturers were sent back on the road,
but returned to Lynn in mid-March with few additional orders.
During the late winter and early spring, requests for assistance from

the City Mission came in heavily from the unemployed and from those who depended on boarders for their livelihoods. One poor woman asked the mission for a little coal, as she was unable to obtain boarders because of the long delay in starting up the season. Once begun, the spring season shut down unusually early in 1873, and everyone hoped for better business in the fall. Shoe manufacturers wrote off the dull spring trade to poor business conditions caused by the disastrous fires in Chicago and in the Boston leather district, by an equine disease that ravaged the horse population, and by severe winter weather.[1] The care that the larger Lynn manufacturers had taken not to begin production in early 1873 before they had orders in their hands and had checked the credit of their buyers seemed a prudent policy in uncertain times. However, this cautious policy, which depended on the postwar factory system of swift production by steam-powered machinery in a short period of time, brought the depression to the shoeworkers of Lynn six months before the financial panic in September.

In October with the fall trade a disappointment and the financial community in disarray from the panic, Lynn manufacturers grew even more cautious and conservative. This deflation proved worse for the shoe industry in Essex County than those of 1857 or 1861. As the end of 1873 approached, it seemed even more vital "that demand should be the precursor of supply," a policy that the shoe industry followed as long as possible.[2] In 1873 at least twenty-five manufacturers in Lynn closed their doors, victims of the depression and, in the words of the sorrowful editor of the *Lynn Reporter*, of the laws of nature that decreed the eating of little fish by big ones.[3] With production geared to the limited number of orders received, unemployment grew and wages continued to fall. The Lynn manufacturers, seeking to supply whatever retail trade remained, changed their styles to plain, utilitarian shoes with no fancy stitching. Demand failed to pick up in 1874 or 1875.

Desperate to locate customers for Lynn shoes, the manufacturers began in the 1870s to explore the Latin-American market where British and Continental firms were well established. It was impossible, however, to sell shoes with uppers of wool serge for wear in the South American climate. By 1877, manufacturers in Lynn and Haverhill were making small lots of all-leather ladies' shoes and boots of fine morocco and kidskin with thin, beveled soles and high, concave French heels to sell in Brazil.[4] Although this market failed to develop for Essex County factories and rich Brazilian women continued to purchase $20 French shoes, the shift to all-leather styles was a harbinger of postdepression production in the 1880s.

Unemployment and downward pressure on wages created widespread discontent among Lynn shoeworkers in 1873 and 1874. The head of the City Mission, W. F. Mitchell, reported misery, degradation, and want in Lynn at the organization's first annual meeting in October 1873. He called on the community to provide any kind of manual labor for unemployed men and housework and plain sewing for women. He also urged the mayor to support a new city ordinance to create jobs for the unemployed, shoveling snow from the city's streets.[5] Working women pawned their sewing machines for food. Stitchers who found themselves stranded in Lynn without money for train fare to get home had to appeal to the City Mission for charity. The mission, funded by private donations and the churches, ultimately ran out of money and closed down in 1877. The Woman's Union for Christian Work, which had functioned as a recruiting agency as well as a protecting shelter for women workers, reversed its policy during the depression years. The superintendent of the Market Street reading room, Miss Abbie M. Bowen, advised young women who had come to Lynn looking for work to return to their parents. Unemployed residents were offered domestic work. Indifference and disillusion had eroded the membership of the organization. Oblivious to the desperation of unemployed women who sought work in Lynn factories, Bowen urged the mothers of Maine and New Hampshire to make their homes so attractive that their daughters would stay there and not come to Lynn until they were old enough to take care of themselves.[6] While hard times persisted, the Woman's Union urged women workers to return to their hometowns and tell others not to come to Lynn.

Shoeworkers found themselves at the mercy of the forces of supply and demand in a severe depression in the local labor market and the national wholesale market for boots and shoes. With the KOSC in shambles after its defeat in 1872 and the DOSC barely alive in Lynn, shoeworkers bore the wage cuts and poor seasons of 1873 and 1874, but not without widespread dissatisfaction. The Lynn manufacturers, having weathered several disastrous seasons in an attempt to cling to their policy of producing shoes only for advance orders, finally broke ranks in the summer of 1874. Factory owners, desperate for orders, underbid each other's prices. Buyers, eager to shave five percent or less from an agreed-on price, countermanded orders already in production. Cutthroat competition and chaos seized the industry and drove wages down further. Even the *Lynn Reporter*, the perennial champion of the manufacturing interests, now spoke for the smaller factories, local retailers, and real-estate interests and decried "unfair competition" as suicidal for Lynn.[7] The rigors of supply and demand were tearing the city apart. In this atmosphere of community anguish, Crispinism slowly revived in 1875 and 1876 as a defensive barrier against the worst that the depression could bring.

In an effort to meet the competitive pressures, Keene Brothers, the sons of George W. Keene who died in 1874, cut their lasters' wages in half in January 1875. The Crispin lasters decided they could stand no more and struck the Keene brothers' factory just as their precious orders began to be filled. A mass meeting of Crispins on January 26 denounced the "injurious competition" between local manufacturers over labor costs and invited them to arbitrate a general level of wages that would prevent any further reductions and guarantee that whatever orders were in the hands of the manufacturers would be filled. By striking just as new orders arrived, Lynn shoeworkers were learning to play the supply and demand game in the interests of equal rights. Faced with an overabundant supply of labor in a depression, they took advantage of the manufacturers' desperate desire for business. As one shoeworker had put it earlier: "The time has come that the keen, intelligent mechanic has been looking for. The most of the orders received must be filled in a specific time. When this is not complied with, the orders are frequently countermanded, resulting in serious losses to the manufacturer. Therefore time is money and delay is dangerous."[8]

Between 1875 and 1878 the Crispin board of arbitration used negotiations to prevent further wage cuts and to settle strikes well timed to catch the manufacturers with fresh orders. The board appointed committees of shoeworkers to arbitrate prices and prepare wage lists agreeable to both bosses and workers. If the first committee failed to arrange a settlement, a second committee carried the authority of binding arbitration. As long as these pro-

cedures prevented cutthroat competition in Lynn and guaranteed
the orderly processing of whatever business the sluggish economy
called for, arbitration seemed beneficial to the community.[9] Large
manufacturers immediately insisted, however, that local cooperation to stabilize wages placed them at a disadvantage in the national
market. Supply and demand, one shoe boss argued, simply had to
be endured by all, for any attempts to avoid the immutable laws of
the market would be useless and incompatible with free trade and
property rights.[10] Still, small manufacturers, retailers, real-estate
interests, and shoeworkers joined together during the depression
years to use arbitration, as they had in the early 1870s, to stabilize both profits and wages and protect property values in the
community.

In response to the actions of the KOSC to prevent further wage
cuts in 1875 and 1876 through its policy of arbitration, shoe manufacturers tightened their control of the work process. In Haverhill the five-man team headed by a laster made up the prepared
upper stock that they received from the cutters and stitchers. The
team members customarily received their wages once the cases had
passed through the lasting process and on to the finishers. By 1877,
foremen directed the teams in Haverhill, and wages were paid only
after the shoes were finished and ready for packing.[11] A year earlier, the P. P. Sherry Company had broken the custom in Lynn of
paying each worker after the shoes had passed through his or her
hands. The new policy stipulated that shoeworkers be paid only
after the work arrived at the packing room, forcing stock fitters
(who prepared the sole leather for lasting) as well as the lasters and
McKay stitchers to wait over a week to be paid from the time the
work left their hands.[12]

Haverhill shoeworkers continued to work as teams, while manufacturers in Lynn began to abolish teamwork in 1878. The *Vindicator*, a new Crispin newspaper edited by Benjamin B. Scully, a
longtime member of the KOSC and a former editor of the *Record*,
analyzed the two systems in relation to the overall decline in wages
in the 1870s. The string teams of Lynn no longer organized themselves as groups. The employer hired each member individually,
and foremen assigned each worker to his group. This broke up
the team as a cooperative, self-determined entity. The hiring of
individuals rather than units facilitated further divisions of labor

and the application of machinery. All lasters were grouped into a separate department with a quota of eighty to ninety pairs a day. In Haverhill, team workers including lasters held to their customary stint of forty-two pairs a day. Lynn's reorganized system could produce only medium-grade shoes because the lengthy delays between processes that worked the stock allowed the leather to dry out, making it less pliable and more easily damaged. Teams of Haverhill shoeworkers finished up specific pairs of shoes over a shorter period of time. These finer grades sold for higher prices; and the Haverhill manufacturers also made slippers, which had a less definite season of production. Scully concluded that the Haverhill shoeworker had kept more direct contact as a team member with his employer, while enjoying more regular work in a customary environment, and more self-reliance and manly independence.[13] Despite these work arrangements, which to Scully more closely reflected the values of the equal rights tradition, wages in Haverhill were lower than in Lynn. High-priced shoes did not sell well during the depression, and the shoeworkers of Haverhill also competed with country shoemakers in a well-developed system of decentralized hand production on turned shoes and slippers that Haverhill bosses had operated for decades in the towns of northern Essex County and southern New Hampshire. This system of handwork continued until the mechanization of the turned shoe process in the 1880s.

Stitchers' wages had also been cut repeatedly after 1873 as the national market for shoes declined and manufacturers abandoned styles with fancy stitching. The adoption of a folding machine for upper pieces and a mechanism for pasting linings replaced handwork and led to reductions in piece rates. Manufacturers also substituted cheap, brittle cotton thread for the expensive but strong silk thread for topstitching the vamps of button boots, a change that made stitching more difficult because of thread breakage and produced a less durable shoe upper. By 1876, stitching room operations had been subdivided into thirty-one different jobs on various pieces of the upper.[14] Aside from the stitching machine, mechanization was still minimal, but these divisions of work suggested to the inventive mind how the various buttonhole and button-sewing operations might be mechanized. The large Swiss shoe manufacturer Bally visited Stoneham in 1877 to examine shoe machinery and its impact on productivity. Bally complained that his own shoemakers often interrupted their work for weddings and festivals and expressed his admiration of the efficiency and industrial discipline of American methods. He praised the way stitching machines were arranged for sewing uppers so that the pedal and the feed were coordinated. The thread was cut at the moment that the operator's foot lifted from the pedal and the right hand removed the finished upper. When the left hand reached for and positioned the next, the foot depressed the pedal and the sewing appeared to be continuous at a rate of 800 stitches per minute.[15] In early 1876 the Lynn manufacturers readied more wage cuts for stitchers.

While the KOSC board of arbitration prevented new wage cuts and negotiated an end to Crispin strikes at eight large factories in early 1876, the stitchers went out on strike at two shops on Union Street near Market. Encouraged by leaders of the KOSC locals to revive the DOSC in Lynn, 200 women met at the Knights' hall on January 11 and listened to B. B. Scully urge them to form a protective association to defend their wages. On January 18 ten stitchers who worked for Amos Fawcett walked out in sympathy over one of their coworkers who had been fired for being "quarrelsome and impudent." Fawcett hired replacements and criticized the strikers for behavior that he denounced as "ridiculous and unbecoming in any ladies."[16] The editor of the *Lynn Reporter* deplored the timing of the strike activity in 1876: the system of production only for advance orders was vulnerable to interruptions in late December and early January, while the additional divisions of labor meant that "the few" could stop all work in a large factory.[17] The manufacturers counted on the desperation of the unemployed eager for work even at low wages at the outset of the busy season to get their orders filled. In the context of the manufacturers' strategy of production, the Crispins were forced to confront their employers at the moment of greatest mutual tension and anxiety over the prospects of the busy season.

On January 29 the entire crew of stitchers left the shop of Joseph N. Smith on Union Street. This strike tested the viability of the reawakening DOSC in Lynn among the nearly 3,000 female operatives. Smith had cut their wages by an average of 20 percent on goods of better than medium grade that required fine stitching.

The firm also required additional work for a new style, an extra handworked buttonhole, at no additional pay. Over fifty stitchers walked out after confronting Smith over the wage cuts. Reductions had resulted in earnings as low as two dollars a week, and work was so irregular that stitchers were often in debt for board and forced to do fancy needlework during the dull seasons. Smith had sent his wage list into the stitching room where the operatives waited for work. They sent him back a "remonstrance" rejecting his cuts, which they signed with all of their names in a circle so the leaders of the group remained secret and the blame would be equally shared.[18] Admitting he had been foiled, but denying the severity of the wage reductions, Smith advertised for new stitchers in Lynn and in the surrounding towns. The striking stitchers established their headquarters across the street from Smith's factory and conducted their activities in a self-consciously ladylike and genteel fashion. They appealed to all Lynn stitchers not to take jobs at Smiths, and when a female operative approached the factory, one or two strikers would slip across the street, politely intercept her, invite her inside their headquarters, and appeal to her to find work elsewhere.[19] The KOSC offered to arbitrate the situation, but the striking stitchers tried to hold out alone.

The strike was lost as Smith easily found replacements among the underemployed stitchers in Lynn. Most stitchers responded to wage cuts by leaving one factory and seeking better pay in another. The polite appeals of the strikers to other stitchers had prevented public criticism of their demeanor, but failed to dissuade other women from taking their jobs. The context of the depression undercut the viability of the DOSC as an effective union. As a group the stitchers were unorganized and undisciplined. High turnover, hard times, and mobility in and out of the shoe factories during the busy season weakened their efforts. In April, when the male workers walked out at C. H. Aborn's factory on Market Street over a proposed wage cut of 20 percent, the stitchers, although their wages too were threatened, kept on working. When the Crispins won the strike, it was done without the help of the stitchers. While the DOSC functioned as a social group, holding parties and other entertainments in association with the KOSC, they lost their strikes in 1876 and were a union in name only.[20] Their role in labor activity during the depression became that of a women's auxiliary to the

KOSC rather than a union representing self-supporting women workers.

In 1877 B. B. Scully and Charles Litchman of Marblehead, the Grand Scribe of the new International KOSC, visited Haverhill to help revive the local Crispin lodges. They advocated arbitration and a strong national organization of shoeworkers in order to force the manufacturers to consult with their employees on wages and abandon rules that altered work customs and offended the idea of manly labor. The policy of the Scully's *Vindicator* in Lynn opposed strikes in 1877 and 1878. Scully also published with approval the debates within the New England Labor Reform League that rejected any identification with woman suffrage, women's rights or any work arrangements that altered the "harmonious division of labor" between the sexes, the "natural" distinctions between men and women, or their mutual interdependence.[21] Many members of the DOSC agreed with these views, but Scully and the *Vindicator* represented only a portion of the Crispin movement in Lynn. By late 1877 in an interview with the *Boston Globe*, Scully complained about the lack of interest among the shoeworkers of Lynn in the revival of the Crispin organization. The failure of Lynn residents to attend meetings and pay their dues resulted in "outsiders" from Maine and New Hampshire taking over as officers of the local lodges and, more important, dominating the board of arbitration. These men, Scully wrote, were incompetent and irresponsible, and he predicted trouble for the Crispins if the large manufacturers got together to force down wages.[22] A strike called by the KOSC in early 1878 filled Lynn with tensions unseen since 1860 and ended the Crispin movement.

In 1878 the large manufacturers in Lynn destroyed the Crispin board of arbitration as they had wrecked the KOSC price agreements in 1872. Competitive pressures during the lingering years of the depression from shoe manufacturers in New York State and Ohio had cut into Lynn's share of the national market. The large manufacturers, seeing their profits and sales declining and hungry for orders, attacked the Crispin arbitration system in order to break the level of wages in Lynn and restore their competitive advantage over producers west of the Hudson River. Led by Samuel Bubier, just elected mayor, sixty-five Lynn manufacturers organized in late

1877 to end arbitration. They represented an estimated $18 million of the $20 million invested in the local shoe industry. Bubier, speaking for them, criticized the Crispin board as composed of incompetents without education or experience in the industry. The board members, he contended, "stand over us like masters" who possessed the ability to ruin any businessman they chose by unfair arbitration settlements. The power of the arbitration committees to act as mediators offended Bubier's sense of the proper deferential position of employees. Employers, he insisted, should negotiate wages with their shop workers, Crispin or non-Crispin, without the interference of any third party. For Bubier and other large manufacturers, uniform wages in Lynn that negated competition over labor costs made a prosperous shoe business impossible.[23]

Most Lynn manufacturers, although unhappy with arbitration, disagreed with Bubier's stand on Crispinism. Many smaller manufacturers feared a return to the cutthroat competition of 1874 and 1875; they opposed Bubier's move to destroy the general wage level in 1877. As a result of this dissension, Bubier was forced to distinguish between the right of shoeworkers to organize collectively and the practice of arbitration. The Crispins, however, remembered well the aftermath of their defeat in 1872 when they were weeded out of shop crews, one by one, and wages fell precipitately. Many believed that without arbitration their organization would be powerless.[24] To block wage cuts, the Crispins threatened to strike any manufacturer who refused to pay the previous season's wage scale. In response, the large manufacturers locked out all Crispins and began to recruit other workers. A number of the manufacturers who backed Bubier's policy against arbitration also ran other shoe factories in Newburyport, Massachusetts; Norway, Maine; and Pittsfield, New Hampshire. When their employees arrived in Lynn as strikebreakers, they were hooted, jeered, and stoned by striking Crispins.[25]

Throughout the strike of 1878 the large manufacturers demonstrated their determination to break the board of arbitration in Lynn and reduce labor costs. As mayor, Bubier used the police force against the presence of strikers in the streets and at the central depot of the Eastern Railroad. The mayor's office ordered the removal of rifles from their racks at the Lynn Armory, putting them out of the reach of local militia units. In an effort to force smaller manufacturers to join the lockout, Bubier shut down both of his steam engines on Oxford and Market Streets early on the morning of January 18, cutting off power to some of the forty or fifty smaller establishments that continued to manufacture shoes and were profiting, according to Crispin rumor, from orders lost by the large manufacturers. These small firms threatened to sue Bubier, and power was restored after a few hours, but Bubier then announced that his engines needed urgent repairs, raising the threat of unscheduled interruptions.[26] The lockout continued for five weeks, and the large manufacturers refused all offers to compromise.

The attack of Bubier and the large manufacturers on the smaller manufacturers for supporting Crispin arbitration procedures fractured the coalition of community interests that had sustained wage levels for several years in Lynn. Scully and other Crispin leaders believed that their best course lay in cooperation, not confrontation, with their employers. Scully supported a compromise in 1878 whereby settlements were arranged shop by shop, recognizing the right of workers to be Crispins, but sacrificing arbitration. Although the Crispins won the right to organize collectively, which manufacturers conceded to their "manhood," their organization would thereafter wait until the manufacturers invited arbitration rather than involve itself in disputes from the start. As a result of the settlement, some Crispin crews returned to work as units; others were forced to work beside strikebreakers from out-of-town factories.[27] Without the backing of active intervention and mediation by a board of arbitration supported by the community, the Knights of St. Crispin organization in Lynn fell apart within a year. Wage rates became subject again to competitive forces in the national market.

An 1879 study of wages over two decades in the shoe industry by the Massachusetts Bureau of Labor Statistics reflected the declining levels during the depression years, further aggravated by Crispin defeats in 1872 and 1878. Ostensibly the evidence in the Bureau's *Tenth Annual Report* had been designed to demonstrate that wages had risen 10 percent between 1860 and 1878 despite increases in the cost of living. The report compiled average weekly wages for 1860, 1872, and 1878, but calculated percentage increases or decreases only for 1860 and 1878.[28] For most Lynn shoeworkers the report might have made more apt comparisons between average wages in 1872, when the Crispins had an arbitrated wage scale, and wages paid in 1878 after a similar system had been abolished. In all categories of men's work between 1872 and 1878, wages had fallen from 16 to 31 percent, a reflection of the hostility of manufacturers to Crispin prices and the effects of the depression. In women's work, wages had dropped 16 percent from 1872 levels.

The major complaint of shoeworkers interviewed in the 1879 study was not, however, lower piece rates, but the extreme seasonality of the work, which resulted in reduced earnings. A woman who had supported herself since she was sixteen working as a teacher and as a retail clerk had stitched shoes for six years. She liked the work, but admitted that she preferred steady employment at fair wages to the seasonal rush when she was forced to work at an exhausting pace for weeks. One shoemaker stated simply: "I am underpaid because I am underemployed."[29] Cutters complained that bankruptcies among the manufacturers during the depression years caused them loss of work and wages and created difficulties in collecting claims from their former employers.

Many of the shoeworkers interviewed in 1878 by the investigators for the Bureau of Labor Statistics expressed an acceptance of the validity of market forces as an explanation of the behavior of wage rates. One cutter who said he was satisfied with his wages asserted that his labor was for sale on the market "like a side of leather." Another cutter, also reportedly satisfied with his wages, believed that inescapable laws of supply and demand governed all business and manufacturing. Other shoeworkers rejected labor legislation and trade unions as unworkable in the market place. They felt that the whole labor question rested on supply and demand forces and on hard money. These attitudes reflected the extent to which the manufacturers' ideology had influenced the views of some shoeworkers. The acceptance of supply and demand arguments relieved the manufacturers of responsibility for the length of the busy season and for wage levels. As one manufacturer put it in the 1879 report, market forces caused the exhausting pace of work during the busy season: "The demand for goods, for a time, is greater than we can supply." Likewise during the dull season: "It would be impolitic to make up stocks of goods in advance of orders, so we have to wait till the busy season opens."[30] Neither seasonality nor wages could be legislated or arbitrated. All seemed beyond the control of manufacturers and shoeworkers. An acceptance of this ideology, which seemed to subject wages and work to natural forces as far beyond human control as the tides, ignored the decisions that had been made for two decades by capitalists in the Essex County shoe industry in an effort to organize their production system to dominate the national market and to destroy any labor association or organization that threatened their competitive advantage.

Only the Crispin ideology based on the equal rights tradition in the craft and on the mutual obligations between employer and employee opposed supply and demand. B. B. Scully of the *Vindicator* demonstrated the erosion of equal rights during the depression years in an editorial, "Supply and Demand," in early 1879, the year that his paper went out of business and the Crispin movement in Lynn folded. Scully believed that uncontrollable market forces explained the movement of wages and the differences between the situations of shoeworkers in Lynn and in Haverhill. His conclusion, given the premise, was obvious and painful: surplus labor in Lynn must be gotten rid of. For Scully, the concentrated seasons of production themselves were proof of surplus labor in the shoe industry. He estimated that 10,000 to 12,000 shoeworkers in Massachusetts and 30,000 nationwide should find other work. Until the surplus of workers was eliminated, he argued, shoeworkers could not expect higher wages. Money spent on "ill-timed" strikes would be better spent organizing farm colonies in the West and the South for surplus workers. Although he criticized "Utopian philosophers" who wasted their time creating alternative systems, Scully himself supported colonization as a solution to surplus labor in Massachusetts and an escape from the rigors of the market. In the fall of 1879 and with considerable bitterness, he declared the KOSC dead and condemned "the swarming" of country youth to the cities, which threatened those colonization schemes that represented the wreckage of Crispin hopes.[31]

The strike and lockout of 1878 temporarily revived DOSC activity in Lynn, although the stitchers did not join the strike or actively aid the men in their battle to preserve arbitration. Central Lodge #1 DOSC continued to exist in Lynn, although all traces of the national organization vanished after 1874. During the 1878 strike, women shoeworkers held meetings to revive their organization. They formed a new lodge called Liberty, but women who identified themselves as DOSC members or protested wage cuts were fired by their employers. Liberty Lodge held regular meetings in 1878, but there was no activity in defense of wages or against mistreatment. One stitcher who claimed as her customary right to see "what was to be seen" was summarily fired from her job in a stitching room in Bubier's Block on Market Street. While watching a circus parade from a doorway, she had failed to respond immediately to the call of her forelady to return to work. Her shop mates meekly resumed their work.[32] Crispin sympathizers encouraged the DOSC to cooperate with the KOSC and warned the stitchers that if the manufacturers failed to cut men's wages, they would reduce the wages of women workers. Liberty Lodge showed no signs of response, and the feeble organization faded away in early 1879.

Hard times, the decline of Crispinism in Lynn, and the ideological struggle between equal rights and the laws of the marketplace caused women workers to reconsider the meaning of the equal rights tradition. This debate centered on the relationship of women to labor protest and the capacity of women to act together to defend themselves as workers. It reflected the shift in the DOSC from a militant union led by self-supporting New England and New York State women to an organization dominated by Lynn women who had been drawn during the depression into the work force both in factories and in homework and who earned wages to supplement their families' incomes.

The central figure in this debate was "Americus," the pen name of a stitcher who had migrated to Lynn from a country town in New Hampshire, married, borne seven children, and worked off and on as a homeworker and as a vamper in a factory.[33] Americus was a DOSC member and a fervent supporter of the Crispin movement. She corresponded with the *Lynn Record* and the *Vindicator*, whose readers relished her dry Yankee humor, her stands against hypocrisy, prejudice, and greed, and her critiques of contemporary Christian doctrine and woman suffrage. Her intellectual stance was one of common sense and skeptical rationalism. In her published correspondence with other stitchers, Americus debated the issue of women's rights, the capacity of women to organize effective organizations to protect their wages, and their ability to advance their rights as workers. In their exchanges, Americus and her sister workers debated the central political issue of the meaning of equal rights for women and explored the very nature of womanhood itself.

Americus opened the debate with her first letter to the *Lynn Record* in early 1874, taking up the arguments that Emma Lane had maintained against woman suffrage. Displaying a talent for satire, Americus mocked the demands of suffragists for privileges equal to men: to smoke, snore, and drink, to spit tobacco, lounge about the streets, talk in slang, and vote. For her part, she wished to engage in none of these activities.[34] Americus's letter against suffrage stimulated a brisk discussion in 1874 among Lynn stitchers. DOSC member Ella A. Little, a thirty-one-year-old unmarried stitcher from New Hampshire who boarded in Lynn, supported suffrage based on her belief in the equality of men and women. Although she was vague about the specific advantages of the vote to female factory workers, Little argued that laboring women would benefit from political power. She defended the unmarried woman against society's jests about old maids and admired those who sought advancement in the professions and in politics. Convinced that she spoke for the majority of women shoeworkers, another stitcher who signed herself "Tryphosia" questioned the utility of suffrage for working women. She had, she declared, read all of the stitchers' letters on suffrage, but regarded the arguments about differences between men's and women's rights as irrelevant. For her, the great issue was economic, not political: "[T]he question which most affects us as a class is a fair compensation for our labor."[35] In a second letter Tryphosia developed her argument that society was divided into two classes and the laboring people did not gain a fair share of the profits from the combined efforts of labor and capital. Union as a class was the paramount objective, a unity that should not be divided over "collateral issues" or "contests" between men and women over suffrage. Tryphosia urged instead a combination of working people on a "liberal and manly basis" in which the elevation of "humanity" stood first.[36]

Tryphosia's challenge to the suffrage debate went unanswered. Instead, Ella Little responded to critics who insisted that men and women were equal but different, neither sex being superior or inferior, but each possessing natural and complementary duties and responsibilities that were best harmonized within marriage and the family. Little believed that society denied women their God-given equality and restricted their opportunities for work and education under a system disguised as natural and separate spheres. Suffrage would permit women an active role in society as workers, as mothers and wives, and as citizens.[37] Little's arguments were dismissed by older women who saw her generation as materialist, greedy, and selfish. Writing on behalf of these critics, Americus concluded that common sense would guide the "sensible woman" not to trouble herself about her rights and rely instead on the protection of her father, brothers, and husband. Public action by women, she believed, caused unhappy homes.[38] Americus reiterated these views in a letter against woman suffrage to the *Vindicator* in early 1877 and was applauded by the editor as "a good, sound, whole-hearted woman, truely womanly."[39] The issue of women's rights continued to provoke additional dissension among Lynn stitchers as tensions rose in 1876 over wage cuts and unsuccessful strike action by the DOSC.

To explain the failures of DOSC activities in 1876, Americus and other stitchers complained about the impact of low wages and of disunity among women workers, but they located the source of the trouble within the nature of women themselves. News stories about the DOSC strike at Smith's factory prompted Ella Little, who had married and moved to Chicago, to write to the *Lynn Record* in support of the strike. She viewed the action as resistance to injustice on behalf of "the cause of women" and denounced the repeated wage cuts that she had experienced for four years in Lynn.[40] But once the strike was lost, Americus reflected on the failures of the DOSC and on the nature of womanhood. Answering the persistent queries of the editor, she wrote to the *Record* that the reason women workers did not organize was that women were "peculiar." As individuals, women were equal to men; they knew as much, could accomplish as much, and behaved themselves better. But in groups, they were foolish, undependable, avaricious, and unprincipled. Dress, hair style, and gentlemen friends distracted them from their duties. Rather than expect united and disciplined action from working women, she wrote, "I should sooner see a flock of geese marching to a fife and drum." Americus described the disunity within the local DOSC lodge in harshly critical terms: weakness, cowardice, selfishness, fear, prejudice, and self-righteousness.[41] After this assault on the character of DOSC women, her appeals to stitchers to join the organization during the summer and fall of 1876 went unheeded.

Americus greatly admired and envied the success of the Knights of St. Crispin in Lynn and believed that guidance from the KOSC would resolve some of the difficulties within Central Lodge. She vigorously defended the Crispin strategy of striking in 1875 and 1876—just as the manufacturers received their orders—against cries of treachery from the *Lynn Reporter*, which she charged with "cringing servility."[42] In a letter to the *Vindicator* in June 1877, she reduced the logic of supply and demand forces in the market to absurdity: overproduction is the cause of hard times; produce less and people will have more. If crops are abundant, people will starve; if there is scarcity, everyone will eat. Destroy the inventories of boots and shoes, and no one will go barefoot. Men are without work because of overwork last year; if more are idled, everyone will have a job.[43] Angered by the pious hypocrisy of Henry Ward Beecher's recommendation during the strikes of 1877 that a diet of bread and water was sufficient for any man, Americus dismissed Beecher as ignorant, overfed, and overpaid, while boldly stating: "When a man is starving in the midst of plenty, and a part of that plenty is justly his, I think he would be less than a man if he did not help himself to bread, even if he walked through blood. . . . [T]he men who have lost their lives as 'rioters,' have not died in vain, if by this means they have taught the nation that law and order, to be efficient and abiding, must be founded upon justice and equality instead of avarice and greed."[44] She strongly defended trade unions for workingmen as the best foundation for labor politics and reform. Her sense of manliness as synonymous with courage and justice contrasted sharply with her views on the nature of womankind.

While bemoaning the nature and capacities of women in contrast to those of Crispin men, Americus and other women correspondents began to describe and analyze the nature of the female work force in Lynn and the impact on their lives of low wages during the depression years. Many stitchers were economic heads of their families, supporting widowed mothers, children, or other relatives.

These female heads of families faced low wages during hard times even for the most skilled work of vamping, the fine topstitching that determined the finished quality of the shoe's appearance. Subcontractors, whose operations outside of large factories sprang up again in the depression years, often held back wages from workers or required fees from novices to learn to operate the machines and then kept the money but failed to teach them properly. Stitchers with responsibilities for self-support or the support of others could not exist on such low wages. One correspondent wrote in 1876 that starvation wages in Lynn threatened to produce the very immorality that Reverend Cook had warned about in 1871.[45] Female heads of families and self-supporting women criticized girls with homes and friends in Lynn and those with working husbands, but who stitched uppers in shoe factories with little regard for the level of wages or for the merits of union organization. The Woman's Union had earlier distinguished the young, native-born women who came from New England country homes as ladies with "fine tastes and appreciation," indicating the "great extent to which they were educated and refined beyond the same class of city girls" in Lynn.[46] Those city girls by the 1870s were also somewhat more likely to be Irish Catholic and daughters of immigrants.[47] Some stitchers began to perceive the divisiveness of competing groups within the female work force: women who were self-supporting and often supported others and those who derived some support from families or husbands.

The increasing number of married women in the work force during the depression of 1873 and the reappearance and growth of homework as an appendage to factory production resulted in divisions within the female work force. In comparison with 1870, the percentage of wives who worked in shoe production in Lynn had doubled by 1880, representing nearly 20 percent of the factory work force. A shift in the average age of working wives between 1870 and 1880 suggests that while newly married women (at an average age of 22.0 years in 1870) continued to work in factories before the birth of their first child, the depression forced older wives (average age of 32.0 years in 1880) to return to the work force. One-fifth of all married women listed as shoeworkers in 1880 either boarded or lived with relatives, but had no husband actually reported in residence. The absence of spouses for these wives, who were reported neither as widowed nor divorced, probably reflects the impact on families of widespread unemployment and social dislocation during the depression. Almost all working wives who boarded in Lynn had no children in residence, suggesting that children were being cared for elsewhere while their mothers stitched shoes during the busy season.[48]

In addition to wives involved in factory work, large numbers of married and single women labored as homeworkers. The Massachusetts state census of 1875 reported that nearly 30 percent of the over 2,000 female shoeworkers in Lynn did homework. The reemergence of homework was not solely a product of the depression, but represented a continuing attempt by shoe manufacturers and subcontractors in the 1870s and 1880s to cut labor costs. Women in Haverhill beaded and trimmed slippers at home by hand for shoe factories, while in Marblehead the home use of treadled sewing machines was common in the late nineteenth century.[49] Mechanization and centralization of shoe production did not eliminate the involvement of women who worked at home, especially as the costs of their labor undercut wages in factories.

One stitcher active in the DOSC vividly expressed this sense of division and competition among women workers in 1879 and became involved in a debate with Americus over the role of "half supported" women in the work force of stitchers. Signing herself "A Stitcher," she argued that the shops were crowded with girls whose fathers provided them with all the necessities and comforts of life. These girls worked in the shops because of "their inordinate love of dress and a desire to compete with their more wealthy sisters in personal adornments." The result was competition for stitching jobs and lower wages. If these girls were asked to join the DOSC, she went on, they refused. They did not need better wages; they had homes, no board to pay, and they worked only for pin money in order to dress better. Even the wives and daughters of manufacturers worked in the shops, she wrote, to add to "their hoards" the wages that might go to poorer girls. Young and beautiful girls who accepted money for board from friends did not care about the level of wages. Responding to the perennial question of the editor of the *Record* as to why the stitchers did not organize, the writer concluded bitterly that men were able to organize to prevent wage cuts, but for women there was no hope; the bosses could cut the stitchers down each season instead of reducing men's wages, knowing that married women and half-supported daughters of local families would take the work at any price. This explanation of low wages as a result of abundant local supplies of female labor suggests that some DOSC members saw supply and demand forces as the basis of their difficulties. The editor of the *Record* agreed with this analysis, criticized the few women who took men's jobs as lasters and finishers, and encouraged the DOSC to resolve its difficulties and organize all women workers.[50] However, a woman's primary obligation to the family rather than to coworkers appeared both divisive and irrevocable.

Americus replied quickly to the charge that married women and local daughters undercut wages and refused to join the DOSC. She had, two years earlier, raised the question herself in a letter in which she had appealed to stitchers not to compete with each other over work available in the shops without regard for the economic circumstances of individuals. In early 1879, however, she defended married women as the most active and ardent members of the DOSC.[51] Americus insisted that the wives who worked in the shoe shops did so out of necessity and frequently because their husbands' wages were too low. Few women, she declared, bent over their machines from early morning until late in the evening for four to six dollars a week because they had a fondness for luxuries. The reason women did not organize, according to Americus, was simple: the majority of working women lacked intelligence and energy; they were ignorant and apathetic.[52] "A Stitcher" was not convinced. Her explanation of the divisions among women workers rested on the structure of the work force, not on woman's nature. Married women, she argued, did not share the economic hardships of the hundreds of homeless girls or those who were the main support of their families. If married women paid board and laundry bills, lived alone in cheerless boarding houses, and had only their own "miserable pittance to live on," she claimed, they would be more energetic and willing to organize. Stitcher concluded that a better appreciation of the fate of the unmarried factory girl who boarded in Lynn or the stitcher who supported herself and others would encourage all women to unite for protection.[53] Her appeals for sympathy did not, however, move Americus.

Before Americus could respond, "A Married Stitcher" contributed to the debate by raising the issue of women workers who violated the sexual division of labor in shoe factories. This stitcher reported that she had worked in the shops from necessity for several years and claimed that she had never met a married woman who stitched shoes except as a result of economic hardship. The reason so many wives were found at work was the presence of "girls who [would] rather work with a crowd of men [as lasters] than in the stitching room with their own sex." Female lasters, she argued, depressed men's wages and forced their wives to work. She not only worked to feed her children, Married Stitcher insisted, but during the lockout of 1878 she was along with many wives in Lynn the mainstay of her family. She felt herself to be a Crispin in principle, but she strongly disapproved of the KOSC admitting girls to the lasters' lodge.[54] Americus responded first to Stitcher in her familiar style of sarcasm and condescension. My dear child, she wrote, married women being such selfish and useless creatures, it seemed the only remedy was to take them all out and shoot them.[55] In an earlier letter, Americus herself had acknowledged that girl lasters were paid less than men for the same work, a situation that she admitted did not make it "nice" to be a woman, but she did not make this point in her reply to Married Stitcher.[56] Instead, Americus agreed with her that wives worked reluctantly and because their husbands' wages were low. Nonetheless, she defended wives working not only for family subsistence, but to educate their children, pay the mortgage, put money in the bank or simply to avoid being idle.[57]

Americus and Stitcher had one final exchange on the issue of married women in the shoe shops and their relationship to labor protest. Stitcher, who worked as a young woman without family assistance, described herself as being "thrown here and there by circumstance." She cited a surplus of 60,000 females in Massachusetts and the need of three-quarters of them to be self-supporting. She wrote in apparent envy of the life that the true married woman should lead: hard at work brightening her home to cheer her tired husband on his return from work. Wives who insisted on working challenged the manly self-reliance of their husbands, lowered wages for deserving homeless girls, and were motivated by jealousy and foolish extravagance. Stitcher concluded hopelessly that ever since Mother Eve, women have been at "the bottom of nearly every trouble."[58]

Americus responded forthrightly. She again defended the presence of married women in the shoe shops and Mother Eve as another wife who deserved more respect: "I always thought Eve was entitled to a little more mercy than she received, in consideration of the poor material from which she was made."[59] Americus ridiculed the notion of a bright, cheery little home as suitable recompense for the overworked and underpaid shoeworker: "If a man had no work and no money, and his stock of provisions had dwindled down to a few baked beans on a tin plate, do you mean that his wife ought to stay at home, eat the beans, and scour the plate up bright for his home coming? You say: —'What could be more cheering to a tired, weary man?' I think the proper answer to that question is—beans."[60] Empty dishes however bright would cheer no one. In hard times, Americus argued, the first duty of a wife was to work for the support of her family. Furthermore, she stated that single girls outnumbered married women in the shops by three to one and that the membership of the DOSC proved that married women were more willing to organize to resist wage cuts than single girls. Men alone, she concluded, were the persons responsible for the sins of the nation and for the faulty social and political system that governed it. As "the weaker vessel," woman could not be blamed.

According to a one in ten sample of women workers in Lynn from the federal census of population schedules in 1880, the female work force in the shoe factories was divided evenly between resident daughters in male-headed households and married women, on the one hand, and women living in female-headed households or as unmarried boarders on the other. The majority of resident daughters in male-headed households were native-born, living in nuclear families with the highest percentage, among the four groups, of foreign-born fathers, three-quarters of whom were natives of Ireland. These daughters were the youngest among the four groups, but one-quarter of them were the eldest child resident in the family. These were the half-supported girls who contributed their wages to their family's income. According to a survey of family budgets in 1875 by the Massachusetts Bureau of Labor Statistics, nearly one-third of the daughters of forty-three families of male shoeworkers were employed, and they contributed an average of 26 percent of the family's total annual income.

Wives, who as workers had doubled their proportion of the work force between 1870 and 1880, resided and boarded with their husbands, many of whom were also shoeworkers. Very few working wives had children in residence, but their average age was the highest among the four groups of women workers. They seemed to be either young wives who worked before bearing their first child and older wives whose children no longer resided with them. In the 1875 family budget survey, only two wives out of forty-three earned wages, one as a homeworker and mother of a school-age child and the other as a newly married woman who boarded with her husband in the residence of a private family. The contrast between the earning power of homework and factory work for wives was striking. The homeworker earned $100 on her sewing machine or 16 percent of the total family income for the year. The factory worker earned $380, which represented 40 percent of the total family income, most of which became savings.[61]

Three-quarters of the unmarried self-supporting women who lived in female-headed households resided with their widowed mothers, and one-third of them were the eldest child in residence in the family. Their average age was second highest among the groups of women workers. Single, boarding stitchers represented the highest percentage of foreign-born women workers, most of whom were from Nova Scotia. The vast majority boarded with private families in Lynn rather than in large boardinghouses, and their average age ranked third eldest. Americus argued that single women outnumbered married women in the work force by three to one. Her estimate was low. Eighty-three percent of the work force in 1880 were single women or widows. The threat of married women in the shoe shops of Lynn to wage levels or to the DOSC organization seemed minimal. However, if married women and resident daughters in male-headed families were content to work only to supplement family income at low wages, as "A Stitcher" argued, their combined numbers at 51 percent of the work force could have had a significant impact on wage levels.

The debate among the stitchers of Lynn in 1879 over the propriety and motives of wives working in the shops was fundamentally an argument that rested on the ideology of separate spheres for men and women. Men, especially husbands, were responsible, public persons who protected women. Women without protection deserved special consideration and pity. Wives owed their loyalty and their work, especially during times of economic hardship, to their families, but all women had basic flaws of character, which was naturally different from the character of men. During the depression years of the 1870s the separate spheres of men and women and their natural if compatible differences remained the foundation of gender relationships in the minds of many articulate working women. Advocates of women's rights or suffrage seemed to assault and challenge the very nature of womanhood and relationships within the family. Unity in the DOSC foundered on the divisions within the female work force and on the perceptions of many of its members of the limited nature and destiny of women.

Not all young women who worked as stitchers in Lynn shared the views of Americus and her correspondents in 1879 about woman's nature and her proper place in society. Another view of the meaning of equal rights for women and its implications for labor protest paralleled and continued to challenge Americus's definition of the nature of womanhood. "Amelia" responded to an editorial in the *Record* in late 1877 that was critical of families who allowed their daughters to stroll about the streets of Lynn at night at the risk of their reputations. She made this an issue of unequal treatment of men and women. If, Amelia argued, her own brother was permitted on the streets "to tempt and allure" her shop mate Julia, shouldn't *he* be kept at home and not Amelia and her friend? She criticized the behavior of young men who stood about on street corners, making ungentlemanly remarks to ladies and staring at them, smoking bad cigars and nasty pipes, and making a cesspool of the streets with tobacco juice and peanut shells. This kind of behavior by men offended public order, but Amelia concluded by suggesting that if both sisters and brothers conducted themselves properly, no one would have to remain at home.[62] Other writers in 1880 and 1881 took up the arguments made earlier by Ella Little and advocated equal rights for women as a foundation for achieving a defense of their rights as workers. In this debate Americus, who had easily dispatched the arguments of most of her critics, found herself caught up in the contradictions of her expressed disdain for woman's nature and her advocacy of collective resistance for women workers.

In the summer of 1880, "Columbia," who described herself as a humble female vamper, criticized shoe manufacturers in Lynn who refused to allow women workers the chance to ride the elevators between the floors of the shoe factories. The issue of riding elevators became a metaphor in a lengthy debate between Americus and Columbia over the capacity of women workers to protest their grievances. Columbia complained that since stitching rooms were generally located on the top floors of factories, women workers had to climb three or four flights of stairs four times a day as they came to work in the morning, left for their noon meal, and departed at night. This, she argued, caused unnecessary, additional fatigue and aggravation. The elevators carried foremen, foreladies, cases of shoes, and even the "precious little bodies" of the owners themselves between floors. She described the shoe factories as hierarchies of power and privilege, as "little despotisms," and dismissing any danger from riding on elevators, she advocated that factory girls be permitted to ride them or that stitching operations be relocated to a lower floor in the buildings.[63] Columbia was asking for changes in working conditions based on her apprehension of an unjust structure of power and status within the shoe factories of Lynn. The initial response of Americus to her proposal was harshly negative. She wondered why the *Record* had published such a letter? She reduced Columbia's desire for factory girls to ride elevators to a personal impulse to break her own neck. A flock of girls, Americus insisted, was like a flock of sheep, not to be trusted around machinery and liable to injure themselves. Elevator rides were, furthermore, less important than other wrongs in factories, such as poor ventilation.[64] Americus defended the wisdom of shoe manufacturers in refusing to allow girls to ride on elevators.

In her reply, Columbia, well acquainted with the style of debate used by Americus in thwarting her other correspondents, began to twit and challenge her on her own ground of common sense. She addressed Americus as "my dear child" and "my dear girl," appropriating her opponent's pose of older and wiser maternal condescension. Was she now opposing free speech and efforts on behalf of the cause of labor? Columbia defended her plan for factory girls to ride elevators operated by male employees as perfectly reasonable and entirely feasible. She compared Americus with her prudish maiden aunt, who threw cold water on her young niece's excited anticipation of holiday plans by warning: "If you live, my dear."[65] In her next response Americus, challenged to show her common sense as a supporter of the cause of labor, relented only a little. She admitted that if the manufacturers would provide safe rides on elevators run by male operators, the lot of the stitcher would improve. However, she added that this was unlikely and anything else would result in a heap of mangled bones and human gore at the bottom of the elevator shaft, ample testimony to the panic that seized girls when they confronted machinery.[66] Columbia in turn seized on this melodramatic example to accuse Americus of sentimental sensationalism and an overexcited imagination—in short to accuse her of being what Americus deplored: a nervous woman.[67] Americus rejected this accusation, insisting that she was a matter-of-fact kind of person, and labeled Columbia's proposal as what "might be" rather than what was likely to be. On this note, she attempted to end the debate by stating that she had no more to say about elevators.[68]

Columbia had none of this. She reiterated her argument and insisted that if the elevators were unsafe, the manufacturers should make them safe. If her plan was visionary, she taunted, then all labor reform was impractical and what Americus herself had advocated for years was hypocritical nonsense. Columbia refused to let the argument end. If Americus did not reply, she would know that she had made a convert.[69] A letter from "A Shoe Manufacturer" interrupted this increasingly acerbic exchange. Identifying himself as one of the largest manufacturers in Lynn, the writer backed Americus's position on the elevator question, citing state laws that held an employer liable for damages suffered by an employee resulting from an injury on an elevator.[70] Columbia pounced on this commendation and congratulated Americus on the appreciation offered by a manufacturer for her labors on his behalf. Americus was then treated to the uncomfortable experience of having herself and her views dismissed in print.

Borrowing and mocking her opponent's rhetorical techniques, Columbia categorized Americus at one point as an inexperienced, foolish young person, unworthy of a hearing. Her opposition to plans for changes in working conditions revealed Americus as "a regular old-fashioned croaker." The position of the shoe manufacturers on the elevator question, Columbia pointed out, was determined by their concern over their legal liability, not over any possible injury to their employees.[71] After several weeks of silence,

Americus finally responded with considerable sarcasm and uncharacteristic ill-humor. Columbia's efforts on behalf of the elevator question were useless, she wrote. The reason was the fundamental character of working girls. Girls were not properly constituted to ride on elevators, even if the manufacturers guaranteed them to be safe. Putting a crowd of chattering, giggling girls on an elevator was as dangerous as permitting a crowd of lunatics to ride.[72] With this dismissal of the nature of her own sex, Americus wrote no more to Columbia.

Columbia had the final word. Farewell, my dear little girl, she wrote. I am not squelched, squashed or annihilated by your withering sarcasm. She gave up on Americus as too obstinate and ignorant to convince with reasonable arguments. In a shrewd estimate of the motives of the owners of the shoe factories, Columbia pointed out to the readers of the *Record* that if the shoe manufacturers wanted factory girls to ride, they would quickly find a way to do so. If by state law each manufacturer was fined five cents for every stitcher who failed to ride, the elevators would be made safe and the girls would be hustled up and down with astonishing efficiency. They should, she concluded in her last letter, make the elevators safe and let us ride them.[73]

This long debate over the propriety of women demanding specific changes in working conditions in shoe factories represented much more than the vigorous exchange in 1880 between two hardy, articulate, and opinionated New England working women. The depression years of the 1870s had reopened the debate over the relationship of women to labor protest and their role in family life. Arguments over the restrictions that confined women to separate spheres of action based on their unique and biologically determined character created a sense of weakness within the female labor force that helped to undermine collective protest. Columbia's vision of the inherent capacity of women workers to identify the injustice in the hierarchical arrangements of work and power in shoe factories and demand changes in working conditions seemed a better ground from which they could sustain efforts to question the authority of their employers. A positive sense of gender was essential for unified action. The conception of womanhood that Americus shared with other women workers in Lynn rested on an eternally defective female nature, which decreed a restricted social

TWO HANDSOME SHOES, MADE BY THE GEO. E. BARNARD CO., LYNN.

The two standard products of Lynn: serge and all-leather high-buttoned boots. *Boot and Shoe Recorder*, August 10, 1892, p. 95, courtesy of Lynn Public Library.

place. These attitudes discouraged women from joining together effectively with others in a fight for justice. When this discouragement was added to the structural divisions within the female work force, the sense of competition among groups of working women, and the hard times of the 1870s, the burdens that faced the DOSC efforts to unite women workers for protest became too formidable. Like the Crispin organization for men, the DOSC did not survive the depression of the 1870s.

The brisk spring trade in 1880 marked an end to the long depression in Essex County. Anticipating the development of new prospects in the national market, manufacturers in Lynn and Haverhill began to diversify and expand their lines of goods. Haverhill factories had enjoyed eleven months of production in 1879, making slippers and sandals of velvet, silk, and brocade and low-cut shoes for sale in the South.[74] Manufacturers in Lynn, Stoneham, Marblehead, and Beverly concentrated on the production of medium-grade, high-cut ladies' button shoes for street wear. They offered styles that varied widely in price, design, and finish, in an effort to sell them in the developing western market that stretched between Mexico and Canada. The uppers of serge button boots, the mainstay of the Lynn product line, were cut out of black and white checked wool with black leather foxing, available in medium grade for $1.25 to two dollars or with a fancy finish from two to four dollars. In 1880, Lynn manufacturers also offered to the domestic market all-leather button boots that had been developed as a style during the depression years to attract sales in Latin America. These boots featured soles with edges beveled on new trimming machines and French heels of various styles. They were lined in linen or cotton drill and faced with lambskin. The uppers were cut from goatskin and grain leather, while those for fancy grades were made of French kidskin.[75] Within two years, the phenomenal sales of these all-leather button boots drove serge boots out of production.

Between 1880 and 1884, shoe production in Lynn adjusted to the new opportunities seen by manufacturers in the domestic market of fifty-two million people. Lynn factories would sell quantities of solid, serviceable, medium-grade shoes to customers in growing urban areas. In their eagerness to obtain orders in the reviving market, manufacturers also produced numerous samples of various styles between 1880 and 1882, including baseball and lawn tennis shoes with canvas uppers to fill what manufacturers perceived to be a new market for sports apparel. However, a large line of goods that required frequent changes in work raised costs of production, and by 1882 the numbers of sample styles had been reduced. For several years Lynn manufacturers experimented with the heels of button boots, from extremely concave French heels to flat heels, before compromising in 1883 on a button boot with a half French heel, a medium-cut vamp, and a scalloped button flap. They abandoned fancy stitching in silk thread on vamps and quarters, but all fine Lynn goods featured handworked buttonholes, while the buttonholes of cheaper grades were outlined in silk cord. Better quality shoes arrived at stores packed in individual paper cartons.[76] By 1884 these decisions had produced an excellent, medium-priced ladies' button boot for mass consumption.

The reviving shoe market of the early 1880s stimulated additional competition over advance orders. Salesmen with their sample cases full of the new product lines were sent westward as early as September for the spring trade and in April for the fall trade. In Lynn, manufacturers built new, larger factories of brick with the latest in steam power and machinery. In early 1882 the shoe district in Haverhill was gutted by a devastating fire, which forced most manufacturers to scramble for any available temporary space in the city while the central business district was being rebuilt with modern, brick factories.[77] Shoeworkers did not share in the bustling recovery of the early 1880s. Wages rose only slightly above depression levels, and by 1883, men and women workers in Essex County began to organize themselves into assemblies of the Knights of Labor to insist on a fairer portion of returning prosperity.

CHAPTER EIGHT

New England Shoeworkers in
the Knights of Labor

Sisters, we constitute a large body, so be careful that
every member be useful, as in "union is strength." . . .
Never try to convey the wrong idea to the public that
because you bear the name of Union Girl, you will be
sustained in unladylike and wrong doings, as you know
our organization has nothing of the kind in its
constitution, and you will bring the censure of the
community on the whole for the rash folly of one.
> —"Union Girl,"
> Lynn *Knight of Labor*,
> December 19, 1885

Shoe production in Essex County in the decade of the 1880s concentrated on the mass production of all-leather, high-cut ladies'
buttoned boots, which sold in the domestic market everywhere
but the South, where the climate required low-cut shoes. "Leather
goods will take the lead; . . . [a] good, solid, well-made, honest button boot is the regular thing."[1] Made of supple materials
including costly kidskin, morocco, grain, and glove leathers, these
boots required skilled stitching and buttonhole work. Laced shoes
for women nearly vanished from retail stores. The production of
leather button boots increased rapidly outside of New England,
especially in the New York shoe factories of Utica and Rochester,
which became prime competitors with Lynn. Competition was
intense in the reviving shoe market of the 1880s, and manufacturers
searched for ways to cut costs and undersell each other.

Despite long seasons of production and hard work to fill heavy
floods of orders, the shoeworkers of Essex County still faced low
wages, slashed by the depression years and unresponsive to the

return of prosperity. In 1884 the Knights of Labor swept through Essex County, organizing thousands of shoeworkers to demand higher wages and seek power in Massachusetts politics. Women workers became an important part of this outburst of popular fervor for the Knights. They organized to demand wage increases and participated in the local, district, and national organizations to advance the interests and concerns of their sister workers in other industries. On the national level, they provided a link on behalf of equal rights with women's organizations for temperance and suffrage. Women shoeworkers in the Knights of Labor continued the search begun by the Daughters of St. Crispin for a national organization that combined gender and class consciousness to serve their collective interests as industrial workers.

Essex County women in the Knights of Labor adapted and utilized the status of lady stitcher that Lynn manufacturers had developed in the late 1860s to protect their rural New England sources of seasonal female labor. The depression years of the 1870s obliged many women to stay in the work force after marriage. This had eroded the image of a genteel young woman who blithely stitched fancy patterns on fine leather or cloth uppers, while dressing fashionably and waiting for the right young man. The experience of low wages and scarce work made the image of the lady stitcher irrelevant to many women. However, the return of prosperity in the early 1880s and the demands of shoe manufacturers for skilled work on the uppers of button boots encouraged collective action. Women shoeworkers invoked the image of the lady stitcher for protection in the streets and in the shops and also utilized it during strikes and confrontations with their employers to unify a female work force divided by age and ethnicity.

Women shoeworkers also faced a Victorian sexual ideology that seemed to exclude working women from the concept of respectable womanhood by considering paid work outside the home and ladyhood as incompatible.[2] Most working women in the late nineteenth century rejected standards of ladylike behavior, but the women shoeworkers of Essex County attempted to use the status of lady stitcher to defend their wages and working conditions and to hold together the diverse elements within the female work force. Nonetheless, tensions developed between native-born women of an older generation who identified with independence and a decorous, defensive gentility and younger, activist working women, many from immigrant families. The image of the lady stitcher served for a time as an umbrella of status that linked native-born women with daughters of immigrants under its protective shelter. By overcoming divisions within the work force, it enabled women workers inside and outside of the Knights of Labor to combine effectively to confront their employers. Although women in the Knights recognized the limits that gentility placed on public action and came to understand the importance of obtaining political power for women in local elections, they succeeded in uniting working women for action where the Daughters of St. Crispin had failed.

Women shoeworkers invoked ladyhood for protection and defense against unwanted or threatening contacts with the community in which they worked. In June 1875 a shop girl had written angrily to the editor of the *Lynn Record*, complaining about the lack of decorum on the railroad cars that she took every morning to her work in Lynn.

> I wish to warn my young lady friends of that class of young men who come to Lynn from Boston on the eight o'clock morning train, and who find no other employment for their time than staring at women all the way, like great idiotic, grinning, country school boys. They are a set of indecent hoodlums, and deserve to be kicked from the cars by their male companions. . . . Of course we have no protection against these half-dozen, ill-mannered boobies and can only say "beware of them."
>
> A Shop Girl [3]

The writer was claiming her right to courteous treatment as a young lady stitcher. Lady stitchers exhibited standards of behavior and decorum that entitled them to respect, especially when away from their homes and families. This shop girl called on the male community to respond and protect her and her friends from mistreatment, a protection, however, on which she no longer counted.

An incident that occurred in a Lynn stitching shop on Market Street in August 1880 illustrated the defensive use of the status of lady stitcher by women workers to ward off attacks on their public position as respectable women. This incident involved an alleged assault by a forewoman on a stitcher and also revealed tensions between Yankee and Irish-American women in the shoe shops.[4] Mrs. Hannah Barbour, who had been fired from the T. C. Murphy stitching firm, visited the shop one morning to inquire about work and to talk to a friend. The forewoman, Miss Sarah McGaughey, ordered her to leave. Barbour told the municipal court that she had said good morning to McGaughey, who looked at her contemptuously and told her to get out or she would be thrown out. When she did not leave, the stitcher said she was hit in the face with a bunch of shoe linings and that McGaughey tried to push her down a flight of stairs while using "indelicate" language. To save herself, Barbour pushed the forewoman into a corner, and then several Irish shop girls rushed up and struck her. Barbour described a rude, excitable, and violent young woman in contrast to her own correct behavior and self-defense.

Sarah McGaughey denied using any "unladylike" language and insisted that she had good reason to ask Barbour to leave, but that Barbour had become violent and seized her by the throat, a grip from which she had been rescued by the shop girls. Witnesses for McGaughey testified to Barbour's own use of "profane" language and to the unprovoked fury with which McGaughey had been attacked. Barbour's witnesses, however, told the court that neither party had used indecent language, but had only exchanged angry words, during which Sarah McGaughey had gestured with a bunch of linings. The accused and the plaintiff defended themselves against accusations of unladylike language and behavior, which for them and for their witnesses represented the fundamentals of the case. Both of their lawyers, however, disagreed. They emphasized the age differences between the two women and debated whether the forewoman had the right to order Barbour out of the shop. They discussed the nature of the evidence given by witnesses, who were described by the plaintiff's attorney as "a tribe who had all told their stories glibly" on behalf of their employer, while McGaughey's counsel dismissed the incident as "but a woman's quarrel."[5] The court found Barbour guilty of assault. Both groups involved in the dispute at the Murphy shop demonstrated in their testimony the importance to stitchers of the status of ladyhood as a part of their shop floor culture and public image.

Women shoeworkers had to negotiate the liabilities of ladyhood not only on railroad cars and in shop disputes, but also in confrontations with their employers. To be a lady stitcher seemed to imply passive, decorous behavior that required others to act to protect and defend women's interests. However, the status of ladyhood and memories of its positive connotations in the 1860s and early 1870s appealed to a cohort of unmarried Yankee women shoeworkers in Lynn who had entered the shops in the post–Civil War years and continued to work as stitchers for a decade or longer. In 1880 well over half the women workers who resided in female-headed households or boarded in Lynn as single, widowed, or divorced persons were thirty years of age or older.[6] These women provided continuity between the Daughters of St. Crispin and the Knights of Labor organization. During a wage dispute in 1888 one such stitcher, who spoke on behalf of higher wages, was described as "[a] lady stitcher of Lynn, a maiden lady, most active in organizing her sisters, and who had actively participated in all of the union schemes for twenty years or more."[7] The status of lady stitcher provided an important sense of dignity and self-worth for an older generation of self-supporting women who worked in the Lynn shoe shops. A sense of self-worth had been successfully used to unify and embolden DOSC stitchers in disputes with their employers and as such was a valuable heritage for labor protest.

Women active in the Knights of Labor succeeded in utilizing the image of lady stitcher aggressively to defend standards of respectful treatment and good wages, while they attempted to overcome the limitations inherent in ladylike speech and conduct. The male workers in the Knights of Labor assemblies in Lynn responded willingly to their calls for community support to protect and defend them during strikes and arbitration proceedings. In December 1883 the stitchers of Lynn received their charter from the Knights of Labor national organization to form local assembly #3016, Lady Stitchers' Union. This assembly was also commonly referred to as the Daughters of Labor, presumably to identify the organization with the Daughters of St. Crispin. By early 1884, stitchers in Beverly, Haverhill, and Salem had also organized local KOL assemblies of lady stitchers. Organized as a secret association during the lockout of 1878, the 8,000 KOL men in Lynn formed eleven assemblies led by Master Workman Charles Litchman of Marblehead in D.A. 30, the district assembly representing Massachusetts. By late 1885 the assemblies of Lynn, Marblehead, Salem, and Beverly split off into a separate D.A. 77 dominated by shoeworkers with fifteen assemblies, the largest of which was the Lynn stitchers' assembly with 1,500 members or nearly half the female work force.[8] An executive board of seven Knights led the activities of D.A. 77 and arbitrated disputes over wages.

The stitchers' list of prices for the spring season in 1884 had been arranged by the local board of arbitration, a device that the Knights in Lynn had borrowed from the Crispins to replace strikes and lockouts and assure shoeworkers steady work at fair wages. Strikes by stitchers in the summer and fall of 1884 were a response to the impact of intensive competition in the national wholesale shoe market, which kept shoe prices low and held down wages. Low prices for leather stock also contributed to the decline in wholesale prices. The Lynn high-cut button shoe that had sold for two dollars in the early 1870s became a dollar shoe, while "cheap work" sold for less. Manufacturers began to contemplate selling their goods directly to retailers through their salesmen rather than allow jobbers to cut into profits, while they sent their sales force out on the road earlier each year to get the jump on competitors.[9]

Stitchers also faced mechanization and changes in the organization of their work, which cut piece rates and undercut the skills they had learned from years of experience. The shift to the all-leather button boot in the 1880s had eliminated fancy stitching on uppers, but the scalloping, finish stitching on vamps, and button-hole work required new skills. A missed stitch on a wool serge vamp of the 1870s could be pulled out and restitched, but a mistake on morocco or kidskin was a puncture, less easily repaired. Women lasters, who specialized in the wool serge uppers of the 1870s, did not work on leather and began to disappear from the work force.[10] Some of them returned to stitching.

By 1885, manufacturers had separated the high cost of scalloping, vamping, and buttonhole work from the less expensive stitching on the body of the upper. The quarter, toe, and heel pieces were assembled or "closed on" by machine operators who were capable of putting in 600 stitches per minute. The seams were then rubbed down, usually by hand, and the stayer securely stitched two rows of thread parallel to the seam for strength. Linings of cotton cloth were seamed on machines for low wages by beginners eager to move to closing-on or staying and later to vamping. After the

A double needle attachment fit the Wheeler and Wilson machine, which
reduced the work of vampers. *Boot and Shoe Recorder*, July 30, 1890,
p. 67, courtesy of Lynn Public Library.

linings were pressed, they were stitched together with the leather upper on the wrong side out, turned, and stitched along the edges to give shape and definition to the upper. Meanwhile the scallops on the outer flap of the boot or the button fly were stitched on a sewing machine and each buttonhole was stitched individually or inserted into the automatic Reece buttonhole machine, which worked a buttonhole in each scallop. The vamper then put the button fly piece or overlap together with the sewn quarter, using two or three rows of stitching for strength. After inspection, the finished upper was passed on to the lasting room.[11]

Between 1873 and 1885 several steps on upper work became mechanized. Machines to fold uppers and sew on buttons at a rate of three per second eliminated relatively expensive and time-consuming handwork. An automatic eyeletting machine punched holes and set eyelets in uppers for laced shoes. The Amazeen skiving machine with a whirling blade that sent out sparks as its emery wheel sharpened the edge also eliminated handwork, beveling the edges of uppers so that seams would lie smooth and flat. An attachment for the sewing machine performed the dual function of trimming the edges of seams while they were being closed on, thus eliminating the trimming done by hand with scissors. Another machine rubbed down or flattened seams prior to stay stitching. Decisions made by manufacturers in the 1870s to divide the labor on upper work seemed to shape the process of further mechanization in the 1880s.

More important in terms of labor costs were the machines designed to cut expenses in vamping and buttonhole work. By 1886 the Wheeler and Wilson Sewing Machine Company of Boston had developed its #12 machine with a two-needle attachment, which cut the costs in half for parallel stitching on vamps and for staying. The Reece Button-hole Machine automatically cut, spread, and stitched around the edges of buttonholes, while the operative simply positioned the button fly piece and started the process.[12] The ultimate machine to eliminate skill from buttonhole work was developed by the Goodyear and McKay Sewing Machine Company, which counted many Lynn manufacturers as stockholders. The process required only one piece of leather rather than the two thin pieces that were commonly stitched together around the buttonhole to form the button fly. On the grounds of protecting the buttonholes against stretching and gaping during buttoning, the new work would be done on one thickness of leather with the buttonholes stamped out by a die and the edges of scallops and buttonholes embossed by machine to imitate stitching. The promoters of the new machine extolled the savings on lining work, scalloping, and buttonholing, but the appearance of the machine-embossed button fly was so unattractive that the machine never caught on.[13] By 1888 the highest labor costs in stitching operations remained vamping, scalloping, and buttonhole work.

One traditional solution for high labor costs that persisted and grew in most shoe centers in Essex County despite centralization was homework. Stitching by hand or by machine for low wages in the home continued during the prosperity of the 1880s. In 1885, 32 percent of the female work force of Haverhill worked at home, and the number of homeworkers in Marblehead doubled between 1875 and 1885.[14] Beading the vamps and bows of ladies' slippers, decorating the uppers of low-cut shoes, and skiving and pressing upper pieces by hand continued as outwork for very low wages.[15] Homeworkers also ran machines for shoe manufacturers in rural areas. Irena M. Knowlton, wife of George K. Knowlton, a small shoe manufacturer in Hamilton, Massachusetts, northeast of Danvers, stitched the uppers of ladies' button boots at home for her husband in the 1870s and 1880s. She also cared for three children, fed boarders, did house and garden work, and kept poultry. Her diary (1870–86) is a litany of fatigue and illness. She worked almost daily on uppers along with her other chores. Under the pressure of her summer activities of preparing chickens for sale, berrying, churning, baking, and stitching uppers, she wrote in despair on August 2, 1879: "went berrying, done some shoes, scot to breakfast and dinner   George went away today but O dear what a life to live *God* help me to do my duty   baked 5 pies   *drove cow.*"[16] Her exhausting duties as mother, wife, housekeeper, and homeworker bore little resemblance to the lives of the factory stitchers of Lynn. With returning prosperity, the percentage of homeworkers in Lynn had fallen from 28 percent of the female work force in 1875 to only 4 percent in 1885. However, one unsuspecting stitcher who found herself during the dull season without any work to do took 60 pairs of serge uppers to work on at home. "I had to press all the tops of the outsides and linings with a hot iron before I could stitch them; it took me two days and until 11 o'clock one night before I got them done. The foreman said they were well done, and paid me 60 cents. I have to find the thread, etc., and was five cents out of pocket by the transaction."[17] Factory stitching, although seasonal, offered a far more attractive work setting for those women able to leave their homes.

Unlike the Crispins, the Knights of Labor in Lynn included the stitchers in the arbitration process that they organized in 1884. The stitchers' assembly was not represented directly on the new board of arbitration, but accepted the initial efforts by the KOL on their behalf. However, in the summer of 1884 the Lynn stitchers' organization was forced to oppose attempts by manufacturers to evade the union price list set by the KOL board. In June the stitchers struck the subcontract shop run by Gustavus Austin on Union Street, which did upper work for the large manufacturer B. F. Doak. The two forewomen at the Austin shop had been switching the tags that identified the various grades of work, compelling the operatives to work on second-quality goods for third-quality wages. A white tag indicated first-quality goods, while red and blue tags identified second and third grades. The board of arbitration negotiated a settlement of the strike at the Austin shop, but the forewomen, Mrs. Jenness and her sister Mrs. Knox, hired other stitchers to replace some assembly members and sent the work out to other shops. The union stitchers again struck the Austin shop to get the forewomen discharged and asked the Lynn Knights to boycott work on shoes for Doak to bring the significance of the dispute home to the large manufacturers.[18] In addition, the operatives in the buttonhole department of the V. K. and A. H. Jones factory struck in mid-July over the sending of their work to "outside shops" to be stitched at less than union prices. The stitchers' assembly meant to drive out of Lynn these "back" or subcontract shops, which stitched uppers for cheap shoes.[19] Most of the rest of the stitchers joined the buttonhole operators, leaving only about fifty women or one-quarter of the female work force still in the shop. The stitchers' assembly set up its headquarters on Market Street and began to focus on the women still at work in the Austin and Jones shops.[20] The confrontations between the strikers and nonstrikers on Union Street revealed serious divisions within the female work force and highlighted the weaknesses involved in a public stance of passive ladyhood for women workers.

About thirty-five of the Austin stitchers refused to obey the strike order by the stitchers' assembly and disagreed with the charge that the forewomen had acted unjustly. After the strike had been on for a few days and persuasion had failed, the unorganized stitchers, now regarded as strikebreakers, were hooted at and called "scab" as they made their way to the Eastern Railroad depot or to their boardinghouses. Although one operative from Peabody was pursued into the ladies' waiting room at the depot, the strikers singled out the forewomen for special attention. The Austin shop owner, eager to divide the female work force, continued to pay union wages to the nonstrikers and defend his supervisors.[21] The daily confrontations on Union Street raised the issue of the use of the street as an arena for dissension among women workers and the propriety of the language and behavior of the union girls. The *Lynn Transcript* called the proceedings in front of the Austin shop "degrading" and defended the nonstrikers from the "opprobrious and insulting epithets" that the crowd used. The "shameful" behavior of the strikers appeared to the editor to be ignored by sympathetic police.[22] Public pressure on the mayor over the neutral position adopted by the police toward the Austin strikers led to intervention by a special police force directed by Deputy Marshal John A. Thurston, who attempted to separate strikers and nonstrikers. Pushing and shoving led to the arrest of striking stitchers for assault and using insulting language toward the Austin workers. After the arrests, the stitchers' assembly switched its tactics and called off the street confrontations, but extended the strike to the Amos Fawcett shop, another stitching operation that did work for B. F. Doak. The extension of the strike had the backing of the local KOL board, but also resulted in a divided response by stitchers to the assembly's strike call and a replication of tension between strikers and nonstrikers.[23] The result was a standoff.

As the municipal elections approached in late 1884, the striking stitchers went into the streets again after the strikebreakers, confident that the political power of the KOL men in Lynn, about one-third of the voting population, would force the mayor to hesitate before using the police against them. After the jeering of a young lady clerk who was mistaken for a stitcher at Austin's, the *Lynn*

Item blamed the mayor and the police for public disorder in the streets of Lynn. "There is hardly a woman in Lynn who is not liable to be insulted or assaulted by the shameless crowds, who are now permitted to carry on their unlawful acts in a high-handed manner, and with little or no fear of being interfered with."[24] Strikers and their supporters were arrested and convicted of what amounted to verbal assault: the use of "profane" language or "creating a disturbance."[25] The union girls, who had walked out of the Austin shop months before, found work in other shops and gave up on the strike in the face of police intervention and the controversial nature of their public behavior.

The political implications of the lady stitcher image divided the female work force during the 1884 strikes over the relationship of the individual stitcher to the KOL assembly and its objectives. Most stitchers, including the entire crew at Austin's, had eagerly supported collective action when the issue was unfair wages, but when the stitchers' assembly tried to get the two forewomen fired and pressured stitchers who disagreed with their concerns to comply, many women workers refused to cooperate. Fair treatment and good wages were acceptable goals for which lady stitchers would organize and act, but they would not support the aggressive pursuit of power in the shops. Answering the appeal of a "Union Girl" in the prolabor *Lynn Bee* for all stitchers to join the assembly, one of the Austin stitchers, who claimed to speak for all of the nonstrikers, replied in terms suggesting the genteel disapproval with which lady stitchers might regard the public behavior of union girls and their receipt of strike benefits from KOL men: "No, thank you; we prefer working honestly for our living to having our board bills paid by men who would be in better business if they supported their wives, rather than girls who worked in Austin's shop."[26] The writer made it clear that the issue of the strike at Austin's shop divided the contingent of boarding stitchers in the Lynn work force and reflected disagreement between generations of female workers about the proper behavior and tactics in a strike. Writing on behalf of those who had worked in the shop for years, this Austin stitcher insisted that "though we, as individuals know our rights and mean to have them, we also know that we are occupying a subordinate position." In her opinion, if operatives became their own supervisors, there would be nothing but chaos and confusion in the shops. The tensions expressed during the 1884 strikes revealed the divisions that existed within the female work force between age groups of stitchers, between residents of Lynn and boarders, and between Irish-American strikers arrested for assault, like Margaret McGeogh, the daughter of a KOL leader in Lynn, and the independent Yankee ladies beset by union girls.

Another issue from the 1884 strike that continued to rankle women workers was their inability to utilize the power of the Lynn Knights in municipal politics on behalf of their grievances and interests. As the municipal elections of 1885 approached, the Lynn *Knight of Labor* printed several letters from stitchers who expressed their dissatisfaction with the continued presence in city government of their opponents during the recent strikes. A letter from "Daughter of Labor," entitled by the editor "What a Lady Says," expressed her wish to vote in the municipal election in order to defeat the incumbent mayor, who had sent the police to intervene in their strikes.[27] She particularly wanted the removal from office of "that old and useless ornament, Captain Thurston." Mistreatment by police threatened her status as a respectable woman and led her to realize the importance of political power for women.

Another attack on Deputy Marshal Thurston came from "Closer-On." She charged him with behavior injurious to "poor striking girls" and recalled that as a striker she had been "manhandled," seized by the shoulder, and pushed up against a factory wall to keep her away from the Austin stitchers.[28] She regarded this public violation of her personal dignity as an outrage. Closer-On was especially irate to find that even after the Workingmen's party had elected the mayor in the municipal elections and chosen a new police chief, Thurston had not been discharged as an example to others, but had been kept on for sentimental reasons, "as an old veteran." Closer-On questioned the political commitment of the men in the Lynn Knights to the interests of the stitchers.

> It is fight for bread and life itself with the shop girls of Lynn, and no enemy of theirs should be allowed to remain in a position where he can do them injury. If the male organizations have not members who are gallant enough to take up the cause of their sisters and see that this old veteran sympathizer of the manufacturers is removed

and placed where he can do no more harm to working girls, then let the daughters assembly, Knights of Labor, rise to the emergency and see what they can do. Let them teach old men as well as young, that if they would be policemen, they must treat Lynn working girls respectfully.[29]

Closer-On might also have noted that in late 1885 members of the Workingmen's City Committee, which met to nominate candidates for municipal office on the Workingmen's party ticket (a coalition of reformers, politicians, and workers), opposed the nomination of any woman for the Lynn School Committee. John A. Willard of the Second Ward, who had served on the school committee with a "lady member," remembered that she had created "a disturbance" and declared the committee to be "no place for women."[30] The political interests of Lynn stitchers seemed peripheral to the local Knights.

The Lady Stitchers' Assembly in Lynn continued to recruit members in 1885 and 1886 and confront their employers, searching for ways to overcome the divisions between lady stitchers and union girls that had disrupted the 1884 strikes. The assembly boycotted the boardinghouse of a relative of the Millan family who ran a shop that specialized in stitching button fly pieces at less than union prices. Emphasizing the prospect of a 20 percent wage increase for union rates over the customary piece rate paid at Millan's, the leadership encouraged all the women workers in the shop to join their ladies' assembly.[31] In September 1885, the stitchers at Austin's struck again, and Mrs. Jenness, the forewoman, was forced to resign. The jubilant stitchers announced they had at last gotten "her scalp."[32] At John McNair's shoe factory located on the outskirts of Lynn at Glenmere, twenty stitchers who were KOL members were fired in December 1885. The stitchers' assembly struck McNair's, but shrewdly avoided antagonizing those women who remained at work. Several were recruited by the striking stitchers. The rest were encouraged to form an independent Stitchers and Button-hole Association, which agreed to honor the strike at McNair's and support arbitration of the dispute by the Knights in pursuit of a citywide scale of wages for stitching. This independent women's organization represented a significant number of workers who participated in strikes and in the arbitration of wages, but who resolutely refused to join the Knights.³³ Acting together, the stitchers' assembly and the stitchers' association called their organization the Lady Stitchers' Union of Lynn.

Members of the stitchers' assembly also tried to bridge the political gap between lady stitchers and union girls over objectives and decorum. Addressing herself in late 1885 to the Lynn manufacturers, "Union Girl" articulated the purposes of the women's union in elegant language that reflected a level of education unusual for female industrial workers, yet carried a message of defiance and strength. "Gentlemen, we have an ambition yet that is hard to tame to dependence. . . . Had we not ought to claim a recompense to warrant us a comfortable livelihood as we toil patiently on?"³⁴ She distinguished the Lady Stitchers' Union as more than simply an organization dedicated to the struggle for higher wages. The fundamental cause, she argued, was equal rights and resistance to tyranny—a life's work. But the writer warned her sister workers that their standing as union girls depended on the correct behavior of each individual to maintain community support and respect. "Never try to convey the wrong idea to the public that because you bear the name of Union Girl, you will be sustained in unladylike and wrong doings. . . . [Y]ou will bring the censure of the community on the whole for the rash folly of one."³⁵ Their organization, she cautioned, was designed to elevate, not to degrade.

This Lynn stitcher also wrestled with the problem of maintaining the womanly virtues of charity, civility, and courtesy along with firmness and militancy.

> Charity is a much-needed trait in one's character, especially at the present time; but we want a well-balanced judgment to know when to exercise this gift and not use it too freely. I am sorry to say it has come to that pass where most employers evince the spirit that honor is recompense enough for our labor. But that does not buy bread and clothes, and while we are willing to toil patiently on, we must and will not submit to tyranny, as such was never the intention of the Almighty. It is our duty to be courteous and civil to our employers, yet the task would be less irksome if by kindness they would win our voluntary admiration and respect.³⁶

Lynn stitchers tried to balance the need for militancy against their employers with the special requirements of respectable womanhood for female industrial workers. Although ladylike behavior created obstacles in strike situations, dignity and decorum also encouraged unity among generations of stitchers and assured the support of the community, strengths on which their organization depended.

The Lady Stitchers' Union in Lynn, which had organized almost 3,000 women by 1886 (2,000 in the assembly and 1,000 in the independent association) and represented over two-thirds of the female work force, refused, however, to admit women who were not stitchers. The *Knight of Labor* criticized the stitchers' assembly for not allowing lady clerks, bookkeepers, dressmakers, and seamstresses to join their organization, thus forming a mixed assembly for women in Lynn. The editor especially insisted that the beneficial influence that women wielded in society should be organized into the KOL. "Our wives and daughters, mothers and sisters, and every true woman who is interested in the well-being of her sex, should avail herself of the protecting arm of the Knights of Labor." [37] The stitchers' assembly refused. Their objective was to recruit all stitchers in Lynn to their trade organization; women in other kinds of work had to organize their own assemblies for box makers and heel seaters and a mixed assembly of male and female laundry workers. [38] The assembly members insisted that their organization represent only women shoeworkers. This became their guiding principle as members of the Knights of Labor.

The rapid growth of the Knights of Labor in Massachusetts had prompted members in Lynn and the surrounding towns of Salem, Marblehead, and Beverly to organize into a separate district assembly in late 1884. The organization of the new D.A. 77 cut the Knights in Lynn off from the original D.A. 30, which represented large numbers of workers in the Massachusetts textile mills as well as other industries and trades. Shoeworkers dominated D.A. 77; D.A. 30 represented a coalition of shoeworkers from Haverhill, Marlboro, Natick, Brockton, and other shoe centers as well as the textile workers of Lowell, Lawrence, and Fall River. The interests of D.A. 30 included political objectives that addressed the needs of workers in textiles and other industries, such as legislation setting up a state board of arbitration and the mandating of weekly payment of wages, both measures subsequently passed by the state legislature in 1886.[39] Tensions grew in the late 1880s between the two district assemblies over the implications of a trade district primarily for shoeworkers and over the question of which district assembly best represented the equal rights tradition in Massachusetts for industrial workers.

The lady stitchers' assemblies outside of Lynn and outside of D.A. 77 were also active in 1885 and 1886. Like the DOSC, the stitchers in Lynn had developed close ties with the stitchers' assembly in Stoneham.[40] In Haverhill the stitchers' assembly with the support of the local Knights arbitrated an end to a charge for steam power that had been deducted from stitchers' wages ever since its installation in Haverhill shops in the early 1870s. The effect was to increase wages by 10 percent, although stitchers continued to furnish thread, paste, and blacking for their work. Unlike Lynn, the Haverhill Board of Arbitration included female representatives who negotiated directly with their employers, and KOL stitchers joined in successful strikes against the Thom Hat Company and the Gale Brothers shoe factory in early 1885. The lady stitchers of Salem won a strike at the McLean and Appleton shoe factory over the firing of Miss Lizzie Ramsdell as a KOL member. She was reinstated after the local Knights threatened to strike the factory and ordered the stationary engineer, who was a Knight, to shut down the steam power at the shop. In addition, the *Laborer* of Haverhill, the voice of D.A. 30, reported thriving stitchers' assemblies in Marlboro and Brockton in early 1886.[41]

After the Lynn Knights had won a significant victory in 1885 over Kimball Brothers, who operated a large shoe factory in Lynn as well as a factory at Gardiner, Maine, they were able to reorganize the board of arbitration into a permanent body that included representatives of the manufacturers. The Knights and the independent Lasters' Protective Union of Lynn identified the low wages paid to shoeworkers in the country shops as the most serious threat to their own wages. The country shop system had begun in the early 1870s when several Lynn manufacturers, facing the first Crispin wage list, had opened up shoe factories in southern New Hampshire and Maine for their cheapest grades of work. Low wages in Massachusetts shoe cities during the depression years of the 1870s discouraged the expansion of the country shops, but with prosperity returning in the 1880s, more and more large shoe manufac-

1885]   SHOE AND LEATHER REPORTER.—Rubber Supplement.   ix

FRANCIS W. BREED,
MANUFACTURER OF LADIES' FINE SHOES.

New Factory
at
Rochester,
N. H.

Capacity
for
3,000 to 4,000
Pairs Daily.

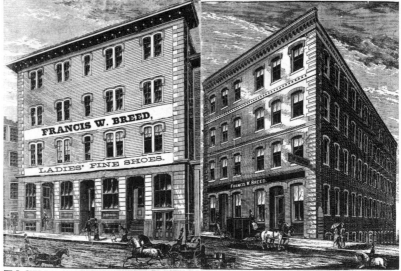

FACTORIES AT LYNN, MASS., AND ROCHESTER, N. H.
ACTUAL RUNNING CAPACITY OF LYNN FACTORIES, 6,000 to 7,000 PAIRS DAILY.

The country shop system. *Shoe and Leather Reporter*, July 30, 1885, p. ix, courtesy of Library of Congress.

turers in Lynn and Haverhill who had an eye on the profits of mass-produced, cheap shoes began operations in the country. Country factories in New Hampshire were scattered in towns well north and east of Rockingham County where Haverhill manufacturers had developed a network of decentralized production for turned shoes among the farming and village population. As in New Hampshire, the country shops in southern Maine were located in towns along the railroad network, away from competitors, and where the only industry was shoe production. In one New Hampshire town, a hundred miles north of Boston, the picturesque New England setting of white church and houses, barber shop, post office, and hay scale was dwarfed by a country shop in 1885: "Looming hugely above its surrounding neighbors, the new shoe factory stood like a leviathan swept hither by some flood and stranded."[42] The isolation of the country factories in widely scattered locations was intended to give the owners a free hand with the community and the local labor supply to guarantee low wages. The estimated savings of rent (50 percent) in factories that grateful townspeople erected at their own expense and in wages (25 percent) were balanced, however, by high freight charges, the costs of maintaining a large inventory of leather stock, the extra expense of supervisory personnel and travel, and the lack of convenient banking facilities.[43] But the real savings, according to the Lynn Knights, was to be realized in levering down wages in Massachusetts. By 1886, twenty-three large Lynn manufacturers had set up country factories in New Hampshire and Maine, including Francis Breed in Rochester, New Hampshire; Charles D. Pecker at Great Falls, New Hampshire; Morgan and Dore at Pittsfield, New Hampshire, and at Richmond, Maine; John Shaw at Keene, New Hampshire; and Keene Brothers at Skowhegan, Maine. B. F. Spinney had been in a factory at Norway, Maine, since 1874. Unlike most Haverhill manufacturers who built their country factories in central New Hampshire, John Pilling moved his entire operation west to Lowell in 1887 where he hoped to demonstrate that the low wages common to textile centers could be utilized to the advantage of the shoe industry.[44]

The KOL victory in the Kimball Brothers strike at Gardiner, Maine, in late 1885 represented a promising regional strategy of organizing country shoeworkers to prevent wage cuts in Lynn and raise wages in Maine. Striking simultaneously in Lynn and Gardiner, the KOL shut down the Kimballs' entire operation. The Lynn Shoe and Leather Association, composed of manufacturers, then voted unanimously to accept a joint board of arbitration as the best way to settle the interstate strike and avoid additional confrontations with the Knights. The joint board of seven Knights and seven manufacturers arbitrated wage lists for an initial six months' period beginning in December 1885. Both employers and employees pledged no strikes or lockouts, but the lasters insisted that rules that applied in Lynn not restrain their ability to conduct sympathy strikes on behalf of country shoeworkers. Manufacturers agreed to fire no worker for being a member of the KOL and to refuse to hire workers deemed obnoxious to the Knights by order of their executive committee. Subcommittees of the joint board began to meet, hear testimony, and submit wage lists to local assemblies for their approval. The conduct of arbitration by the KOL in Lynn contrasted with similar procedures in Philadelphia, where arbitration was used only for deadlocks between manufacturers and local assemblies.[45]

In early December, Kimball Brothers sat down in Maine to arbitrate wages with the local KOL assemblies in Gardiner and, significantly, with representatives of the Lynn Knights as well.[46] The joint board in Lynn then took up the settlement of all wage disputes in 1886, while the Knights continued to put pressure on country factories in other towns. The Lynn lasters with KOL backing struck the Spinney and Keene factories in Maine, while the lasters of Haverhill struck the country shop of Gale Brothers in Exeter, New Hampshire. In early 1886 the Lynn Knights were acknowledged to be at the height of their power and "all the rage."[47] Like the Crispins, the Knights of Labor arbitrated wages to combat the pressure of marketplace competition and seasonality on their work.

The agreement of the stitchers in Lynn to let the KOL executive board negotiate a citywide wage list on their behalf did not, however, include the placing of women workers on the joint board of arbitration. Unlike the women shoeworkers in the Garfield Assembly in Philadelphia or in the Haverhill stitchers' assembly, the Lynn stitchers did not negotiate directly with their employers and named James H. Carr as their secretary to represent them on the executive committee. This lack of direct participation by stitchers in the wage negotiations in Lynn caused immediate trouble.

When the Knights announced the wage agreement for stitching in February 1886, serious and prolonged dissension among the stitchers forced the Knights to reopen negotiations for several categories of work. The stitchers had asked the joint board to increase their wages generally by 10 to 15 percent, but the wage list cut prices on some work, such as closing on, and on the third grade of goods, while raising wages only on the scarcer first-quality work. Manufacturers' representatives had persuaded the Knights on the board to tie stitching wages to the sale price of the shoe. Harried by the demands of cutters and other shoeworkers to settle their wages for the season, the KOL executive board suggested that if the stitchers worked under the new wage list for six months, then the board would reopen negotiations. The editor of the *Knight of Labor* appealed to them: "Give the new system a fair trial, girls."[48] But there were so many protests from the stitchers that by late March the board was forced to reopen the question of the stitchers' wages. The adjustments in the price list, announced in mid-May, finally proved acceptable. Some Lynn manufacturers reacted to the initial wage increases for stitching in 1886 by establishing stitching shops outside of Lynn, but these country shops could rarely produce a similar quality of work. A few country factories even sent their stitching work to be done in Lynn.[49]

The trouble over the wage list for stitching in 1886 revealed weaknesses in the operations of the joint board. Subcommittees met frequently to deal with the complicated problems of setting prices for subdivisions of labor. Members of the joint board admitted that stitching wages represented "perplexing" problems that concerned unfamiliar work and produced delays. The time-consuming work of the board was also hampered by the need to settle minor grievances. Although the Knights counted on competition among manufacturers to prevent a unified front by employers on the joint board, this also led to high turnover among manufacturers' representatives, which postponed deliberations. The complexities of arbitration in Lynn convinced shoeworkers in D.A. 77 to oppose the creation of a state board of arbitration in 1886 as impractical.[50]

After the success of its strategy of holding production in Lynn factories hostage for better conditions and wages in country shops and the arbitration of a general increase in wages in 1886, the

Lynn Knights attempted to encourage other shoe centers in Massachusetts to raise their wages to a level closer to Lynn's.[51] The problem was that the other shoe centers were in D.A. 30. The Haverhill Knights were not interested in pushing the level of wages higher, fearing competition from turned-shoe workers in rural Rockingham County. The Lasters' Protective Union had equalized wages between the two cities, but the cutters, stitchers, and other workers in Haverhill were receiving wages from 10 to 30 percent lower than those paid in Lynn.[52] The Knights and the popular press in Lynn became convinced that orders were being redirected from their city to Haverhill because of the lower wages paid there. Despite the fact that Haverhill still specialized in low-cut turn shoes and slippers and shipped smaller cases of shoes, containing not sixty but twelve pairs per case, the volume of production in Haverhill seemed a sharp contrast to a dull season in Lynn. The *Lynn Saturday Union*, which grew increasingly critical of the KOL in early 1886, taunted the Lynn shoeworkers for enjoying high wages, but having no work to do. The editor admonished the Knights to respect the laws of supply and demand: "Wage earners may learn very soon that to push such matters is clearly against their every interest, and that they cannot exceed the natural laws."[53] For shoeworkers, the solution seemed to be more regional organization.

In the spring of 1886 the Knights in D.A. 77 proposed that a trade district of shoeworkers be formed for New England that would equalize wages in the region. However, the Knights in D.A. 30 regarded this proposal as a dangerous extension of their mistaken decision in late 1884 to allow D.A. 77 to be organized out of the original district. The proposed trade district was strongly opposed by many groups within D.A. 30 and became a major issue for their delegation to the General Assembly of the Knights meeting at Richmond, Virginia, in October 1886. At the semiannual district conventions for 1886 held at Lowell in January and at Worcester in July, D.A. 30 delegates voted overwhelmingly and in secret session to reject the New England trade district and ejected members who supported the idea.[54] The April 10, 1886, editorial of the Haverhill *Laborer* expressed the fears of the leaders of D.A. 30. Although the trade district might have a powerful influence on the manufacturers in one particular industry, they feared that the development of trade districts for skilled workers would divide the Knights of Labor in Massachusetts, leaving the "great mass of cheap and unskilled labor . . . to founder in disorganized poverty." "When by the force of numbers or superior skill a part of our Order think they can travel faster unencumbered than by being harnessed to unskilled, unorganized and poorly-paid masses, then comes the appeal for a trade district. Brothers of St. Crispin, it is a retrograde movement."[55] The *Laborer* also warned the Lynn Knights that unless the general wage level for all workers in New England increased, skilled workers would suffer:

> An enlightened self interest demands of the best organized branch of industry in Massachusetts that it stay with the factory people of Lawrence and Lowell, with the poverty paid stonecutters of Cape Ann, with the seamstresses and laborers of Boston—with the rank and file of the army of labor, and that the advance onward be made in one solid, well disciplined, irresistible column, whose aim shall be not to make an aristocracy among the working people themselves, but to give every honest working man and woman the largest possible share of that wealth by labor alone created.

In their own self-interest, shoeworkers had to continue the powerful coalition with all other industrial workers in the major cities of the commonwealth. Leaders of D.A. 30 also opposed the trade district for political reasons, fearing the weakening of the influence of the Knights on the state legislature. One case in point was the passage of the bill under consideration in the state legislature requiring the weekly payment of wages, legislation designed to benefit the large number of textile workers in D.A. 30.

These issues of strategy and philosophy dominated the KOL press in Massachusetts during the summer of 1886. Those who defended the trade district argued that the large mixed district had failed to oppose the power of capital effectively. The trade district had the advantage of being built on a foundation of fraternity, experience, and a shared work environment, which made organization and discipline possible.[56] The Lynn *Knight of Labor* argued that rivalry between shoe towns over the level of wages hid impulses of aristocracy among workers where equality was essential. Organized labor must, one of the editors wrote, exorcise the demon of caste. Nonetheless, he expected Lynn workers would be at the forefront both in influence and in wages. "We are all laborers and all struggling in the one common battle of life and we hope to see this matter of Lynn, Beverly, Haverhill and other shoe centers, prices equalized as near as possible, of course, always allowing some little margin in favor of this city on account of the superior workmanship of its laborers." [57]

The men and women in the Lynn Knights were well on their way to embracing trade unionism in 1886. They saw the shoeworker as enmeshed in the wage system and influenced by the forces of supply and demand in the national shoe market. In defense of the boycott as a legitimate weapon in labor struggles, one of the leaders of the Lynn KOL accepted the implications of supply and demand. "The theory of supply and demand ruling business may be an axiom in regard to manufactured articles, but in regard to the labor which produces them, we propose to demonstrate its reality by giving it a market value like every other commodity to be bought and sold by two agents, the buyer and the seller." [58] The Lynn Knights developed regional strategies and promoted the trade district to oppose those manufacturers who were attempting to use competition from the country factories to force down wages. If Haverhill was not yet a serious competitor in the production of high-button shoes, new large factories were being planned by manufacturers eager to realize the profits in mass production of the cheaper grades and intensify regional competition.

Supporters of the mixed district of various industries within the Knights, however, saw the issue of the trade district in 1886 as one of justice as well as power. D.A. 30 could not operate successfully on behalf of the general interests of labor in Massachusetts without the effective organization and militancy of its shoeworker assemblies. How could the shoeworkers of Essex County successfully oppose the competition from the country shops without the help of workers in other shoe centers in D.A. 30? Could the equal rights tradition be realized within the existing wage system or in trade unions? Was the trade district or the mixed district the better vehicle for equal rights? These were the terms of the debate between D.A. 30 and D.A. 77 in 1886.

Replying to a socialist critic just prior to the Richmond convention, Frank K. Foster of Haverhill, editor of the *Laborer*, confessed that the Knights in Massachusetts were at a crossroads. If the wage system was to be recognized and accepted as the dominating influence in the economy, then the trade union offered the most powerful force to oppose it. If the Knights decided to work to abolish the wage system, then the trades must be retained within the larger organization. If the Richmond convention did not settle this issue, he wrote in September, the result would be confusion and disorder within the KOL in Massachusetts.[59] The Richmond convention sidestepped the issue and adopted a policy of trying to control the trade district movement within the organization.[60] The result, as Foster predicted, was dissension within the Knights of Labor in Massachusetts.

Women workers in D.A. 30, especially in Haverhill, played much more active roles in the executive bodies on the local and district level than in Lynn. The KOL board of arbitration in Haverhill included shoeworkers, male and female, hatters, and morocco dressers.[61] When Mrs. A. M. Barrows, forelady of a stitching shop for the Jennings and Stevens Company, fired several French-Canadian stitchers because she could not understand their English, the local stitchers' assembly called a strike and, discovering that Barrows was herself a KOL member, blackballed her from their assembly. When she appealed their decision to the D.A. 30 headquarters in Boston and was reinstated as a "Lady Knight," the Haverhill stitchers pursued the matter to the executive committee of the district and won their case against Barrows.[62] The native-born and immigrant women in the Haverhill assembly acted together to achieve justice for their members. Mrs. Lizzie H. Shute of Haverhill, who had personally pursued the obnoxious Barrows, had been a delegate representing her local assembly to previous KOL national conventions. In 1886 she went to the Richmond convention as an elected member of the district executive board.

D.A. 30 sent the largest delegation to the General Assembly in Richmond, among whom were Annie Moran, shoeworker from Natick; Maggie Burke, shoeworker from Marlboro; Mary A. Ferry, dressmaker from Milford; and Mary Ward, weaver from Taunton. With Lizzie Shute, they represented one-third of the total female delegates. The Knights in D.A. 77 sent a much smaller delegation, which included only one woman delegate: Mrs. Nellie Hardison, a Lynn stitcher and former Daughter of St. Crispin.[63]

The Richmond convention became the high point of activity for KOL women on the national level.

Even after its initial years of secrecy, the Knights of Labor as a national organization was slow to involve and organize women workers. The first convention in 1878 endorsed the principle of equal pay for equal work as a tactic to prevent women from replacing men in industrial jobs, but did not act to admit women as members. In 1881 the male shoeworkers of Philadelphia in D.A. 64 led by local organizer Henry J. Skeffington inducted women shoeworkers who were involved in a successful strike led by Miss Mary Stirling into the first women's assembly in the Knights.[64] The Garfield Assembly #1684, which received its charter in September, represented shoe stitchers and was the first to send a woman delegate to a KOL General Assembly in 1881, and in 1883, Stirling won several votes for a national office and was awarded the honorific title Grand Venerable Sage.[65] Other representatives of autonomous women's assemblies joined her as delegates to KOL conventions; by 1886, women represented over 50,000 members of the KOL or 9 percent of the membership. D.A.s 30 and 77 had the largest concentrations of women members where over 13,000 Massachusetts women were Knights of Labor, 80 percent of whom were textile operatives and shoeworkers.[66] At the 1884 convention in Philadelphia, however, women Knights had to fight for the control of Garfield Assembly against efforts by Philadelphia KOL men to organize a rival assembly of women shoeworkers.

Mary Stirling was not a delegate to the 1884 convention from her district assembly in Philadelphia, indicative of the conflict over the status of Garfield Assembly. Instead Miss Mary Hanafin made the case for women's control of the local.[67] Although employed as a salesclerk in 1884, Mary Hanafin's devoted efforts on behalf of female industrial workers in the Knights of Labor General Assemblies between 1884 and 1887 would be difficult to account for without recognizing her background as a shoeworker and a charter member of Garfield Assembly. Some Philadelphia Knights had persuaded Harry Skeffington, who had aided the creation of Garfield Assembly in 1881, to organize a new assembly of women shoeworkers and to ask the district of Philadelphia to request a charter from the General Assembly in 1884. Defeated at the district level, the leaders of Garfield Assembly appealed to the 1884 convention not to undermine their control of the organization. Hanafin argued that Sister Stirling wished to organize all women shoeworkers in Philadelphia into one body strong enough to oppose the shoe manufacturers. She denied that the assembly was unwilling to accommodate all women shoeworkers in the city or unable to direct its affairs according to KOL principles. Hanafin challenged the Philadelphia Knights, who had criticized assembly leaders for blackballing scabs, to admit that this was precisely the policy that the brother Knights themselves had taught the sisters. Her arguments exposed the tensions within the Philadelphia Knights over the autonomy of Garfield Assembly.

Skeffington, who believed in the strength of female assemblies and supported woman suffrage, backed Hanafin's arguments by reporting that the supporters of the proposed assembly told him 450 women wanted to organize when there were only twelve.[68] Swayed by his speech, the convention voted to sustain the position of Mary Stirling and Mary Hanafin. Encouraged by this, the two Philadelphia women and Lizzie Shute of Haverhill organized a national committee at the 1885 convention to collect statistics on women's work. This convention, held at Hamilton, Ontario, nominated Mary Hanafin for the national executive board and again dubbed the vindicated Mary Stirling Grand Venerable Sage.[69] By 1885, women shoeworkers had aggressively defended the autonomy of female assemblies and introduced an active concern for the welfare and advancement of women workers at the conventions of the Knights of Labor.

At both General Assemblies in 1886, women shoeworker delegates pushed this work further. At the special session in June at Cleveland, Mary Hanafin and Lizzie Shute were appointed to a committee to respond to an appeal by the Ohio Woman Suffrage Association for the Knights to endorse woman suffrage. A special committee of Hanafin, Shute, and Charles Litchman of D.A. 30 persuaded the General Assembly to endorse the work of the Woman's Christian Temperance Union. This endorsement of temperance also contained a sweeping commitment by the Knights to equal rights for its women members at work and in wages and an equal voice in the making and administration of the laws of the order. "We believe," the convention's resolution read, "this equality had never before been accorded by any organization of labor." But the ideology of the Knights of Labor represented two conflicting positions on women's involvement in their organization: a general commitment to equal rights and a moral critique of capitalism based on values shaped by family life and domesticity.[70] Although the Knights welcomed all women into their ranks, the natural sphere for women remained the home, not the workplace. The Knights supported participation by women in political action, but the ideology of the Knights discouraged a critique of capitalism from the special experience and needs of female industrial workers. Many shoe stitchers, carpet weavers, and textile operatives in the Knights developed a different vision of equal rights and woman's place in the labor movement that involved the exercise of power on behalf of the interests of working women.

Long before the Richmond convention in October, the Committee on Woman's Work had sent out questionnaires to local women's assemblies requesting information on wages, hours, and conditions of work. The results indicated that on the average, women worked a ten-hour day and earned five dollars a week in industrial work, except for shoeworkers who, as the committee members well knew, earned more and worked fewer hours.[71] The committee reported its findings to the Richmond convention, enlisted almost all of the female delegates in 1886 (most of them textile operatives and shoeworkers) in their activities, elected officers, and most important, persuaded the convention to name Leonora Barry, a hosiery worker from Amsterdam, New York, as a permanent general investigator for a Department of Woman's Work in the KOL. Barry became a walking delegate on behalf of women workers. At Richmond, Mary Hanafin, the most experienced female delegate, formally presented the committee's recommendations, which the convention accepted. She also answered the appeal of the Ohio suffragists by emphasizing that the first objective for working women was not suffrage, but organization to obtain better wages and conditions. Nonetheless, the Knights endorsed woman suffrage in 1886, and Leonora Barry's activities as general investigator between 1886 and 1889 led her into close contacts with both the suffrage and the temperance organizations.[72] However, when women shoeworkers in Massachusetts and Philadelphia followed their brothers out of the Knights late in 1886 into a national trade assembly and later into trade unions, the solid foundation in the KOL that supported Barry's work and equal rights for women workers fell apart. Beginning in 1887 no female representatives of D.A. 30 or D.A. 77 or from Garfield Assembly appeared at the national conventions, and Barry presented her three historic reports on women's work to a General Assembly rapidly losing interest in the subject.[73] This loss in 1887 of the successful female champions of assemblies led by working women in their own interests led to the abandonment of efforts by the Knights to organize women workers.

Historians of women's involvement in the Knights of Labor have focused much of their attention on Leonora Barry's work and her reports on the conditions of female wage earners in 1887, 1888, and 1889 for the General Assembly. This focus on the national reports and their contents shifts attention away from the rank and file except as seen through the eyes of the increasingly discouraged and pessimistic Barry.[74] She concluded after three years of arduous work that women could not and would not be organized as autonomous units, a conclusion that contradicted the experience and hopes of those activist women in the Knights who had initially sponsored her work as an investigator.[75]

Barry's first report in 1887 immediately demonstrated that the investigations in 1885 by the committee of Hanafin, Stirling, and Shute were an unrealistic assessment of the experience of the average woman worker. Rather than five dollars a week for a twelve-hour workday, the women garment and textile workers contacted by Barry reported an average workday of fourteen hours for $2.50 to three dollars a week.[76] She was uncovering a female work experience unknown to the shoe stitchers of Massachusetts and Philadelphia. By 1888 Barry reported mass defections in district assemblies where women's organizations had flourished in 1886. The numbers of women members in the KOL shrank alarmingly from over 50,000 in 1886 to about 10,000 in 1888.[77] Barry dismissed the shoe strike of 1887 in Philadelphia that pulled the Garfield Assembly apart as the result of the "folly" of its members. Although she had held KOL men accountable for malice and opposition to organized women in her first report, Barry's recital of her activities in 1888 blamed the troubles in female assemblies on lack of education and maturity and overwhelmingly difficult work conditions. The new realities of industrial work appalled her: the crowding of the labor market with immigrants, children, and married women, the speedups and mechanization. Barry wrote in discouragement of starvation wages and the threat of immorality among women workers. She worried about the impact of overwork and harsh conditions on the health of the future mothers of the country and began to advocate protective legislation as a solution for working women's problems.[78] As she despaired over the lack of organization by women workers, Barry embraced the rationale of protective legislation.

In her third report in 1889 Barry recommended abandoning all attempts to organize women workers. The time of separate interests along sex lines, she wrote, was past.[79] The penalties of being a woman as well as a worker were too much; the job of organization belonged to the brother Knights. Woman's natural pride and timidity coupled with the effect of restrictive social custom made it harder for women to struggle against their oppressors than for men. Women lacked industrial training and had no trades or skills, which rendered them victims to machine work and competition. The effect of such industrial work created apathy and hopelessness and inculcated habits of submission and acceptance. On the other hand, women earning good wages, she reported, were indifferent to others, and all saw marriage as an escape from the labor market. These natural and acquired disabilities led Barry to the conclusion that women should, if they could, withdraw from wage-earning entirely and devote themselves to domestic duties.[80] She ended her last report by advising the Knights to close down the woman's department. Her recommendation that women workers be submerged in the general organizations of workers cut the Knights off from the heritage of activism by autonomous women's assemblies such as Garfield Assembly and the lady stitchers' organizations of Essex County.

The contents of Barry's three reports for the KOL indicated that growing numbers of female industrial workers in the late nineteenth century experienced their work in ways totally unlike those of New England shoeworkers. The traditions, cultural background, and expectations of lady stitchers contrasted with the situations of garment workers, textile operatives, and other women workers. Stitchers were distinguished among female industrial workers for their high wages, their access to skilled work, traditions of militancy and organization, their noncompetitive work relations with men, their positive sense of their gender, and for their cultural background as native-born Americans, many of whom were New England Yankees. All of these characteristics separated New England stitchers from most female industrial workers. The Knights of Labor organization in Massachusetts, especially D.A. 30, had offered a brief chance for female shoeworkers and textile operatives to work together as a coalition, but the stampede of the shoeworker assemblies in D.A. 77 after 1886 into trade districts amid serious and disruptive jurisdictional disputes cut off the possibility of an alliance between native-born and immigrant working women in Massachusetts. The cost of this disunity was heavy: one of the greatest fears haunting New England shoeworkers in the late nineteenth century was a descent to the level of the immigrant textile workers in adjoining cities and towns.

Despite the disintegration of the KOL in Massachusetts in the late 1880s, the stitchers' assembly in Lynn continued to function effectively as an organization to protect the interests of women shoeworkers. The stitchers faced serious threats to their wages and working conditions. While retaining a firm foundation for resistance, they also began to criticize the mythology of the lady stitcher and in doing so they would develop a stronger consciousness of themselves as a hard-working industrial work force, an experience closer to that of the masses of working men and women.

The assemblies of male shoeworkers in the Essex County Knights faced division and decline in the late 1880s. The Lasters' Protective Union remained independent, and the McKay stitchers formed their own organization. Strikes called by leather workers in Salem and Peabody in 1887 drained the treasury of D.A. 77. After the 1886 General Assembly, the leaders of D.A. 30 persuaded Terence V. Powderly to visit Lynn to try to block the development of a new national trade assembly for shoeworkers. At a convention held at Brockton on June 8, 1887, Harry Skeffington, who had been blacklisted and forced to leave Philadelphia, pulled together shoeworker delegates from ten states into a national trade organization that named him Master Workman. Knights from Lynn participated in the convention, but did not play a major role in the organization of the national assembly. A stitcher from Brockton represented women workers on one convention committee, and James H. Carr of the Lynn stitchers' assembly, Lizzie McElwee of the Garfield Assembly, and a stitcher from Marlboro became members of the national executive board of the new assembly.

At the convention, Skeffington, a longtime supporter of autonomous female assemblies and of woman suffrage, addressed the major complaint of stitchers about the power structure of arbitration. He proposed an arrangement that guaranteed that female members of stitchers' assemblies would participate directly in arbitration settlements on an equal basis with other shoeworkers. Stitchers' assemblies committed to equal rights and full representation for women workers helped shape the new national trade organization. When Skeffington met Powderly in Boston a few days after the convention, the national trade assembly was already an entity that Skeffington defended as functioning within the Knights as one wheel turned within another. Backed by D.A. 30, Powderly visited Lynn on June 12 to prevent the absorption of the local Knights by Skeffington's organization. Powderly, however, offered them little. After avoiding a public reception by a delegation of D.A. 77 leaders including members of the stitchers' assembly, he addressed a large and friendly audience of Knights at the Music Hall. Ignoring the Brockton convention and the national trade issue, he emphasized arbitration, temperance, and land reform.[81] He concluded by criticizing strikes as the equivalent of war—unwise in a speech to Lynn shoeworkers, whose very success at arbitration rested on militant confrontations with the manufacturers based on a strong regional trade organization.

Additional troubles plagued both men and women shoeworkers in the Knights when the state board of arbitration, established in 1886 at the height of KOL political power in Massachusetts, took over the settlement of wage disputes in Lynn in 1887 and 1888. One of the first arbitration cases heard by the three-member board, which represented labor, capital, and the public interest, involved the Lynn Knights and Francis W. Breed, who operated a country shop in Rochester, New Hampshire. Breed epitomized the large manufacturers who had moved the production of cheap grades of shoes out of Lynn. The arbitration decision in February 1887 represented a victory for the large manufacturers and a defeat for the Lynn Knights.

For years the manufacturers had blamed the movement of the production of cheap shoes to the country shops in Maine and New Hampshire on high wages in Lynn. The result was fewer orders, less work, and the threat to Lynn of slipping from preeminence in the national shoe market. Smaller manufacturers in the city shifted partially into the production of medium and fine grades of ladies' button shoes for sale in New England, but the larger manufacturers counted on the mass production of cheap button boots to yield profits on huge quantities of sales. After the initial establishment of a few country shops during the period of Crispin wage agreements, twenty large Lynn manufacturers set up country factories in the late 1870s and early 1880s to gain a competitive advantage in labor costs. Many of the manufacturers complained about the uncertainties of dealing with organized workers in Lynn, especially with the lasters. Their risk-taking, preparations, and profits from the busy season could all be upset by labor disputes. One manufacturer claimed in 1888 to have been forced to the country by the arbitrary demands of the Lynn lasters. "Even if you want merely a change that involves a decrease of work, they ask for extra pay for it, their idea being that the manufacturer is getting profit from the change in some way, and that they therefore ought to have a share of it." [82]

Another firm criticized the KOL policy of demanding the same wage for all grades of work on the grounds that whatever the quality of the materials or the anticipated sale price, the amount of labor to last, stitch, or burnish a shoe was essentially the same. As a result, the manufacturers argued that the otherwise abundant work on cheap grades could not be done in Lynn and had to be performed in the country. They argued that the return of cheap work to Lynn could mean steadier employment and higher annual earnings, even if piece rates were reduced on the cheap work. The price to be paid for a return of cheap work to Lynn was a general wage reduction to be negotiated with the Knights, but some manufacturers had begun to advocate nonunion "free shops." Lynn manufacturers believed themselves beset by competitive pressures from shoe manufacturers in the West, which by the 1880s meant

Chicago, Cincinnati, and St. Louis as well as cities in New York State, and by regional competition from a country shop system that many of them had helped to build and operate. Men like the two Keene brothers who argued for wage reductions in Lynn talked constantly of competition, whether from Haverhill or Stoneham or the country shops, and were pointing in 1888 to the "prairie shoemaker" as Lynn's newest nemesis.[83]

The Lynn Knights knew that the country shop system had been created by the large manufacturers to force down wages in their Massachusetts factories. As much as shoeworkers were eager for more work, many of them understood that if wages were cut in Lynn, wages would also be cut in the country factories and the result would be a general wage reduction for all shoeworkers in New England. The very men who complained about competition, one laster explained, were the ones who ran country shops. "They work Lynn against the country and the country against Lynn, and they have done that for a long time."[84] When the KOL was at its peak in the mid-1880s, the Knights attempted to organize the country shops, raise wages throughout New England, and maintain Lynn as the industry's high wage standard. But in 1887, unsure of the future of organized labor in Massachusetts, the Knights accepted the settlement of the Breed case by the state board of arbitration.

The board had been persuaded by the large manufacturers to give them a chance to return the cheaper grades of work to Massachusetts. The Breed decision established a new, lower level of wages for third-grade work, reducing wages by 7 percent on all operations except lasting, McKay stitching, and upper stitching. As the Knights feared, Breed then proceeded to cut wages in all other grades of work and used the wage cuts in Lynn to beat down his labor costs at his country shop in Rochester and his newly opened factory at Athol in central Massachusetts.[85] These wage cuts in addition to the country shop competition shook up shoe manufacturing in Lynn. As one manufacturer said in 1888: "The competition grows stronger everyday, . . . we must either make a shoe cheap enough to compete with the country manufacturers or retire altogether from the business."[86] Some shifted totally into medium and fine goods. Others, still eager to share in the profits of production in volume and mass sales, searched for ways to cut their labor costs in Lynn. The stitchers, especially the highly paid vampers and buttonhole makers, became one of the targets of these efforts.

In late 1887 Samuel Crossman, who operated stitching shops in Lynn and Beverly, made an attempt to pay his women buttonhole makers by the week rather than by the piece. The Lady Stitchers' Union, which still represented 1,500 women in 1887, took the case to the state board of arbitration in November. Crossman proposed a daily stint of 4,000 buttonholes on good grades of work and 5,000 on the cheap grade, for which women would work nine and a half hours a day and receive ten dollars a week for ten months' work. He was paying six cents per 100 as a piece rate in Lynn and Beverly, but told the board that he could get better quality work with weekly wages. The stitchers who testified at the hearings rejected Crossman's offer. Lizzie M. Waite of Salem said she greatly preferred the piece rate to the weekly wage, and all of the women workers supplied personal experiences of earnings on piecework well above the proffered ten dollars a week. At the six cents per 100 piece rate, buttonhole operators could produce 4,000 per day and earn over fourteen dollars per week. They saw Crossman's proposal for what it was: a wage cut. Miss Eliza Merrow said she felt "freer" on piecework and criticized the stint of 5,000 buttonholes per day as excessive. Despite Crossman's promise of ten months' work, the women knew he could not guarantee orders. Others argued that if they worked by the week, only some of the operatives would be furnished with work throughout the year, while on piecework, the custom was to share whatever work was available during the dull season. Most complained about the aggravations and additional effort involved in working on cheap leather stock with brittle cotton thread. They preferred to work on fine grades, but wanted steady work at current piece rates. The state board accepted the testimony of union stitchers and did not endorse the Crossman proposal. The failure of the board to support Crossman prompted J. H. Winchell, who operated the largest shoe factory in Haverhill, to withdraw his application for a hearing to settle a strike with his lining makers in early December. Winchell decided to cut his labor costs by shutting down his stitching room, which employed 200, and having his work sent to country shops.[87]

As in the Breed case in 1887, the state board was more amenable to arguments by Lynn manufacturers who insisted that wage reductions for stitching were essential to attract shoe production back to Massachusetts from the country shops. In the spring of 1888 Henry C. Mears, the proprietor of a stitching shop that did work for large factories, brought a grievance to the state board concerning wages paid by his competitors in Lynn. The board seized the occasion to set up a general wage schedule for all grades of stitching in the city that equalized wages paid by the factories and the subcontract shops and attempted to lure stitching work back to Lynn from the country by reducing rates on cheap work.[88] The reductions in wages for overlap vamping, buttonhole work, and staying on the cheap grade of work announced in the state board's decision on June 19 caused a revolt among the Lynn stitchers. They threatened to strike all stitching operations in Lynn unless the board reopened the arbitration process. In an unprecedented move, deplored by the manufacturers and the trade journals, the board held hearings in Lynn on July 13 to listen to additional testimony from the female operatives.[89]

During the hearings on the Mears case, the stitchers described their experiences and their expectations as workers. All were conscious of the need to earn as much as possible on piecework during the busy season. Their goal was to earn about ten dollars a week as a yearly average in order, according to a sympathetic female stitching shop proprietor, "to live properly in Lynn." Average weekly expenses for boarding stitchers were room rental at two dollars a week, board at $2.75, a dollar for fuel in the winter, and 50¢ for laundry. But most earned less than ten dollars a week, and the higher paying jobs of staying, buttonhole making, and overlap vamping required skill and experience. Improved machinery and competition from country shops had reduced the wages of even the most skilled workers; that of overlap vampers had been cut sixty cents a case over the past three years.[90]

Like the functionally autonomous craftsmen in the late nineteenth-century factory, the stitchers in Lynn had developed a set of customs about their work that they used to defend their position as workers.[91] In 1887 their common sense of a reasonable quota or stint of work done by the piece and their custom of sharing work during the dull season had enabled them to resist Crossman's weekly wage proposal. They defended the skills they had learned as stayers, vampers, and buttonhole makers. The stitchers also had developed an ethical code of behavior that emphasized self-support and womanly respectability. David Montgomery's discussion of mutualistic and manly behavior and the development of work rules based on craft traditions represents the response of male shoeworkers to the challenges of the factory system. The cultivated sense of self-worth that women had as lady stitchers was constructed from their gender and work experiences, the diverse nature of the female work force, and their estimate of the community's response to women's involvement in militant action. Women shoeworkers were, however, less self-directing than craftsmen; they had no helpers to supervise or craft tradition to inspire them. They actually preferred piecework to weekly wages; to them it meant more autonomy, higher wages, and better working conditions.

Montgomery equated the experience of shoeworkers in the Knights of Labor with that of workers in the garment industry, which suggested to him "that unionization of women operatives was likely to have a remarkably radicalizing impact on the organization."[92] The organization of women prevented the employer from using one set of unskilled workers against another group of skilled workers. But the sexual division of labor in the Essex County shoe industry did not mean that male workers were skilled and female workers were unskilled. Women shoeworkers had developed their own hierarchy of skills from pasting and lining making to overlap vamping as a result of their exclusive control of stitching work. The power they acquired from the total organization of all workers in the KOL did encourage resistance and antagonized their employers, particularly in comparison with the weak position of the stitchers after the collapse of the Daughters of St. Crispin in the late 1870s. However, the restricted position of women in the local and district administrative structures within the KOL, especially in D.A. 77, and their lack of political power meant that however radicalizing the impact of their presence in the Knights of Labor, the effect was limited to confrontations with the shoe manufacturers.

Most stitchers who testified at the second hearing on the Mears case had worked for five years or more in the Lynn shops and estimated that the average capacity for work was between two and two and a half cases during a nine and a half hour day. In direct contradiction to the testimony of the stitching shop operators, almost all preferred stitching in silk on the finer grades of work because they believed that they could make more money at it. James H. Carr, who had been the secretary of the stitchers' union since 1885, pointed out to the state board of arbitration the different groups of women who stitched shoes: daughters with homes and families, wives, and poor widows with dependents. But he insisted that the union represented foremost the interests of "that large class of women who had no homes here, but lived in rooms and who must have work to earn an honest living."[93] The threat of reduced wages in those categories of work: staying, buttonhole making, and vamping, on which self-supporting women depended for their livelihood and self-respect, prompted the rebellion among the stitchers against the Mears decision. Wage reductions in those categories for cheap work were rescinded by the board, but lower wages in general, the prospect of working exclusively with cotton thread on cheap leather, and the difficult fight to support themselves decently forced the stitchers of Lynn to confront the mythology surrounding the lady stitcher.

The occasion of this confrontation was an investigative report on Lynn written by a female journalist for the *Boston Sunday Herald* just after the second Mears decision in July 1888.[94] Under the title of "The Shoe Girls of Lynn," the long feature article, which was reprinted in the shoe trade journals and in many New England newspapers, described the stitchers as genuine American working women from New England homes and compared them to the factory girls of the pre–Civil War Lowell textile mills. More desirable than schoolteaching or saleswork, stitching was represented as easy work at facile machines for high wages among women so respectable that they could easily be mistaken for the wives of New England clergymen or the principals of girls' schools. Descriptions of older workers emphasized their intelligence, dignified respectability, and common sense, which set them apart from other female factory workers. Prettily dressed and independent, with enough extra money to indulge in extravagances or start bank accounts, the younger shop girls, with "sea-shell complexions" and dimples "playing hide and seek" with rosy mouths, led lives that were depicted as essentially frivolous. Rollicking times both during and

A SHOE STITCHER.

Illustrations from "The Shoe Girls of Lynn," *Boot and Shoe Recorder*, August 8, 1888, pp. 25 and 27, courtesy of Lynn Public Library.

A BUTTON HOLE MAKER.

after working hours testified to the mischievous spirit of Yankee girls and their sense of equal social status with their employers. But the worst, given the resolution of the Mears case, was the writer's conclusion: "Among all the long list of working women you will find none better circumstanced, more content, more physically strong and attractive, better cared for or more generously dealt with than the shoe girls of Lynn."[95]

In response to these enthusiastic impressions of the situation of Lynn shop workers, thirteen stitchers took the train to Boston to set the *Herald* editor straight.[96] They warned young New England girls not to believe the estimates of average wages that the *Herald* story had put at eighteen dollars a week; the average wage was closer to seven dollars. The stitchers insisted that the figures for an average day's work were exaggerated; even for an experienced shoeworker, two cases were the limit, not three. Beginners could earn only the barest subsistence, perhaps three dollars a week with which they could not hope to cover their expenses for room and board. Poverty and hardship waited for homeless, inexperienced girls. One stitcher described shops in Lynn designed to teach learners where girls worked for nothing on cheap grades of shoes supplied by the large manufacturers. Young women, they argued, should not come to Lynn under false impressions. Decent wages could be earned only during the busy season by experienced workers, and even then had to be stretched to cover expenses throughout the year. Only in the best shops that produced the finer grades and provided work more steadily could a stitcher earn over ten dollars a week as a yearly average, and these women were experienced vampers or buttonhole makers. Inexperienced girls sometimes subsisted on bread and water when out of work and far from home and family, and sickness drove them in desperation to seek the charity of their fellow workers. In contrast to the youthful frivolity, easy work, and attractive wages of the *Herald* story, the stitchers described the darker side of their experience: uncertainty caused by the seasonality of work, a fear of slipping from respectability into poverty, and long years of hard work by experienced workers for wages that seemed barely enough to cover their expenses and under constant danger of reduction. The recruitment of young women with empty promises of easy work and high wages became an additional threat to the work force of lady stitchers in the Knights of Labor.

By 1890 all shoeworkers faced the growth of supervisory methods and mechanization by which the manufacturers intruded more deeply into the work process in order to control and reduce labor costs. Accounting procedures used by new female clerical workers to figure wages allowed managers to keep tabs on every case of shoes as it moved through the various operations. The advantage was clear. "You are enabled to push your goods through the factory more rapidly. . . . Best of all, it enables the manufacturer to keep the entire labor account in the office. . . . It is desirable that the manufacturer know, or be in a position to know, just what each individual is earning, especially when introducing new machinery."[97] In 1912 John Tobin, president of the Boot and Shoe Workers' Union, testified to the Commission on Industrial Relations that this system developed in the late 1880s was the equivalent of scientific management. He recalled timing his work as an edge-setter with his own watch in an effort to raise his level of productivity as the piece rate for edge-setting was cut and cut again. "The piece work task," he explained, "is the incentive to high speed." The division of labor, the level of mechanization, and the use of the piece rate system made the shoe industry so efficient that time and motion experts "would starve to death in a shoe factory."[98] The employer used the coupon or tag system to keep track of how much work every shoeworker performed each day. This system intensified and internalized time discipline for shoeworkers and needed no supervision. The problem for shoeworkers was too much speed; by the 1880s there were already plenty of pacemakers in shoe factories.

As the Knights of Labor in Massachusetts declined, shoe manufacturers pushed harder to mechanize shoe production. In early 1889 virtually every process in the shoe factory seemed mechanized, even lasting and cutting.[99] Machines to assist lasters by driving tacks into the stretched upper or by using cement and metal pincers to hold the upper to the last were the precursors of the Consolidated Hand Method Lasting Machine, patented in 1884 and introduced in 1889, which utilized moving, fingerlike metal pincers to draw the upper smoothly over the last while a mechanism drove the tacks in automatically. This machine seemed to whisper to the laster: "I've got your job."[100] Cutters who worked on morocco, kid or calfskin cut the leather by hand, but cloth or leather that had been grained over to cover the cuts, bruises, and scratches on the hide and the mistakes of the tanner could be cut with metal dies. A stitching room with a new seam finishing machine opened in 1887 in the Jones factory in Lynn completely run by electric motors furnished by the local Thomson-Houston Company.[101] By 1892 the homework system for stitching the uppers of the very cheapest kinds of shoes in Haverhill had developed the characteristics of the worst work in the sweated garment trades: fourteen to fifteen hours of labor a day for fifty to seventy-five cents, performed in tenements by women with no work alternatives. Manufacturers admitted that if they had figured their profit too narrowly, the only way out was to get the stitching done at "bedrock prices."[102] All of these changes in the work process were introduced during the period of dissension among the Massachusetts Knights of Labor after 1886.

The disintegration of the KOL in Massachusetts, the reduction of wages in Lynn in 1887, which was followed by a general reduction of wages in the country shops throughout New England, and the prospect of remorseless competition among shoe manufacturers in the national market stimulated new efforts among labor organizers. The initial phase of this activity to pull together all shoeworkers in New England into one trade organization was marked by great division and conflict. Harry Skeffington had been recognized as the Master Workman of the Knights' national trade district of shoemakers in 1888, but he quarreled with Powderly. In February 1889, Skeffington called all shoeworkers to join an independent trade union, the Boot and Shoe Workers' International Union. This move was strongly opposed by KOL assemblies in Lynn and in Marlboro.[103] Initially, the BSWIU began to organize in the country shops of Maine, New Hampshire, and central Massachusetts. By late 1889 the new group had moved into Essex County, concentrating on Haverhill, the former center of D.A. 30, and Danvers.[104] The BSWIU organizers were careful to cooperate with the Lasters' Protective Union and the McKay stitchers' organization, and they encouraged the lady stitchers' unions in Lynn, Beverly, and Marblehead to support strikes by BSWIU stitchers in North Adams,

Massachusetts, and in Utica, New York.[105] However, the leadership of D.A. 77 viewed Skeffington with great distrust based on their experience helping him organize the original trade district in June 1887 and the national trade district in 1888. One element of this distrust concerned the lower standard of wages paid to shoeworkers in Haverhill that the new union used as the basis for its wage settlements with New England manufacturers.[106] For Lynn shoeworkers, cooperation with the new trade union meant wage cuts.

The fledgling BSWIU faced its most serious challenge from the nine largest manufacturers in Haverhill in early 1890. The Nine, as they were called in the local press, had decided to deal with national and regional competition by setting up nonunion shops and reducing wages. Shoeworkers had to sign an "ironclad" contract, specifying that they would work for several years at set daily wages on any machines assigned to them and guarantee their employer that they would not join any union.[107] Competition from the country shop system had become so severe for Haverhill manufacturers in 1888 and 1889 that profits were reportedly shrinking fast. "Their only way, they say, is to build big factories, turn out enormous quantities of shoes, take big risks and invest large capital. By doing this they can meet competition and do a profitable business." [108]

Competition, according to the editor of the *Haverhill Bulletin*, induced concentration. Large factories meant relative savings in expenses, including rent, insurance, and other operating costs, and reduced expenses gave large manufacturers a competitive edge.[109] The nine Haverhill manufacturers were in the process of building new large facilities outside the central business district, some of them freed from dependence on steam power by the introduction of electric motors. J. H. Winchell was just completing his new seven-story factory with an additional two-story brick tower, reportedly one of the largest shoe factories in New England. The costly establishment, which opened in January 1891, employed 1,000 workers. A barred gate on the front entrance operated from inside the main office and controlled their comings and goings. Winchell explained: "This keeps intruders out, and prevents interruption in the work." Shoeworkers dubbed it "the Fort." [110] The Haverhill Nine also tried to avoid selling their products to jobbers and sent many cases of shoes directly to the retailer, while some contemplated establishing their own retail stores.[111] In late 1889, when the BSWIU workers at Winchell's walked out over a wage cut, all nine of the largest manufacturers backed Winchell by locking out their 2,500 workers in a general shutdown of their operations in Haverhill. This confrontation with the BSWIU was timed to destroy the emerging trade union before it had grown strong enough to impose a citywide wage list like that of the Knights in 1886.[112]

With very large investments of capital at risk in 1890, the conflict between the Nine and the BSWIU was marked by a bitter rhetoric unknown to the conflicts of the Crispins or the Knights. Large manufacturers castigated the smaller firms as weak and afraid of their employees, allegations that deeply divided the Haverhill business community. Representatives of the Nine spoke of battle lines, a war to the death, and a knife in the heart of every labor union.[113] They hired an agent of the Pinkerton detective agency as a labor spy, a man who was later identified as involved in the defeat of the Molly Maguires in Pennsylvania.[114] In response, the editor of the *Haverhill Bulletin* became indignant over the terms of the lockout: get out and starve until you agree to be entirely subservient. The terms suggested to him that Haverhill's workers were being reduced to the wage slavery of cotton mill centers. Even the chairman of the state board of arbitration, which was called in to arrange a settlement, characterized the behavior of the Haverhill manufacturers as "tyrannical."[115]

The lockout was a total failure, and during the conflict the BSWIU recruited hundreds of shoeworkers in Haverhill including many stitchers into its ranks. The nine large manufacturers had each given a $5,000 personal bond as a guarantee of their support for the lockout, but those firms with workers under contract were forced to pay them daily for doing nothing while production was suspended. In order to keep their employees away from BSWIU organizers, some shops that participated in the lockout even arranged parties and suppers during working hours. To everyone's astonishment, 100 nonunion stitchers at the Jennings, Friedman, and Stevens Company were paid for dancing their afternoons away. After only one week, a settlement was arranged on January 18. Winchell agreed to negotiate with his union workers, and local legal opinion declared the ironclad contract unenforceable. Chick

Brothers held out against the settlement, but in early February they too accepted the wage list negotiated by the BSWIU with Winchell, their chief competitor in the production of cheap ladies' button boots.[116]

The settlement with Chick Brothers by the BSWIU immediately involved the new union in Haverhill in a struggle with the KOL cutters of Lynn. A fire in the central factory district in Lynn in late 1889 had destroyed many factories and shops, sending cutters to look for work in Haverhill, where they faced the organizing drive of the BSWIU. Instead of joining the BSWIU, Lynn men organized the Haverhill cutters into the KOL national trade district to demand a wage scale similar to that paid to cutters in Lynn, a difference of two dollars a week. The success of the BSWIU during the lockout, however, had prompted Skeffington and local organizer Harry C. Moulton to try to organize all shoeworkers except the lasters. The two groups confronted each other over the loyalties of the Haverhill cutters, whose ranks in early 1890 included many men from Lynn.

Master Workman Allen B. Stevens of the KOL national trade district and James Carr of the Lynn stitchers' union attended a public meeting in Haverhill where Skeffington tried unsuccessfully to win over the KOL cutters. In April, after organizing the stitching and making rooms at Chick Brothers, the BSWIU moved to sign an agreement with the company that covered the cutters but not the lasters. When the KOL cutters struck Chicks over the reductions in the BSWIU wage list for cutting, they were replaced by BSWIU men. In early May the KOL and the BSWIU held another public debate in Haverhill before a large audience that included many stitchers, but it resolved nothing and the local labor war continued.[117] The previous January, Skeffington and Moulton had sent a BSWIU organizer, Joseph Pettell, to Lynn. When he was discovered in mid-May working as a buffer for B. G. Patten and negotiating with his employer on behalf of the trade union, the Knights called the cutters and the stitchers at Patten's out on strike. The strike forced Patten to fire Pettell and abandon the talks with the BSWIU, while settling with the KOL and granting a wage increase to the stitchers.[118] The invasion of Lynn by the BSWIU was nipped in the bud. By the early 1890s, Haverhill had become the New England stronghold of the new trade union for shoeworkers, which identified itself with the American Federation of Labor, while Lynn remained loyal to the Knights of Labor.[119]

In Lynn, the sense of craft and community that underlay the local traditions of labor militancy sometimes prevailed over wider forms of organization.[120] But in the 1880s, the activities of New England shoeworkers in the Knights of Labor included both regional and national concerns. In addition to building a strong foundation of community organization, Essex County Knights, Lady Stitchers, and the LPU overcame divisions within the work force, organized workers in other shoe towns into two powerful KOL districts, and reached out into the New England region to develop a trade organization able to confront the threat of the country shop system. Men and women in the Knights fought to create a regional trade union to unite shoeworkers as the best solution to their class needs.

Working women in the Knights utilized the cultural imagery of ladyhood, which guaranteed them the status of respectable womanhood and provided a means to overcome divisions within their ranks. Yet they also came to understand the general condition of the masses of female industrial workers and fought on the district and national level of the Knights for power to represent working women. Their vision of a union that could reflect both class and gender interests inspired their activity as lady stitchers in the 1880s and provided a foundation for future activism. As the Knights declined as a force for regional and national cohesion, Essex County shoeworkers became seriously divided by internecine conflict, but the cruel depression of the 1890s would force them into a new national federation.

CHAPTER NINE

Militancy and Disintegration,
1892–1910

I, as an individual, was at the mercy of the manufacturer and was forced to continue to work at low wages,
until as a crew, backed by the union, we struck. The
plea of individual agreement sounds well, but the
individual is always offered Hobson's choice: Accept
my proposition or get out.

—"A [Female] Striker,"
Haverhill Gazette,
January 23, 1895

During the wage cuts and general hard times produced by the
depression of the 1890s, the BSWIU locals in Haverhill called a
strike that in turn prompted the organization of a new national
federation of shoeworkers' unions. Crucial to this federation were
the stitchers in Haverhill and Lynn who, relying on their virtual
monopoly over stitching skills, organized women shoeworkers in
their communities and throughout the region in 1895 and again in
1903. They supported the work of Mary A. Nason, who played
a significant role in the new organization, renamed the Boot and
Shoe Workers' Union. Nason's position as one of the first women to
represent female industrial workers on a national union executive
board created opportunities for her successors, Emma Steghagen
and Mary Anderson, to utilize their positions in a union bureaucracy and work in alliance with middle-class reformers for the
organization and protection of women workers. However, a split
developed in 1903 between the female supporters of the BSWU and
the women shoeworkers in Essex County who rejected the policies
of the national union. This division meant that significant sources
of class militancy and gender solidarity in New England would be

lost to the BSWU, to the Women's Trade Union League, and to female trade unionists in the AFL in the early twentieth century.

The large manufacturers in Haverhill continued to oppose the growth of the BSWIU after the failure of the 1890 lockout, but the union concentrated much of its organizational work in the early 1890s on midwestern cities and areas outside New England where shoe production was growing rapidly: Rochester, Cincinnati, Chicago, St. Louis, and Detroit. In Massachusetts, the growing BSWIU organizations in Haverhill and Brockton were balanced by the strongholds of the Knights of Labor National Trade Assembly in Lynn and Marlboro. Profiting from the dissension between the BSWIU and the KOL cutters in 1891 and the increasingly shaky position of the Lasters' Protective Union as the use of the lasting machine spread in New England, the large producers of cheap women's shoes in Haverhill adopted new techniques to cut labor costs. J. H. Winchell and Chick Brothers established antiunion shops employing labor at low wages under three-year ironclad contracts and bought machines to undercut the wages of the local lasters who still worked by hand methods. The Goodyear turn machine for low-cut shoes had already mechanized the jobs of the only other major group of handworkers in Haverhill: the turn workmen. By 1895 the Chick operation reputedly had captured the medium-grade, ladies' button boot business from Frank W. Breed of Lynn.[1]

The use of the contract system and new machinery allowed large manufacturers to introduce immigrant labor into the Haverhill work force, a move that began to shift the Essex County shoe industry away from its nineteenth-century base of native-born workers. Labor leaders in Haverhill denounced the contract system as designed to ensnare unwitting Russian Jews and impoverished French-Canadians, two groups unable to read the English-language contracts they were forced to sign and unaware of the violations in those contracts of American civil rights.[2] The challenge of a new foreign-born, contract labor force in Haverhill and the resentment of shoeworkers against the wage cuts and increased mechanization of the depression years precipitated the 1895 strike.

Two years earlier, the failure of shoe manufacturers in New England to collect on the credit that they had advanced to retailers led to widespread business failures, a reflection of the general collapse of demand and the development of a national industrial depression. During these hard times, firms in both Haverhill and Lynn that had produced medium to fine grades of women's shoes, rather than compete with the large factories in the cheap shoe market, themselves shifted to the cheaper grades.[3] The collapse in customer demand, the use of the Goodyear machine for turned work, and the general reduction in wages also undercut the advantages of country factories in New England. In 1893 the *Boot and Shoe Recorder* dismissed the country shop system as declining and inefficient.[4] An increase in the price of leather stock, especially sole leather, was attributed to the impact of the depression on the consumption of meat. Fewer cattle slaughtered for the Chicago packinghouses meant fewer domestic hides to be tanned. This decline in the demand for meat kept the supply of hides restricted for several years, and the "inexorable law of supply and demand" seemed to place great pressure on shoe manufacturers either to raise the prices of their goods to offset higher leather costs or cut wages still further.[5] Facing low demand even for cheap goods, shoe manufacturers agonized over the 1895 season. Samples were delayed, the price of leather carefully scrutinized, and the future of the industry bemoaned.

In reaction to market uncertainty, some firms designed new styles of goods in an effort to stimulate a little demand for novelties. An extremely narrow, pointed toe, variously called the needle or razor toe, was popular for both high and low-cut women's shoes as well as for men's wear in 1894 and 1895. Machine operators and lasters complained that this extreme style resulted in broken needles and ruined stock, led to delays that reduced their weekly wages, and caused them great physical strain over their work. Low-cut oxfords with two buttons rather than lacing struck a compromise between the style and fit of the high-button shoe and the reduction in labor costs of producing low-cuts. Lynn manufacturers began to add inexpensive oxfords to their product lines in 1894 and 1895.[6]

Stitchers, especially vampers, who had been in short supply in Essex County shoe towns during the prosperous years of the early 1890s, faced wage cuts and slack time. By early 1894, women shoeworkers in Lynn rallied around the local stitchers' assembly in an attempt to oppose additional wage cuts. Many complained

A Lynn vamper, 1895. Photograph by Frances Benjamin Johnson, courtesy of Library of Congress.

of being unemployed since the spring season of 1893 and of being forced to subsist on two meals a day. The prices for vamping had been cut by more than half, and the average worker could earn only five dollars a week for seven months of work. For the self-supporting stitchers of Lynn, this was not a living wage. For the first time, the stitchers organized themselves within the assembly, department by department, from lining makers to vampers and foxers (who did fine stitching on ornamental leather overlays) in an attempt to avoid competition among skill groups.[7] In Haverhill, many stitchers sought individual rather than collective solutions to the wage cuts and extended slack seasons of the early depression years.

By 1895, Haverhill was a city of 30,000 with over 150 shoe factories of various sizes. There were 8,200 shoeworkers, of which 2,500 or 30 percent were female. Many of the women workers had come to Haverhill from small towns in New England or from French and English Canada seeking work as stitchers. Two-thirds of the women who worked in the shoe shops of Haverhill in 1895 were native-born Americans of Yankee, Irish, and French-Canadian background. The remaining third were immigrants from Quebec or the Maritime Provinces. Many of these native and foreign-born females boarded in Haverhill during the busy season.

> Those who live in the Merrimac street boarding houses . . . constitute but a fraction of the hundreds, yes thousands, who board and room in Haverhill. . . . [But] it is in . . . home boardinghouses where the great majority of the girls live. In one boardinghouse visited there were 25 girls rooming. The proprietor said that when the dull times came about 10 of this number would go away; some to their homes in Maine and New Hampshire, some to Lynn, Brockton or other shoe towns, and others to room with friends, or go off he could not tell where. This was about the average, he claimed, of the number who came and went as the work fluctuated, buffeted about from place to place, but always willing to stay where they could get work.[8]

Their status as lady stitchers offered these geographically mobile workers respectable womanhood while they labored in the shoe centers of Essex County. In addition, the position of many Haverhill stitchers as boarders or roomers in private families meant that their lives as transient industrial workers were accepted by the community. These close ties between the social lives of local residents and boarding shoeworkers created strong ties of sympathy for the strikers in 1895.

The depression years of 1893 and 1894 forced severe wage cuts on all shoeworkers, and by the end of 1894 the wages of the stitchers of Haverhill had been cut by one-third. Chances at the elusive ten-dollar weekly wage of the 1880s had vanished. Skilled native-born shoeworkers faced the reality of being no better off than the immigrant textile workers of Lawrence or Fall River. In early 1895 the BSWIU members in Haverhill resolved to fight to prevent the introduction of "mill wages and mill customs" into shoe factories.[9]

The severe cuts in stitching wages during the depression put pressure on self-supporting women workers to seek supplementary work or cooperative living arrangements. After a ten-hour day in the factory during the busy season, women sewed or copied letters at night to earn extra money. Others slipped away from the shops a few minutes before noon to serve at tables during the lunch hour in hotels and restaurants crowded with hungry shoeworkers. Co-operative living with other women cut the costs of boarding. Some women arranged to rent single rooms in their flats to other workers. Others simply rented unheated rooms and spent the evenings in public halls. Boardinghouse keepers reported that female lodgers moved in with friends to save money or disappeared. Others grudgingly accepted work as domestics.[10] Despite the hardships, there was little evidence of union activity among the stitchers of Haverhill until the opening of the 1895 spring season.

The central issue of the 1895 strike was the ironclad contract adopted by three of the largest shoe factories: Spaulding, Spaulding and Swett, and Chick Brothers, all located on River Street a mile west of the crowded central shoe district of smaller manufacturers. The high costs of leather in 1894 encouraged these manufacturers of cheap shoes to revive the contract system to reduce labor costs and remain competitive in a sluggish market. In addition to low wage rates, the ironclad contract, which ran for three years for immigrant labor and one year for native, required the worker to leave a dollar a week with the company as a security deposit against leaving the factory without notice or joining a strike. Although manufacturers claimed the deposit would be repaid at 7 percent interest, the worker received no receipt for the money and the full weekly wage was entered on the pay envelope. The worker's good behavior was the only assurance of receiving those wages. The shoeworkers of Haverhill feared that the manufacturer would break the contract by discharging the worker on some excuse, such as poor work or misbehavior, and cut labor costs by keeping the deposit. The initial targets of the ironclad contract were the immigrant workers: Armenians, Russian Jews, French-Canadians, and Italians.[11] Native-born shoeworkers, male and female, believed they would be next.

The ironclad contract became the rallying point of the strike in the eyes of the community, the work force, and the smaller manufacturers, who negotiated wages through a local board of arbitration and still resented the behavior of the owners of the larger new factories during the 1890 lockout. These smaller manufacturers, having lost much of their market for the medium and finer grades of goods in the depression, were turning to the production of cheaper grades in competition with the River Street shops. The successful adoption of the ironclad in any Haverhill shops would force the smaller firms, by their own admission, to cut wages.[12] The unions in Haverhill faced a crisis over community standards of wages and conditions. The community feared its transformation into a grimy industrial city filled with immigrant labor.

As the busy season for the spring trade started up in December 1894, three of the River Street shops and a few of the larger shops in the central factory district applied the ironclad contract to their entire work force, native and foreign, skilled and unskilled. The stitchers at Spaulding, Spaulding and Swett, and Chick Brothers joined the strike called by the BSWIU during the last week in December. The LPU lasters had already struck several shops over the impact on their wages of the adoption of the Consolidated Lasting Machine, which sharply cut the wages of men assigned jobs as pullers-over, work reluctantly done by former lasters who assisted the lasting machine operator. Some of the Jewish, Armenian, and Italian men who worked at the three factories were persuaded to forfeit their deposits under the ironclad contract and join the strike. These immigrant workers, who could be trained on new machines or assigned work as pullers-over or stitchers, threatened the jobs, status, and wages of both male and female shoeworkers. Their participation in the strike was a blow to the strategy of the contract factories.[13] The strike of 1895 began with a commanding show of militancy and unity.

On January 1 the strikers held a giant parade through the snowy streets of the city's business and factory district. At the head of the line of march, 400 women stitchers led the 2,000 men on strike. The demonstrators carried banners that included the slogans "The Women Are with Us" and "Daughters of Hannah Duston." A commemorative statue of the colonial heroine Hannah Duston that depicted her as a formidable and aggressive figure, hatchet in hand, had been erected in 1879 near City Hall, adjacent to the boardinghouse district where many of the stitchers lived.[14] The parades of strikers often passed the statue, which served them as a cultural symbol of Yankee female strength and courage.

The procession on January 1 disclosed the general plan of the strike leadership: to unite all nationalities and both sexes to fight the common enemy. The new capitalists on River Street and their allies in the old industrial district were using the ironclad contract to hire foreign labor, lease new machines, and beat down the wages of native-born shoeworkers. Speeches in French, Italian, and Yiddish conveyed the message to the new immigrant workers, who were featured in the strike parades as the innocent, suffering victims of the contract system. Other trade union members joined the march in sympathy with the shoeworkers, and 300 KOL cutters, although not on strike, marched to demonstrate the support of all skill groups.[15] Not since 1860 had New England shoeworkers so openly demonstrated their discontent.

Following the parade, the strikers and their supporters jammed the city's public halls, where they heard speeches by strike leaders and by Frances Willard, president of the Woman's Christian Temperance Union, and by her two English companions, temperance leader Lady Henry Somerset and trade unionist Amy Hicks. In the late 1880s Frances Willard had encouraged the membership of the WCTU to examine the causes of poverty beyond intemperance and to link its activities with the Knights of Labor.[16] In what appeared to be her first public statement on behalf of strikers, Frances Willard supported their demand for a living wage, denounced the contract system, and endorsed the eight-hour day. Giving her blessing to the stitchers as an "elder sister," Willard concluded with an eloquent plea "to stand as a unit in the struggle which is being fought for the nation, in Haverhill." [17] Two days later at a WCTU banquet in Boston honoring Lady Somerset, all three reiterated their support for the strike and called on the temperance and labor movements to join forces. [18]

Mary Nason made the last speech to the strikers on the night of the giant parade. Mary A. Caldwell Nason was born in 1856 in South Paris, Maine, a small town just outside of Norway, where B. F. Spinney of Lynn had opened his country factory in 1874. Mary Caldwell probably learned to stitch shoes at Spinney's in her late teens, an occupation to which she returned after her marriage to Fred W. Nason ended in divorce. Nason was thirty-five years old in 1891 when, as the president of the small BSWIU stitchers' local #4 in Haverhill, she participated in the activities of the Joint Shoe Council. As a self-supporting New England native, her cultural background and work were consistent with that of the lady stitchers in the Knights of Labor. But while a BSWIU official in Haverhill, Nason became interested in women's participation in trade unions and in socialism. She brought Socialist Labor party lecturer Mrs. Martha Moore Avery of Boston to speak to the Haverhill stitchers about equal rights and socialist principles. Nason also sponsored the appearance in 1892 of Mary Kenney of Chicago, who as an organizer of women workers for the AFL spoke to the Haverhill stitchers about their sister shoeworkers in other cities and urged them to recruit local women into their union. The connections that Nason established with activist women in the WCTU, SLP, and the AFL helped to sustain the Haverhill stitchers during the 1895 strike.

On the night of January 1 she praised the ability of the women workers of Haverhill to take action as a unified body. "Yesterday was the proudest day of my life because I regained faith in the women. The events of yesterday raised the women of Haverhill 100 percent, not only in my estimation, but in the estimation of everybody on earth." [19] Nason invoked the equal rights tradition by categorizing the struggle over the ironclad contract as a question of the survival of the free men and women of New England. She concluded her speech by asking the audience whether after listening to the fine women who had proceeded her as speakers, anyone could say it was not respectable for women to organize? Nason, Willard, Somerset, and Hicks challenged the stitchers of Haverhill to abandon their aspirations to ladyhood and to redefine their sense of womanhood to emphasize strength and courage rather than passivity and gentility. Willard told the stitchers: "There is nothing attractive about weakness in either man or woman. Men need women with a mind of [their] own." [20]

In the 1880s the lady stitchers and the union girls of Lynn had debated the implications for their respectability of public action and the pursuit of power in the shoe shops. They fought to influence local arbitration decisions and municipal politics. Haverhill women had enjoyed more formal representation in their local and district assemblies, but the women's local in the BSWIU remained small. Women shoeworkers had used ladyhood to encourage social respectability and collective action, but many stitchers in Essex County clung to individual solutions to class problems. As lady stitchers, the women workers of Haverhill were not organized effectively in 1895. Fearful of losing status by being engaged in industrial work, they demonstrated gender pride by dressing well and cultivating respectability. Lady Somerset privately expressed surprise at the appearance of the striking stitchers. "They are well-dressed, some of them elegantly, and their conduct is a credit to them. In my country young women of their station and occupation spend their money in saloons, and they do not compare with these in looks and bearing." [21]

New labor activity required unity with male shoeworkers, but it also promised chances for female participation in politics and in trade unionism. If ladyhood and power for female industrial workers were incompatible, then the image of the lady stitcher would have to be abandoned. In that event, stitchers needed to fashion a new sense of womanhood, combining strength and action with respectability. The hard times of the 1890s and the changing nature of the work force in the industry forced the Haverhill stitchers to reexamine the meaning of being a working woman during the course of the 1895 strike.

The strategy of the strike leadership was to confine the strike to the three River Street factories and use the women's monopoly on stitching skills to close down production, while permitting the competitors of the three largest manufacturers in Haverhill to fill their orders. This strategy would also demonstrate the uselessness of the ironclad contract to prevent collective action and held out hopes of a quick victory over the contract system, goals manageable financially for the various small unions in Haverhill.[22] Like the Crispins and the Knights of Labor, the overall objective was to arbitrate a citywide wage agreement to end local competition over labor costs.

In addition, James F. Carey, one of the strike leaders and a Populist candidate for the state legislature in 1894, expressed a larger vision on the day of the great strike parade: the cooperative commonwealth. He insisted that the state government should assume responsibility for stabilizing capitalism by regulating and encouraging industrial production. As wages rose with the eight-hour day, the increased buying power of the masses would end the illusion of overproduction. Cutthroat competition that led to wage reductions had to be eliminated, he argued, along with middlemen, high salaries for managers and capitalists, and unearned interest on invested capital. He predicted that within five years mass political action organized by the forces of urban populism would create new government policy that could benefit all.[23] This socialist vision sustained and inspired many Haverhill strikers in 1895, including Mary Nason, and convinced them of the need for action.

The initial phase of the strike received widespread support from the community, led by the smaller factory owners, the professional class, almost all of the Protestant and Catholic clergy, local businessmen, and retailers. The largest manufacturers bought their shoe findings and supplies, their packaging materials, and other items at lower cost in Boston or New York City, thereby alienating local small businessmen. Three shoe factories released their workers during the middle of the workday to participate in one of the strike parades. The unions had been active in local politics, and the city government was openly in sympathy with the strike. A clear identity of interest between the skilled, native-born shoeworkers and the community of Haverhill explains the depth of local support for the strike.[24] There was a frequently expressed fear that if the strikers lost this contest, the character of the city would change, especially if a new and unpredictable, low-wage, foreign-born work force replaced the native workers. The community stood together against undesirable change.

Two outside factors, however, disrupted the early strategy of the strike and its local support. The Massachusetts State Board of

Arbitration investigated the situation in early January and recommended that the strike end and wage arbitration begin in June after the close of the spring busy season. The strike committee immediately rejected this proposal. Secondly, the state superior court at Salem issued a temporary injunction on January 15 at the request of Chick Brothers to prevent the strike leaders from directing the strike and its massive, noisy parades, which provided the major source of enthusiasm against the contract system.[25] The implications of both events undermined local support for the strike.

In retaliation against the injunction, strike leaders widened their activities to three other large manufacturers, including J. H. Winchell's Company and its new box-making and shoe factory operation at Island Park surrounded by the Merrimack River, which the strikers named contemptuously: "Little Pullman." In an important move, the KOL cutters at Winchell's, which had the largest cutting room in the city, now joined the strike. On January 16, as the strikers marched by Chick Brothers to the beat of muffled drums and called out the shop crews at Winchell's, the Gale Company, and the Byron Noyes factory, every man and woman's face in the line of march was turned in defiance toward the figure of William Chick lounging in his doorway, but not a word was spoken. None of the strike leaders were in sight. Shoeworkers poured out of the three factories to join the parade of strikers, while onlookers and shop crews at other factories cheered.[26] But as a result of this enthusiastic action, hundreds of additional strikers were added to the financial burdens of the strike committee.

By mid-January, six of the largest shoe factories in Haverhill and their stitching subcontractors had been struck by 3,000 workers. Meanwhile, the city authorities found themselves responsible for the enforcement of the superior court injunction against the strike leaders. Retailers, hurting from the loss of trade as the strike dragged on, appealed for a settlement. The Consolidated Lasting Machine Company of Beverly sent strikebreakers and offered to train new men on their machines. The River Street shops tried to identify picketers for blacklisting by using the new photographic technology of "kodaks."[27] Militancy and money became critical to sustaining the strike; the stitchers and their leader Mary Nason provided both.

Nason's leadership of the stitchers' strike and their local union was energetic and effective. She organized parades and meetings, while recruiting new members. She addressed shop crews, settled problems, and headed off rumors. Nason represented the stitchers on the strike committee and at the meetings of the state board of arbitration. As head of the stitchers' union and a symbol of their strike activity, Mary Nason raised funds for the strike through her contacts among sympathetic upper-class women and trade unionists in Boston. Nason had known Mary Kenney in 1892 while Kenney was working as an AFL organizer. During her brief stay in Boston, Kenney had become acquainted with a number of settlement house residents and upper-class reformers, such as Mrs. Charles Gordon Ames and Ida Mason, people whom she described as "wealth with a social vision." On her return to Boston from Chicago in 1894, she married John F. O'Sullivan, an AFL organizer. Mary Kenney's work as a labor organizer in Chicago reflected both her interest in organizing women into female-controlled unions by trade and her close connections with middle-class women reformers and feminists at Hull House. She met Samuel Gompers through her Hull House friends in 1892, a meeting that led to her brief appointment as a national organizer. In Boston she sought to set up the same kind of connections between concerned middle-class women and female industrial workers.[28] Mary Kenney O'Sullivan probably provided Mary Nason with her Boston contacts.

The alliance in 1895 between the Haverhill stitchers and upper-class women reformers in Boston represented an early example of cross-class support for female labor militancy. These contacts provided Nason and the strikers with respectability as women unionists, with financial support for their efforts, and with favorable publicity in the Boston press. One example was Mrs. Charles Gorden Ames, factory inspector and the wife of a Beacon Hill clergyman, who organized a public meeting of the Young Men's Christian Association to discuss the shoeworkers' strike. Frances Willard, Lady Somerset, and Amy Hicks joined Mary Nason and T. T. Pomeroy, the chairman of the Haverhill strike committee, to present the strikers' case to Boston opinion.[29] Josephine Shaw Lowell, a Boston and New York socialite, reformer, and feminist who headed the New York Consumers' League, concluded the prestigious Parker Memorial lecture series with a speech supporting the

Haverhill strikers. The *Evening Transcript*, the voice of Brahmin Boston, commented favorably on her remarks.

Through these contacts, Mary Nason was able to address private meetings in Back Bay and Beacon Hill drawing rooms, receiving large donations after the meetings. A committee of five led by the socially prominent Boston philanthropist Robert Treat Paine visited Haverhill in February and issued a report in mid-March that supported the strikers' demands for the end of the contract system and urged arbitration of all grievances.[30] The news that Nason and the stitchers had tapped the wealth and influence of Brahmin Boston gave them respectability, support, and excellent publicity. The expenses of the strike, estimated at $4,000 a week for twelve long weeks, were covered in part by the many sources drawn upon by these contacts. Nason successfully linked the local solidarity of working women in Haverhill to an alliance with upper-class Bostonians and national temperance reformers who pressured manufacturers and shaped public opinion on behalf of the striking native-born shoeworkers and in support of cooperation between capital and labor.

The action of the stitchers was the decisive factor in the 1895 strike. This was recognized by all: the Haverhill strike committee, the local newspapers, the major newspapers in the state, and the journal of the Massachusetts AFL, the *Labor Leader*—even by the owners of the River Street shops. The first reaction of Spauldings and Chicks to the great parade of January 1 was to send out their forewomen in hired carriages to visit the striking stitchers at their boardinghouses and persuade them to come back to work. This failing, all the women strikers were warned to return to work at the old wages or face a blacklist. In a few days, there were rumors that the fainthearted would go back to work, but a parade at 6:30 A.M. on River Street by striking stitchers averted any such move. The major stitching subcontractors desperately appealed to the stitchers' union to finish up their work under contract to the River Street factories, but the union refused most of these requests.[31] The River Street shops then gave up trying to break down the unity of the stitchers in Haverhill and tested instead the regional solidarity of New England stitchers.

Manufacturers circulated notices of employment at good wages throughout northern New England, while agents seeking stitchers visited the shops of Lynn and Brockton. Rumors of the arrival of stitchers from Lowell and from South Royalton, Vermont, proved groundless. One group of women from Exeter, New Hampshire, did appear in Haverhill, but no boardinghouse would accommodate them, and their new employers had to pay their expenses at a hotel. Agents from Haverhill promised Lynn stitchers good wages and jobs, if necessary, for their husbands. Most labor leaders in Massachusetts considered the possibility of women strikebreakers arriving from other states as remote and believed that the women of Lynn and Brockton would refuse to undercut their sisters in Haverhill. The River Street shops also tried to find stitchers in Massachusetts among Armenian, Jewish, and Italian men with needle skills in stitching and tailoring, but there was not enough skilled help willing to come to Haverhill. The River Street shops sent their unlabeled upper work to Lynn and other shoe towns in Essex County to be stitched. When the unions of Lynn discovered a consignment of Chick Brothers' work in a Lynn shoe shop, they set up a search committee to visit all the shops to look for the scab work. The Lynn stitchers held "indignation meetings" and threatened to strike in sympathy with the Haverhill stitchers if any establishment in Lynn took the work. Stitchers in Lynn and Newburyport sent donations to the Haverhill strikers. Anger at the actions of the Haverhill agents, revulsion at the ironclad contract, and the sense of a general threat to native-born shoeworkers caused the membership of the Lady Stitchers' Union of Lynn to increase in 1895 by 700.[32] The women shoeworkers of New England were demonstrating the power of their sisterhood and craft solidarity.

By mid-January the stitchers of Haverhill faced anger and rough treatment from their bosses in recognition of their demonstrated power to halt production. J. H. Winchell, fearing a strike, personally visited his stitching room and threatened to discharge any stitcher who even discussed the strike. The management of the Gale Shoe Company, which with Winchell's was struck on January 15, locked out its eighty female stitchers and threw their belongings at them from the windows.[33] Such treatment only increased the stitchers' sense of importance and militancy. The hard times of the depression seasons and a new sense of power and urgency persuaded the Haverhill stitchers to renounce any connection with the lady stitcher imagery of the Knights of Labor era. During the course of the strike, they renamed their organization the Women Stitchers' Union.[34] The wage cuts, the depression, and the strike convinced the stitchers of Haverhill that they had no choice but to accept working-class status and unionism.

Approximately 500 stitchers struck the three River Street shops in late 1894, and 300 more were added by the extension of the strike in mid-January. Attendance at the stitchers' union meetings ranged between 600 and 800, and the formal membership was put at several hundred by the treasurer, Margaret C. Barnett. Half were native-born women of Yankee and Irish parents and half were of French-Canadian background, both native and foreign-born. Gender and craft consciousness in the 1895 strike united women shoe-workers from diverse ethnic backgrounds. Although half of the women in the shoe shops of Haverhill were reportedly married, wives seemed to take less of a role in the strike parades and meetings than self-supporting women. Mary Nason's public statements on the lack of response from married women to the union's call to organize and her expressed desire to prohibit wives from industrial work indicated some difficulty in organizing married stitchers. The other three leaders of the women's strike in addition to Mary Nason were unmarried, native-born, and self-supporting women. Older, experienced stitchers provided mature leadership, while the rank and file of younger women, the majority of whom were under thirty, contributed high spirits and energetic commitment.[35]

The stitchers' union organized its members into shop crews that met every other day to exchange information and keep up each other's courage. On three occasions the striking stitchers heard Martha Moore Avery of the Socialist Labor party praise their determination. Avery's socialism, which was a blend of Yankee reform, gender consciousness, and socialist principles, struck a resonant chord among them. Members addressed each other as "sister" and identified themselves resolutely as "Chick's crew #1." Strike benefits of four dollars per week went to women who were self-supporting or who had dependents; married stitchers received three dollars.[36] Some striking stitchers left Haverhill to seek work in other cities, while others returned to their New England homes, but for those who stayed with the strike, individualism gave way to collective consciousness. One of the striking stitchers expressed this shift in a letter to the *Haverhill Gazette* on January 23:

So much has been said about the manufacturers being willing to treat with their help individually that perhaps an instance of individual treatment of the wage question may be of interest. Last June in the stitching room in which I was at work a cutdown was proposed. I knew that the price paid was less than was paid for similar work in other factories and remonstrated, and was assured by the superintendent that my employer was willing to pay what others did. I at once secured the figures from two other factories and proved that they were paying from 20 to 100 percent more than we were getting, presenting the figures to the superintendent. The result was only that the cut was prevented, but the promise made to me that the wages should be the same as in other factories was forgotten. It was at the end of sales. I, as an individual, was at the mercy of the manufacturer and was forced to continue to work at low wages, until as a crew, backed by the union, we struck. The plea of individual agreement sounds well, but the individual is always offered Hobson's choice: Accept my proposition or get out.[37]

During the 1895 strike, the stitchers' union in Haverhill also attempted to extend the equal rights tradition to women workers. Union members worked hard to protect their respectability by preventing the strike committee from using the phenomenon of striking females to attract the curious or the excitable to the fund-raising benefits that featured entertainment and dancing. They refused to accept the idea of special, cheaper tickets for women to these benefits. Two of the striking stitchers voiced their objections:

"I don't see why they want to charge less for women than for men. Why don't they make it [the admission price] the same for both? We can pay as much as they can."

"Yes," put in another, "if we ever intend to become independent and get equal rights, we might as well begin right away."

Haverhill stitchers also resented the small number of male workers in stitching rooms who received higher wages for the same work. Under pressure from the stitchers' union, the strike committee adopted a statement supporting equal pay for equal work. However, most stitchers realized that many male unionists in Haverhill were skeptical of their commitment to the strike. Mary Nason and the women strikers understood that they had to prove their militancy if they were ever to count in the trade union movement. They did so by marching, like the women of Lynn in 1860, in the frequent strike parades, 200 to 400 strong, in long skirts and thin boots through streets that were alternately icy, snowy, slushy, and muddy from January to mid-March.[38]

The solidarity and militancy of the Haverhill stitchers was severely tested during the strike by a blunder committed by strike leader Pomeroy during a speech that he made in Boston on January 18, which the *Boston Herald* picked up and turned into a sensation. Pomeroy had pointed out the relationship between low wages for women workers and prostitution, declaring that there were 300 women living in Haverhill's central business district whose room rent was "paid by men." Reports of the *Herald*'s story and refutations of the charges dominated the front pages of the Boston press for several days and immediately called into question the morality of the stitchers of Haverhill and of the female strikers in particular. After her hard work to identify the stitchers with respectability and propriety, Nason publicly rebuked Pomeroy for his statement, but she did not permit this dangerous incident to divide the stitchers' local or weaken its resolve during the strike.[39] Nevertheless, as geographically mobile, self-supporting women, the moral status of many of the Haverhill stitchers remained open to public question.

The community of Haverhill, especially the clergy, vigorously defended the stitchers' morality. The Reverend Calvin Clarke of the Centre Congregational Church defended the many operatives who attended his services as good country people from small towns in New England and the Maritime Provinces who had been drawn to Haverhill by the work in the shoe shops. Father O'Doherty of St. Joseph's Church, who had served the parish for seventeen years, used a network of sodality members to counsel those even suspected of immorality. Of the 450 young women in his parish, he estimated that 350 were shoeworkers. "My girls," he asserted, "are good girls." Statements by the city missionary and the chairman of the Overseers of the Poor confirmed the opinions of the clergy. Even W. W. Spaulding, one of the River Street manufacturers whose workers were on strike, denounced the allegations of immorality among stitchers. When a *Boston Journal* reporter sought more mundane opinion, a brakeman at the Boston and Maine Railroad station in Haverhill stated that he had seen something of life and that the Haverhill girls were "slow" and "too strict." [40] The community defended and protected the morality of the striking stitchers, and the controversy slowly and painfully subsided. The citizens of Haverhill had not been shocked to see these women marching through its streets.[41] They saw the strike as an effective defense of community integrity by respectable New England women who had for years been welcomed into their homes, factories, and retail stores during the busy seasons.

By the first week of March, however, the strike funds were nearly exhausted. On March 10 and at the strike committee's recommendation, those remaining out on strike voted 239-199 to return to work, but the striking stitchers cast the majority of votes against the motion. The leaders of the committee argued that the strike had served its purpose. The ironclad was dead in Haverhill, wage cuts had been halted, 118 factories had signed a new agreement to arbitrate wages, and the strength of the new stitchers' organization had been proven.[42] The real hope for change lay with a national union of all shoeworker organizations. The three major groups representing workers in the industry, the BSWIU, the national trade assembly of the Knights of Labor, and the Lasters' Protective Union, met in Boston in mid-February to plan a convention for such an organization. On March 7 the call went out to all shoeworkers to meet in Boston on April 10. Representatives of the Haverhill strikers, including Mary Nason, were active in the deliberations at the convention and in the organization of the new federation.

The Boston convention drew together the major organizations of shoeworkers in New England, including the new United Turn Workmen's Union, and linked them with the BSWIU organizations in Chicago, St. Louis, and other midwestern cities. Carey, Pomeroy, and Nason of the Haverhill strike and four of the additional seven women delegates from Haverhill and Marlboro served on convention committees. Some ran for office in the new organization. Neither Lynn nor Brockton sent female delegates. Nason was nominated for permanent chair of the convention and received twenty-one votes, but withdrew, throwing her support to Carey, who was elected. Nason and Pomeroy served on the steering committee that organized the new federation along with representatives from Baltimore, St. Louis, Lynn, Marblehead, Rochester, Brockton, and Detroit. Stitchers Louise Holstein of Haverhill and Mary Burns of Marlboro participated in drawing up the organization's constitution.[43]

A debate over a minority report on the preamble to the constitution offered by John F. Tobin of Rochester, a member of the Socialist Labor party, raised the question of the ideological and political orientation of the new BSWU. Tobin wanted the shoeworkers to commit themselves to political action to replace private ownership of the means of production with collective ownership. Nason moved adoption of the minority report, which Carey and Pomeroy supported, but the Tobin proposal was defeated 81 to 23. The convention rejected the vision of radical change advocated by leaders of the 1895 strike in favor of a simple federation of existing groups. Furthermore, Tobin had to promise not to allow his connections with the SLP to influence his actions before the delegates elected him general president of the new organization. Mary Nason was nominated for general treasurer, but lost by ten votes. The delegates then elected her as one of the seven members of the general executive board. This action recognized the role of the stitchers in the Haverhill strike and represented an unprecedented acceptance by male unionists of the importance of women workers to policy-making on the national level of trade unionism. The delegates also settled on a low rate of dues, ten cents a week, and rejected a differential initiation fee for men and women, deciding on one dollar for all. The convention endorsed equal pay for both sexes, the eight-hour day, and the abolition of the contract system and child labor, and adopted a union label.[44] However, this coalition of shoeworker organizations proved an uneasy one. As a result of the first year of his presidency of the BSWU, John Tobin began to advocate a stronger centralized union management and a high dues policy to an organization dominated by representatives of New England shoeworkers whose traditions and experience rested on local autonomy and equal rights.

After the Boston convention, Nason returned to Haverhill, where she headed the Women Stitchers' Union #6 and helped to organize stitchers in Stoneham and Lynn. Her work extended the nineteenth-century basis of stitcher militancy by urging women workers to reject mixed locals with male shoeworkers, which threatened to submerge their interests, and instead organize themselves as autonomous units. In Brockton, Haverhill, and Lynn, the stitchers' locals retained autonomy, but in Stoneham, despite Nason's efforts, BSWU stitchers joined a mixed local. Nason also maintained close ties with the stitchers' local in Marlboro.[45] Her most potentially powerful position was, however, on the general executive board. Tobin quickly found the board too unwieldy for decision-making because of the scattered residences of its members, and he worked to centralize authority into the hands of the union leaders located near Boston. There were two Boston area members: Mary Nason and John H. Murray of Marlboro.[46] The centralization of decision-making in Boston on the important questions of authorizing strikes and awarding the union label to manufacturers intensified Nason's influence on national policy. Murray (apparently speaking for Tobin) openly opposed her presence on the executive board at the BSWU convention in 1896.

Tobin's major problem in establishing the BSWU as a national bargaining agent was merging with the KOL and the LPU, organizations that had strong traditions of militancy and local control. He regarded the payment of dues to the new union as a test of the commitment of the rank and file, while he sought to centralize decision-making in the hands of the general officers. Male organizers would promote the BSWU label to create a demand in the national market for union-made shoes. At the same time, he pressed the delegates in 1896 for a commitment to socialist principles. But representatives of New England shoeworkers continued to dominate the convention, which rejected Tobin's efforts to raise dues, increase benefits, centralize decision-making, and endorse socialism and the political activities of the SLP. Only four women attended the 1896 convention of 105 delegates: two women from Marlboro, Mary Burns and Nellie Trainor, who had participated in the first convention; Annie G. Smith, representing the newly formed Lady Stitchers' local #108 of Lynn; and Mary Nason. Nason represented her Haverhill local, but (for some unknown reason) only after the committee on credentials acted on her petition to be seated as a delegate. Tobin was reelected as general president despite the rejection of his proposals to reorganize the BSWU and the lukewarm reception of his policies to hire organizers and advertise the union label.[47]

John Murray of Marlboro began his attack at the 1896 convention on Nason's position on the executive board by proposing to add Boston area representatives to the body, but insisting that the board was no place for women. He pointed out that only two members of the board resided in Massachusetts—himself and Sister Nason—and "she, being a woman, was not called upon to adjust differences." [48] If Murray was referring only to the limitations on the knowledge of shoe operations by women because of the sexual division of labor, the effect nonetheless was to render women shoeworkers alone unable to function on a general level in the union. Objections from the convention floor by Massachusetts men forced Murray to apologize for this attack on a person regarded as one of the best organizers on the board. The convention then adopted a resolution to require one female, should permanent organizers be authorized by the BSWU officers; they intended Nason to be that woman. Murray failed to persuade the delegates to reorganize the executive board, but with Tobin's support was able to sponsor a temporary change in the election procedures for the board. Instead of being elected by the convention delegates, a ballot would be mailed to all union locals, and Nason, little known outside of Massachusetts, was eliminated from the board by January 1897. [49] At the next convention, only the stitchers' union in Lynn remained controlled by women workers. Murray himself served as a delegate from the Marlboro stitchers' local, and Tobin represented a mixed union in Rochester that included stitchers.

Nason's deteriorating position in the BSWU reflected the disappearance of her base of support among the stitchers of Haverhill and her inability to sustain effective women's locals elsewhere. Dissatisfaction with Tobin's policies of avoiding strikes and confrontations with employers cost the BSWU the support of Haverhill workers who, after their partial success in 1895, were eager to seize the momentum of the new organization to pressure the manufacturers to negotiate a wage list. By the spring of 1896, the membership of the stitchers' union had melted away, most expelled for nonpayment of dues. The men's locals in Haverhill suffered a similar erosion of members. In May 1897 the BSWU revoked the charters of all of the Haverhill locals for inactivity, "anarchy," and nonpayment of dues. They were reorganized later that year, but the impetus in Haverhill was leading shoeworkers away from the national organization into an independent, local movement. No delegates from Haverhill attended the 1897 convention. [50] Nason resigned from the stitchers' local and the Joint Shoe Council and left the city for Boston, where with the help of the reform-minded women who had supported the stitchers' strike in 1895 she became a state factory inspector. She worked in Boston until 1920.

Mary Nason tried to connect the late nineteenth-century idea of respectable womanhood and the requirements of twentieth-century labor activity for women shoeworkers. From her experience as a self-supporting Yankee stitcher, Nason came to understand the need for a permanent organization on the local level linked with a strong national union. She rejected the lady stitcher imagery and its pursuit of social status for an open acceptance of class reality and socialist principles. She worked hardest to organize self-supporting women as that portion of the work force most in need of protection, but she recognized the importance of unified action with women workers in local families. She also worked to maintain among the stitchers the sense of gender consciousness that had sustained labor militancy in the late nineteenth century. Nason was willing to cooperate closely with men's locals and the national union, but she fought to keep stitchers in control of their own locals. She acted as a representative of New England women's interests in the BSWU. Along with the middle-class women identified by Estelle Freedman as female institution builders in the late nineteenth century, Mary Nason and the stitchers of Essex County sought to create and maintain separate and autonomous organizations for working women.

The new and rich meanings of womanhood fashioned by Mary Nason and the Haverhill stitchers during the 1895 strike meant little to John Tobin and the BSWU leadership. Her identification with autonomous women's locals and with local strike militancy contradicted Tobin's efforts to transform the BSWU into a business union. But in eliminating Nason from its national leadership in 1896, the BSWU lost contact with the gender consciousness and craft solidarity that had inspired the labor protest of the women shoeworkers of New England.

The BSWU convention of 1897 marked a year of general defection and the revocation of many local charters for the nonpayment of even the low dues required of members. Tobin underscored the disintegration by denouncing Allen B. Stevens of Lynn, the Master Workman of the Knights of Labor trade assembly, who in defiance

of the BSWU continued to recruit cutters to the Knights, not only in
New England but in midwestern cities as well. A lockout in Stoneham destroyed the BSWU locals in 1897. No women delegates
appeared at the convention from Brockton, although Mattie Rowe
of Lynn and three other women from Marlboro including Nellie
Trainor participated in the convention's activities. Even this strong
delegation of Marlboro stitchers disappeared in a ruinous strike
during the winter of 1898–99 to which Mary Kenney O'Sullivan,
an invited observer at the 1897 convention, lent her support.[51]
Devastated by its losses in New England, the BSWU searched for
another constituency and a new direction.

In 1899 John Tobin, who led the remnants of a tottering BSWU
of only about 5,000 members, shifted to business unionism and
a policy of high dues, sick and death benefits, no strikes, and the
union label as leverage to arbitrate wages. The union sought a new
basis of support among shoeworkers west of the Hudson River.
To the thirty-three delegates who assembled in his hometown of
Rochester in 1899, Tobin said: "For many years it has been my
firm conviction that an economic organization based on high dues
and the payment of sick, death and strike assistance, would produce much better results for its members than a union whose only
source of solidarity is the class conscious sympathy of the workers
one for another."[52] Abandoning any pretense to being a socialist,
Tobin was reelected in 1899 to lead a union willing to cooperate
with manufacturers who would adopt the union label, while developing ties to middle-class reformers and consumers to pressure
antiunion factories to accept the BSWU. The only women delegates
at the Rochester convention were Emma Steghagen and Vennie
Collins of Chicago, but Steghagen was elected by the convention
to sit on the general executive board, thereby reviving the policy
of reserving one seat for a representative of women shoeworkers.
Mary Nason's legacy of autonomy for women workers within the
labor movement was sustained in the BSWU only in this respect.
Emma Steghagen and her successor on the board, Mary Anderson of Chicago, used this position to work for the unionization of
women through the BSWU and later through the Women's Trade
Union League organized in 1903. Anderson later became the first
head of the Women's Bureau in the Department of Labor.[53] Their
position on the national level of a union bureaucracy enabled them

to work with middle-class women after 1903 to organize working women and to lobby for protective legislation and for woman suffrage.

The new direction of the BSWU was confirmed at the 1902 convention in Detroit. The push to organize shoeworkers was tied to the adoption of the union label stamped on each pair of shoes by the manufacturer. Tobin discouraged BSWU members from expecting that union label contracts with their employers would mean higher wages. To link the union label with wage increases, he believed, would prevent its adoption; higher wages would come only with total organization. Tobin defended the concession to the employer made in most BSWU contracts of the right to discharge workers and to determine the way work was conducted in the factories. The BSWU stamp would guarantee the employer freedom from labor troubles through the arbitration of wages and specified only that any shoeworkers hired be BSWU members.[54] To the shoeworkers of Essex County who had followed a tradition of local and regional arbitration of wages, but only after powerful demonstrations of militancy and unity by the workers in the cities where the shoes were made, this policy appeared weak and unrealistic.

Tobin argued at the 1902 convention, however, that shoes were sold not in local or regional markets, but in the national market; and that the union label would guarantee more work and income to the BSWU member once consumer demand for stamped goods was sufficiently organized to be an influence on the national market. The real danger to BSWU members, he claimed, was not from the shoe manufacturers, who would see the economic sense and business advantage in the union label, but from the unorganized or the independent-minded shoeworker. In pursuit of unity among all groups of workers in the shoe industry, Tobin had negotiated conciliatory agreements with the Lynn KOL cutters in 1900 and the LPU in 1901, whose delegates had walked out of the BSWU over the level of wages negotiated for lasters. Tobin insisted that union label contracts would help the BSWU organize and discipline its members, while the union label promoted consumer demand for BSWU shoes in the national market.

The 1902 convention delegates in Detroit endorsed these policies. Among them were Emma Steghagen and Mary Anderson and strong delegations of women from Rochester and from a new stitchers' local in Haverhill. Steghagen reported to the convention on the success of the Ladies' Label League of Chicago, which was at work trying to stimulate consumer demand for union goods in the ladies' shoe industry. A federation of these label leagues in the AFL, under the name Women's Trade Union Label League, later became one of the elements in the creation of the Women's Trade Union League in 1903. Steghagen urged additional efforts among working women and middle-class consumers on the national level to pressure manufacturers to accept the BSWU.[55] When led by women shoeworkers loyal to Tobin and to business unionism, efforts to promote unity among women promised influential connections with middle-class reformers and consumers. The BSWU was attempting to use cross-class support among women for its own organizational purposes. The loyalty of New England shoeworkers, especially the stitchers of Haverhill, to the BSWU and to its new policies would be tested in a showdown with the Lynn Knights of Labor assemblies in 1903.

The depression years of the 1890s did little to change the composition of the work force of Essex County stitchers. The vast majority of women shoeworkers remained native-born Americans from Yankee homes and native-born daughters of Irish and French-Canadian families. Many were young unmarried women who along with older single women, widows, or divorcées needed to support themselves and frequently needed to provide for dependents. Samples of one in ten female shoeworkers from the Lynn census of population in 1900 and 1910 indicate strong continuity with the patterns of the female work force in the 1880 census.[56] However, the percentage of geographically mobile women who boarded during the busy season declined and the number of wives in the work force rose.

The percentage of boarding stitchers in Lynn continued at about 20 percent of the female work force in 1900 and 1910, but this represented a decline from 28 percent in 1880 and 36 percent in 1870. The nineteenth-century pattern of geographical mobility for about one-third to one-quarter of the work force of stitchers was being slowly replaced by a dominant pattern of local residence for female workers in the early twentieth century. Among the residents, the percentage of wives in the Lynn female work force grew steadily to 21 percent in 1900 and 29 percent in 1910, in comparison with 17 percent in 1880. By 1910 more and more wives supplemented their family's income by doing shoe work during the busy season.

Young single women from male-headed resident families remained a stable percentage of the work force (34 percent in 1880, 35 percent in 1900, and 31 percent in 1910). They continued to represent the youngest age group of women workers with the highest percentage of foreign-born fathers. The percentage of residents living in female-headed families, who were largely unmarried and who supported themselves or widowed mothers, also remained stable between 1880 and 1910 at about 22 percent of the work force. Men in stitching work (2 percent) represented only a distant threat to Lynn stitchers in 1900. Despite the hard times of the 1890s and the consolidation of much of Lynn's shoe production into large, complex factory operations, the general composition of the work force of Lynn stitchers had not changed much since 1880.

Table 5. Shifting percentages of women shoeworkers in Lynn, 1870–1910, based on marital status and residence

	1870	1880	1900	1910
Boarding stitchers	36%	28%	19%	18%
Wives	9%	17%	21%	29%
Single residents in male-headed families	34%	34%	35%	31%
Single residents in female-headed families	21%	21%	25%	22%
Total Lynn female work force	100%	100%	100%	100%

This table is based on the federal manuscript censuses of population; see Appendix B.

The relative status of women shoeworkers in industrial work in Massachusetts also remained high in the opening decade of the twentieth century. In a study of women's work prepared in 1901 by the Women's Educational and Industrial Union of Boston, women who worked in the shoe factories of Lynn and Haverhill represented the highest paid and most satisfied workers, except for their general desire for more work during the slack season.[57] Another WEIU study in 1911 indicated that women shoeworkers remained the highest paid female industrial workers in the state.[58] In 1901, when compared with female textile workers in Fall River and Lowell and with retail clerks and waitresses in Boston, shoe stitchers enjoyed more flexible hours, a higher level of education, more job satisfaction, and even some enthusiasm for their employment and for their social contacts with other women shoeworkers. The twenty stitchers interviewed in this study reported that they had begun to work at an average age of 18.6 years and had been at their jobs for nearly nine years. Three-quarters were unmarried and native-born. Most lived in boarding or lodging houses, although the study was directed at self-supporting women, which excluded wives and resident daughters. Their major complaint was the effect on their health of the straining pace of work during the busy season. Their average annual earnings, which ranged between seven and twelve dollars a week for piecework in the prosperous post-depression years, yielded an average weekly wage of $6.45 after living expenses of four dollars per week. This was almost twice the weekly net income ($3.82) of retail clerks, whose work, according to the study, if less remunerative, offered better conditions for health and status. Of the twenty stitchers interviewed, only one from Haverhill was a union member, and few were members of social clubs. Most attended church, but their favorite amusements were the theater in Lynn and Boston, cycling, dancing, and shopping, activities that indicated discretionary income to spend. In the early years of the twentieth century, female shoeworkers remained an elite among working women in Massachusetts, enjoying the highest standard of living as well as social and educational status. They still faced the disadvantages of a highly seasonal industry, but their levels of wages and skill meant they could live relatively comfortably, save money, and enjoy their free time.

In late 1901 Miss Marie Van Vorst spent three weeks in Lynn among the women shoeworkers, disguised as a working girl. Van Vorst and her sister-in-law, Mrs. John Van Vorst, were typical of middle-class, reform-minded ladies who concerned themselves with the impact of industrial work on the lives of women and with the threat of class conflict in the 1890s.[59] Women like the Van Vorsts observed working-class life as temporary participants in order to provide irrefutable evidence to justify social reform. Some gathered statistics; others transformed themselves into working girls in order to publish their experiences and expose the reality of working-class life to the American public. For the Van Vorsts, the result was *The Woman Who Toils: Being the Experiences of Two Ladies as Factory Girls*, published in 1903. Their middle-class perceptions, however, overwhelmed their abilities to understand working-class experience, and they concluded melodramatically that working girls lived among sordidness and squalor, "condemned to slow death—mental, moral, physical death!"[60] When Marie Van Vorst presented herself as "Bell Ballard" from Paris to a French-Canadian family in Lynn, she was welcomed to live with them and their six other boarders, who included three French-Canadian "young ladies who work[ed] in the shops." Her boardinghouse keeper was a kindly, maternal woman who reassured Marie: "Ici nous sommes toute une famille" and promised her that the other young women would help her find work in the shops.[61] Marie Van Vorst found this work experience incompatible with any middle-class conception of ladyhood.

Marie's first contacts with the shoe factories shocked her sensibilities: the noise, the bad smells, the close air, and the pandemonium of the stitching room. She was frightened by the men in the shops and the pace and bustle of the factory operations, but was immediately hired as a presser on piecework, a job of folding and gluing uppers, which required experience, patience, stamina, and quick fingers to earn a reasonable wage at existing piece rates. Maggie McGowan taught her the job and impressed Marie with her kindness and encouragement despite the time it took from her own work. Marie left the shop after her first day's work having earned seven cents and with overpowering impressions of the stinking glue, tobacco smoke, "horrid din," and dirty surroundings. Maggie, who had been a presser for ten years and earned $12.00 a week, suggested to Marie that she consider doing domestic work instead.

After a trying and upsetting first day, Marie was revolted by the evening meal taken in the crowded kitchen amid smoke, frying odors, and stifling heat. She ate nothing. Her fellow boarders and her boardinghouse keeper were concerned, courteous, and sympathetic, and Marie, unable to explain her reactions, experienced a chasm of class difference. Physically irritated by the cheap, coarse clothing she wore as a disguise and fascinated yet repelled by the sight of Maurice, a boarding laborer in the house whom she described as sensuous, dirty, and powerful, the epitome of "Labour," she gratefully sought her room but could not sleep. Her second day as a presser was no different, and after several more she quit her job and sought another. The only work she could find was cleaning the corrosive shoe dye from between the vamp and sole of the almost finished shoe: the filthiest job in the industry. As a cleaner she earned twenty-five cents for five hours' work that left her smooth, white hands stained and ruined. After three weeks in Lynn, Marie put her notes in her purse and took the train for Boston, but could not avoid being snubbed by the dining car waiter because of her working girl's clothing.[62]

The Woman Who Toils provides a progressive, middle-class but essentially limited perspective on life in the shoe shops for Essex County women. Marie presented herself as an unskilled learner who was offered the worst jobs at the lowest wages. With no experience on a sewing machine, stitching was out of the question for her. She caught only a glimpse of the well-dressed shoe operatives who belonged to the union, but whom she observed as pale and "tired-out." The most significant evidence in her report revealed the extent of fellowship among women shoeworkers. Her relationships with other women in the shops and at her boardinghouse were marked by sympathy and support. Generous, helpful Maggie McGowan had taken time from her own work to teach her pressing. Her sister boarders who were stitchers and wore much finer clothing did not condescend to her appearance, but treated her with "sisterhood and kindness."[63] Her treatment by the men in the shops, of whom she was deeply frightened, was also considerate. A pale, thin, old edge-setter noticed that Marie's cramped position at her workbench tired her and suggested an adjustment that eased her aching back, but he carefully made his remark through another woman worker. Marie silently blessed him. Even her foreman seemed encouraging. The conditions of the work were hard, dirty, noisy, and fatiguing, but her fellow workers in the shoe factory, especially the women, offered Marie human solace and support. This system of support and sisterhood sustained the women workers of Lynn and Haverhill in 1903 when they confronted not their employers, but the leadership of the BSWU.

Even after the easing of the depression in 1897, shoe manufacturers in New England still faced serious problems with market demand. Leather prices stayed high, but there was great resistance from jobbers and retailers to raising prices to customers. Demand remained uncertain, and profits small. Consequently, there was great interest among shoe men in New England in a speech given by Massachusetts Senator Henry Cabot Lodge in late 1898 that advocated the use of the American consular service as an agent in seeking foreign markets for domestic manufactured goods; but for many Lynn firms the domestic market still offered unexplored possibilities. Those manufacturers who made ladies' high-buttoned boots tried to capture the market for bicycle footwear, while others searched for new ways to attract the customer's eye. "Mannish" shoes with flat heels, broad toes, and substantial soles were novelties manufactured specifically for women swept away by the national craze for athletics at the turn of the century.[64] Louis XV heels and low-cut shoes provided foils for fancy hosiery fads. This search for new ways to attract and please the consumer undermined the production of the standard styles of ladies' buttoned boots and low-cut shoes in Essex County. The giddy change of styles, season by season, included new colors and leathers and required new lasts and heel shapes. In Lynn, according to the *Boot and Shoe Recorder*, only the innovative and enterprising young manufacturer could survive the pace of this constantly changing market.[65] Many older, smaller firms vanished in the 1890s, victims of the depression years and the demands for constant novelty. However, the most serious attempt to capture a predictable share of the shifting consumer market was made by Lynn manufacturers who began to make "speciality" shoes in large quantities.

The attraction of speciality shoes to the manufacturer lay in the avoidance of severe competition in the national shoe market. Before the panic of 1893, some Lynn manufacturers who made high-priced goods began to put their trademarks in the shoes to attract repeat orders based on quality and customer satisfaction. Most of these firms had shifted to cheaper grades during the depression, but with the return of prosperity after 1897, they began again to make shoes with trademarks to sell for between $1.25 and $2.50. Each had a specific name for these goods: Mizpah, Peerless, Try-Me, Superior, or simply the firm's name, such as Sorosis. Many of these shoes were advertised both in the trade journals and to the public, and some were sold in special retail stores. The manufacturers intended that the price of the shoe should not fluctuate with the judgment of market demand by the jobber or retailer but remain fixed, while the idea of quality and style attached to the trademark would persuade the customer to meet the advertised price.[66]

As the shoe industry searched for ways to stabilize demand, the trade journals assessed the activities of the BSWU. Local jurisdictional disputes in Essex County between the Knights, the LPU, and the BSWU, the loss of major strikes in Massachusetts, and the limited number of union label factories by 1900 meant that the new national union offered little immediate threat to employers. In August 1897 the idea of convincing the public to buy shoes because they had union labels seemed absurd and "contrary to human nature," but the need felt by shoe manufacturers to use trademarks to avoid the competitive pressures of the national market left them willing to listen to the arguments of the BSWU leadership, especially after the union shifted its policy to the union label and arbitration of wages in 1899.[67] The *Boot and Shoe Recorder* allowed John Tobin, Horace Eaton, the secretary of the BSWU, and Edward Daley, the former president of the LPU, to use its pages in 1900 and 1901 to present to shoe manufacturers the union label contract as a method of gaining a competitive advantage. Eaton put the proposition plainly in July 1901.

> [W]ith the assistance of our union stamp as a selling factor, he [the manufacturer] will crush his non-union competitor or drive him into the union. The conditions of competition are in our favor. . . . The keener the struggle for "orders" the more valuable the advantage to the user of our stamp, and the surer we are to secure a complete combination of our craftsmen, provided we do not foolishly retard or destroy our chance by putting obstructions in the way of manufacturers who wish to adopt it, such, for instance, as to demand an increased bill of wages, and thus place him at a disadvantage with his non-union competitors.

Out of organizational weakness and failure, the BSWU had embraced the manufacturers' ideology of supply and demand as an organizing rationale. The Knights of Labor in Lynn had also accepted the rigors of market forces, but used arbitration and a strong regional organization to limit the power of manufacturers and end competition over wages by establishing a union standard. Tobin and the leaders of the BSWU accepted market competition among large manufacturing units as a permanent feature of the economy. They sought to encourage cooperation between labor and capital by organizing a national union that would use arbitration rather than strikes to settle grievances but pose no immediate threat to employers. In December 1900, Tobin attended an early conference of the National Civic Federation, and the BSWU convention in 1902 commended the NCF for its efforts to improve industrial relations.[68] Like Samuel Gompers, Tobin had rejected socialism and abandoned direct action against employers or control of work as goals of unionism.

By late 1901, as the *Boot and Shoe Recorder* correspondent from Lynn noted, the demand for the union label on shoes appeared to be growing rapidly, while a BSWU contract promised no strikes and a three-year agreement on wages with all disputes to be submitted to arbitration.[69] In 1903, although there was trouble from many KOL cutters and stitchers in Lynn who refused to join the BSWU, the union had negotiated ten label contracts in the city and twelve more in Haverhill. With the help of the union label contract and the desire of the shoe manufacturer to gain a competitive advantage in the national market, the leadership of the national union believed that New England shoeworkers would slowly be drawn back into the BSWU.

Massachusetts was crucial to the efforts of the BSWU to establish itself in the national industry. In 1900, 44.9 percent of the total value of product in the boot and shoe industry was manufactured in Lynn, Haverhill, and Brockton, and 41 percent of the industry's work force was employed in the state.[70] Between 1899 and 1903 the BSWU signed contracts with factories in all three cities and reorganized locals for various skill groups, including a mixed local in Lynn for female stitchers and for male finishers and bottomers. All the Lynn cutters remained independent in the Knights' assembly. The 1900 agreement that the cutters had signed with the BSWU guaranteed the recognition of KOL cards in Lynn until the BSWU had organized 250 cutters, whereupon all cutters would join the trade union. This the Lynn Knights were determined to prevent. The Lynn lasters did become members of the BSWU, but the majority of the stitchers in Lynn remained unorganized, neither attached to the mixed BSWU local, unless they were employed in union label factories, nor members of the Lady Stitchers' Union, which had faded away as an organization after 1895. In Haverhill the BSWU had twelve union contracts, some of them with large firms such as Thayer, Maguire and Field, J. H. Winchell, and Hilliard and Taylor, and others with smaller manufacturers of high quality, low-cut shoes. Many shoeworkers who rejected the BSWU in 1896 remained in their local independent organizations. In 1901 the Turned Workmen's Union organized a coalition of Haverhill workers into the Shoe Workers' Protective Union.[71] The Haverhill lasters had left the BSWU in 1898, but returned in 1902 under an agreement similar to the one negotiated with the KOL cutters in Lynn. The Haverhill stitchers had their own women's local in the BSWU, but the SWPU also had a stitchers' local with about 900 members.

During the spring of 1902 the BSWU and the SWPU struggled with each other over control of the Joint Shoe Council in Haverhill, while the BSWU leaders moved aggressively to eliminate dual unionism from the two principal centers of shoe production in Essex County. Tobin sent organizers from Rochester to Lynn in late 1902 to set up a cutters' local in violation of the 1900 agreement with the Knights.[72] In Haverhill, shoeworkers inside and outside of the BSWU had strongly opposed the signing of union label contracts with the notoriously antiunion factories of J. H. Winchell and John W. Russ, firms that paid wages much below union scale and employed predominantly immigrant workers. The signing of union label contracts with these firms would swell the BSWU membership in Haverhill with foreigners who earned low wages. The union itself seemed to be restoring the obnoxious features of the ironclad contract that had been defeated in 1895. Jeremiah Donovan, who had organized the two firms for the BSWU at the behest of Tobin, was ousted by the Haverhill Shoe Council as its agent in 1902. Donovan had also angered the SWPU stitchers by replacing their representative on the shoe council with a BSWU stitcher.[73] He was, however, retained as the agent of the local AFL-dominated Central Labor Union.

The union label contracts with the other ten factories in Haverhill forced the raising of local union dues in accordance with the BSWU high dues policy. The endorsement of this policy by the Rochester convention in 1899 had at the time created immediate and widespread opposition, especially from stitchers. At subsequent BSWU conventions, some delegates made efforts to lower the dues for women workers. The female delegates from Chicago, however, strongly resisted any alteration in the dues schedule, despite organized protest in 1900 from women shoeworkers in Illinois. In 1913 Charles Baine, general secretary of the BSWU, recalled with contempt the opposition to the twenty-five cents weekly dues in 1899, which when demanded by insistent union organizers reportedly left many stitchers in tears. Tobin and the BSWU leadership regarded the women members as no different from the rest of the membership in respect to dues, but Tobin admitted in 1905 that as far as he was concerned, women members had little influence in the organization and no real leaders.[74] BSWU leadership was indifferent to the special needs, interests, or traditions of women shoeworkers.

By 1902 the signing of union label contracts with low wage factories and the high dues policy had undermined the BSWU locals in Haverhill, a situation that brought John Tobin and BSWU organizer Frank Sieverman of Rochester to the city to answer their critics. Tobin defended the issuance of the union stamp to low wage firms as a strategy to organize first and raise wages later. The manufacturer, he argued, would not adopt the union stamp if it meant higher labor costs and a competitive disadvantage. Sieverman reminded the Haverhill workers that the shoes they made were sold in a competitive national market and that their share and their employers' share of that market was dependent on the union stamp. Both men defended high dues as essential to pay union benefits and conduct effective strikes, but only when those strikes were authorized by the BSWU national leadership.[75] The shoeworkers of Haverhill listened, but many were not convinced. In January 1903 the SWPU opened talks in Lynn with three firms that made low-cut shoes and began to organize their turn workmen. They also encouraged the Lynn Knights to organize all the cutters of Haverhill. When the KOL cutters struck W. H. Tuttle, a BSWU stamp factory in Lynn, on January 10, the SWPU and the turn workmen of Haverhill backed the Knights against the BSWU.[76] The showdown over the loyalties of shoeworkers in Essex County was on.

The role of the stitchers in the Lynn strike of 1903 continued to demonstrate their power as a gender-conscious group of skilled workers. Most women workers in Lynn had rejected the mixed BSWU local and had on several occasions between 1897 and 1903 joined with the KOL cutters to oppose the BSWU.[77] When the cutters extended their strike in January 1903 to all ten stamp factories in Lynn, the BSWU stitchers at the Nicholson shop rebelled against the wage reductions they claimed had been made since the union stamp had been issued to the firm. They also criticized the closed shop, which forced them to pay high dues, and many expressed sympathy with the Knights. Their grievances as BSWU members were essentially over their loss of income as women workers and their lack of power in the local. Stitchers came forward with evidence to prove that as a union shop Nicholson's had cut wages in 1902 on vamping, staying, and other machine operations. One vamper complained that a group of women had sent for the BSWU agent to protest the wage cut, "but he never came near us."[78]

The stitchers' strike quickly spread to other union stamp factories: the Donovan Company, Walton and Logan, Watson and Jones, and Harney Brothers. A mass meeting of 400 to 500 stitchers and the striking KOL cutters on January 17 revived the stitchers' assembly. Mrs. Jeanette Hamilton, vice president of this new Lady Stitchers' Assembly and a vamper at Donovan's, voiced the grievances of women workers with the BSWU that violated their sense of dignity and independence and penalized those without skills. The twenty-five cent weekly dues were a hardship, she argued, especially on women workers in nonstitching jobs at low piece rates. For the table girls, who pressed, glued, basted, and prepared the uppers for stitching, the twenty-five cents a week in dues represented a substantial proportion of their wages. She knew one girl who frequently earned only a dollar a week, which paid for her room, while she worked as a waitress for her meals. This girl was often forced to borrow money from her shop mates to pay the union dues that permitted her to work. Stitchers who earned higher wages did not earn them consistently because of the seasonal nature of the work and had to pay twenty-five cents a week during slack times and periods of unemployment. Jeanette Hamilton pointedly contradicted the claims of Mary (Mamie) Donovan, secretary of the mixed BSWU local #205, who cited high wages earned by stitchers and insisted that the twenty-five cents in dues represented only a very small sum from their earnings.[79] For self-supporting women used to stretching their wages over dull times, high union dues were an unwelcome addition to their budgets. As the BSWU made no pretense of increasing wages and tolerated wage cuts at union shops, the payment of weekly union dues seemed an additional and outrageous wage reduction.

Jeanette Hamilton traced the source of these grievances to the lack of control of the BSWU local by the stitchers. She insisted that women members had taken their grievances to the union without success. Furthermore, during the election of local and national officers, stitchers had been given marked ballots. When Hamilton demanded an explanation, she was told it was "for the good of the organization." She refused to vote under such circumstances. There were few, she added, who were not "heartily disgusted" with the BSWU.[80] One stitcher complained: "I became a member of the organization in its infancy in this city and was in it for two years. There was not a week during that time that I earned $5 and there were others who earned little more and still others who earned less. If we didn't have the 25 cents dues, they would be very indignant. . . . I deprived myself of the necessities of life to pay an unfair tax of 25 cents for the privilege of the firm to use a label or stamp of organized labor."[81]

The stitchers also disapproved of the use of the mixed local's share of the weekly dues, eight and one-half cents, for recreational activities that promised ice cream and cake for the ladies, but often delivered only beer for the men. Other BSWU stitchers' locals outside of Lynn used their dues to create emergency funds to keep their women members in good standing and eligible for sick benefits during the dull seasons. Reacting to the dissatisfaction of the Lynn stitchers, Frank Sieverman, who was troubleshooting for Tobin during the Lynn strike, criticized the mixed local for ignoring the needs of the stitchers and brought Emma Steghagen from Chicago in March to organize a women's local.[82] Sieverman's action was too late to save the situation. By then, the grievances of the Lynn stitchers extended far beyond control of their local.

The BSWU leadership in Boston reacted to the strike action against the union factories in Lynn by trying to blame and isolate the Knights, while demonstrating the ample resources of their organization and allies to crush any opposition. Samuel Gompers, interested in protecting the union label in other industries, openly backed the BSWU, as did the Central Labor Unions in Lynn and Haverhill. Tobin pilloried the Knights as enemies of organized labor, as has-beens, and as backbiters who manipulated the stitchers for their own benefit. Striker Nellie Cunningham, a stitcher who worked at Walton and Logan, reacted sharply to Tobin's attempts to discredit the Knights and the stitchers as their dupes. The stitchers, she wrote to the *Lynn Item*, had been tricked or manipulated by no group and would prove it by their actions in the strike.[83] BSWU officials also characterized the cutters as "labor aristocrats" and used insults to shame the Knights for hiding behind the skirts of women stitchers. But the cutters' defiance of the BSWU and its formidable allies had already won them the admiration of the community and the region for their courage. Sympathetic shoeworkers in Lynn turned the accusation back at the union, jeering and hissing from factory windows at the cutters whom the BSWU brought to the city to work in the stamp factories, challenging them to "be men once more!"[84]

The source of Tobin's unremitting hostility to the Lynn strike and its Essex County supporters was his determination to stick with business unionism and his fears that successful demonstrations of local militancy and autonomy would show up the BSWU as a weak partner to its allies among union label manufacturers and middle-class reformers and to Gompers and the AFL. This was the test of Tobin's leadership of the new BSWU, and the Knights in Lynn seemed to represent all that was backward-looking and ineffectual. Tobin unwisely belittled the 1903 strike as a "tempest in a teapot" and a "puff of smoke," while he attempted to break the strike by bringing hundreds of BSWU members to Lynn, to be paid from a $20,000 strike fund he placed in local banks. In collusion with the stamp manufacturers he filed a petition for an injunction against the strike leadership that named nine stitchers. However, the BSWU cutters brought in from New England shoe cities did not stay. Most of those from Maine and New Hampshire were persuaded by the Knights to leave Lynn, while the KOL in

North Adams kept the cutters of western Massachusetts at home. No BSWU cutters from Brockton appeared at all.[85] The national union faced an opposition with formidable regional solidarity.

One day after the Lynn cutters struck, the SWPU in Haverhill created a diversionary action by calling their turn workmen out on strike at Hazen B. Goodrich, a BSWU stamp factory. Despite the efforts of BSWU organizer Gad Martindale of Rochester, who had replaced the unpopular Donovan, other turn workmen and cutters at two more stamp factories in Haverhill followed. These moves, coordinated with anti-BSWU groups in Lynn, presented the national union with grave difficulties in New England. The skilled turn workmen of Haverhill were virtually irreplaceable, and additional substitutes for striking cutters in Haverhill would now have to be found. The secretary of the local SWPU pointed out that the BSWU stamp may once have been a warranty against strikes, but now its presence in Essex County shoe factories guaranteed labor trouble.[86] Every manufacturer in Lynn and Haverhill could imagine his work force during this busy and prosperous season melting away to serve the BSWU as strikebreakers or to strike in defiance of the organization.

The 1903 strike of cutters and stitchers received widespread support from New England shoeworkers and from other groups of shoe and leather workers in Lynn, such as the grain counterworkers, treers, McKay stitchers, and lasters, many of whom contributed to the strike fund rather than pay their union dues to the BSWU. In retaliation, Tobin ordered a strike on March 6 at the union shop of William Porter in order to stop contributions by sympathetic stitchers to the anti-BSWU strike fund. The community of Lynn eagerly supported the fund-raising benefits of the stitchers, which included balls and a May breakfast, while the police and the mayor's office received harsh criticism from the BSWU and the stamp manufacturers for favoring the strikers.[87]

During the union war in Essex County, BSWU cutters from Rochester, Cincinnati, Chicago, Minneapolis, and St. Louis arrived in Lynn, but the community met them with great demonstrations of hostility and many left. Illegally imported cutters from Montreal departed quickly after the Lynn Knights informed the U.S. Immigration Service in Boston of the circumstances of their arrival. An inspector and several U.S. marshals appeared in Lynn to investigate allegations that the BSWU had violated the alien contract labor law, while Gompers intervened on Tobin's behalf with the immigration service. In his consuming desire to defeat the Knights and other independent shoeworker organizations in New England, Tobin utilized every antiunion tactic of the most hostile manufacturer. Many of the striking KOL cutters quickly found jobs with other Lynn shoe firms, and the stamp factories tried to fill their orders by using cutters of less skill and experience. The BSWU was forced to make up out of its own treasury the difference in wages between the customary quota and quality of work expected of skilled Lynn cutters and the lower output of the BSWU strikebreakers.[88]

Much of the BSWU strategy to break the 1903 strike centered on the stitchers. Tobin later admitted that "without the girls the contest would have ended the first week or two," and the Knights acknowledged that the stitching rooms of the stamp factories became the real battlefield of the strike.[89] At first, BSWU leaders from the Boston office tried to talk the striking stitchers into going back to work, while agreeing to make concessions that would resolve their grievances. One shoeworker, William James, scoffed at these efforts by Frank Sieverman to conciliate the women:

> You are kind and pleasing to the lady stitchers at present but you will not convince them they are wrong. . . . The stitchers are the key to all shoe troubles and if they [the BSWU] had worked to give them more wages and less ice cream their local treasury would be fuller than the lasters. . . . The Lynn shoemaker knows what unionism is. It does not consist of threats, ice cream parties, strike breakers, or being a party to an injunction against your fellow shoeworkers, especially when some enjoined are those dearly beloved ladies you think so much of.[90]

Union officials then went to the BSWU stitchers' local in Haverhill and promised women members "first places" in Lynn stamp factories, which guaranteed them abundant work at the best piece rates. Nearly all of the stitchers in the Haverhill BSWU refused to come to Lynn as strikebreakers and those in the SWPU threatened a sympathy strike against any shop in Haverhill that tried to stitch uppers for stamp factories in Lynn. Stitchers in Salem also refused to go to Lynn and threatened to strike any shop doing Lynn work.[91] When union loyalty conflicted with their interests as shoeworkers, the majority of Massachusetts women stood together against the BSWU.

Cooperation among women shoeworkers proved to be as effective in the region as in Essex County. Striking stitchers took the train to Exeter and Dover, New Hampshire, where they convinced other stitchers to stay away from Lynn. One young BSWU stitcher from Farmington, Maine, who was persuaded to travel to Lynn, grew suspicious at strike rumors and found that she had been hired as a strikebreaker. After talking to the Lynn women, she refused "to stand out against members of her own sex." She was a BSWU member, she said, only because she was forced to be, but begrudged every cent of dues she paid, referring indignantly to a wage cut that she had experienced in a BSWU factory in Maine.[92] A former Massachusetts vamper who was working in Cincinnati, the principal source of the BSWU stitchers who came to Lynn as strikebreakers, wrote the Knights to offer her help in dissuading Ohio women from aiding the BSWU on the grounds that stitchers were being deceived about the nature of the troubles in Lynn.[93] The inept policy of the BSWU toward women stitchers in New England made sisterhood an easy choice for them in 1903.

The naming of stitchers in the BSWU petition for an injunction represented the first citation of women in such proceedings in Massachusetts and created great anger among the strikers. This was reported to Mary Kenney O'Sullivan, who covered the Lynn strike for the *Boston Globe*. O'Sullivan sympathized with the BSWU against the strikers, but her account also conveyed the indignation of those named in the injunction, such as Miss Mary E. Peabody: "I am mad clear through. . . . [I]f I had known that this [injunction] was coming I would have 'had the deed as well as the credit.' The only thing I am sorry for is that I did not take some part in the riots." Miss Katherine McLellan protested: "I do not like the insinuation that the charge implies, that I am rowdyish, unladylike and riotous. I am not that sort and I deeply resent the whole proceedings."[94] Both were stitchers who boarded in Lynn and had become charter members of the new stitchers' assembly. Efforts to locate the leaders of the stitchers' assembly in 1903 in the 1900 Lynn census and the city directories between 1900 and 1905 yielded the names of thirty women, or over half of the fifty-eight identifiable activists, who were either officers, participants in the benefits and fund-raising activities, members of investigating committees, or persons named in the injunction. Of these thirty women, two-thirds were unmarried and nearly three-quarters roomed, boarded, or lodged in Lynn. The leaders in 1903 were native-born, self-supporting boarders, like many of the stitchers active in the DOSC and in the Knights. Mary Kenney O'Sullivan's account of the stitchers' activities carried hard judgments on the strikers by BSWU women in Lynn who called them traitors to the union cause. Mary Donovan, the secretary of the BSWU mixed local and a resident daughter related to the owner of the Donovan factory, insisted that the union had maintained and even increased stitching prices in stamp factories and that union benefits were well worth twenty-five cents a week.

The nineteenth-century traditions of gender and craft loyalty that supported collective action among women shoeworkers were, however, severely tested during the 1903 strike. An identity of interests among women workers, useful during the 1895 strike to dissuade other New England stitchers from taking the places of their striking sisters, created feelings of betrayal and anger in 1903 toward those women who chose to stay with the BSWU or came to Lynn from cities outside New England as strikebreakers. Some stitchers in Lynn did not strike, and others returned to work at the stamp factories after a few days. Stitchers who went back to work did so on the grounds of personal independence and self-support. One wrote: "I don't want anybody to [throw] it up to me when this strike is over that I subsisted on the charity of the Knights of Labor or any of the men or women employed in other factories."[95] M. E. Lee, a stitcher who continued to work for Harney Brothers, made her position plain: a mixture of personal self-interest and stubborn independence. She was a BSWU member, but thought the dues were too high. As a woman old enough, she claimed, for the Old Ladies' Home, she saw no advantage for herself in the strike, which seemed to her to be a conflict among men. Impervious to charges of disloyalty to her sister workers, she stated: "Other people's opinions of me will not get me my bread and butter."[96] The Lady Stitchers' Assembly did not initially target such nonstriking local BSWU women for harrassment, but reserved most of their hostility for stitchers brought into Lynn by the BSWU. However, as the strike went on and tempers got out of control, female members of the local BSWU were set upon in the streets by women strikers and pelted with rotten eggs. The effect of this anger against BSWU loyalists began to erode sisterhood as a viable basis for protest.

Many of the female strikebreakers from other towns and states were easily identified to the strikers by their escorts of BSWU men. Among them was Mary Anderson of the BSWU in Chicago. Some were politely persuaded to return to their homes. One case especially embarrassing to the BSWU was that of the Livingston sisters, Belle and May, the daughters of the secretary of the BSWU locals in Rochester. Frank Sieverman had prevailed on them to come to Lynn. Intercepted in Boston by alert members of the stitchers' assembly, the Livingston sisters joined the ranks of the strikers and arrived in Lynn not as strikebreakers, but to attend the theater with their delighted new friends, escorted by the Knights. When their brother also came to Lynn on behalf of the BSWU, he told his sisters their father would "shoot them on sight" when they returned to Rochester. Other BSWU stitchers from midwestern cities, primarily Cincinnati, who worked in the stamp factories were hounded daily as they made their way to their places of work from a large boardinghouse located near the central industrial district. Jeering crowds and showers of rotten eggs greeted their appearance, and rocks were hurled against their windows at night. Many of the insults and eggings were administered woman to woman. Leaders of the stitchers' assembly, although eager to avoid appearances in police court on disorderly conduct charges, nonetheless denied rumors that men dressed as women were the perpetrators of these actions. A man in a woman's dress, assembly members pointed out, could not run at all, much less escape an arresting officer.[97] The strikers wished to bear public responsibility for their hostile behavior toward disloyal sisters, even when such behavior put their own respectability at risk.

Women's purses conveniently hid eggs, and a lady's sense of public humiliation prompted the idea of using asafetida as a weapon against female strikebreakers. Sprayed on a woman's clothing from behind without her knowledge, this vile-smelling substance, defined discreetly in the Lynn press as *teufels dreck*, ruined her clothes and made her a menace to public noses. One young woman from Beverly experienced a spraying of asafetida on her clothing as she waited in the ladies' room at the central depot. Once seated in the railroad cars, the smell of her became so powerful that all other passengers retreated while she burst into tears. Other acts of hostility by female strikers against strikebreakers included ink sprayed on light-colored clothing, hair-pullings, and slapped faces.[98] The disloyal sister was punished by the destruction of her lady's garb and her aura of respectability.

Many Lynn stitchers rejected the arguments of BSWU women members that union benefits were worth the union dues. For them, the problem was the ability of the BSWU to represent the stitchers as wage earners. One stitcher who worked at a nonunion shop said that her sister workers would welcome a union if it served the employee, not the employer. Stitchers, she said, were no longer concerned with saving money for the dull season, but "getting a day to day living." The issues for her were wages and equal rights: the "liberty" for which "our forefathers fought." Another stitcher complained that the BSWU's attempt to organize a woman's local was a bluff. "Until now women have been of the very least importance to the BSWU except to donate their weekly 25 cents." She dismissed the BSWU as "corrupt," arguing: "Our labor is our most valuable possession; we realize unions have come to stay and it would be better to have a union where we can unite under one head as long as that head is wise enough to protect the working people as much as the manufacturers."[99] The striking stitchers of Lynn and their sympathizers in the local female work force rejected the advice of one of their forewomen who had supervised stitchers in Lynn and in other cities since 1883 and who insisted that the interests of the employer and the employee were identical. Noting the scarcity of experienced stitchers during the past several seasons, she argued that the quality of stitching was more important to the sale of ladies' shoes than a union stamp. "The skilled Lynn stitchers—the best on earth—God bless them. I have had charge of help in Maine, New York and Boston but give me two teams of the real Lynn help and we can produce better shoes than 5 teams of any other."[100]

The scarcity of skilled stitchers and the effective use of acts of hostility against loyal BSWU women led Tobin to seek other ways to replace the Lynn female strikers. The BSWU sent young men and boys to Lynn as stitchers from Brockton and from the nonunion shop of Thomas G. Plante in Boston, a firm that had left Lynn in 1896 after a lockout. Harney Brothers hired Jewish men from stitching shops in Chelsea where they stayed on after the strike as active BSWU members and antagonists of the KOL stitchers.[101]

These acts by the union leadership challenged the traditional sexual division of labor in shoe production and undermined the ability of women to organize themselves and represent their interests as shoeworkers.

The most controversial move by the BSWU, designed to intimidate independent stitchers in both Lynn and Haverhill, and in other New England cities if need be, was the establishment of a stitching operation in Boston run by the union. BSWU funds would be used to teach the trade to young women who as learners would pay union dues and stitch uppers for union stamp factories throughout New England. Many manufacturers were dubious about the practicality of such an arrangement, but were eager to break the stitchers' strike. Infiltrators from the stitchers' assembly in Lynn reported, however, that only a few learners had been employed at the Boston stitching shop by early March, and the whole operation proved a costly failure.[102] The use of union funds to pay for the training of new women workers to undercut the resistance of those already in the trade ruined any chance for the BSWU to recover even its slim hold on Essex County stitchers.

By mid-March, the owners of the stamp factories in Lynn, Haverhill, and Brockton were calling for a settlement of the 1903 strike. In early April and with the strike still effective in the stitching rooms of the Lynn stamp factories, the independent shoeworkers organizations in Essex County created a new if tenuous federation of shoeworkers. The membership consisted of the Knights assemblies of cutters in Lynn and Haverhill; the lady stitchers (KOL) of Lynn and the stitchers of Haverhill; the turn workmen of Lynn, Haverhill, and Marblehead; the SWPU in Haverhill and in Lynn; the LPU in Haverhill and North Adams; the stock fitters of Lynn; and the leather workers of Lynn, Haverhill, and Marblehead. Organized formally in early May at a convention in Haverhill, the Federated Shoe and Leather Workers' Union represented an alliance of Essex County shoeworkers outside of the BSWU. On June 12, Harney Brothers, one of the largest union stamp factories in Lynn, abruptly abandoned the union label and promised its striking stitchers to restore their former positions and their old machines. In retaliation, the BSWU called a strike against Harneys', but within days lasters from Haverhill had replaced striking BSWU lasters, while other BSWU loyalists were warned by their female relatives who were stitchers to pack their bags if they intended to stay out on strike at Harneys'. With the BSWU's effort at Harneys' a failure and the season's orders for stamped shoes either filled or canceled, Nicholson's and Donovan's also abandoned their union stamps and contracts. In April, two Haverhill shops returned their stamps, and the turned workmen in other BSWU factories nailed their dues books to the wall. Most of the Haverhill union shops abandoned the stamp before the fall production season.[103] By the end of the summer of 1903 the BSWU had collapsed in two national centers of shoe production. The defeat of the BSWU in Essex County represented a significant victory for local autonomy and equal rights, the basis on which labor militancy among New England shoeworkers had flourished in the nineteenth century. The BSWU organization in Brockton remained strong, however, based largely on the appeal of the union label in men's shoes to the AFL's two million organized male members.

The 1903 strike was a valedictory expression of the cultural and regional solidarity of the most skilled workers in the New England shoe industry: the cutters, the stitchers, the turn workmen, and the lasters. These native-born Americans, many of Yankee background, relied on nineteenth-century traditions of equal rights to justify their protests against the tyranny of the BSWU. However, this cultural basis for protest was narrowing in the early twentieth century, as the number of immigrant workers in shoe production increased and mechanization continued. Equal rights faced the danger of developing into an exclusionary tradition.

Likewise, the militant uses of gender loyalty among women shoeworkers had fractured the female work force in 1903. Essentially a cultural response to class problems and based on nineteenth-century social distinctions, gender solidarity among women workers was undercut as the sexual division of labor in shoe production changed in the early twentieth century. When combined with skill and experience at their work, sisterhood among late nineteenth-century women shoeworkers furnished the basis for effective moments of resistance both to employers and to unresponsive and indifferent union officials. But this female protest tradition had not been enough to sustain a permanent organization. Even in Lynn, the center of persistent militancy by women workers, the toll of marriage, the claims of the family, and the mobility of many self-supporting women undercut the chance to build enduring class institutions based on gender experience.

The BSWU did not immediately abandon its efforts in Essex County, but shifted the fight against the Knights into the hands of the AFL. The Massachusetts State AFL Convention in 1903 denounced the Knights of Labor in Lynn and the SWPU in Haverhill as unfit to associate with the legitimate labor movement. In September the Lynn Central Labor Union sponsored the appearance of AFL national organizer Stuart Reid to promote the activities of the Women's Trade Union Label League. Reid joined forces with the remaining BSWU stitchers and the Lynn Equal Rights Club, the local suffrage organization, to form a chapter of the label league to organize women as consumers and encourage the purchase of union label goods. The target of these efforts was ladies' shoes. Men who represented the vast majority of organized labor bought their own shoes, hats, and cigars, and the label on these products had succeeded in creating a demand for union goods. Women who were not organized into unions to any extent and who bought their shoes for style and price were to be persuaded by the label league to use their buying power to support union labor. This meant the BSWU. Miss Ellen F. Wetherell, leader of the Lynn suffrage organization who had written a pro-BSWU account of the 1903 strike, was made president of the Lynn label league.[104] The stitchers in the Knights of Labor immediately organized to oppose these activities.

The Women's Trade Union Label League in Lynn was also used by the BSWU and the AFL to criticize the stitchers as well as the cutters in the Knights. Reid denied that the stitchers had any real grievances against the BSWU and dismissed the 1903 strike as "a silly squabble." Early in 1904, however, the Lynn branch of the label league awarded gold watches to two BSWU stitchers from Chicago, Mary Anderson and Mary Doyle, who served as strikebreakers in 1903. Reid also recruited Mary Kenney O'Sullivan to address the Lynn organization. She argued that the union stamp was the salvation of the worker and strongly defended the BSWU. In response, the stitchers' assembly dismissed Reid and his criticism and remained loyal to the courtly leader of the KOL cutters, L. Boyden Armstrong, whom they greatly admired as a hard-working Lynn resident who drew no salary as a union leader and spoke the language of the equal rights tradition. They also made it clear that they objected only to the BSWU label and supported the policy of union labels in general. In an open letter to Reid, the stitchers' assembly announced that they knew they were the key to the labor situation in Lynn and would not be coerced into the BSWU by tricks or wiley tactics. The letter concluded: "Give us no more advice, man-from-nowhere with your hat on." [105] The label league in Lynn never became a viable organization.

The divisions that BSWU policies had created among the women workers of Lynn during the 1903 strike and the subsequent opposition of the local stitchers' assembly to the efforts of the AFL women in the Women's Trade Union Label League weakened efforts in Massachusetts to promote union membership for women workers and suffrage. At the AFL national convention held in Boston in November 1903, the organization briefly considered a national boycott of Lynn and Haverhill-made shoes, but, more important, endorsed the Women's Trade Union League, a cross-class coalition of middle-class women and trade union women dedicated to organizing women workers into the AFL. The headquarters of the WTUL was located in Chicago, a BSWU stronghold. In April 1904, Mary Kenney O'Sullivan, Mary Morton Kehew, president of the Women's Educational and Industrial Union of Boston, and Emily Balch, Wellesley College economist, organized the Boston chapter of the WTUL. The treasurer of the Boston WTUL was Mary (Mamie) Donovan, the BSWU stitcher who had fought the Lady Stitchers' Assembly in 1903 and served as the secretary of the Lynn Women's Trade Union Label League. The WTUL in Boston closely associated its organizational activities with an AFL union that had been rejected by Essex County stitchers.

According to Nancy Schrom Dye, the historian of the WTUL, the Boston league was unable to raise funds or attract working-class members and remained less successful than the WTUL in other cities.[106] Dye argued that the WTUL was an outgrowth of nineteenth-century female networks, but the policies of the BSWU had divided women shoeworkers and disrupted their sense of gender consciousness and class identification. By accepting these divisions, the WTUL in Massachusetts cut their new organization off from those women shoeworkers who possessed the longest tradition of interest in women's rights and suffrage and the best record of effective labor protest as industrial workers. Furthermore, the political heritage and social status of the native-born stitchers of Essex County might have helped resolve some of the tensions between middle-class and working-class women that haunted the national WTUL. Militancy among women shoeworkers in Essex County survived in the early twentieth century only in independent unions outside the AFL. In addition, the alienation of these organized stitchers led the AFL leadership to disregard the possibilities of organizing a similar group of young, native-born, single working women. When female clerical workers tried to organize themselves in the early twentieth century, AFL leaders told them that "organizing unions was not appropriate for respectable women."[107]

The BSWU made the lot of women shoeworkers more difficult by moving quickly to punish dissident women in Haverhill after the events in 1903. In January 1904 the general executive board heard two appeals from Haverhill stitchers who were refused sick benefits by the local BSWU. Mrs. Alice McMenamon had worked late into her pregnancy, fainted one day in the shop, and miscarried. Three days later, she filed for sick benefits. The local executive board had determined that the miscarriage had been brought on by bronchitis, as confirmed by her doctor, but decided that her activities since her illness, which included a trip to Boston and the resumption of her work, disqualified her from benefits. The general executive board agreed that confinements were not to be regarded as sickness in accordance with union policy and that Alice McMenamon's miscarriage was a confinement. The second case involved Miss May Mack, McMenamon's sister, who had typhoid fever, recovered, and applied for sick benefits. The local BSWU board had denied her benefits because within three weeks of her attack she had been observed attending a musical performance in Haverhill on a rainy night. In May Mack's case, the general executive board made a sweeping judgment on the motives of Haverhill stitchers who applied for sick benefits:

> There had for some time past been a disposition on the part of members in Haverhill to secure all of the sick claim money possible from the General Organization and that the receipts from the various local unions in Haverhill were quite frequently of less amount than the sick claims. The members seem to show a disposition to get even with the General Union by endorsing anybody's claim whether

justifiable or not, and [we] believe that it would be very poor policy on the part of the General Board not to sustain the local executive board in that city who had the courage to turn down a sick claim.[108]

May Mack was denied her benefits. The general board then voted to categorize all miscarriages as the equivalent of confinements, not covered by sick benefits. The effect was to penalize all women in the BSWU.

The Federation of Shoe and Leather Workers, organized as an anti-BSWU coalition in 1903, quickly broke apart into independent, local groups. Rejecting the national union's decision to bow to market forces, Essex County shoeworkers resumed their traditions of local arbitration of wages backed by direct action and local autonomy based on craft and gender solidarity. Haverhill shoeworkers remained in the SWPU with the BSWU surviving only at J. H. Winchell's, and the local leather workers were later drawn into the Industrial Workers of the World. Most of the former BSWU members in Lynn organized the United Shoeworkers' Union, which by 1912 absorbed the cutters and the stitchers' assemblies. The BSWU hung on in Lynn only in two stamp factories. The work force in these two Essex County cities remained in separate labor organizations until the 1920s. The 1903 strike also proved costly to the BSWU outside Essex County. The union's membership, which had grown substantially between 1899 and 1904, leveled off and remained static between 1904 and 1910. The exhaustion of the union treasury in the 1903 strike left the BSWU unable to support Chicago shoeworkers caught in a lockout in 1904, which led to the organization of another rebellious, independent movement, the Progressive Shoeworkers. There was also serious trouble with the cutters and stitchers in the St. Louis locals in 1903 and 1904.[109]

In 1907 the lasters in Lynn and Brockton bolted the BSWU to form an independent movement, and it was feared the BSWU stitchers' local in Brockton, the strongest in the East, would follow. In contrast, the lady stitchers' assembly in Lynn continued to grow after 1903, so rapidly that by 1907 they seriously considered forming a new national trade assembly for women within the Knights of Labor. The stitchers retained their very close ties with the KOL cutters, electing a Lynn cutter as their Master Workman every year between 1903 and 1912. In 1911 the stitchers' assembly in Lynn had 2,000 members, while only 150 belonged to the straggling BSWU local. By 1920 there were more women shoeworkers organized in the United Shoe and the SWPU (21,000) than in the national BSWU (14,000).[110] Alice Kessler-Harris, who sought the reasons for the general decline in the numbers of organized women in the AFL after 1902, concluded that women's subordinate role in industrial production and the opposition of employers and the AFL to the organization of women workers kept them unorganized. Discouraged from unionization, working women turned to middle-class allies and protective legislation.[111] Many women shoeworkers in Essex County, however, avoided this path and remained active and effective in the labor movement after 1903, but outside the AFL. The stitchers of Essex County had rejected the BSWU, one of the major unions in the AFL, which supported protective legislation and cross-class efforts to promote trade unions for women.

Gender solidarity among women shoeworkers in Essex County was slowly undermined by many other factors in addition to the policies of the BSWU. Resident wives and daughters who were secondary wage earners tied to family economies formed an increasing percentage of the female work force. Since the recovery from the depression of the 1890s, there was a persistent and growing scarcity of experienced stitchers for the New England shoe industry. This regional scarcity had given stitchers leverage during the 1895 and 1903 strikes, but had also encouraged manufacturers in Lynn and in Haverhill to recruit new immigrant men into their stitching rooms. In 1900 only 2 percent of the Lynn stitchers were male, a figure not much different from the 1 to 3 percent of the work force who were men and worked in nineteenth-century stitching operations. Over three-quarters of these male workers in 1900 were native-born, largely in Massachusetts. By 1910 the number of men in female-typed shoe work had jumped to 20 percent of the total work force employed in these jobs. Only half of these male workers were native-born, while of the 49 percent foreign-born men, half were immigrants from Southern and Eastern Europe and from the Middle East, where men did needle work on garments and leather. Jews from Russia and Poland, Italians, Greeks, and Armenians from Turkey worked as vampers, stitchers, finishers, packers, trimmers, and pressers.[112] Not only did this shift represent a change in the sexual composition of stitching and other traditionally female work in shoe production, but a major shift was occurring in the ethnic composition of the work force as well. By 1920, male stitchers and vampers were common in the Essex County shoe industry, and foremen and male instructors worked in stitching rooms beside forewomen and female teachers. Foreign-born male stitchers were described in a 1915 study of the Massachusetts shoe industry by the Women's Educational and Industrial Union as "a menace to women's historic employment as shoe stitchers." [113] The study predicted that native-born women would not associate with foreign men in the stitching rooms.

Male immigrants worked for the same piece rates as native-born women, allowing manufacturers to keep labor costs steady, even if women stitchers were scarce. Furthermore, foreign-born men could be legally worked for more than the limit on women workers of fifty-four hours a week, a distinct advantage for them and their employers during the busy season. This protective legislation was intended primarily to limit the workweek of women who were supplementary wage earners rather than to assist self-supporting women. A fifty-four hour law became effective for women and children in Massachusetts in 1912 and permitted male stitchers to work longer hours and thus earn, especially as vampers, higher wages than women.[114] In 1919, Massachusetts adopted additional protective legislation for women that reduced the legal workweek to fifty hours. In an industry organized into concentrated seasons of production, the limits that protective legislation placed on the workweek of women shoeworkers restricted their ability to earn wages during the busy season. These limits undercut the level of annual income earned by self-supporting women that had sustained them during the dull seasons. Protective legislation in Massachusetts enacted in the 1910s encouraged the replacement of self-supporting female stitchers with immigrant men. Ironically, the strongest advocates of protective legislation for women in Massachusetts were the Women's Educational and Industrial Union and the WTUL in Boston. The contradictions between the successful politics of these groups and the interests of self-supporting women shoeworkers were reflected in a general decline in the numbers of females in the stitching rooms of Essex County.

The decline in the percentage of women in industrial work after 1900 and the shift of young, native-born women into retail, clerical, and other occupations may have also reduced the attractiveness and status of stitching as women's work. In Lynn, shoe manufacturers regarded the employment opportunities for women at the expanding General Electric operation as siphoning off potential stitchers. Styles in footwear before and after World War I undermined the popularity of the standard high-buttoned or laced shoe that required experienced vampers. While the War Industries Board insisted on standardized products for the duration, the influence of French styles on American fashion during the war years created a vogue for low-cut shoes, shorter skirts, and higher heels and promoted the idea that each dress or outfit required a matching or contrasting pair of shoes. The depression of the early 1920s, as in the 1890s, stimulated both the production of novelties and very intense competition. Novelty footwear with a maximum of style at a minimal price produced to be merchandised in department stores replaced standard goods made to fill orders from wholesalers and retailers.[115] By the 1920s, the patterns of marketing this new product and the cultural, sexual, and residential composition of the work force of stitchers in Essex County shoe production had undergone fundamental and irreversible changes. The basis of labor militancy for men and women shoeworkers would have to shift from a tradition of nineteenth-century equal rights to a new strategy for the twentieth century.

Conclusion

This study of class, gender, and labor protest for nineteenth-century Essex County shoeworkers demonstrates that the sexual division of labor has a history that reflects the interplay of changes in the organization of production and the social experience of men and women. The origins of the sexual division of labor in New England shoemaking lay in the expansion of production and the shifting control of profits in the late eighteenth century, evidence of the penetration of the household and family by new market forces; but social life shaped the form and context of work in both preindustrial and industrial production. Women workers especially found their class experience divided by the claims of family and the potential of gender consciousness.

Industrialization affected men and women shoeworkers in significantly different ways. Artisan life provided a cultural setting for an ideology of resistance based on decentralized group work and the social status of craftsmen. In contests with shoe manufacturers, this ideology was expressed as a demand for an equality of rights between employer and employee. After 1865, factory work—centralized, increasingly mechanized, and geared to the rhythms of busy and dull seasons—meant skill degradation and decreasing autonomy for male shoeworkers. Loss of apprenticeships, subdivided work procedures, and lower wages made the factory system a negative experience for former artisans.

Women's experience in preindustrial production had provided neither a setting of group work nor craft training. Although the common bonds of womanhood did inspire some shoebinders to a vision of labor protest in the early 1830s based on a shared experience of work, involvement in outwork meant low wages and periodic exhaustion in isolation from fellow workers. The factory system transformed women's work into a group experience in central shops. The busy seasons encouraged employers to pay relatively high wages in order to recruit additional numbers of New England women into industrial work. Geographical mobility for a portion of the female work force separated them from the direct supervision of family and kin and gave them control over their wages.

The sexual division of labor that persisted in the shoe factory gave women a virtual monopoly over the stitching process. As stitching operations became subdivided, a hierarchy of skills developed giving some women access to skilled work and good wages. The factory system rewarded skill and mobility for women workers, centralized their work experience, preserved the sexual division of labor, and permitted some women to be self-supporting. These women often became leaders of strikes and autonomous women's labor organizations. In spite of the continuation of homework, the factory meant positive changes for most women shoeworkers.

The equal rights tradition also had different meanings for men and women. The artisan tradition of protest and the mechanic ideology included women's experience only when their work was seen as part of the family economy headed by the artisan himself. Contradictions between the household work of women and their new involvement in shoe production moved shoebinding onto the wage labor market and out of artisanal control. Labor protest by artisan men defended decentralized work and the role of working women as supplementary to the family economy. When shoebinders attempted to build labor protest in the 1830s, they based their appeal on a shared sense of gender and work. For some, labor protest required an extension of the equal rights tradition to include new public rights for females, but ideological, economic, and social submersion in artisan family life circumscribed and defeated their efforts. In the 1840s the artisan conception of women as moral and apolitical narrowed the ways in which shoebinders could contribute to labor protest. Gender differences in work arrangements, ideology, and politics separated the experience of preindustrial shoeworkers and made it difficult for journeymen to regard women as fellow workers whose experience in many ways anticipated changes in the organization of production.

When a new industrial work force of young, unmarried New

England women began to operate sewing machines in centralized locations, male and some female activists regarded the interests of these factory operatives as in conflict with those of female contributors to the family economy. An opportunity was lost during the strike of 1860 to build an alliance between women who worked at home and those employed in the shoe shops, a promising alternative for working women to the family wage. The Lynn strike committee opposed the objectives of this new female industrial work force and failed to incorporate their interests into collective efforts against the shoe manufacturers. The resulting divisions among shoeworkers weakened their ability to resist changes in the industry during those years when mechanization and centralization were transforming shoe production.

In the post–Civil War shoe factory, the equal rights tradition of labor protest provided a setting within which tensions continued between self-supporting female industrial workers and women workers tied to a family economy. The primacy of marital status and the different obligations of women to their families became issues that divided and weakened their resistance. While the equal rights tradition was utilized to justify labor protest by both male and female shoeworkers, their conceptions of equality were different. The debates of the 1860s and 1870s between Emma Lane and Jennie Collins, Americus and Columbia, "Married Stitcher" and "A Stitcher" over the relevance for working women of access to formal political power and over the capacity of women to contribute to labor protest revealed some of these differences. For wives and daughters who supplemented family income, their role in family life defined the boundaries of their work and the meaning of their womanhood. Political rights belonged to the male head of family and the proper role of women in labor protest was that of auxiliaries to men's organizations. For Mary Damon, Emma Lane, and Americus, gender solidarity meant cooperation with other wives, mothers, and daughters in support of family interests.

On the other hand, for self-supporting and providing women whose economic needs approached those of men who headed families, a different sense of gender experience became an integral part of their commitment to work. They organized separate unions to represent the interests of all women workers and sought equal rights in the labor movement and as citizens. For Mary Russell,

Clara Brown, Martha Wallbridge, Mary Nason, and Jeanette Hamilton, gender solidarity meant cooperation with other women to achieve their rights at work and in society. The difficulties of resolving these differences between wives and daughters and self-supporting and providing women limited the effectiveness of their labor protest, despite the possibilities inherent in the coalitions of women that occurred during the strikes of 1860, 1871, 1895, and 1903. For working women, marital status and relationship to family could be potentially as divisive as ethnicity and race.

For a time, the development of a justifying image in the 1870s and early 1880s by self-supporting women based on their ascribed social status as lady stitchers concealed these divisions within the female work force and lent the prestige of respectable womanhood to female industrial workers. But the separate organizations and activities of the DOSC and the KOSC, the failure of the Knights of Labor to structure the interests of shoe stitchers in D.A. 77 into their institutional arrangements and politics, and the conflicts between women workers in Essex County and the national leadership of the BSWU indicated that male perceptions of female gender continued to restrict working women from the public world of men's activity.

Nonetheless, some women shoeworkers pursued equal rights on the regional and national levels: in the National Labor Union, the General Assemblies of the Knights of Labor, and in the Boot and Shoe Workers' Union. They sought equal pay for equal work, equal access to skilled work for women in other industries, and formal representation of the interests of working women in labor organizations. As Daughters of St. Crispin, as Lady Knights, and as organizers of the BSWU, women shoeworkers tried to sustain a national trade union to give them strength in regional contests with manufacturers. They formed connections with the post–Civil War women's rights movement. This essentially female tradition of labor activism in the late nineteenth century was based, however, on a historic conception of womanhood that proved to be limiting and restricting as a basis for class action. In the early twentieth century, women shoeworkers relinquished nineteenth-century gender categories, abandoned the mythology of the Yankee factory girl and the lady stitcher, and sought a more viable foundation for collective resistance.

Women workers used the historic content of gender as a cultural source of resistance. They justified pre–Civil War labor protest by calling themselves females: the daughters and wives of New England mechanics, much as the New England textile operatives, had used their status as daughters of freemen in their labor protest. They carried over this terminology to vindicate their political involvement in the antislavery and temperance movements. In 1860 many women saw their role in the regional shoe strike as a defense of the New England family, but the changing character and location of women's work had by then created a new female work force of factory girls whose independence, mobility, relatively high wages, and strategic position in centralized production gave them a new sense of what it was to be a woman shoeworker.

Yet geographical mobility carried special meanings for women. It opened the way to transcend family and community loyalties for relationships with sister workers and for regional and national collective action. But mobility also made them vulnerable to recurrent charges of immorality as homeless women. Appropriating a defensive imagery based on an assumed status as ladies, New England stitchers successfully tied this elevated social role to their position as industrial workers and extended its protection to the daughters of immigrants who joined them in the stitching rooms. The lady stitcher bridged the chasm in the ideology of Victorian America between wage-earning and respectable womanhood. However, as industrial production became more concentrated and shoe manufacturers recruited immigrant workers while continually adopting measures to cut wages, the stitchers of Essex County ultimately abandoned ladyhood as an inappropriate concept for their status as workers. They chose to be union women. Their justifications for labor protest reflected the redefinitions of gender for nineteenth-century women workers.

Although the shoeworkers of nineteenth-century Essex County prevented capitalists from using women to undercut the jobs and wages of men, divisions within the work force based on sex maintained an exaggerated sense of difference between men and women workers, separated their organizations, and ultimately led to the subordination of women's influence within larger groups such as the Knights of Labor and the BSWU. Nonetheless, the sexual division of labor created opportunities as well as limitations for women shoeworkers: access to skilled work with relatively high wages and the chance for self-direction and autonomy based on gender and class consciousness. Despite the exclusion of women from full participation in the structures of power within labor organizations and their subordinated position within the equal rights tradition, there were moments of unity and strength when men and women joined together in powerful coalitions in the late nineteenth century. Gender and class solidarity worked together successfully in the strikes of 1871, 1884, 1895, and 1903 and indicated the possibilities inherent in resolving the divisions among the men and women of New England who made shoes.

The experience of the women workers of Essex County reveals the complexity and diversity of working-class women's lives: their divisions and their struggles over gender and class consciousness, family loyalty, the meaning of their work, and their efforts to formulate effective means to defend their interests. Their heritage of sisterhood, autonomous organization, and self-direction provides an alternative to competition between men and women over industrial work and to the family wage as a strategy for the defense of working-class family life. Evidence of their diversity should force historians to abandon a concept of female industrial workers as an undifferentiated mass, uncommitted to their work and dependent on the family economy.

In combination with the work of other historians on female industrial workers in the nineteenth century, this history of the labor protest of women shoeworkers suggests the outlines of a woman's tradition within the American labor movement, a tradition of simultaneous organization and action independent of yet connected to the labor protest of men. The setting of any study of the American worker should include the experiences and interrelationships of both genders and the uses of the sexual division of labor by both employers and workers. Finally, historians must recognize that both gender and class are fundamental to consciousness and to the structure of organizations.

Appendix A

Account of Charles Fisher, June–July 1837

Dr. [debits]

Cr. [credits]

June 6
to amount page 93
        1,026.56
June 11 to an order on P. H.
        12.00
    to 4 qts pegs   .40
    to 1 strap   .20
    to 1 peck pegs   .64
    to closing 60 pr brogans
        1.80

June 26 to closing 60 pr
brogans
        1.80
    to 6 lasts   1.08
    to 1 skaine twine   .06
June 29 to an order to Fisher
    P. H.   6.00

July 1 to 2 qts pegs   .16
    to an order on P. H.
        12.00
    to an order on P. H.
        8.00

June 6
By account page 93
        1,040.71
    by closing and binding
70 pr [@]3 1/2   2.10

June 26 by 60 pr Wom[en's]
Boots
        15.00

July 1 by 60 pr Wom Boots
        12.00

    By closing & binding
    2 pr childs   .60
    by 6 pr brogans   1.26

Sophronia Guilford Fisher closed and bound children's and women's shoes, but not the brogans listed in the debit column of her husband's account. Charles Fisher made both brogans and women's boots and relied on an unidentified shoebinder outside his immediate family to provide him with bound brogan uppers for the 60 pairs that he made in June and July 1837. The other 60 pairs of bound brogan uppers were presumably returned to the Prestons to be given out to another brogan maker. Brogan uppers did not have linings, thus they were "closed," not bound.

Account of William Peabody, January–May 1835

Dr. [debits]   Cr. [credits]

Jan 3, 1835
to amount page 67   By amount page 67
                        155.57   211.52
Jan 20 to 4 qt. pegs   .32   by 60 pr Brogans   15.90
Jan 27 to cash   25.00   Jan 20 by 60 pr brogans [@]
                                            25 1/2
                                                                15.30
Feb 2 to closing 120 pr.   Jan 27 by 60 pr brogans 30
brogans
                         5.40   13.20
        to closing 60 pr. brogans   Feb 2 by 60 pr brogans
                         2.70   13.20
Feb 9 to closing 60 pr. brogans   Feb 9 by 60 pr brogans
                         2.70   15.30
March 14 to closing 60 pr   Feb 17 by 60 pr brogans
brogans
                         2.70   15.30
        to Bushel pegs   2.56   Mar 2 by 60 pr brogans
                                                                15.30
        to #1 Thread   .62   Mar 14 by 60 pr brogans
                                                                15.30
Mar 20 to cash
twenty five   25.00   by 60 pr brogans

Mar 29 to 4 qts. pegs .37 By closing 60 pr boys brogs
                                                    2.40

to 2 knives .33 Mar 29 by 60 pr brogs
                                                   15.30

April 10 to cash ten doll 10.00 by 50 pr
                                    by 10 pr   10.10

April 25 to closing 120 pr April 8 by 50 pr brogs 20 1/2
brogs
            5.40   10.25

May 1 to closing 60 pr brogs April 17 by 60 pr brogs
            2.70   12.30

to 1/2 peck pegs .32 " 25 by 70 pr brogs
                                                   14.35

                      May 1 by 60 pr brogs second
                        cut   10.00

Female members of William Peabody's family closed only 60 pairs of boys' brogans in early 1835. William Peabody made 15 lots of adults' sizes of brogans and depended on a nonfamily shoebinder for 8 lots of sewn brogan uppers. The Prestons supplied the rest of the brogan uppers to Peabody.

Appendix B

The 1860 census: Lynn, Haverhill, and Marblehead

Information on women's occupations first appears in the federal census of population in 1860, but there are many difficulties involved in using the census schedules to locate the women shoeworkers of New England. No occupations for wives in male-headed families appear for Lynn, Haverhill, or Marblehead; only daughters and sisters living in male-headed families are recorded by occupation. The federal census of manufacture for 1860 does not distinguish between handwork and machine work, homeworker and factory worker, Lynn resident and outworker. The data in the manufacturing census for 1860 reports 3,803 female workers employed by manufacturers in Lynn and 2,008 employed by Haverhill shoe bosses, but some undetermined number of these lived in neighboring towns.

The census data also underenumerates female factory workers by recording information on Lynn and Haverhill residents between June and August of 1860, a period that coincided with the slack season of production. Seasonal periods of work began in Haverhill before 1855, according to the *Haverhill Gazette*, November 24, 1855, and probably appeared in Lynn somewhat earlier. The total number of migratory female factory workers who left the shoe towns in early May at the end of the busy season is unknown. The city directory of Lynn ignored female shoeworkers entirely. The Haverhill city directory listed only 115 female shoeworkers, but the data reflected information gathered in early December just before the start of the busy season. There are reliable numbers for neither homeworkers nor factory workers in Lynn and Haverhill in 1860.

Census enumerators also used terminology that makes it difficult to interpret the categories of the few shoeworkers who are listed. In Haverhill the census listed all 225 female shoeworkers as "binders," despite the mechanization of work in factories. In Lynn, female workers were reported as "stitchers" (a term for machine operator both in the home and in the factory) and as "binders" or "trimmers" (handwork that also could be conducted in the home or in the factory). The census data, however, can be compared to estimates found in newspaper reports on the numbers of homeworkers and factory girls involved in the 1860 strike meetings to yield some sense of the proportions of homework to factory work for women in 1860.

To eliminate outworkers residing in the neighboring towns of Marblehead, Salem, Beverly, and Swampscott, I subtracted my estimate of 1,000 workers from the total of 3,803 in the 1860 manufacturing census for Lynn, leaving 2,803 as an approximate number of homeworkers and factory workers who either resided or boarded in Lynn. On March 6, 1860, 1,700 women workers or 60% of the total approximated work force signed the low wage list and represented homeworkers or their supporters. Of the 1,700 signers, the 1,000 women who met on March 17, 1860, with the machine bosses were undoubtedly machine operators in the home. The other 700 may have been binders or factory girls sympathetic to the homeworkers' cause. The remaining 1,000 or nearly 40% of the work force were probably factory girls, always in a minority in the total work force, but as full-time machine operators in centralized production, capable of crippling the work process. For Haverhill I subtracted a smaller estimated number of outworkers in nearby towns (700) from the 2,008 reported in the 1860 census of manufacture, leaving 1,308 female shoeworkers, which included the 300 machine girls who worked in factories, as estimated by local newspaper sources in 1860. Machine workers in Haverhill were about a quarter of the work force, and the remaining 1,000 women appear to be handworkers, as Haverhill shoe bosses did not rent sewing machines. The numbers in the population census for Lynn and Haverhill were too small to sample, and the numbers may not be representative of the total work force. My calculations throughout were done without the assistance of a computer. The general characteristics of the female shoeworkers found in the census, however, accord with the words and actions of the homeworkers and the factory girls during the women's strike meetings.

Lynn, 1860. The Lynn census of 1860 lists a total of only 371 stitchers and 117 binders. Two of the stitchers were men. Of the female stitchers, over half (52%) boarded in the city, usually living with families in households that boarded from one to three additional stitchers. A common pattern in the Lynn census consisted of a household of a young cordwainer in his twenties or early thirties with a wife of similar age, several small children, and one or two female stitchers as boarders. Boarding stitchers represented a chance for a Lynn wife (perhaps a former stitcher herself) to supplement family income. Only twenty stitchers lived in large boardinghouses with other workers, while three lived alone. Of the stitchers who boarded, 31% were native-born outside of Massachusetts, primarily in Maine and New Hampshire, and 19% were foreign-born, principally in Nova Scotia (8%) and in Ireland (7%). The remaining 48% of the boarders were natives of other cities and towns in Massachusetts. In addition to the boarders, 23% of the stitchers were resident daughters or sisters in families where the male head or one relative worked on shoes, and another 23% were members of resident families with no males employed in shoemaking. Most resident and boarding stitchers were unmarried (98%); only eight stitchers were listed as married and these women were apparently either widows or were living separately from their spouses. No occupations were recorded for wives living with their husbands in 1860. The average age of the resident stitcher was lower (21 years) than that of the boarding stitcher (23.7 years). Of the total number of stitchers reported in the Lynn census, 28% resided or boarded in female-headed families, while 19% either appeared to be the sole support of widowed mothers, grandmothers, and small children related to them or lived with their sisters. These arrangements implied reliance on female wage-earning for family support and as such were incompatible with the family wage objectives of the homeworkers in the strike.

Although it is difficult to estimate the proportions of factory workers and homeworkers in Lynn from vague or incomplete data and with no surviving company records, the 52% of the Lynn stitchers listed as boarders were likely to be factory workers. A stitcher did not commonly run a rented sewing machine on shoe leather in a house where taking boarders supplemented family income and space was precious. On the other hand, the resident family involved in shoemaking was more likely to recognize the economic return of renting or purchasing a sewing machine for a wife, daughter, or sister to operate on a part-time basis at home, thus avoiding the long hours of factory work. It appears somewhat less likely that the nonshoemaking family in Lynn, e.g., the grocer, salesman, or carpenter, would rent a machine for a female family member unless the consideration of working at home prevailed over factory work. Therefore, the 23% of resident daughters and sisters of shoemaking families who were stitchers, along with the unknown number of wives who worked on shoes and who were uncounted in the census, probably represented the backbone of the female work force of homeworkers. They were members of shoemaking families in Lynn and accepted the customary role of female homework.

A sample of one in ten (255) of 2,550 male shoeworkers, all designated as "cordwainers" in the 1860 census of Lynn, suggests the differences between the male shoeworkers and the majority of unmarried stitchers listed in the 1860 census.

	Shoemakers (outwork)	Stitchers (factory)
Average age	34	22
Boarders	15%	52%
Married	57%	2%
Resident in female-headed households	4%	18%
Native-born outside of Massachusetts	13%	31%
Owned personal property	56%	1%
Owned real estate	28%	0%

Differences in age, marital status, residence, place of nativity, ownership of property, and most important, relationship to centralized, mechanized production created different interests in the 1860 strike, especially between residents of local families and boarders.

Haverhill, 1860. Over half of the female shoeworkers listed in the Haverhill city directory for 1860–61 and in the Haverhill census for 1860 were boarders. The majority of boarders in the census were probably factory workers; no machine work was done at home in Haverhill. Sixty percent of the female shoeworkers resided or boarded in households unconnected with shoemaking activities (10% lived in large boardinghouses and 10% lived in female-headed families), and the remaining 40% resided or boarded in shoeworker families. Of the female shoeworkers in the Haverhill census, 96% were unmarried, and the wives probably worked as binders. As in Lynn, fewer than 10% were Irish by birth or parentage. Of the 60% of the work force that boarded, 46% came from out of state, principally from Maine and New Hampshire; 53% from cities and towns in Massachusetts; and a few were English-Canadians. In all, the situation of the female factory workers who boarded did not directly identify their interests as workers with the local family wage economy.

Marblehead, 1860. The Marblehead census of population for 1860 listed as shoebinders almost all of the 252 women working in shoe production. A very few were identified as rosette makers, stitchers or "compo" workers, indicating employment in the Joseph Harris shop that was struck by its female employees just before the bottomers' strike in early March. No distinction was made between home and factory workers by occupation. Of the 252 women workers enumerated in the Marblehead census (no sample was taken), 19% were boarders and 81% were residents of the town. Only 13% of the total number of women workers were born outside of Massachusetts, including twenty born in Nova Scotia. A small number of wives (sixteen) were listed as shoeworkers, but newspaper estimates in 1860 indicated that about 300 women worked at home and 300 more as factory workers. Among the women workers resident in the town, one-third lived in female-headed families and nearly half resided in families in which no male relative was involved in shoemaking. Of the total of women workers enumerated in 1860, 44% were either boarders or residents in female-headed families, circumstances that were not compatible with the family wage as an objective of the bottomers' strike. As for Lynn and Haverhill, the census for Marblehead in 1860, with all of its problems for identifying women shoeworkers, yields some indirect evidence on a different set of residential, family, and economic circumstances for important portions of the female work force that suggest the basis for divisions among shoeworkers over the objectives of the 1860 strike.

The 1870 census: Lynn

The underenumeration of women shoeworkers in the population census persisted as a problem in the censuses of 1870, 1880, 1900, and 1910. The census data continued to be collected in June and July after the close of the busy season for the spring trade. As a result the number of women who boarded in Lynn and constituted "the floating population" was probably undercounted. For 1870, the census manuscripts yield only 1,480 women workers or 54% of the 2,756 stitchers reported in the census of manufacture for 1870. Of the total work force of stitchers, 3% were men, drawn presumably to the work by the relatively high wages paid for stitching in the immediate postwar period. Also undercounted was the number of women, married and unmarried, who worked at home on machines. The Massachusetts state census of 1875 reported 575 homeworkers in Lynn, representing less than one-third of the total work force in 1875, reported as 2,056. The *Sixth Annual Report* of the Massachusetts Bureau of Labor Statistics in 1875 provides information on the household budgets of twenty-three families of shoeworkers in Lynn (pp. 240–53), but offers evidence on only one female homeworker and one wife who worked in a factory.

The 1870 census enumerators in Lynn used varying and unsystematic terms for occupations in the shoe industry. In the Sixth and Seventh Wards all women shoeworkers were "shoefitters." In the First, Second, and Third Wards the categories included stitcher, shoe stitcher, shoe trimmer, and machine operator. In the Fourth Ward, a center of working-class population, the terms were shoe stitcher, shoe trimmer, and shoe finisher. The Fifth Ward listed stitcher, works in shoe factory, and shoefitter. The variety of terms used make it difficult to distinguish factory workers from homeworkers with certainty.

The 1870 census provides information on residence by ward, dwelling, and family, on sex, age, place of birth, and place of parents' birth. Marital status and relationship to head of household must be inferred from the information on the members of the household although married couples and their children are grouped together as families, and brothers and sisters are distinguished from married couples by listing them in the reverse order of their ages the youngest first. Boarders and lodgers with different names from the head of household were listed last. Some boarders with different names may in fact have been relatives.

Based on the perceptions of women shoeworkers in Lynn before 1870 of various groups within the female work force, I divided the one in ten samples taken from the censuses of Lynn, 1870, 1880, 1900, and 1910 into four categories.

1. Unmarried residents, usually daughters, living in male-headed families.
2. Wives, resident or boarding, whether husband was present in the census returns or not.
3. Unmarried residents living in female-headed families.
4. Boarders or lodgers, whether single, widowed, or divorced.

The majority of the stitchers sampled in the Lynn census of 1870 were unmarried residents, representing over half (55%) of the work force of stitchers. Thirty-four percent lived as daughters in male-headed families. Their average age was 20.2 years, the lowest of the four groups analyzed, but nearly half of them represented the oldest child living in the family and providing supplemental income from their wages. The nativity of their fathers indicates that 36% were American-born daughters of immigrants. Half of these fathers also worked in shoe factories along with substantial numbers of other family members. Sisters and brothers in 76% of the families were also shoeworkers. One-quarter of these families had other relatives or boarders living in the household. The majority lived in nuclear families.

Residents in male-headed families:
Nativity: 90% native-born New England
          10% foreign-born (80% Ireland)
Father's nativity:
          54% native-born New England
          46% foreign-born (76% Ireland)
Marital status:
          100% single
Average age: 20.2 (youngest group)
Percentage of work force: 34%

The married women shoeworkers enumerated in the 1870 census were assumed to be factory workers rather than homeworkers. They represented 9% of the total work force, and the large majority had no children present. Nearly 80% of their husbands also worked in shoe factories. Only 15% of these married couples were residents of Lynn; the rest boarded, principally with resident families rather than in large boardinghouses. Over 90% of the married stitchers were natives of New England. They probably came to Lynn as single boarding stitchers, married in the city, and stayed in the shoe factories until the birth of a first child.

> *Wives:*
> Nativity: 92% native-born New England
>   8% foreign-born
> Father's nativity: no data
> Average age: 22 (second-youngest group)
> Percentage of work force: 9%
> Residence: boarders 85%; residents 15%

When boarding wives are combined with the 36% unmarried boarding stitchers, a total of 44% of the stitchers who worked in Lynn in 1870 fell into the category of boarder, regardless of their marital status.

Of the total work force, 21% lived in female-headed families in Lynn as single women. Over three-quarters of these families were headed by the mothers of stitchers and most of these contained other siblings. The large majority of these mothers who headed families occupied themselves with housekeeping, but 35% took in boarders. A tiny number boarded as families in resident households. The *Sixth Annual Report* of the Massachusetts Bureau of Labor Statistics in 1875 contained information on household budgets only for male-headed families, but economic survival was likely to be even more difficult during the depression years for female-headed families. About 15% of the native-born were daughters of foreign-born mothers. Their average age of 24.3 years was the second oldest to the boarding stitchers, possibly indicating a decision to postpone marriage in order to contribute wages to their mothers' households. In 29% of these families, the stitcher represented the eldest child in residence. The sister of the stitcher or the stitcher herself headed the remaining one-quarter of these female-headed resident families. These families represented unmarried sisters living together or unrelated, single stitchers residing together. These groups were counted in the census as families, but might have represented former boarding stitchers who had taken up residence in Lynn, rather than return to their parents' homes after each busy season. They probably lived together for economy and companionship. They might have been sample-makers, who earned higher wages and enjoyed steadier work than other stitchers.

> *Residents in female-headed families:*
> Nativity: 81% native-born New England
>   19% foreign-born (two-thirds Ireland)
> Mother's nativity (Father's nativity unknown):
>   45% native-born New England
>   35% foreign-born (two-thirds Ireland)
>   20% no data
> Marital status: 100% single
> Average age: 24.3 (second-oldest group)
> Percentage of work force: 21%

Unmarried boarding stitchers represented over one-third of the total work force in 1870.

> *Boarders:*
> Nativity: 74% native-born New England
>   6% native-born United States
>   20% foreign-born (80% Nova Scotia)
> Father's nativity: no data
> Marital status: 96% single; 4% widows
> Average age: 25.4 (oldest group)
> Percentage of work force: 36%

Eighty percent boarded with resident families. Seventy percent boarded in households with other stitchers, and 22% boarded with their sisters, most of whom were also stitchers.

Alan Dawley dismissed the use of the federal manuscript census of population in 1870 as a source of information on the floating population of shoeworkers (p. 143). He divided the male shoeworker population into categories of "stable" (living in Lynn for ten years or more) and "mobile" (for residents of less than ten years). Predictably, given Lynn's growth in the 1860s, 79% of the male shoeworkers are "mobile," a definition so general as to be meaningless. Given his categories, Dawley was forced to describe his third group, the floating population, as "tramping workers," propertyless, without skills or personal connections in the community, buffeted about by seasonality; in effect, a reserve army of labor (pp. 135–42). None of these categories are useful in understanding the experience of women shoeworkers in the postwar period. Exact information on their numbers is scarce, but the category of boarding is a clear indicator of mobility. In 1873 the Lynn city missionary complained that many of the young members of the floating population who were church members did not even obtain official letters of transfer to churches in Lynn and therefore did not appear on local church records as members (*LR*, Oct. 1, 1873). Perhaps the only way to identify this floating population is the category of boarding in the census manuscripts. For a defense of the reserve army of labor argument, see Alexander Keyssar, *Out of Work*, (Cambridge: Cambridge University Press, 1986), pp. 69–76.

The 1880 Census: Lynn

The tenth federal census of population for Lynn adds direct information on the relationship of the woman shoeworker to the head of the household. Information is also provided for occupation, nativity, and the place of birth of both parents. Occupational categories, which varied widely with individual enumerators, include: shoe turner, shoe trimmer, stitcher on shoes, shoe "sticher," works in shoe factory, bow maker, sews on shoe buttons, buttonhole maker and finisher, shoe buttoner, shoe liner and tier, button sewer, lining maker, stitcher for shoe factory, works on shoes, makes shoe trimmings, top turner, boot binder, and shoe stitcher. It is difficult, given the inconsistent and undefined categories used by the enumerators, to tell how much of the work was homework or factory work. A bow maker or button sewer could have worked in either setting. The 575 homeworkers reported in the state census of 1875 shrank to 201 or 6% of the total female work force in 1885, presumably wives with small children. I excluded from the category of female shoeworker jobs performed in heel shops or in sole preparation as part of the leather goods industry. Also excluded from the sample were forewomen, one female laster, and eighteen male stitchers (the number of male stitchers had shrunk from 3% of the total work force of stitchers in 1870 to 1% in 1880, presumably the product of declining wages for stitching). The sample represents 2,620 women or 80% of the total of 3,274 based on information in the United States Bureau of the Census, *Report on Manufactures of the United States, 1880*, (1883), p. 410.

Unmarried residents in male-headed families composed 34% of the female work force in 1880. Eighty-five percent lived with their fathers; the rest lived with other male relatives: brothers, grandfathers, cousins, or uncles. Based on their fathers' nativity, about one-third of the native-born were second-generation Americans. Of these male heads of families, 40% were shoeworkers. Seventy-two percent of the young women resided in nuclear families; 28% in extended families or households with boarders or servants. One-quarter of the women were the eldest children resident in their families.

> *Residents in male-headed families:*
> Nativity: 86% native-born New England
>   1% native-born United States
>   13% foreign-born
> Father's nativity:
>   48% native-born New England
>   2% native-born United States
>   49% foreign-born (74% Ireland)
>   1% no data
> Marital status: 100% single
> Average age: 22.2 (youngest group)
> Percentage of work force: 34%

The single residents in male-headed families in 1880 represented the same percentage of the work force (34%) as they had ten years earlier. Their average age had risen from 20.2 to 22.2 in 1880, possibly as a result of delayed marriage or increasing family need during the depression years after 1873. The shoe industry of Lynn continued to recruit one-third of its female work force from young unmarried resident, native-born daughters, one-third of whom had Irish-born parents.

The percentage of wives who worked in shoe production in Lynn in 1880 represented 17% of the female work force, doubling the number in 1870. Another 6% (according to the state census of 1885) were presumably involved in homework, while those reported in the federal census of 1880 probably were factory workers. Wives did not drop entirely out of shoe production as a result of mechanization or centralization and actually increased their labor force participation rate during the depression years. The average age of working wives was 32.0 years, a sharp increase over 22.0 years in 1870, indicating that during hard times some married women returned to the work force after child-bearing or delayed their age of marriage. Ninety-three percent of the working wives who boarded in 1880 had no children in residence, while half of the resident wives had children living with them, but of these, most had only one child. Furthermore, 20% of the working wives did not reside or board in Lynn with their husbands, but were not listed as separated or divorced; they lived with relatives or boarded. Over half of the resident husbands were also shoeworkers. Based on the nativity of their fathers, about 10% of the native-born were second-generation Americans.

Wives:
Nativity: 85% native-born New England
          15% foreign-born
Father's nativity:
       74% native-born New England
       24% foreign-born
       2% no data
Average age: 32 (oldest group)
Residence: boarders 30%; residents 70%
Percentage of work force: 17%

Tamara Hareven and Maris Vinovskis studied fertility differentials at the household level in towns in Essex County based on a sample of married women twenty to forty-nine years old drawn from the 1880 census enumerations of Salem, Lynn, Lawrence, Lynnfield, and Boxford, but did not analyze labor force participation (p. 125). They suggested, however, that working wives probably had lower fertility rates than those not employed, but noted that their involvement in paid work was limited. Work, they argued, was more likely to curtail fertility through the postponement of marriage rather than through direct family limitation ("Patterns of Childbearing in Late Nineteenth-Century America: The Determinants of Marital Fertility in Five Massachusetts Towns in 1880," in *Family and Population: Nineteenth-Century America*, edited by Tamara K. Hareven and Maris A. Vinovskis (Princeton: Princeton University Press, 1978), pp. 85–125.) My sample of working wives in 1880 yields no evidence on age of marriage or fertility, but suggests that married women responded to hard times and reductions in the wages of male shoeworkers by doubling their numbers in the work force. Over half of these working wives were thirty years of age or older, which indicates that they were different from the young wives in the 1870 sample who stayed in the work force only until they had a first child.

Resident, unmarried female shoeworkers who lived in female-headed families, many of whom had special responsibilities for supporting widowed mothers, represented the same percentage of the work force in 1880 (21%) as in 1870. Their average age had risen from 24.3 years in 1870 to 26.8 in 1880. Nearly 20% of these women workers headed families themselves, while 73% lived with their mothers. The remainder lived with older sisters or aunts. One quarter of the native-born were daughters of immigrant fathers. About the same percentage were eldest children in residence, 33% in 1880 and 29% in 1870. This group also demonstrated a remarkable persistence in characteristics between the 1870 and 1880 censuses, except for a rise in average age.

> *Residents in female-headed families:*
> Nativity: 84% native-born New England
>   5% native-born United States
>   11% foreign-born (83% English Canada)
> Father's nativity:
>   62% native-born New England
>   38% foreign-born (52% Ireland)
> Marital status: 80% single; 20% divorced or widowed
> Average age: 26.8 (second-oldest group)
> Percentage of work force: 21%

The proportion of boarding stitchers in Lynn in 1880 was 28% of the work force, a decline from the 36% of the work force in 1870. This decline may represent perceptions of shrinking opportunities for work in Lynn during the depression years, but the increased number of married women who boarded in 1880 may represent boarding stitchers who had changed their marital status, but continued to work and board in Lynn. Their average age, 25.4 in 1870 and 25.7 in 1880, changed only slightly. About the same percentage boarded in large boardinghouses in 1880 (22%)

as in 1870 (24%). About 10% of the native-born were daughters of immigrants.

> *Boarders:*
> Nativity: 72% native-born New England
>   1% native-born United States
>   26% foreign-born (68% Nova Scotia)
>   1% no data
> Father's nativity:
>   58% New England
>   35% foreign-born (60% Nova Scotia)
>   7% no data
> Marital status: 93% single; 7% divorced or widowed
> Average age: 25.7 (second-youngest group)
> Percentage of work force: 28%

Karen Oppenheim Mason, Maris Vinovskis, and Tamara Hareven studied women's labor force participation in Essex County based on a sample drawn from the 1880 census. Their sample included data from the textile city of Lawrence, from Lynn, and from several rural towns, but no other shoe towns. The result of the study indicated that life course stage (youth and single marital status), community job structure, and family economic status were more important determinants of women's paid work outside the home than cultural values associated with ethnicity, although the results apply to communities and industries other than shoe production, and New England Yankees were not regarded as an ethnic group with distinct cultural values. The Lynn female shoeworker earned the highest wages among the female occupations. ("Women's Work and the Life Course in Essex County, 1880," in *Transitions: The Family and the Life Course in Historical Perspective*, edited by Tamara K. Hareven, (New York: Academic Press, 1978), pp. 191–92, 212.) My sample of the Lynn census of 1880 confirms that young single women dominated stitching work, but also suggests that their status as shoeworkers and involvement in labor protest reflected a set of social expectations derived from their cultural values as Yankee women. The Essex County sample from the 1880 census also noted a higher rate of involvement of wives in paid work in Lynn than in Lawrence, attributable to relatively higher wages in shoe work and the availability of homework

(p. 212). Another important factor was the impact of six years of serious economic depression just preceding the 1880 census.

All of the categories of female workers were remarkably persistent in the censuses of 1870 and 1880. The female work force in Lynn were still overwhelmingly young, single, native-born New Englanders whose parents were also predominantly New Englanders. Even the foreign-born from Nova Scotia with Scottish and English backgrounds shared basically similar cultural values with the Yankees. The depression years of the 1870s and a decline of nearly 20% in wages, however, revealed a basic division within the female work force: 49% of the women shoeworkers (single boarders and those living in female-headed families) were self-supporting, while 51% worked as "half supported" wives and daughters who supplemented family income.

The 1900 and 1910 Census: Lynn

The occupational categories listed in the 1900 and 1910 censuses reflect the minute division of labor and complex job specialization that continued to vary widely in usage within enumeration districts. The two major divisions that I used to distinguish work in the samples were stitching-related work: tip fixer, vamper, stayer, top stitcher, shoe barrer, staymaker, tip maker, and closer-on; and secondly, all other shoe operations performed by women: gummer, presser, eyeletter, lacer, polisher, etc. The one in ten sample for 1900 represents 2,890 female shoeworkers or 80% of the total 3,600 women operatives reported in the 1900 census of population in its report on manufactures. A similar sample from the Lynn census of 1910 rests on 4,120 female shoeworkers or 85% of the 4,849 reported as the total female work force published in the 1910 statistics on occupations.

Unmarried residents living in male-headed households and families represented 35% of the sampled work force in 1900. Eighty-five percent were single daughters living with male-headed families; the balance were sisters, nieces, or cousins of the male head. Based on the nativity of their fathers, over 40% of the native-born were daughters of immigrants. Sixty-eight percent had other shoeworkers in their families, while one-quarter were the eldest children or the only employed children in the family. Only 61% had jobs related to stitching operations, the lowest percentage among the four groups with access to this better paying work, a reflection of their relative youth and inexperience. These young, unmarried women performed the least skilled work of cleaning, lacing and tying, and glueing and pasting as well as the various categories of "girl in shoe shop" and "shoe helper."

> *Residents in male-headed families, 1900:*
> Nativity: 77% native-born New England
>   3% native-born United States
>   20% foreign-born
> Father's nativity:
>   33% native-born New England
>   3% native-born United States
>   64% foreign-born (46% Ireland)
> Marital status: 100% single
> Average age: 23.6 (youngest group)
> Percentage of work force: 35%

In the census of 1910 among the same category of resident females in male-headed families, the sample exhibited essentially the same characteristics as in 1900, while dropping to 31% of the work force. Of the four groups analyzed in 1910, their fathers represented the highest percentage of foreign-born, as in 1900: 66%, nearly half of whom were born in Ireland. Eighty percent were daughters in male-headed families, and the remainder were nieces, sisters, sisters-in-law, and cousins of the male head. Only half had stitching-related jobs in the shops. As in 1880, the shoe industry in Lynn in the first decade of the twentieth century continued to recruit one-third of its female work force from young unmarried resident, native-born women, and in 1910, 41% were daughters of immigrants.

> *Residents in male-headed families, 1910:*
> Nativity: 70% native-born New England
>   5% native-born United States
>   25% foreign-born
> Father's nativity:
>   29% native-born New England
>   5% native-born United States
>   66% foreign-born (43% Ireland)

(By 1910, some of the fathers reported as New England–
born may have been the American-born children of the
Irish famine generation of the 1840s.)
Marital status: 94% single; 6% divorced or widowed
Average age: 24.7 (youngest group)
Percentage of work force: 31%

The percentage of wives who worked in shoe production in
Lynn was 21% of the sampled work force in 1900 and 29% in
1910. This reflects a steady growth in the proportions of married
women working in the industry since 1880 (17%). Their average
ages, 34.7 years in 1900 and 35.1 years in 1910, represent the
oldest group of females in the work force, indicating that many
had returned to industrial work during or after their child-bearing
years. About 15% of the native-born in 1900 and about 20% in
1910 were second-generation Americans. In 1900, 61% of working
wives resided or boarded with their husbands, while a surprisingly
high 39% resided or boarded in Lynn with no husband present in
the household at the time of the census count. In 1910, 78% of the
wives resided or boarded with husbands, while 22% had no spouse
present. Many of these working wives, however, resided with their
families or kin, while a much smaller number resided or boarded
alone.

Wives, 1900:
Nativity: 65% native-born New England
         2% native-born United States
        33% foreign-born (80% English Canada)
Father's nativity:
        52% native-born New England
        48% foreign-born (49% English Canada)
Average age: 34.7 (oldest group)
Residence: boarders 23%; residents 77%
Percentage of work force: 21%

Wives, 1910:
Nativity: 68% native-born New England
         6% native-born United States
        26% foreign-born
Father's nativity:
        52% native-born New England
         3% native-born United States

45% foreign-born
Average age: 35.1 (oldest group)
Residence: boarders 19%; residents 81%
Percentage of work force: 29%

Over half of the wives in 1900 had no children listed in residence for the census tabulation, but of these only 23% of the wives in the sample were over forty years of age and liable to be past child-bearing or have children old enough to have left home. Nearly two-thirds of the wives involved in shoe work in the 1910 census had no resident children, but only one-third of these working wives were forty years of age or over. The unusual phenomenon of a relatively high number of older, married women employed in the industry and the effects of this on fertility was one of the concerns of a study of the Massachusetts shoe industry conducted by the Women's Educational and Industrial Union of Boston.

The WEIU conducted an investigation in 1911 and 1912 of four shoe cities in Massachusetts as centers for the employment of women, including Lynn but not Haverhill. The researchers chose three representative shoe factories in Lynn for questionnaires on nativity, length of residence, and marital status, and conducted interviews with about a hundred shoeworkers. The study indicated that married women represented 31% of the Lynn work force, according to both the state census of 1905 and the 1911 data, a number that was reported as "unusual" relative to other shoe centers and unexpectedly higher than the 29.3% of wives who worked in Massachusetts cotton textile factories in 1905. The "distinctly American training" and "mature age" of many of the working wives of Lynn marked them as an unusual "feminine factory force" (p. 22). This, the study concluded, was the result of the demands of stitching work, which paid good wages and required mature judgment and experience.

Although lacking data on ages of working women, the 1911 study surmised that married women from thirty to fifty years of age formed a large proportion of the total work force. In my sample of the 1900 group of Lynn wives, 68% were thirty years or older; in the 1910 sample of Lynn wives, 65% were thirty years or older. In addition, among the single residents in female-headed families and households, 58% were thirty years or over; among female boarders, 47% were thirty years or older. The average age of the 1910 Lynn sample was 31.3 years of age, but the maturity of the female work force was not confined exclusively to married women. Skill, experience, and judgment in stitching shoes plus relatively high wages for industrial work seemed to keep women in shoe production longer than other factory work. The WEIU study also suggested that married women shoeworkers in Brockton were limiting their fertility in order to remain in the work force and that the divorce rate in that city, the highest in the state, reflected the chance for female self-support in the relatively high wages paid women shoeworkers (p. 27).

Females resident in female-headed households in the 1900 Lynn sample comprised 25% of the work force. Over 40% of the native-born were daughters of immigrants. One-third headed households or families themselves, and two-thirds supported widowed mothers. Of this group, 29% were the oldest employed children in the residence.

> *Residents in female-headed families, 1900:*
> Nativity: 80% native-born New England
>   3% native-born United States
>   17% foreign-born (two-thirds English Canada)
> Father's nativity:
>   41% native-born New England
>   59% foreign-born (61% Ireland)
> Marital status: 77% single; 23% divorced or widowed
> Average age: 31.4 (second-oldest group)
> Percentage of work force: 25%

Female residents in female-headed households in the 1910 Lynn sample represented 22% of the sampled work force, a slight decline from 1900. The primary characteristic of these groups in both 1900 and 1910 was their need for economic self-support. Forty-two percent headed households themselves in 1910, while 41% supported widowed mothers and 16% lived with unmarried sisters or aunts. The percentages of the foreign-born, both of residents and their fathers, were increasing by 1910, shifting this group significantly away from native-born status. One-third were daughters of immigrants.

> *Residents in female-headed families, 1910:*
> Nativity: 70% native-born New England

2% native-born United States
28% foreign-born
Father's nativity:
    36% native-born New England
    1% native-born United States
    62% foreign-born
    1% no data
Marital status: 75% single; 25% divorced or widowed
Average age: 34.5 (second-oldest group)
Percentage of work force: 22%

Boarders in 1900 in Lynn represented 19% of the sampled work force with the second-highest average age at 32.9 years. Sixty percent boarded with private families in Lynn. About 10% of the native-born were daughters of immigrants. This group of boarders in 1900 had the highest percentage of stitching-related work at 74%, as if their very presence in Lynn depended on the availability of stitching at good wages.

Boarders, 1900:
Nativity: 65% native-born New England
    35% foreign-born (74% English Canada)
Father's nativity:
    52% native-born New England
    48% foreign-born
Marital status: 83% single; 17% divorced, widowed, or unknown
Average age: 32.9 (second-oldest group)
Percentage of work force: 19%

In 1910 the percentage of boarders remained stable at 18%, but their average age of 31.0 years dropped behind female residents in female-headed families. Nativity stayed steady at 62% native-born, but of these about 10% were daughters of immigrants. The 1911 data in the WEIU study revealed that women workers in the shoe industry from New England states had slipped to "but a handful," but the 1910 census sample indicates that that handful was still 12% of the female shoeworkers in Lynn. Two-thirds of these boarders in 1910 had stitching-related jobs.

Boarders, 1910:
Nativity: 57% native-born New England
    5% native-born United States
    38% foreign-born (61% English and French Canada)

Father's nativity:
       46% native-born New England
       5% native-born United States
       49% foreign-born
Marital status: 88% single; 12% divorced or widowed
Average age: 31 (second-youngest group)
Percentage of work force: 18%

Social historians who have used census data to identify female industrial workers and their social circumstances tend to categorize working women who headed households by their marital status, usually as widows, rather than as self-supporting wage earners or they identify working women in terms that emphasize their temporary status as workers. A major exception is the work of Carole Turbin on the Troy collar workers, "Reconceptualizing Family, Work, and Labor Organizing: Working Women in Troy, 1860–1890," *Review of Radical Political Economics* 16 (Spring 1984), pp. 1–16. Turbin used the term "provider" to distinguish those elements in the female Irish work force in Troy who were persistent and seemingly permanent workers. In addition to self-support, the term provider conveys the obligation to support dependents. Evidence in my samples of the Lynn censuses of 1870, 1880, 1900, and 1910 also supports the need for a term like provider that defines the persistence of a large group of self-supporting women workers regardless of their past or future prospects of marriage. In addition to the numbers of native-born, unmarried boarders who persisted at about one-quarter of the female work force, female workers in female-headed families who often supported widowed mothers and those who headed families themselves and sometimes lived with other female relatives constituted another quarter of the Lynn female work force that persisted throughout these decades. Their combined numbers ranged from 57% of the total female work force in 1870 to 40% in 1910.

Percentage of self-supporting (residents in female-headed families plus single boarders) women in the Lynn female work force:
1870: 57%
1880: 49%
1900: 44%
1910: 40%

Evidence on their involvement in labor activity suggests (as does similar data on the Troy collar workers) that these self-supporting or providing women who constituted nearly one-half of the female work force in Lynn played an important role as leaders in organizing collective protest by women shoeworkers.

The characteristics of female shoe workers in Lynn in 1900 and 1910 are remarkably consistent. Changes occurred in rank order of average ages; the number of married workers rose; and the percentages of foreign-born workers and of daughters of immigrants edged up. The change detected in the 1910 Lynn data that had the greatest potential for altering the nature of the female work force and the sexual division of labor was the growing percentage of male immigrant workers in stitching-related jobs and in other female-typed shoework. In 1900, only 2% of the female-typed work was performed by male workers and of this number, 78% were native-born, largely in Massachusetts. Half were heads of families, and the industry customarily paid a higher wage rate to native-born men who worked at stitching. By 1910, the total number of men in female-typed shoework was nearly 1,000 workers, or 20% of the combined male and female work force in stitching. Fifty-five percent were single men, and the rest were married. Most lived with family or kin; less than a quarter boarded. In addition to the growth in numbers, the nativity of these male workers shifted. Only 51% were native-born in comparison with 78% in 1900. Of the foreign-born, half were from Ireland, Canada, and Northern and Western Europe, while the other half came from Southern and Eastern Europe and the Middle East. Most noticeable were Jews from Russia and Poland (11% of the number of men in female-typed work), Italians (5%), Greeks (5%), and Armenians from Turkey (5%). Of the nearly 1,000 men, one-quarter were vampers and stitchers, one-third were finishers and packers, and another third were trimmers and pressers. The remainder were scattered in various jobs such as cleaner, skiver, liner, and cementer. Immigrant and native-born men were beginning to displace women in all job categories formerly women's work.

This shift in the ethnic origins of stitchers in the Lynn shoe industry was predicted in general terms by the 1911 *Report of the Im-*

migration Commission (based on data from a 1905 report on the 1900 federal *Census of Manufacture*) concerning the shoe industry in New England, which contained a study of 710 households in New England shoe cities. The report noted a growing percentage of foreign-born workers in shoe production since 1880 and claimed that since the initial recruitment of Southern and Eastern Europeans between 1890 and 1900, the labor force had been principally recruited from these sources. This may have been the case in Brockton or in Marlboro where, for example, Greek workers were allegedly recruited to break the 1898 strike, but the report does not identify the location of the households under study or indicate in what ways these recent immigrants fitted into the job structure of the shoe industry. The study did, however, state that primarily male foreign workers were recruited to shoe work in 1905, while their wives took in boarders, and that over 50% of the Italians and Russian Jews had had previous work experience in shoemaking (pp. 211–73, 325).

Summary of female shoeworkers in Lynn, 1870–1910

Table 6. Percentage of female shoeworkers and average age

	Percentage of female shoeworkers				Average age			
	1870	1880	1900	1910	1870	1880	1900	1910
Boarders	36%	28%	19%	18%	25.4	25.7	32.9	31
Residents in male-headed families	34%	34%	35%	31%	20.2	22.2	23.6	24.7
Residents in female-headed families	21%	21%	25%	22%	24.3	26.8	31.4	34.5
Wives	9%	17%	21%	29%	22	32	34.7	35.1
All female shoeworkers	100%	100%	100%	100%	23	26.7	30.7	31.6

Table 7. Nativity of Lynn female shoeworkers

	Percentage of native-born				Percentage of American-born daughters of immigrants			
	1870	1880	1900	1910	1870	1880	1900	1910
Boarders	80%	73%	65%	62%	no data	9%	13%	11%
Residents in male-headed families	90%	87%	80%	75%	36%	36%	44%	41%
Residents in female-headed families	81%	89%	83%	72%	16%	27%	42%	34%
Wives	92%	85%	67%	74%	no data	9%	15%	19%
Average for all female shoeworkers	86%	84%	74%	71%	26%	20%	29%	26%

Table 8. Sex ratio of Lynn shoeworkers, 1865–1905

	Men	Women	Total
1865	6,984 (58%)	4,984 (42%)	11,968
1875	5,440 (73%)	2,056 (27%)	7,496
1885	9,334 (68%)	4,461 (32%)	13,795
1895	9,885 (72%)	3,757 (28%)	13,642
1905	15,237 (71%)	6,028 (29%)	21,540

Table 9. Sex ratio of Haverhill shoeworkers, 1865–1905

	Men	Women	Total
1865	3,039 (75%)	1,001 (25%)	4,040
1875	1,486 (57%)	1,102 (43%)	2,588
1885	4,010 (66%)	2,057 (33%)	6,067
1895	5,755 (69%)	2,534 (31%)	8,289
1905	6,608 (70%)	2,886 (30%)	9,494

Sources: *Census of Massachusetts*, 1865–1915; U.S. *Census of Population*, 1860–1910. Figures reported in the U.S. *Census of Manufacture* for 1905, p. 238, indicate that the percentage of women employed in the Massachusetts shoe industry rose between 1890 and 1905: 1890, 27.6%; 1900, 31.8%; 1905, 32.1%. Figures for Lynn rose slightly and those for Haverhill show a slight decline.

Abbreviations

Newspapers and Trade Journals

AmW	*American Workman*
BAd	*Boston Advertiser*
BCit	*Beverly Citizen*
BG	*Boston Globe*
BH	*Boston Herald*
BJ	*Boston Journal*
BP	*Boston Post*
BrEnt	*Brockton Enterprise*
BSR	*Boot and Shoe Recorder*
BSt	*Bay State*
BT	*Boston Traveler*
DGSA	*Dover Gazette and Strafford Advertiser*
FLINews	*Frank Leslie's Illustrated Newspaper*
HB	*Haverhill Bulletin*
HG	*Haverhill Gazette*
KL	*Knight of Labor*
L	*Laborer*
LAm	*Lawrence Daily American*
LB	*Lynn Bee*
LG	*Little Giant*
LI	*Lynn Item*
LL	*Labor Leader*
LPS	*Labor Problems Scrapbook, 1894–1914 (clippings from HG)*
LR	*Lynn Reporter*
LRec	*Lynn Record*
LSU	*Lynn Saturday Union*
LT	*Lynn Transcript*
LyN	*Lynn News*
MJ	*Middlesex Journal*

NEMech	*New England Mechanic*
NOb	*Natick Observer*
NYH	*New York Herald*
NYT	*New York Times*
Rev	*Revolution*
SGaz	*Salem Gazette*
SLR	*Shoe and Leather Reporter*
SLRec	*Shoe and Leather Record*
SLRev	*Shoe and Leather Review*
StA	*Stoneham Amateur*
TWP	*Tri-Weekly Publisher*
Vind	*Vindicator*
WAd	*Workingman's Advocate*

Organizations

AFL	American Federation of Labor
BSWIU	Boot and Shoe Workers' International Union
BSWU	Boot and Shoe Workers' Union
D.A.	District Assembly
DOSC	Daughters of St. Crispin
KOL	Knights of Labor
KOSC	Knights of St. Crispin
LPU	Lasters' Protective Union
MATH	Museum of American Textile History
MBLS	Massachusetts Bureau of Labor Statistics
NCF	National Civic Federation
NLU	National Labor Union
SLP	Socialist Labor party
SWPU	Shoe Workers' Protective Union
WCTU	Woman's Christian Temperance Union
WEIU	Women's Educational and Industrial Union
WTUL	Women's Trade Union League

Notes

Introduction

1. For the discrete approach, see Sean Wilentz, *Chants Democratic: New York City and the Rise of the American Working Class, 1780–1850* (New York: Oxford University Press, 1984); Christine Stansell, *City of Women: Sex and Class in New York, 1789–1860* (New York: Knopf, 1986); Susan Levine, *Labor's True Woman: Carpet Weavers, Industrialization and Labor Reform in the Gilded Age* (Philadelphia: Temple University Press, 1984); and Leon Fink, *Workingmen's Democracy: The Knights of Labor and American Politics* (Urbana: University of Illinois Press, 1983).

2. For the class and community approach, see Alan Dawley, *Class and Community: The Industrial Revolution in Lynn* (Cambridge: Harvard University Press, 1976); Paul G. Faler, *Mechanics and Manufacturers in the Early Industrial Revolution: Lynn, Massachusetts, 1780–1860* (Albany: State University of New York Press, 1981); and John T. Cumbler, *Working-Class Community in Industrial America: Work, Leisure and Struggle in Two Industrial Cities, 1880–1930* (Westport, Ct.: Greenwood Press, 1979). John Cumbler's study and Daniel J. Walkowitz's *Worker City, Company Town: Iron and Cotton-Worker Protest in Troy and Cohoes, New York, 1855–84* (Urbana: University of Illinois Press, 1978) compared work, community, and protest in two cities with different industries.

3. John R. Commons, "American Shoemakers, 1648–1895: A Sketch of Industrial Evolution," *Quarterly Journal of Economics* 24 (Nov. 1909), pp. 39–83; Blanche Hazard, *The Organization of the Boot and Shoe Industry in Massachusetts before 1875* (Cambridge: Harvard University Press, 1921); Don D. Lescohier, "The Knights of St. Crispin, 1867–1874: A Study of the Industrial Causes of Trade Unionism," in the *Bulletin of the University of Wisconsin* 355 (1910); John Philip Hall, "The Knights of St. Crispin in Massachusetts, 1869–1878," *Journal of Economic History* 18 (June 1958), pp. 161–75; Edith Abbott, "Women in Industry: The

Manufacture of Boots and Shoes," *American Journal of Sociology* 15 (Nov. 1909), pp. 335–60; Augusta Emile Galster, *The Labor Movement in the Shoe Industry: With Special Reference to Philadelphia* (New York: Ronald Press, 1924); and Helen L. Sumner, *History of Women in Industry in the United States*, vol. 9 of *Report on Condition of Woman and Child Wage-Earners in the United States* (Washington, D.C., 1910).

4. David Montgomery, *Workers' Control in America* (Cambridge: Cambridge University Press, 1979). Nick Salvatore's biography of Eugene V. Debs explored the changing meaning of manhood in Debs's thought; see *Eugene V. Debs: Citizen and Socialist* (Urbana: University of Illinois Press, 1982). Anna Davin has pointed out the neglect of the sexual division of labor both as an object of study and as a tool of analysis: "Feminism and Labour History," in *Peoples' History and Socialist Theory*, ed. Raphael Samuel (London: Routledge and Kegan Paul, 1981), pp. 176–81.

5. David Brody, "The Old Labor History and the New: In Search of the American Working Class," *Labor History* 20 (Winter 1979), pp. 111–26.

6. Leslie W. Tentler, *Wage-Earning Women: Industrial Work and Family Life in the United States, 1900–1930* (New York: Oxford University Press, 1979), p. 6.

7. Patricia Branca, *Women in Europe Since 1750* (New York: St. Martin's Press, 1978).

8. Susan Porter Benson, *Counter Cultures: Saleswomen, Managers, and Customers in American Department Stores, 1890–1940* (Urbana: University of Illinois Press, 1986); Barbara Melosh, *The Physician's Hand: Work Culture and Conflict in American Nursing* (Philadelphia: Temple University Press, 1983); Thomas Dublin, *Women at Work: The Transformation of Work and Community in Lowell, Massachusetts, 1826–1860* (New York: Columbia University Press, 1979).

9. For the household and family as the basis of labor protest, see Philip S. Foner, *Women and the American Labor Movement: From Colonial Times to the Eve of World War I*, 2 vols. (New York: Free Press, 1979) and Dawley, *Class and Community*, pp. 224, 228–29.

10. Virginia Yans-McLaughlin, *Family and Community: Italian Immigrants in Buffalo, 1880–1930* (Urbana: University of Illinois Press, 1982); Tentler, *Wage-Earning Women*; Daniel J. Walkowitz, "Working Class Women in the Gilded Age Factory: Factory, Community and Family Life among Cohoes, New York, Cotton Workers," *Journal of Social History* 5 (Summer 1972), pp. 464–87; Carole Turbin, "Reconceptualizing Family, Work, and Labor Organizing: Working Women in Troy, 1860–1890," *Review of Radical Political Economics* 16 (Spring 1984), pp. 1–16; Jane

Humphries, "Class Struggle and the Persistence of the Working-Class Family," *Cambridge Journal of Economics* 1 (Sept. 1977), pp. 241–58; Martha May, "Bread before Roses: American Workingmen, Labor Unions and the Family Wage," in *Women, Work and Protest: A Century of Women's Labor History*, ed. Ruth Milkman (Boston: Routledge and Kegan Paul, 1985), pp. 1–21; Louise A. Tilly and Joan W. Scott, *Women, Work, and Family* (New York: Holt, Rinehart and Winston, 1978).

11. Susan E. Hirsch, *Roots of the American Working Class: The Industrialization of Crafts in Newark, 1800–1860* (Philadelphia: Temple University Press, 1978); Walkowitz's study, *Worker City*, compared labor protest among the male iron workers of Troy with the protest of the predominantly female cotton textile workers of Cohoes and used the categories of class, ethnicity, and community.

12. For the importance of gender and class, see Rayna Rapp, Ellen Ross, and Renate Bridenthal, "Examining Family History," *Feminist Studies* 5 (Spring 1979), pp. 174–200; Heidi I. Hartmann, "The Unhappy Marriage of Marxism and Feminism: Towards a More Progressive Union," *Capital and Class* (Summer 1979), pp. 1–43; Sarah Eisenstein, *Give Us Bread but Give Us Roses: Working Women's Consciousness in the United States, 1890 to the First World War* (London: Routledge and Kegan Paul, 1983); Mari Jo Buhle, *Women and American Socialism, 1870–1920* (Urbana: University of Illinois Press, 1981); Jackie West, "Women, Sex, and Class," in *Feminism and Materialism: Women and Modes of Production*, eds. Annette Kuhn and AnnMarie Wolpe (London: Routledge and Kegan Paul, 1978), pp. 220–53; Iris Young, "Beyond the Unhappy Marriage: A Critique of the Dual Systems Theory," in *Women and Revolution*, ed. Lydia Sargent (Boston: South End Press, 1981).

Chapter One: The Origins of the Sexual Division of Labor, 1750–1810

1. Sarah Smith Emery's daughter, Sarah Anna Emery, published several reminiscences of the Newburyport area, including her mother's *Reminiscences of a Nonagenarian* (Newburyport, 1879). See especially pp. 70–89. On the Smith family, see George Thomas Little, *The Descendents of George Little* (Auburn, Me., 1882), p. 197. Sarah Smith married in 1812; therefore this incident occurred about 1810.

2. D. Hamilton Hurd, *History of Essex County* (Philadelphia: J. W. Lewis and Co., 1887), pp. 391–414, 674–747, 929–43, 1058–98, 1901–3.

3. Carol Ruth Berkin, *Within the Conjurer's Circle: Women in Colo-

nial America (Morristown, N.J.: General Learning Press, 1974), p. 3. Louise Tilly and Joan Scott traced the patterns of preindustrial work for European women in *Women, Work, and Family*.

4. On the work roles of colonial and Revolutionary era women: Gerda Lerner, *The Woman in American History* (Menlo Park, Calif.: Addison-Wesley Publishing Co., 1971); Nancy Cott, *The Bonds of Womanhood: "Women's Sphere" in New England, 1780–1835* (New Haven: Yale University Press, 1977); Mary Beth Norton, *Liberty's Daughters: The Revolutionary Experience of American Women, 1750–1800* (Boston: Little, Brown, 1980); Laurel Thatcher Ulrich, *Good Wives: Image and Reality in the Lives of Women in Northern New England, 1650–1750* (New York, Alfred Knopf, 1982); Alice Kessler-Harris, *Out to Work: A History of Wage-Earning Women in the United States* (New York: Oxford University Press, 1982); and Nancy Folbre, "Patriarchy in Colonial New England," *Review of Radical Political Economics* 12 (Summer 1980), pp. 4–13.

5. Deacon David Marsh account book, Haverhill (1721–37), pp. 20–21, Haverhill Public Library. For a similar system of exchanges in kind for services as a hallmark of rural household production, see Christopher Clark, "Household Economy, Market Exchange and the Rise of Capitalism in the Connecticut Valley, 1800–1860," *Journal of Social History* 13 (Winter 1977), pp. 169–89.

6. David Marsh, Jr., account book, Haverhill (1791–1812), pp. 24, 82; unpublished Marsh family geneology (1633–1806), p. 4, Haverhill Public Library. Hannah Black married in 1795 and was able to supply her mother with some cash for shoes, but Sarah Black's account continued to list exchanges of labor with Marsh until 1801. For other dealings of shoemakers with widows, see the Thomas Bartlett accounts, Newbury (1725–30) as cited in Ulrich, *Good Wives*, pp. 45–46.

7. In a 1921 study *The Organization of the Boot and Shoe Industry*, Blanche Hazard made imaginative use of account books and interviewed New Englanders whose memories stretched back as early as 1821, recapturing for her the patterns of preindustrial stages of production that had survived in isolated towns. John Philip Hall used additional account books of both itinerant and custom shoemakers before 1800 in "The Gentle Craft: A Narrative of Yankee Shoemakers," (Ph.D. diss., Columbia University, 1954), pp. 49–59, 95–122. On female shoemakers, see Ulrich, *Good Wives*, p. 35. On a similar system of itinerant artisan tailors, see Joan M. Jensen, "Needlework as Art, Craft, and Livelihood before 1900," in *A Needle, A Bobbin, A Strike: Women Needleworkers in America* ed. Joan M. Jensen and Sue Davidson (Philadelphia: Temple University Press, 1984), p. 4.

8. Alonzo Lewis and James R. Newhall, *History of Lynn, Essex*

County, Massachusetts, 1629–1874 (Lynn, 1865), p. 88; George Wingate Chase, *History of Haverhill, Massachusetts* (Haverhill, 1861), p. 532; J. W. Hanson, *History of the Town of Danvers to 1848* (Danvers, 1848), p. 30; Account book of James Brown of Newbury (1759–89); see entry for Dec. 4, 1759, Haverhill Public Library. As late as 1794, only two shoemakers were said to reside in Haverhill, but Arthur H. Cole doubted that there were so few shoemakers in the town: "The Boot and Shoe Industry of Haverhill, Massachusetts" (Thesis in Economics, Harvard University, 1911).

9. Faler, *Mechanics*, p. 8; Lewis and Newhall, *History of Lynn*, p. 328; Hazard, *Organization of the Boot and Shoe Industry*, pp. 12–15.

10. Faler, *Mechanics*, pp. 10–12; Hazard, *Organization*, pp. 28–29; Hall, "The Gentle Craft," pp. 73–77. Malcolm Keir made dubious and extravagant claims for Daygr and insisted that he introduced a sexual division of labor into production, in *Manufacturing Industries in America* (New York: Ronald Press, 1923), pp. 219–21.

11. Dawley, *Class and Community*, p. 14; Norton, *Liberty's Daughters*, pp. 166–70, 244–45.

12. Keir is the source of the argument; *Manufacturing Industries*, pp. 221–22, see also Hall, "The Gentle Craft," pp. 21–22 and Faler, *Mechanics*, pp. 24–26. Horace B. Davis also rejected Keir's argument, in *Shoes: The Workers and the Industry* (New York: International Publishers, 1940), p. 111. More sensitive to the origins of the sexual division of labor and the family labor system were Hazard, *Organization*, p. 25; Sumner, *History of Women*, p. 167; and Edith Abbott, "Women in Industry," pp. 337–40. Essex County had the most unbalanced sex ratio of all Massachusetts counties in the late eighteenth century: Douglas Lamar Jones, "The Strolling Poor: Transiency in Eighteenth Century Massachusetts," *Journal of Social History* 8 (Spring 1975), p. 34.

13. Keir, *Manufacturing Industries*, pp. 225–26. Faler regarded the introduction of women into shoe work as evolving "inevitably" from preindustrial production and growing markets; *Mechanics*, pp. 25–26. Dawley noted, but did not explain, the use of female labor in shoe production; *Class and Community*, pp. 17–19. Also see William H. Mulligan, Jr., "The Family and Technological Change: The Shoemakers of Lynn, Massachusetts, during the Transition from Hand to Machine Production, 1850–1880," (Ph.D. diss., Clark University, 1982), pp. 8–25. On sewing with bristles, see Hazard, *Organization*, pp. 44, 51–55; William Stone, "Lynn and Its Old-Time Shoemakers' Shops," *Lynn Historical Society Register* (1911), p. 86; and Clarence N. Trefrey, "The Shoemaking Industry in Marblehead: A Reminiscence," *Essex Institute Historical Collections* 117 (July 1981), pp. 220–21.

14. On the involvement of women in central and southern Massachusetts shoe production, see Hazard, *Organization*, pp. 52, 59–71; Commonwealth of Massachusetts, *Statistical Information Relating to Certain Branches of Industry in Massachusetts for the Year, 1837* (Boston, 1837). For earlier evidence, see Secretary of the Treasury, *Documents Relating to the Manufacturers in the United States, 1832*, 2 vols. [The McLane Report] (New York: Burt Franklin reprint, 1969).

15. Alice Morse Earle's classic study in 1898 of the lives and work of women in the seventeenth and eighteenth centuries contains no reference to women's work on shoes: *Home Life in Colonial Days*, (Stockbridge: Berkshire Traveller Press, 1974). Except for an occasional female shoemaker in colonial towns, there is no evidence that women were engaged in shoe production before the 1780s, contrary to Kessler-Harris, *Out to Work*, p. 28. Edith Abbott surmised that a division of labor in the shoe shop preceded the introduction of shoebinding, in "Women in Industry," p. 337. On the Porter family of Danvers who took in apprentices, journeymen, and their relatives, see "Putnamville and the Early Shoe Manufacturers in Danvers" (Lecture, author unknown, Dec. 1905, Danvers Archival Center), based on the Porter Family Accounts (1773–1850).

16. On the preindustrial patterns of household production, see David Newhall Johnson, *Sketches of Lynn; or, The Changes of Fifty Years* (Lynn, 1880), pp. 23–66; Hazard, *Organization*, pp. 4–53; Philip C. Swett, "History of Shoemaking in Haverhill, Massachusetts" (Paper, n.d., Haverhill Public Library); William L. Hyde, "Reminiscences of Danvers in the Forties and Fifties," *Historical Collections of the Danvers Historical Society 5* (1917), pp. 4–6 and Stone, "Lynn," pp. 49–100. For apprentice work on sewing, see Johnson, p. 30, and Stone, p. 86.

17. Dawley, *Class and Community*, pp. 16–25. See also Hazard, *Organization*, pp. 24–32, and Faler, *Mechanics*, pp. 20–23.

18. On Breed, see Dawley, *Class and Community*, pp. 21–23, and Faler, *Mechanics*, pp. 13–17. On Gale and Porter, see Cole, "Boot and Shoe Industry," pp. 5–11, and "Putnamville," pp. 23–26. Faler argued that by the 1830s the artisans of Lynn had all been reduced to the status of wage earners; pp. 81–83.

19. Johnson dates the origins of the ten footer to the expansion of the production in the 1750s; *Sketches of Lynn*, pp. 13–23.

20. Johnson, *Sketches of Lynn*, pp. 23–66, and Stone, "Lynn," pp. 86–95. For the mechanic ideology, see Faler, *Mechanics*, chaps. 3 and 10.

21. Dawley, *Class and Community*, pp. 1–10.

22. For production and population figures, see Faler, *Mechanics*, pp. 12–13. Sharon V. Salinger noted the development of capitalist labor relations that preceded industrialization in Philadelphia. Women

workers were not drawn into production, however, but did replace men increasingly as domestic, indentured servants. "Artisans, Journeymen, and the Transformation of Labor in Late Eighteenth-Century Philadelphia," *William and Mary Quarterly* 40 (1981), pp. 62–84.

23. One of the demonstrations of early nineteenth-century New England village activities at Old Sturbridge Village, Massachusetts, is a shoebinder working in her house using the awl, needle, and a shoe clamp to assemble an upper of a low-cut shoe. The upper is then taken to the shoemaker's shop located elsewhere in the village. On binding, see Johnson, *Sketches of Lynn*, pp. 336–40, and Swett, "History of Shoemaking," p. 12.

24. As evidence of the breakdown of the apprentice system just before 1860, Faler cited the exclusive assignment of sewing shoe uppers to apprentices by their masters, a mark of incomplete training. Some apprentices were thus exploited, he argued, "by limiting their instructions for the first five years to sewing seams [shoebinding]—a tedious, boring task"; *Mechanics*, p. 97.

25. In contrast, Stephen A. Marglin argued that the development of a division of labor in outwork satisfied the capitalist's search for an essential role in production as a coordinator of his workers. "What Do the Bosses Do?" *Review of Radical Political Economics* 6 (1974), pp. 60–112.

26. Alan Dawley noted that in the late eighteenth-century account book of Nathaniel Tarbox of Lynn, who married his master's daughter Abigail, there appears at least one instance of a wage paid to her by her father for shoebinding; *Class and Community*, p. 19. But this may be a payment acknowledging that Abigail's labor as a wife was owed to the family economy of her husband. As of 1987, the Tarbox accounts in the Lynn Historical Society are lost.

27. George F. Dow, ed., *Two Centuries of Travel in Essex County* (Topsfield, Mass., 1921), p. 182.

28. Johnson, *Sketches of Lynn*, p. 331. Johnson implied that this family labor system continued until it was undermined by mechanization in 1852. Dawley correctly suggested that the image applied largely to the pre-1830 period; *Class and Community*, p. 45.

29. Reconstructed in the garden of the Essex Institute in Salem, Massachusetts, are the Lye-Tapley shoe shop of Danvers and the seventeenth-century John Ward house, the kitchen of which is adjacent to the shop. Here, the historian can contemplate the dynamic between the kitchen and the shoe shop. I agree with the interpretation of Lise Vogel, who in a critique of Edward P. Thompson's concepts of task labor and timed labor as they apply to women and children pointed to the necessity of combining both task and timed labor in a preindustrial but capitalist productive sys-

tem. See "The Contested Domain: A Note on the Family in the Transition to Capitalism," *Marxist Perspectives* 1 (Spring 1978), pp. 63–67.

30. This is in contrast to Sean Wilentz's description of working women in early nineteenth-century New York City as "craft workers" (*Chants Democratic*, pp. 10–11) and confirms the conclusions of Natalie Zemon Davis, who saw the work identity of sixteenth-century women of Lyon as subordinated to their gender role in the family and their relationship to shop work as strictly limited. She noted that journeymen did not include women who assisted in the work process in their craft hierarchy and did not seek jurisdiction over them. Boys' training, marked by rituals of commencement and termination, gave them a work identity that was not shared by their sisters. "Women in the Crafts in Sixteenth-Century Lyon," *Feminist Studies* 8 (Spring 1982), pp. 42–80. For a similar lack of training or apprenticeships for seamstresses, see Ava Baron and Susan E. Klepp, " 'If I Didn't Have My Sewing Machine . . .' : Women and Sewing Machine Technology," in Jensen and Davidson, *A Needle*, p. 22.

31. Paul Faler, "Cultural Aspects of the Industrial Revolution: Lynn, Massachusetts, Shoemakers and Industrial Morality," *Labor History* 15 (Summer 1974), pp. 367–94. Faler saw no implications for the mechanic ideology or the artisan community in the physical and social separation of the work places of the shoebinders and the shoemakers, although he argued that class divisions began with a similar separation between the work places of the journeymen in the shops and the master, later the shoe boss, in the central shop; pp. 22, 27, 167. Dawley also did not regard the ten footer as a socially separate work unit; *Class and Community*, pp. 18–19.

32. For a different view of the impact of the rise of outwork on women as family members which emphasized victimization and exploitation, see Christine Stansell, "The Origins of the Sweatshop: Women and Early Industrialization in New York City," in *Working-Class America: Essays on Labor, Community, and American Society*, ed. Michael Frisch and Daniel J. Walkowitz (Urbana: University of Illinois Press, 1983), pp. 78–103.

Chapter Two: The Rise of Early Labor Protest, 1810–37

1. Israel Buffum account book, Lynn (1806–47), vol. 1, Lynn Historical Society. Keney did not appear in the Buffum accounts as a shoemaker and the appearance of credits for shoes in his accounts as a part of his wife's wages suggests that he was not a shoemaker. Abigail Keney probably bound all of the shoes herself, as her two daughters were only

fourteen and twelve in 1808. The Aaron Breed accounts of Lynn (1805–17), Lynn Historical Society, list payments to shoebinders separately from shoemakers in 1809, but Breed paid them only in goods. For another example of an early cash payment, see Rufus Mansfield account, entry for November 1809 in untitled ledger, Lynn, (1790–1824), Lynn Historical Society.

2. On the useful distinction between the family economy and the family wage economy, see Tilly and Scott, *Women, Work, and Family*, pp. 31–60; 105–45.

3. Percy W. Bidwell, "The Agricultural Revolution in New England," *American Historical Review* 25 (July 1921), pp. 683–93. Bidwell analyzed the rise of manufacturing in New England, especially in Middlesex and Essex Counties, from the viewpoint of the rural household.

4. This debate over idle female hands in rural households began with an editorial on July 20, 1831, in the *New England Farmer and Horticultural Register* (1822–46). Responses appear on Aug. 24, Sept. 7 and 14, 1831. Also see Massachusetts, Commissioner for the Agricultural Survey of the State, *Fourth Report* (Boston, 1841), pp. 157–58, 181–82. On the question of the "useful woman" versus idle female hands and the rise of the idea of the lady, see Eisenstein, *Give Us Bread*, pp. 60–65; and Gerda Lerner, "The Lady and the Mill Girl: Changes in the Status of Women in the Age of Jackson," *American Studies Journal* 10 (Spring 1969), pp. 5–15. On outwork, see Bidwell, "Agricultural Revolution," pp. 696–97; Thomas Dublin, "Women and Outwork in a Nineteenth Century New Hampshire Town: Fitzwilliam, New Hampshire," in *The Countryside in the Age of Capitalist Transformation: Essays on the Social History of Rural America*, ed. Jonathan Prude and Steven Hahn (Chapel Hill: University of North Carolina Press, 1985); and Sumner, *History of Women*, pp. 115–20, 139–42. In the mid-Atlantic states, butter-making replaced spinning and weaving as a major home industry: Joan M. Jensen, "Churns and Butter Making in the Mid-Atlantic Farm Economy, 1750–1850," *Working Papers from the Regional Economic History Center* 5 (1982), pp. 60–100.

5. Hazard, *Organization*, pp. 43–44; Faler, *Mechanics*, pp. 26–27; James R. Newhall, *Centennial Memorial of Lynn, Essex County, Massachusetts, 1629–1876* (Lynn, 1876), p. 63. Among the account books that illustrate the shift of shoebinding out of the family labor system are those of Aaron Breed, Lynn (1805–17), Israel Buffum, Lynn (1806–47), Jonathan Boyce, Lynn (1793–1813), John Burrill, Lynn (1819–20), Untitled ledger, Lynn (1790–1824), Lynn Historical Society; Samuel Bacheller, Lynn (1795–1845), James Coburn, Boxford (1804–21), Robert Brown, West Newburyport (1813–28), Caleb Eames, Wilmington (1819–

25), Old Sturbridge Village; John Tappan, Bradford (1827–43), Haverhill Public Library; and Unknown Shoemaker, Environs of Newbury (1837–38), Essex Institute. In contrast, see the Amos Breed accounts, Lynn (1763–81), Lynn Historical Society, in which there is no notation of a separation of making and binding.

6. John Goodwin accounts, Reading (1810–34), in the possession of Mrs. C. Nelson Bishop of Reading, Mass. I am grateful to Mrs. Bishop for access to her personal collection and for her assistance in research. Also see Hall, "The Gentle Craft," pp. 123–45.

7. Alice Kessler-Harris, *Women Have Always Worked: A Historical Overview* (Old Westbury: Feminist Press, 1981), p. 28.

8. Joseph Lye's journals (1819–30), Lynn Historical Society. Henry Fuller Tapley, "An Old New England Town as Seen by Joseph Lye, Cordwainer," *Register of the Lynn Historical Society* 19 (1915), pp. 36–40; Dawley, *Class and Community*, pp. 46–47; Faler, *Mechanics*, pp. 48–49, 81–88; Mulligan, "Family and Technological Change," p. 174.

9. Joseph Lye, Jr., was born in 1792 and was fifteen years old when his father died, suggesting that his apprenticeship was incomplete. In 1819, when she worked as a shoemaker, Anna Lye probably supported her two unmarried daughters and her youngest son.

10. Samuel Bacheller account, Lynn. Anna Lye's work was unacknowledged in her son Joseph's journal, which began in 1819 but makes no mention of his mother or her work.

11. Anonymous daybook, Lynn (1825–27), Old Sturbridge Village, and ledger of Sarah (Sally) Whittaker (1815–41), Haverhill Public Library.

12. No mention is made by Lye that his mother or sisters bound uppers for him. These incidents of waiting for work appear in Lye's journals in 1819, 1820, 1825, and 1829. On March 29, 1820, Lye closed a pair of shoes himself so that he could proceed with his work and did so again in 1822 and 1823. In October 1830, Lye recorded his election as the first treasurer of the Lynn Society of Journeymen Cordwainers. He died in 1834. Also see Stone, "Lynn," p. 89.

13. Ross David Thomson, "The Origins of Modern Industry in the United States: The Mechanization of Shoe and Sewing Machine Production," (Ph.D. diss., Economics, Yale University, 1976), pp. 15–16.

14. Boyce account, Lynn. In addition to Boyce's accounts for Willson and Ston, see his accounts for Thomas Boyce, John Newhall, Daniel Oliver, and Daniel Willson. This interpretation of debits for binding in the accounts of shoemakers was supported in 1981 by a conversation with Mark Simpson, staff member, Old Sturbridge Village.

15. The diaries of Isaac W. Merrill, Haverhill (1828–78), Haverhill Public Library. Merrill's diaries do not contain his personal accounts. On

Haverhill, see Cole, "Boot and Shoe Industry," pp. 9–10, 13a–15; and Swett, "History of Shoemaking," pp. 6–8.

16. Isaac's troubles with Lois had just begun. In 1834, when Merrill took a Portuguese apprentice, Lucio J. DeFreitas, Lois and Lucio fell in love and ran off together. In 1837 Lois and Isaac reconciled.

17. Unidentified shoe manufacturer's stock book, Lynn (1830–31), Lynn Historical Society. Based on the figures of cut stock given out to workers in March 1830 and 1831, the annual production of this shoe manufacturer was about 30,000 pairs in 1830 and over 70,000 pairs in 1831. According to the McLane Report, vol. 1, pp. 224–35 in 1832, only the eleven largest shoe manufacturers in Lynn had the capacity to produce over 30,000 pairs annually. This stock book was from one of those concerns. I abandoned systematic linkage of the shoebinders' names listed in the stock book to the Lynn vital records because the names were frequently illegible, incomplete, or confusing. On the rise of the central shop, see Faler, *Mechanics*, pp. 26–27.

18. John and Charles P. Preston accounts, Danvers (1815–45), Essex Institute.

19. For example, see the McLane Report on Raymond and East Kingston, New Hampshire, vol. 1, pp. 626, 629.

20. Anna Rea account book, Topsfield (1814–40), MATH. Anna Rea's employer was not identified in her accounts, but Topsfield bordered on Danvers, where shoe bosses commonly put out work to rural people; see Preston accounts. As a young, unmarried daughter of a farmer, Anna Rea worked from November 1817 to December 12, 1818, the date on which she collected her first wages for binding 525 pairs of shoes at an average price of three cents a pair. She received $15.75 for her efforts of over one year. During 1818 and 1819 Anna Rea worked steadily as a binder, achieving her greatest production and earning her highest wages. In six months she produced 600 pairs for $18.00; the following eight months she sewed 880 pairs for $26.40. This steady work suggests that she was relatively free of household and farm duties. After 1820, however, there were few entries in Rea's account book for shoebinding.

21. Julia Moffard, unpublished assessment of the Anna Rea account and records of the Essex County Probate Court, MATH.

22. William Richardson papers, Stoneham (1811–39), Baker Library, Harvard University.

23. "Reminiscences of Charles Buffum," *LI*, Oct. 5, 1901. Buffum estimated the price for binding at three cents a pair, but seemed to be referring to the 1840s.

24. For a systematic analysis of the production and wages of shoebinders in Danvers in the late 1830s and early 1840s, see chapter 3.

25. On the intermittent nature of homework, see Cott, *Bonds of Womanhood*, p. 39; Dorothy Richardson Tilton, "The Richardson Family in Stoneham" (Scrapbook, 1963, Stoneham Historical Society); and the Preston accounts.

26. Abbott, "Women in Industry" p. 337.

27. Swett, "History of Shoemaking," pp. 10–15. David Johnson estimated that in the mid-1840s, a "smart" woman could bind four pairs of kidskin gaiter boots a day at prices ranging from seventeen to twenty-five cents a pair; *Sketches of Lynn*, p. 338. Evidence from the McLane Report suggests that the average price per pair in 1832 was four to five cents and the typical production was four to five pairs a day. Isaac Merrill expected his wife Lois to earn twenty-five cents a day in 1831, but it is not clear exactly how many uppers she was expected to bind each day or at what price. The McLane Report on Haverhill indicates that 249 binders earned twenty cents a day, but it is hard to tell exactly how much work this represented. The McLane Report figures on Lynn list 1,060 binders, 60 percent of whom earned eighteen to nineteen cents a day and 40 percent twenty-one to twenty-three cents a day. Edith Abbott found the McLane Report figures for Massachusetts useful ("Women in Industry," p. 341), but Helen Sumner argued that the first reliable statistics appear in the 1837 state report on Massachusetts industry (*History of Women*, p. 168). Hazard had relatively little to say about shoebinding or its prices (*Organization*, p. 44). In his chapter on shoemakers' wages, Faler looked at earnings from the raising of livestock and from garden patches in Lynn that supplemented the family's income, but he did not examine the wages of shoebinders (*Mechanics*, pp. 80–85).

28. Diaries of Isaac Merrill, entries for Dec. 26, 1835, and Jan. 16, 30, 1836.

29. Aaron Breed accounts; Jonathan Boyce accounts; John Burrill accounts; Israel Buffum accounts; John Goodwin accounts. John Burrill first paid some cash to shoeworkers in 1821.

30. Johnson (*Sketches of Lynn*, pp. 86–106) discusses the order system in Lynn; James H. Turner, "Memories of Haverhill," Mar. 28, 1896, collection of newspaper clippings, 1895–1902, Haverhill Public Library.

31. *Marblehead Gazette*, Feb. 1, 1834.

32. The Reading Society asked for prices ranging from two cents a pair on children's strap laced shoes to seven cents a pair on men's and women's strap shoes. A search of the surviving Boston newspapers did not turn up the advertisement of the Reading society.

33. The 1831 issues of the *New England Christian Herald* (later published in New York as *Zion's Herald*) published in Boston are lost, as are the clippings that John Philip Hall used at the Reading Historical Society.

Hall quotes from them at length in "The Gentle Craft," pp. 152–54. Also see the *Lynn Mirror*, Aug. 6, 1831.

34. Hall, "The Gentle Craft," pp. 153–54.

35. "Preamble to the Constitution of the Female Society of Lynn and Vicinity for the protection and promotion of Female Industry," *LRec*, Jan. 1, 1834; and "Address of the Shoe-Binders of Lynn at a Public Meeting," held Dec. 30, 1833, *LRec*, Jan. 8, 1834. The standard work on women's involvement in trade unionism by John B. Andrews and W. D. P. Bliss published in 1910 reprinted the society's constitution, but not the preamble: *History of Women in Trade Unions* (New York: Arno Press, 1974), pp. 42–43. The 1837 statistics of manufacture for Massachusetts indicate that the women of Saugus who met to affiliate with the Lynn Female Society represented nearly the entire work force of binders in the town. The fact that they met in the Methodist Church confirms Faler's argument that evangelical religion in Lynn supported labor protest; *Mechanics*, pp. 104–5.

36. *LRec*, Jan. 1, 8, 1834.

37. *LRec*, Jan. 1, 1834.

38. *LRec*, Jan. 8, 1834. For efforts by New York City working women including shoebinders to organize labor protest on similar terms in the 1830s, see Stansell, *City of Women*, pp. 130–54.

39. For the seventeenth-century idea of "comfortable support" as the proper relation of women's labor as supplementary to the well-being of the family, see Benjamin Wadsworth, *The Well-Ordered Family* (Boston, 1712), as cited in Mary Ryan, *Womanhood in America: From Colonial Times to the Present* (New York: Franklin Watts, 1983), p. 31. A competency for an artisan represented a wage that would enable him to support his family and save something for old age; Faler, *Mechanics*, pp. 172–73.

40. *LRec*, Jan. 8, 1834.

41. Ibid.

42. Ibid. The association of fear and shame with the poorhouse by the shoebinders was one of the products of a new industrial morality analyzed by Faler in "Cultural Aspects," pp. 367–94.

43. *LRec*, Jan. 8, 1834.

44. Faler mistakenly dated the organization of the Lynn Female Society as 1830; *Mechanics*, pp. 197–98. Although the cordwainers who organized the Mutual Benefit Society of Journeymen Cordwainers listed the low wages for binding among their grievances in 1830, the Female Society did not appear until late 1833 under its own leadership. On the cordwainers' society, see the *Lynn Mirror*, Aug. 14, Sept. 4, 1830. Dawley also dated the Female Society as organized in 1830, but noted that the independent action of each sex in organizing separate societies reflected

the fact that men and women were hired as individuals and not as families; p. 62. Susan E. Hirsch observed the same in Newark, in *Roots of the American Working Class*, pp. 28–29.

45. A comparison of the leadership of the cordwainers' society and the Female Society revealed only one family connection: the marriage in October 1834 of Elizabeth K. Keene, secretary of the Female Society, to Pelatiah Purinton, vice president of the cordwainers' society. According to local vital records, Mary Russell, the chair of the Female Society, was not a Lynn native, but probably was the daughter of John and Mary Russell of Marblehead, born in 1812, which would have made her twenty-two years old and unmarried in 1833. Hall referred to her as "Mrs. Mary Russell," but there is no evidence to confirm a Russell marriage before 1833 or suggest that her mother led the society. There were two Mary Russells married in Lynn after the activities of the society had declined: one in August 1834 to Nathanial L. Howard and another in 1843 to William B. Moulton. The Mary Russell who led the Female Society in early 1834 was probably, like Elizabeth Keene, unmarried and in her early twenties. The treasurer of the Lynn Society was Miriam B. Johnson, the wife of a shoemaker. A search of the published vital records of Essex County identified only two of the leaders of the Saugus Female Society: Martha Clark Hawkes, a twenty-one-year-old wife, and Harriet Richardson Newhall, also married, who was twenty-five years old in 1834. London women in the tailoring trades in the early 1830s based their protest activity on family and community ties as well as on their experience as workers, as did the shoebinders of Essex County. However, the tailoresses competed with artisan tailors and faced male opposition to the demands of their organizations; Barbara Taylor, " 'The Men Are as Bad as Their Masters . . .': Socialism, Feminism, and Sexual Antagonism in the London Tailoring Trade in the Early 1830s," *Feminist Studies* 5 (Spring 1979), pp. 7–40. James Schmeichen has argued that female outworkers in London were more "preindustrial" and less "modern" than factory workers but were nonetheless, and in contrast to "preindustrial" men, unlikely to engage in collective protest; *Sweated Industries and Sweated Labor: The London Clothing Trades, 1860–1914* (Urbana: University of Illinois Press, 1984), pp. 66–67, 187.

46. In 1837 the membership of the Female Anti-Slavery Society of Lynn included two former members of the Female Society: Miriam B. Johnson, treasurer of the Lynn Society, and Martha C. Hawks, vice president of the Saugus Society. "Minutes," Lynn Female Anti-Slavery Society, 1836–38, Lynn Historical Society.

47. Alan Dawley and Paul Faler, "Working Class Culture and Politics in the Industrial Revolution: Sources of Loyalism and Rebellion," *Journal*

of Social History 9 (June 1976), pp. 446–71. Critical of this typology is Frederich Lenger, "Class Culture and Class Consciousness in Ante Bellum Lynn: A Critique of Alan Dawley and Paul Faler," *Social History* 6 (Oct. 1981), pp. 317–32. The tailoresses of New York City in 1831 were not singular in their feminism; see Stansell, *City of Women*, p. 133.

48. The divisions within the society became public in an exchange of views in the *LRec* between the society's chair, Mary Russell, who signed herself "A Shoe Binder"; Joshua C. Oliver, a Lynn shoe manufacturer or "Philadelphius"; and an unidentified woman, "Another Shoe Binder." Another Shoe Binder, who described herself as "in a great measure dependent upon this employment for a living," defended Philadelphius. *LRec*, Feb. 19, Mar. 12, 22, Apr. 2, 1834.

49. *LRec*, June 18, 1834. Mary Russell greatly exaggerated the results of the Lowell turnouts in 1834, which failed to prevent a wage cut or even create an organization such as the Female Society; Dublin (*Women at Work*, 89–98). The *LRec* made a brief reference to the wage disputes in Lowell on February 19, 1834. During the same month, a strike by female textile workers occurred at the Cocheco Company in Dover, New Hampshire (Foner, *Women* 1, pp. 32–33), but the Lynn paper carried no notice of it. For the seemingly insurmountable difficulties of organizing female outworkers in New York City based on their alleged ignorance of the economic system and psychological subordination, see Stansell, "Origins of the Sweatshop," pp. 95–97. Yet, there were turnouts among seamstresses in 1831, 1836, and 1845 (p. 87) and much evidence of complaints and grievances.

50. Cott, *Bonds of Womanhood*.

51. On a sense of sisterhood and early labor protest among the Lowell textile operatives in the 1830s, see Dublin, *Women*, pp. 86–107.

52. Johnson, *Sketches of Lynn*, pp. 120, 168–69.

53. Turner, "Memories."

Chapter Three: The Social Relations of Production in the Rural Outwork System, 1838–45

1. This chapter was originally published in a slightly different form in *The New England Quarterly*, Sept. 1987. Ann Swett to Sarah Swett, Feb. 1847, Letters of Ann Swett Appleton, 1847–50, MATH.

2. On Farley, see Harriet H. Robinson, *Loom and Spindle* (Kailua, Hawaii: Press Pacifica, 1976), pp. 87–88. On palm-leaf hatmaking and garment making as outwork, see Dublin, "Women and Outwork"; Sumner, *History of Women*, pp. 115–20, 139–42; Jensen and Davidson, *A Needle*, pp. 20–59; Clark, "Household Economy," pp. 180–81.

3. Duncan Bythell, *The Sweated Trades: Outwork in Nineteenth Century Britain* (New York: St. Martin's Press, 1978), pp. 16, 20. Ivy Pinchbeck examined an experience similar to shoebinding among English outwork spinners in *Women Workers and the Industrial Revolution, 1750–1850* (1930; reprint, London: Virago Press, 1981), pp. 136–47.

4. All figures on the numbers of outworkers and their relation to workers in textile factories are from Commonwealth of Massachusetts, *Statistical Information Relating to Certain Branches of Industry in Massachusetts*, 1837, 1845, and 1855. The rural outwork system remained outside of the community focus of the studies of Lynn by Dawley, Faler, and Mulligan.

5. On the capture of the southern market for women's shoes by New England manufacturers because of lower costs of production especially resulting from the higher proportion of women employed in New England, see Mulligan, "Family and Technological Change," pp. 38–40; Hirsch, *Roots*, p. 27.

6. This argument was suggested by Patricia Branca's discussion of household production as one phase of the development of work and consciousness among European women in *Women in Europe* and by Nancy Cott in *The Bonds of Womanhood*. In contrast, Christopher Clark saw the market, capitalist production, and the rural household in New England interacting initially to preserve family life and the values of rural society; "Household Economy," pp. 180–81. On the putting-out system in worsted woolens in England that involved women workers in a complex and variable system of rural industry, see Pat Hudson, "Proto-Industrialization: The Case of the West Riding Wool Textile Industry in the 18th and early 19th Centuries," *History Workshop Journal* 12 (1981), pp. 34–61.

7. Accounts of John and Charles P. Preston, Essex Institute.

8. Wolfram Fischer, "Rural Industrialization and Population Change," *Comparative Studies in Society and History* 15 (1973), pp. 158–70; David Levine, "The Demographic Implications of Rural Industrialization: A Family Reconstitution Study of Shepstead, Leicestershire, 1600–1851," *Social History* 2 (1976), pp. 177–96; Rudolf Braun, "Protoindustrialization and Demographic Change in the Canton of Zurich," in *Historical Studies of Changing Fertility*, ed. Charles Tilly (Princeton: Princeton University Press, 1978); and Hans Medick, "The Proto-Industrial Family Economy: The Structural Function of the Household and Family during the Transition from Peasant Society to Industrial Capitalism," *Social History* 3 (1976), pp. 291–315. For a recent assessment of the importance of a focus on the rural household in early industrialization, see Jean H. Quataert, "A New Look at Working-Class Formation: Reflections on the

Historical Perspective," *International Labor and Working Class History* 27 (Spring 1985), pp. 72–76.

9. Medick, "Proto-Industrial Family," pp. 309–10; Dublin, "Women and Outwork," pp. 1–4.

10. For the persistence of many of the values of the household economy even as country merchants sought profits in local exchange networks, see Clark, "Household Economy," pp. 177–78.

11. On Danvers, see Hanson, *History of the Town of Danvers*; Hyde, "Reminiscences," pp. 1–20; Edwin Mudge, "The Shoe Trade of Danvers," in *Proceedings . . . at Salem Village, now Danvers*, ed. Charles B. Rice (Boston, 1848), pp. 235–43; and McLane Report, vol. 1, pp. 218–19.

12. Mudge, "The Shoe Trade," in *Proceedings*, ed. Rice, p. 237. On Middleton, see Lura Woodside Watkins, *Middleton, Massachusetts: A Cultural History* (Salem: Essex Institute, 1970). Watkins argued that the outwork system brought "hope and security" to Middleton families and lowered the age of marriage; pp. 118–20.

13. The face-to-face nature of the transactions often resulted in accounts headed simply, for instance, "Mrs. Peabody," a name among others so common in Danvers as to defy identification. Residence was established in the vital records and the Federal Manuscript Census of Population for 1840 for 78 percent of the shoemakers and for 68 percent of the shoebinders.

14. Linkage to the 1850 census of the names of the fathers and husbands of shoebinders who worked for six months or more for the Prestons revealed that only a little over a third (38 percent) were shoemakers. Twenty-seven percent were farmers or had other occupations, while occupations were not found for 23 percent, and 12 percent of the shoebinders were widows. Of the husbands or fathers of the twelve steady shoebinders, two were shoemakers and three were farmers, but six remained unidentified or untraceable. One shoebinder who worked for the Prestons was an elderly shoemaker.

15. McLane Report, vol. 1, pp. 218–19; MBLS, *Sixteenth Annual Report* (Boston, 1885), pp. 331–32. I calculated the average wages for the Preston binders by dividing their total wages by the number of weeks between the date of taking the cut stock from the central shop and the date of the return of the sewn uppers. There is no telling how much time each binder actually spent each day or each week binding shoes, but the traditional statistical sources seem to exaggerate the amount of work that an average binder could complete in a day or in a week.

16. For an analysis of an outwork system that did not supply cash to its workers, see Dublin, "Women and Outwork." For the debate over the relationship of Massachusetts agriculture to the market economy,

see Winifred B. Rothenberg, "The Market and Massachusetts Farmers, 1750–1855," *Journal of Economic History* 41 (June 1981), pp. 283–314.

17. Harriet Beecher Stowe, *Oldtown Folks* (Cambridge: The Belknap Press, 1966), pp. 73–82. I thank Louise Knauer for this reference.

18. Johnson, *Sketches of Lynn*, pp. 336–37.

19. James P. Hutchinson accounts, Essex Institute. I am grateful to Richard Trask of the Danvers Archival Center for information on Sarah Towne Colcord. Sarah Towne's father may have been the Daniel Towne who died in Danvers three years after she was born in 1810. The 1850 census of Danvers recorded her seventy-five-year-old widowed mother, Harriet, residing with the Colcords. It is possible that Sarah's mother also bound shoes, which explains in part the prodigious work listed in Sarah's account with the Prestons.

20. I calculated the average age of marriage in Danvers and Middleton for women married for the first time between 1830 and 1849 from the published vital records of the towns. Ruth McIntire, born in 1804, and Nancy Kemey, born in 1807, do not appear in the published marriage records before 1850. The birth date of Fanny F. Putnam is unknown, but no marriage record appears in this name after her employment ends in 1838.

21. I also conducted a search for the names of unmarried shoebinders in the Massachusetts Vital Records, Boston.

22. I thank Tom Dublin for his patient support while I tried to figure out the meaning of the debits for binding in the shoemakers' accounts, an interpretation for which I am alone responsible. See sample accounts of Charles Fisher and William Peabody, Preston accounts, Appendix A. The ledger of Woodman and George of Haverhill (1841–44), Haverhill Public Library (too damaged for systematic analysis), used its debits column to list both goods and cash and the stock given out, the price and date, balancing on the credit side with the work completed by the shoeworker.

23. Emery, *Reminiscences*, p. 88; Harriet S. Tapley, *Chronicles of Danvers, 1632–1923* (Danvers, 1923), p. 123. James P. Hutchinson of Danvers had worked before 1846 as a shoemaker for the Prestons.

24. Medick, "Proto-Industrial Family Economy," p. 301. On the values of the household economy as resistance to market relations, see Clark, "Household Economy," 180–85.

25. Letter to the editor from "E," *NEMech*, Mar. 19, 1858.

26. Widow Sally Whittaker had to combine many other kinds of work with shoebinding to support her family on her own efforts, including renting her horse and pastures, selling chickens and milk, hiring herself and her children out to neighbors, and taking in boarders. Ledger of Sally Whittaker (1815–41), Haverhill Public Library.

27. Elizabeth Fox-Genovese, "Gender, Class, and Power: Some Theoretical Considerations," *History Teacher* 15 (Feb. 1982), pp. 255–76.

28. *Proceedings of the Convention of the Manufacturers, Dealers, and Operatives in the Shoe and Leather Trade in the State of Massachusetts, March 2, 1842* (Boston, 1842), pp. 70–71.

Chapter Four: Women and the Artisan Tradition

1. All figures are based on calculations from Commonwealth of Massachusetts, *Statistical Information in Massachusetts*, 1837, 1845, and 1855. Dawley, *Class and Community*, p. 75.

2. Dawley, *Class and Community*, p. 75. Of the total female "all hands" employed (39,068) in Massachusetts in 1837, shoebinders represented 39.3 percent. No figures appear in 1837 for outworkers in straw and palm-leaf hats, but in 1845, Massachusetts recorded 13,311 homeworkers in this industry. On the outwork system in hatmaking, see Dublin, "Women and Outwork."

3. Richardson papers; see correspondence file for 1835–39.

4. The letters from Crawford and Reece are dated between 1831 and 1835 and those between Dike and Richardson are dated respectively Aug. 28, Sept. 22, 1828; Aug. 1, 1835, and Sept. 7, 1836, Richardson papers.

5. Benjamin Hosmer to Richardson, Sept. 4, 1826, Richardson papers.

6. The letters are from the Richardson papers. Jesse Reed was a native of Bedford, Massachusetts, in Middlesex County, where other Richardson outworkers lived. He married a Bedford woman in 1819 and may have moved to New Hampshire to try to improve his health. On his death, Costello Hosmer to Richardson, Jan. 5, 1839, Richardson papers.

7. Stone, "Lynn," pp. 86–88. For a description of a central shop in the 1840s, see *LSU*, Dec. 27, 1884, p. 5.

8. Stone, "Lynn," p. 88.

9. Hyde, "Reminiscences," p. 5; Cole, "Boot and Shoe Industry," p. 18.

10. Buffum accounts. A reprint of the Robinson directions is located in the *Lynn Business Magazine* 1 (June 1907), p. 22. The originals are in the Lynn Historical Society.

11. Stone, "Lynn," p. 88. For additional acts of resistance, see Stone, p. 93; Mudge, "Shoe Trade," in *Proceedings*, ed. Rice, p. 238.

12. Stone, "Lynn," pp. 89–90.

13. Ibid., p. 89. For reminiscences of a wage dispute between a journeyman and a shoe boss, see *LB*, Feb. 6, 1886, p. 3.

14. Faler, *Mechanics*, pp. 198–99.

15. Norman Ware, *The Industrial Worker, 1840–1860* (Chicago:

Quadrangle Books, 1964), p. 200; Dawley, *Class and Community*, p. 63.

16. Faler, *Mechanics*, p. 200; Dawley, *Class and Community*, p. 63.

17. Dawley identified the potential of a radical core of thought in the equal rights tradition, but he concluded that when the shoemakers of Lynn turned to political action rather than economic change in the 1840s and 1850s, the ballot box became the "coffin" of class consciousness; *Class and Community*, p. 70. Ware argued that middle-class reformers seized, tamed, and redirected the intensity of labor activity in the 1840s into innocuous channels; *Industrial Worker*, pp. 207–26.

18. *Awl*, July 17, Aug. 29, 1844. Elizabeth Cheever married John Tuttle in 1843 and was probably the daughter of a shoemaker who taught her the trade. Whether she continued to make shoes or train apprentices after the birth of four children between 1843 and 1847 is unlikely.

19. "Centre Street," *Awl*, Sept. 18, 1844.

20. *Awl*, Sept. 18, 1844.

21. *Awl*, Sept. 11, 1844.

22. *Awl*, Dec. 28, 1844. The tone of the toast suggests the survival of traditional eighteenth-century moral values among some men in the cordwainers' society. On changes in social values and labor protest, see Dawley and Faler, "Working Class Culture," pp. 466–71.

23. *Awl*, Dec. 21, 1844.

24. *Awl*, Sept. 18, 1844.

25. Keith Melder, "Women in the Shoe Industry: The Evidence from Lynn," *Essex Institute Historical Collections* 115 (1979), pp. 274–75.

26. Faler, *Mechanics*, pp. 109–38.

27. Dawley and Faler, "Working Class Culture," pp. 446–71. For the problematic issue of moral respectability for working-class women in New York City and the changes during the 1840s in working-class male attitudes, see Stansell, *City of Women*, pp. 19–29, 76–101.

28. For example, see Carroll Smith-Rosenberg, "Beauty, the Beast and the Militant Woman: A Case Study in Sex Roles and Social Stress in Jacksonian America," *American Quarterly* 22 (1971), pp. 562–84.

29. *Essex County Washingtonian*, Dec. 29, 1842; Jan. 26, 1843. On Woodend and temperance in Lynn, see Faler, *Mechanics*, pp. 104, 130–36, 206–10. On New York City working-class women and temperance, see Wilentz, *Chants*, pp. 310–11.

30. Barbara Welter, "The Cult of True Womanhood, 1820–1860," *American Quarterly* 18 (1960), pp. 151–74.

31. "Mechanics' Wives," *Awl*, June 28, 1845. Despite their support for binding as appropriate female work, the editors estimated that some shoebinders worked twelve to fourteen hours a day, earning from two to four cents an hour; Jan. 4, 1845. For the use of the eighteenth-century

concept of the useful woman during early industrialization, see Eisenstein, *Give Us Bread*, pp. 60–65.

32. *Awl*, Jan. 4, 1845. Nathan Chase was regarded as a "grinder" or a bad boss by Lynn shoemakers; Faler, *Mechanics*, p. 178.

33. For the manufacturers' side, see the *Awl*, Jan. 25 and Feb. 15, 1845. For Darlin's side, see Jan. 4 and Feb. 22, 1845.

34. *Awl*, Feb. 1, 22, 1845. However, one of the poems that subsequently appeared, "On the Art of Shoemaking" by "Constance," in *Awl*, Feb. 22, 1845, did refer explicitly to the tensions experienced by one woman who objected to participating in the cordwainers' society as a subordinated female.

> And now the Awl and Needle are combined,
> Ladies your talents show, with intellect refined;
> Though men still take the lead in politics and shoes,
> Yet, when they ask our aid, oh! let us not refuse.

> But help them in this work, with willing heart and hand
> And let not man be left alone, within this happy land;
> Yet when we own this claim, (let not despotic sway)
> Arouse the woman's wrath, (with that *old* term, Obey.)

35. *Awl*, Aug. 28, 1844; Jan. 11, Mar. 15, Apr. 12, June 26, 1845; Dublin, *Women at Work*, pp. 108–31.

36. *Awl*, Oct. 11, 1845; *Voice of Industry*, Nov. 21, 28, Sept. 18, 1845. Dorothy Thompson, *The Chartists: Popular Politics in the Industrial Revolution*, (New York: Pantheon, 1984), pp. 120–51. Thompson, who found evidence on Chartist women difficult to locate, argued that their support was strongest in the 1830s and that activist women drifted into the temperance movement in the 1840s. For the shifting attitudes of New York City working men in the 1830s and 1840s toward women as activist workers, see Wilentz, *Chants*, pp. 350–53, 370–71.

37. *Annual Report of the Board of Health of Lynn* (Boston, 1850), p. 14.

38. Faler, *Mechanics*, pp. 93–94.

39. *LN*, July 13, 1849.

40. Nancy Burkett, head of Readers' Services at the American Antiquarian Society, Worcester, Massachusetts, discovered the diaries of Sarah Trask at the Beverly Historical Society while she was searching for manuscript material for *Women's History Sources: A Guide to Archives and Manuscript Collections in the United States*, ed. Andrea Hinding (Ann Arbor: University of Michigan Press, 1979). I am grateful to her for drawing my attention to the diaries, excerpts of which appeared in Mary H. Blewett, "'I Am Doom to Disapointment': The Diaries of a Beverly,

Massachusetts, Shoebinder, Sarah E. Trask, 1849–1850," *Essex Institute Historical Collections* 117 (July 1981), pp. 192–212.

41. Carroll Smith-Rosenberg, "The Female World of Love and Ritual: Relations between Women in Nineteenth Century America," *Signs* 1 (1975), pp. 1–29; Cott, *Bonds of Womanhood*, p. 16. The need to identify networks of friendship and support among poor and working-class women is discussed in Rapp, Ross, and Bridenthal, "Examining Family History," pp. 174–200.

42. Cott, *Bonds of Womanhood*, p. 16.

43. Sarah Trask was the second youngest of six surviving children of Benjamin and Catherine Foster Trask, *Vital Records of Beverly, Massachusetts*, vol. 2 (Topsfield, Mass., 1907).

44. Samuel Eliot Morison, *The Maritime History of Massachusetts, 1783–1860* (Cambridge: Houghton Mifflin, 1960), pp. 286–87.

45. Lucy Larcom was herself a native of Beverly who had returned to teach school in 1853, after working in the cotton mills of Lowell. She lived that year with her married sister on Cabot Street, the main thoroughfare, and began to write her first poetry, including "Hannah Binding Shoes" and a companion piece, "Skipper Ben." In this poetry, Larcom developed the themes of patient waiting and endured loss, experiences common to the female community of Beverly. It is not hard to imagine Sarah Trask and Lucy Larcom passing each other in the streets of Beverly. Lucy Larcom, *A New England Girlhood* (Boston: Houghton Mifflin, 1889), pp. 93, 96–97, 271; Daniel Dulany Addison, *Lucy Larcom: Life, Letters, and Diary* (Boston: Houghton Mifflin, 1897), pp. 1–6, 44–48, 61–66. For other poems with similar themes of patient waiting and endurance, see Lucy Larcom, *The Poetical Works of Lucy Larcom* (Boston: Houghton Mifflin, 1889), pp. 1–11.

46. The arithmetical errors appear in the original diary entry.

47. Carl Degler, *At Odds: Women and the Family in America from the Revolution to the Present* (New York: Oxford University Press, 1980), pp. 29–50.

Chapter Five: The Early Factory System and the New England Shoe Strike of 1860

1. Faler, *Mechanics*, pp. 223–26; *NOb*, Feb. 18, 1860.

2. *Annual Report of the Board of Health of Lynn*, pp. 13–14; Hazard, *Organization*, pp. 77–76, 109. Hazard regarded the high cost of leather stock as the impetus to centralized supervision.

3. "A Chat with Moses How," *BSR*, Dec. 19, 1888, pp. 48–49.

4. Ibid.

5. *TWP* (Haverhill), Apr. 14, 1860. For a discussion of mechanization as a gradual and discontinuous process during which handwork and domestic production persisted, see Raphael Samuel, "Workshop of the World: Steam Power and Hand Technology in Mid-Victorian Britain," *History Workshop* (Spring 1977), pp. 6–72.

6. Heeled shoes had been replaced in the 1830s by spring heels, which were made with only a few lifts by the shoemaker. Spring heels gave way to flat heels, but heeled shoes came back into style in the 1850s; Hazard, *Organization*, p. 93; Johnson, *Sketches of Lynn*, pp. 340–41. For tensions expressed by bottomers in Haverhill over wages earned by heelers, see *BT*, Mar. 9, 1860; *BJ*, Mar. 23, 1860. For tensions between outwork bottomers and male shop workers, see *NOb*, Feb. 25, 1860.

7. Hazard (*Organization*, p. 92) argued that the beginnings of the factory system could be located in the division of labor in the ten footer, but even after the supervision of work was centralized under the control of the employer, the work process retained some of its preindustrial features.

8. Johnson described the transfer of men's work into early factories as gradual, but regarded the mechanization of women's work as rapid and "revolutionary"; *Sketches of Lynn*, p. 16. He did not distinguish between female homeworkers and shop workers.

9. *Annual Report of the Board of Health of Lynn*, pp. 13–14. Hazard noted that in South Shore Massachusetts shoe towns, girls went into central shops in the 1850s as pasters and trimmers; *Organization*, p. 100. Abbott, "Women in Industry, " p. 346. William Mulligan used the federal census of population for Lynn in 1850 to argue that fertility patterns in shoemaking families were powerfully affected by women's employment, especially the involvement of women in family "work units." Shoemaking families in Lynn had lower fertility rates than other skilled workers and more concentrated periods of childbearing; "Family and Technological Change," pp. 67–71, 83–85. The census of 1850 provides no data on women's employment, and the evidence based on account books in this study indicates that the work of most shoebinders in Lynn had been dissociated from family work units by the 1830s. The fertility patterns that Mulligan described took place in a context of changes in the outwork system. Lower fertility probably reflected the breakdown of the family labor system rather than the continuity of the family as a work unit.

10. Edward Poor accounts, Georgetown (1828–69), Essex Institute. On apprentice training, see Faler, *Mechanics*, p. 97.

11. Andrew Gould accounts, Topsfield (1859–60), Essex Institute.

12. Sumner, *History of Women*, pp. 170–71. On the question of home

and work for women in the nineteenth century, see Elizabeth Pleck, "Two Worlds in One: Work and the Family," *Journal of Social History* 10 (1976), pp. 178–95.

13. *LI* (Reminiscences of John Brooke Nichols), Nov. 10, 1903; Thomson, "Origins of Modern Industry," pp. 63–64; *LI*, (Obituary of John Brooke Nichols), Aug. 30, 1913. As a cutter working in a central shop, Nichols was well acquainted with the inefficiencies of the outwork system. *LyN*, Mar. 18, 1853; Johnson, *Sketches of Lynn*, p. 16; *BSR*, Sept. 22, 1897, p. 91. On Blake, see Mulligan, "Family and Technological Change," pp. 95–96.

14. Grace Rogers Cooper, *The Sewing Machine: Its Invention and Development* (Washington, D.C.: Smithsonian Institution, 1976), p. 24. On the rapid adoption of the sewing machine in Lynn, see Dawley, *Class and Community*, pp. 76–77; Johnson, *Sketches of Lynn*, p. 16; and Abbott, "Women in Industry," p. 348. Most historians overlooked the persistence of homework on machines in the 1850s; the exception was Sumner, *History of Women*, p. 171. For the impact of the sewing machine on garment-making, see Baron and Klepp, "If I Didn't Have My Sewing Machine . . . ," in *A Needle*, ed. Jenson and Davidson, pp. 20–59.

15. Stone, "Lynn," p. 98; *Lynn Weekly Reporter*, Feb. 28, 1863; Swett, "History of Shoemaking," pp. 16–17; "First Introduction of the Sewing Machine into the Shoe Business," *SLR*, Dec. 12, 1867; Thomson, "Origins of Modern Industry," pp. 247–61. Singer produced the first home model in 1856 and a more successful one in the late 1850s, but had difficulty selling them until a system of retail stores was set up in the 1860s; see Baron and Klepp, "Sewing Machine," in *A Needle*, ed. Jenson and Davidson, pp. 36–37.

16. "Moses How," *BSR*, Dec. 19, 1888, pp. 48–49.

17. Swett, "History of Shoemaking," pp. 17–18.

18. Ibid., p. 18.

19. Some customers continued to prefer hand-sewn to machine-sewn shoes; *SLR*, Dec. 17, 1868; May 2, 1872; *Eighty Years of Progress of the United States* (New York, 1864), p. 428. *Annual Report of the Board of Health of Lynn*, p. 14. On binding wages after 1852, see account books of Edward Poor, Andrew Gould, and James Hutchinson. For binders' wages in 1860, see Faler, *Mechanics*, p. 225; *TWP*, Mar. 3, 10, 15, 20, 1860; *HG*, Mar. 9, 15, 1860. On cabbaging, *LR*, Mar. 5, 1870.

20. David Johnson believed machine ownership to be fairly common in Lynn; *Sketches of Lynn*, p. 340. Blanche Hazard, however, suggested that the cost of machinery meant that most stitching operations were carried on in central shops; *Organization*, pp. 95–96. An examination of the Lynn Tax assessments in 1860 and the 1860 schedules of the federal

census of manufacture provided no data on sewing machine ownership by companies or by individuals. The author of *Eighty Years* claimed that ownership of sewing machines by workers was widespread in Lynn and in Essex County (p. 428), as did *Scientific American*, Oct. 6, 1860. As evidence of machine ownership by individuals, Faler cited Massachusetts legislation in 1858 that protected the owner-operator of a sewing machine against its attachment for bad debts; *Mechanics*, p. 225. At least one thousand female homeworkers played an important role in the 1860 strike, and many must have owned or rented machines. For my estimate of the number of homeworkers in Lynn, see Appendix B. Baron and Klepp's study of garment workers suggests that few seamstresses could afford to purchase sewing machines in the 1850s and 1860s even when the price fell below $100. As a consequence, Singer adopted a hire-purchase plan to encourage renting and leasing; "Sewing Machine," in *A Needle*, ed. Jenson and Davidson, pp. 35–36.

21. Fred A. Gannon, *A Short History of American Shoemaking* (n.p., 1919), p. 34; *NYT, BJ*, Feb. 29, 1860. The *NYH*, Feb. 29, 1860, estimated that in Marblehead 300 women worked on machines in factories, while 300 more used machines at home.

22. *LyN*, July 20, 1855. Mulligan cited the installation of sewing machines in "large open spaces known as 'binding sheds' where binders worked under close supervision" ("Family and Technological Change," p. 95). These probably were subcontract machine shops such as those run by Nichols and Blake in Lynn. For a discussion of the nature of the female work force in the 1860 Lynn census, see Appendix B.

23. For this information, see the coverage of the 1860 strike in the *NYT*, Feb. 27, Mar. 3, 1860; *NYH*, Feb. 29, Mar. 3, 1860; *BT*, Mar. 9, 1860; *BJ*, Feb. 24, 1860.

24. Dublin, *Women at Work*, pp. 201–7.

25. The diaries of Martha Osbourne Barrett, Salem (1848–79), Essex Institute. I am grateful to RoseAnne C. Waters for this reference. See entries for Apr.-June 1855, especially July 29, 1855.

26. Ibid., Mar.-May, 1856.

27. *LI*, (Reminiscences of the 1860 strike by Mrs. Eliza Bartlett Keene), Oct. 26, 1895. I did not find Eliza Bartlett in the 1860 census.

28. *NEMech*, Mar. 19, 1859. Improvements in machinery and the use of steam power after 1860 relieved some of this hard physical effort; Sumner, *History of Women*, p. 172. On the ten-hour movement, see Dublin, *Women at Work*, pp. 112–14, who cited Edward P. Thompson's argument that early factory operatives resisted time-discipline and focused on the long hours of daily work as their chief grievance.

29. *TWP*, Mar. 10, 1860.

30. Baron and Klepp argued similarly that inefficiencies in outwork on garments were resolved by new technology, but that technology alone did not cause changes in women's work; "Sewing Machine," in *A Needle*, ed. Jenson and Davidson, pp. 25–27, 41–42, 50–51. Judith A. McGaw cited recent research on the impact of technology on women's work that regards mechanization as producing only superficial changes, while preserving the sexual division of labor, in "Women and the History of American Technology," *Signs* 7 (Summer 1982), pp. 798–828. Also see Joan W. Scott, "The Mechanization of Women's Work," *Scientific American* 247 (Sept. 1982), pp. 166–87. Sally Alexander's study of the working women of London, some of whom were closers (binders) of shoes, emphasized the persistence throughout the nineteenth century of the sexual division of labor, which originated within the patriarchal family and was transferred into production. As closers, women in London were confined to a few specific skills and were seldom included in trade unions; and male shoeworkers strongly resisted any changes in the sexual division of labor: "Women's Work in Nineteenth Century London: A Study of the Years 1820–1850," in *The Rights and Wrongs of Women*, ed. Juliet Mitchell and Ann Oakley (New York: Penguin, 1976), pp. 59–111.

31. *NEMech*, Mar. 19, 1859.

32. I derived these figures from an estimate made by a Boston shoemaker, James Haines, cited in *NYH*, Mar. 22, 1860, and from estimates made in 1864 in *Eighty Years*, p. 428. For general estimates of the productivity of machine operators, see Sumner, *History of Women*, p. 172, and Abbott, "Women in Industry," p. 164.

33. I compiled the figures from the Lynn *Board of Health Report* in 1850, the statistics of industry for Massachusetts in 1855, and from the United States Census of Manufacture, Manuscripts for Lynn, 1860.

34. Dawley argued that the mechanization of women's work solved the problems of the outwork system and created a "new and expansive class" of machine girls; *Class and Community*, pp. 76–78. For the overall decline in standards of work and wages for shoemakers in the 1850s, see Faler, *Mechanics*, pp. 77–99.

35. Thomson, "Origins of Modern Industry," p. 64; Hazard, *Organization*, pp. 101–2. *Essex Banner*, Aug. 13, 1853; Oct. 6, 1855; *LR*, Mar. 3, 1860. See Appendix B for a sample of male shoeworkers in 1860.

36. On German and Irish immigrants in Natick, *NOb*, Feb. 25, 1860. This account noted the attempts made by the Natick shoe bosses to divide the German, Irish, and native American bottomers.

37. *LyN*, Feb. 8, Mar. 7, 1860; *Randolph* (Mass.) *Transcript and Advertiser*, Mar. 24, 1860.

38. On the depression, see Faler, *Mechanics*, pp. 224–25. For press re-

action, see *LR*, Feb. 18, 25, Mar. 31, Apr. 21, 1860; *SLR*, Mar. 15, 1860; *BJ*, reprints of stories and letters from the *Milford* (Mass.) *Journal*, Feb. 18, 23, 1860; *NOb*, Feb. 18, and letter to the editor from "W," Feb. 25, 1860; *Marblehead Ledger*, Feb. 29, 1860. For the origins of the Republican party's position on the tariff as inspired by a critique of the iron law of wages and as an attempt to exempt American workers from the laws of supply and demand, see James L. Huston, "A Political Response to Industrialism: The Republican Embrace of Protectionist Labor Doctrines," *Journal of American History* 70 (June 1983), pp. 35–57.

39. For an expression of these views, see letter to the editor from "Pump Sole," *NOb*, Feb. 25, 1860.

40. *NOb*, Feb. 18, 1860.

41. *BT*, Feb. 24, 1860; *Dover* (N. H.) *Enquirer*, Mar. 1, 1860.

42. *BSt*, Mar. 1, 1860. The regional shoe strike of 1860 was the largest demonstration of labor protest before the Civil War and as such has had attention from historians, but little systematic analysis. Foner analyzed the 1860 strike in detail and regarded it as an outstanding example of working-class unity between men and women. He dismissed the dissension among the women workers during the strike as "some discussion," and stressed the heroic and exemplary aspects of the strike, emphasizing women's militancy (*Women* 1, pp. 90–97). He ended his account by announcing a new era of militancy among factory women in the shoe industry and suggesting a direct (but erroneous) connection between the events of 1860 and the organization of the Daughters of St. Crispin in 1869 (p. 97). Commons, Hazard, Sumner, Johnson, and Galster all fail to mention the 1860 strike. Like Foner, Andrews and Bliss saw the 1860 strike as directly linked with the Crispin movement in the late 1860s (*History of Women*, p. 108), and Barbara Wertheimer based her account on Andrews and Bliss: *We Were There: The Story of Working Women in America* (New York: Pantheon, 1977), pp. 89–90. See notes 85 and 88 below for a discussion of Dawley and Faler on the strike.

43. *BT*, Feb. 24, 1860. Members of the executive committee were Alonzo Draper, John R. Parrott, Samuel Green, S. P. Sanderson, and A. C. Wyman; *BSt*, Feb. 23, 1860. The events of the 1860 strike in Lynn were reported widely in the New England press; *BSt*, Feb. 23, Mar. 1; *LR*, Feb. 25; *BP*, Feb. 25; *BJ*, Feb. 23; *BT*, Feb. 24; *BH*, Feb. 23; *BAd*, Feb. 24. Reporters from two New York newspapers arrived after the outbreak of violence on February 23.

44. Among the hostile reactions were *BAd*, Feb. 24, 25; *LyN*, Feb. 29; *Worcester Aegis and Transcript*, Feb. 25; *BH*, Feb. 27; *Portland* (Me.) *Advertiser*, Feb. 25. On the Marblehead strike, *BP*, Feb. 27 and *NYH*, Feb. 29, 1860.

45. *NOb*, Feb. 25, Mar. 3, 1860 (the masthead carried a wrong date on the latter issue). *DGSA*, Mar. 3, 1860; *ML*, Feb. 22, 1860. James L. Huston noted the strikers' criticism of the operations of the law of supply and demand but suggested that no groups other than proslavery advocates seriously questioned the validity or politics of supply and demand, in "Facing an Angry Labor: The American Public Interprets the Shoemakers' Strike of 1860," *Civil War History* 28 (Sept. 1982), pp. 198–212.

46. *BSt*, Jan. 26, and especially Feb. 2, 1860; the editors of the *LyN* agreed heartily with Josselyn, Feb. 8, 1860.

47. *BSt*, Mar. 8, 1860; *BJ*, Feb. 23, 1860.

48. *BH*, Feb. 24, 1860; *BJ*, Feb. 23, 1860.

49. *BCit*, Mar. 31, 1860. The involvement of E. C. Darlin, former editor of the *Awl*, on various strike committees suggests the direct connection between shoemaker protest in the 1840s and in 1860; *BJ*, Feb. 20, 1860.

50. *BJ*, Feb. 23, 28, 1860; *NYH*, Feb. 29, 1860; *BT*, Feb. 23, 1860; *LR*, Apr. 14, 1860.

51. *BH* and *BJ*, Feb. 24, 1860. The audience at the women's meetings often interrupted or commented on the speaker's remarks. Many of these comments are easily understood in the context of the newspaper reports to be negative or positive in their character. "Shame" was used to convey both agreement and disagreement with the speaker. Later in the February 23 meeting, the cry of "Shame" greeted a description of exploitation of a binder by a shoe boss, but "Shame" was used on other occasions to reprimand the speaker for the use of the term "nigger" (see note 60) and to convey disagreement with the last attempt by Clara Brown to rally the women to her leadership on March 2. Reported in the press as "Shame," the remark conveyed either agreement, "It is a shame," or disagreement, "For shame." In the context of the first meeting, which was crowded with shop girls, the cries of "Shame" that greeted Draper's remarks may have been a negative comment on his description of the economic dependence of women on the male members of their families, but other women in the audience might also have agreed that for females not to be able to marry was indeed a shame.

52. *BH* and *BJ*, Feb. 24, 1860.

53. These comments from the audience did not mean that the speakers were rejecting marriage, but that they were speaking for their interests as self-supporting industrial workers, however temporary. Steven Dubnoff's study of the Irish textile workers of Lowell in 1860 indicated that boarding workers, male and female, displayed "strongly calculative" behavior, acting as if they were responsible only to themselves: "Gender, the Family, and the Problem of Work Motivation in a Transition to Industrial Capitalism," *Journal of Family History* 4 (Summer 1979), pp. 121–36. For

information on the Lynn work force in 1860, see Appendix B. Clara Brown, the leader of the shop girls, was among those who were married in Lynn after 1865. She married a twenty-seven-year-old Lynn shoemaker, William W. Cilley, in 1870 when she was twenty-nine. Maris Vinovskis warned, however, that migration can affect and distort the evidence of marriage registers. Marriages may be performed in the town where the bride lived, yet the new couple may reside in the community where the groom lived and worked. See *Fertility in Massachusetts from the Revolution to the Civil War* (New York: Academic Press, 1981), pp. 49–50. Thomas Dublin traced the patterns of migration to Lynn for three working-class wards based on the state census of 1865 and found very high rates of marriage among female residents who migrated to Lynn, in "Women Workers in the Early American Working Class: Textile and Shoe Workers, 1830–1870" (Paper read at The Future of Labor History Conference, Northern Illinois University, Oct. 1984). Also see Dublin, "Rural-Urban Migrants in Industrial New England: The Case of Lynn, Massachusetts in the Mid-Nineteenth Century," *Journal of American History* 73 (Dec. 1986), pp. 623–44, especially p. 635.

54. The second women's meeting, on February 27, 1860, was covered very briefly by the *LyN*, *BP*, *BSt*, and the *LR*. Long accounts appear in the *BJ*, *BH*, and *BP*, Feb. 28, and in the *NYH*, Mar. 3, 1860.

55. *BJ*, Feb. 28, 1860.

56. *SLR*, Mar. 15, 1860.

57. According to the *BJ*, Mrs. Graham represented the Seventh Ward on the women's executive committee, while a Miss Carrie A. Brown (undoubtedly Clara) represented the Fourth Ward, where Clara H. Brown was listed as a boarder in the 1860 census; *BJ*, Feb. 24, 1860. Mrs. Damon was listed as a dressmaker in the Lynn city directory in 1860. Also see *BJ*, *BH*, Feb. 28 and *NYH*, Mar. 3, 1860.

58. *BJ*, *BH*, Feb. 29, 1860. For the third women's meeting, a reporter for the *NYT* joined the Boston press. They were met at the door by women angered by the reporting of the previous meeting, but were admitted after promising to omit any "nonsense" spoken in the heat of debate; *NYT*, Feb. 29, 1860.

59. *BJ*, *BH*, Feb. 29, 1860.

60. *NYT*, Feb. 29, 1860. Brown's use of the word "nigger" drew negative comments from antislavery members of the audience: "Shame, there are colored persons here." Brown replied, "I meant Southern niggers," indicating a reference to slave labor as opposed to free labor. *BH*, Feb. 28, 1860. Brown's insensitivity to local antislavery opinion suggests her lack of connection with community values in Lynn. On the context of racism in Lynn, see Faler, *Mechanics*, p. 213.

61. *NYT*, Mar. 6, 1860.

62. Ibid. There are six accounts of the fourth women's meeting in the out-of-town press: the Mar. 3 issues of the *BJ*, *BH*, *BAd*, the Mar. 5 issue of the *NYH*, the Mar. 6 issue of the *NYT*, and the Mar. 7 issue of the *BP*. The *LyN* and the *LR* criticized the out-of-town press for making the women's meetings appear ridiculous; *LyN*, Mar. 7 and *LR*, Mar. 3, 1860. The *BSt* carried only a brief account of the fourth meeting, Mar. 8, 1860.

63. *NYT*, Mar. 6, 1860.

64. *BJ* and *BH*, Mar. 3, 1860; *NYH*, Mar. 5, 1860.

65. *NYT*, Mar. 6, 1860; *BAd*, Mar. 3, 1860.

66. *NYT*, Mar. 6, 1860.

67. Ibid.; *BH*, Mar. 3, 1860; *NYH*, Mar. 5, 1860.

68. *NYT*, Mar. 6, 1860; *BP*, Mar. 3, 1860; *BH*, Mar. 3, 1860.

69. *NYT*, Mar. 9, 1860.

70. *BSt*, Mar. 8, 1860.

71. *FLINews*, Mar. 17, 1860. This illustration is often used or described in detail in books and films on women's history and the labor movement; see the cover and title page of Dawley, *Class and Community*; Judith Papachristou, *Women Together: A History in Documents of the Women's Movement in the United States* (New York: Knopf, 1976); *The Emerging Woman* (Film Images/Radim Films, 1975); and Eleanor Flexner, *Century of Struggle* (New York: Antheneum, 1970).

72. *BSt*, Mar. 8, 1860. See also the sketch captioned "Convention of Hemmers and Stitchers, February 28," of the third women's meeting. The artist, Albert Berghause, preceded Leslie to Lynn in order to capture this scene. Other sketches included one of an interior of a stitching shop with six machine girls still at work during the strike; *FLINews*, Mar. 17, 1860. Dorothy Thompson argued that women often headed up Chartist parades and processions or presented banners and gifts as symbols of community values and on behalf of their husbands, brothers, and fathers; *The Chartists*, pp. 120, 126, 129–30.

73. *BSt*, Mar. 8, 1860. Also see *LR*, Mar. 10; *TWP*, Mar. 8; *BAd*, Mar. 8; *BP*, Mar. 8; *BH*, Mar. 8, 9; *BJ* (late edition), Mar. 7, 1860.

74. *NYH*, Feb. 29, 1860; *TWP* and *HG*, Mar. 15, 1860.

75. *TWP*, Mar. 5, 10, 15, 17, 1860; *HG*, Mar. 8, 15, 1860. Of the canvassing committee, three of the five members were identified as daughters of shoemakers.

76. *BJ*, Mar. 19, 1860. On Haverhill stitchers, see Appendix B.

77. *TWP*, Mar. 27, 1860; *HG*, Mar. 23, 1860.

78. *Newburyport Herald*, Mar. 6, 7, 12, 17, 1860; *NYH*, Mar. 8, 29, 1860; *BCit*, Mar. 10, 1860; *SGaz*, Mar. 10, 1860; *MJ*, Mar. 17, 1860; *BT*, Mar. 24, 1860.

79. Quote is from *NYH*, Mar. 19; also see Mar. 29, 1860; *BJ*, Mar. 20, 1860.

80. *NYH*, Mar. 19, 1860.

81. *NYH*, Mar. 29, 1860.

82. *SLR*, Mar. 15, 1860.

83. *HG*, Mar. 2, 1860. The *BSt*, Apr. 12, 1860, listed twenty-seven manufacturers who agreed to raise wages. Of these, I located twenty in the 1860 census of manufacture for Lynn. These twenty raised wages for a total of only 355 bottomers. None of the thirty-seven largest companies signed the list.

84. *LR*, Mar. 31, 1860; *NYH*, Mar. 29, 1860.

85. Paul Faler concluded in his brief account of the events in 1860 that the strike represented a sharp break with the preindustrial past, ending community harmony and introducing industrial conflict and class division; *Mechanics*, pp. 222–23.

86. Louise A. Tilly, Joan W. Scott, and Miriam Cohen challenged Edward Shorter's argument that wage-earning altered the behavior of working-class women and that individualistic and self-seeking attitudes led to sexual emancipation and higher fertility. They disputed the causal connection between increased illegitimacy rates and changed behavior, emphasizing the continuities of preindustrial attitudes among European working women. See "Women's Work and European Fertility Patterns," *Journal of Interdisciplinary History* 6 (Winter 1976), pp. 447–76.

87. Norman Ware developed a typology for the pre-1860 American labor movement, which he divided into defensive and aggressive activities. Ware characterized as aggressive those activities conducted to obtain limited concessions on wages and conditions from employers, rather than to challenge the legitimacy of the employer's authority. Defensive actions were fought from the basis of preindustrial values and represented efforts to restore a traditional relationship between workers and employers; *Industrial Worker*, pp. 198–240.

88. This material suggests that while homeworkers fought against the separation of work and home, they wanted a domestic role that would include wage-earning and household responsibilities in the interest of the family wage. It contradicts Dawley's view that the dramatic and public involvement of women in the strike challenged the prevailing cult of domesticity that separated work and home and designated the private world of family life as the only appropriate place for women's activities; *Class and Community*, pp. 81–83.

89. Hartmann, "The Unhappy Marriage." Hartmann, however, defined the family wage as an early twentieth-century phenomenon by which a male worker could support a family without paid employment by his wife

or children. Much of the evidence to which Humphries referred in "Class Struggle" involves industries where families worked together, e.g., coal-mining and textiles. For an attempt to synthesize in theoretical terms the Humphries and Hartmann debate, see Gita Sen, "The Sexual Division of Labor and the Working-Class Family: Towards a Conceptual Synthesis of Class Relations and the Subordination of Women," *Review of Radical Political Economics* 12 (Summer 1980), pp. 76–86. Temma Kaplan demonstrated the power of gender consciousness to unite housewives and female factory workers in early twentieth-century Spain, in "Female Consciousness and Collective Action: The Case of Barcelona, 1910–1918," *Signs* 7 (Spring 1982), pp. 545–66.

Chapter Six: Crispin Protest in the Post–Civil War Shoe Factory

1. *SLR*, vol. 28, Aug. 14, 1879, p. 229. A 15 percent tariff on imported shoes plus the dislocations of the Civil War cut off the Canadian market to American manufacturers. See Gregory Kealey, "Artisans Respond to Industrialism: Shoemakers, Shoe Factories and the Knights of St. Crispin in Toronto," *Historical Papers*, Canadian Historical Association (June 1973), p. 139.

2. Hazard, *Organization*, pp. 116–18, 124; Seth Bryant, *Shoe and Leather Trade of the Last Hundred Years* (Boston, 1891), pp. 77–78. Saul Engelbourg in "The Economic Impact of the Civil War on Manufacturing Enterprise," *Business History* 21 (July 1979), p. 155, denied that the Civil War created enough demand or profits to alter manufacturing organization in the Massachusetts boot and shoe industry. Alan Dawley argued, however, that inflation and the government's greenback policy made credit easier and cash for domestic orders more available and that this encouraged mechanization and expansion in Lynn (*Class and Community*, pp. 94–95). Many manufacturers found that wartime inflation and easy credit allowed them to shift their business to a cash basis and reduced their dependence on credit. See Glenn Porter and Harold C. Livesay, *Merchants and Manufacturers: Studies in the Changing Structure of Nineteenth Century Marketing* (Baltimore: Johns Hopkins Press, 1971), pp. 10–11. Shoe manufacturer Moses How complained that the demand for light shoes, especially turned shoes, a speciality of Haverhill, did not reestablish itself until 1870; "Moses How," *BSR*, Dec. 19, 1888, p. 49. After Gordon Blake had proven his stitching machine for bottoming shoes a success, a number of Lynn manufacturers organized a syndicate headed by McKay to purchase claims on Blake's patent, which the U.S. Supreme Court upheld in 1865. See Charles H. McDermott, *A*

History of the Shoe and Leather Industries of the United States, vol. 1 (Boston, 1920), pp. 71–72.

3. *LR*, May 23, 1874.

4. *SLR*, vol. 10, Nov. 21, 1867, p. 4.

5. *LR*, Sept. 19, 1868; Feb. 2, 1870; Hazard, *Organization*, p. 120.

6. The term "ladies' shoe" in the 1860s indicated a sole sewed on a McKay machine with an upper of glove kid, serge, or other fine material. "Women's work," also commonly made in Essex County and in southern New Hampshire, was classified as the coarser kinds of shoes with uppers of calfskin, pebbled goatskin or other medium-heavy leather and soles that were machine-pegged. *SLR*, vol. 10, May 30, 1867, p. 4. For an analysis of this shift in production during the Civil War, see *SLR*, vol. 28, Aug. 14, 1879, p. 229.

7. *LT*, Mar. 9, 1872.

8. *LR*, May 8, June 5, 1869; Jan. 13, 1872.

9. *SLR*, vol. 10, Dec. 12, 1867, p. 4.

10. *LR*, Jan. 24, 1872.

11. Commonwealth of Massachusetts, *Statistical Information Relating to Certain Branches of Industry in Massachusetts for the Year, 1865* (Boston, 1865), pp. 158–61 (Lynn), 148–50 (Haverhill), 136–39 (Danvers), 164–66 (Marblehead). A higher proportion of women (42 percent) worked in Lynn shoe factories than countywide; see Secretary of the Commonwealth, *Abstract of the Census of Massachusetts, 1865* (Boston, 1867), pp. 142–43, 150–51.

12. *Massachusetts Census of 1865*, pp. 2–3, 16–17, 155–57, 166–67, 286–89.

13. See the manuscript schedules of the Federal Census of Manufacture of 1870 for Lynn, Haverhill, Marblehead, and Danvers.

14. John Cumbler argued that the most rapid period of economic change in shoe production occurred in the decade 1855–65, in *A Moral Response to Industrialism: The Lectures of Reverend Cook in Lynn, Massachusetts* (Albany: State University of New York Press, 1982), pp. 5–6, but the impact of the depression of 1857 on shoe manufacturing and the disruptions and loss of markets during the Civil War delayed change. The decade of 1865–75 represents a period of the rapid maturation of the early factory system that was partially in place before the Civil War. Dawley and Cumbler both tended to regard technological change as an abstract and overwhelming force; Dawley, *Class and Community*, p. 94; Cumbler, p. 8. William Mulligan has also argued that the process of mechanization, rather than decisions by capitalists, transformed the family work system in shoe production ("Family and Technological Change," pp. 127–31).

However, married women were only in part driven from the work force and not by machines, but by centralization and time-discipline, and later by the application of steam power to replace foot power. Mechanization and centralization did not cause extreme seasonality in the industry, but capitalists used machines and factories to attempt to dominate the national market and increase profits.

15. *LR*, July 15, 1868. The *SLR* of June 13, 1867, contrasted the speed of steam-power manufacturing with the small quantities, lost time, inefficiencies, and low productivity of decentralized production. The interests of the manufacturers were expressed in the *SLR*, published weekly in New York City and alternately in Boston and New York by 1874 and in the *SLRec*, published in Boston from 1870–75.

16. *LR*, Jan. 23, 1869.

17. *SLRec*, Dec. 19, 1870, p. 173; *SLR*, vol. 10, May 9, 1867, p. 4; May 16, 1867, p. 4; vol. 12, June 17, 1869, p. 2; vol. 14, June 15, 1871, p. 4. For an overall appraisal of these policies, see *LT*, Mar. 9, 1872.

18. *SLR*, vol. 12, June 17, 1869, p. 2. In *Merchants and Manufacturers* Porter and Livesay argue that changes in distribution and marketing are as important to understanding post–Civil War economic structure as changes in production (pp. 1–2). Mass production and the rise of factories increased productive capacities and created falling prices as supply outstripped demand. The response of many large producers was to search for ways to control the market (pp. 10–11).

19. *SLR*, vol. 10, May 23, 1867, p. 4; Sept. 5, 1867, p. 4; Nov. 21, 1867, p. 4; vol. 15, Dec. 28, 1871, p. 1. For the attitudes of freedmen toward russet brogans, see *SLR* vol. 45, Nov. 8, 1888, p. 1037.

20. *SLR*, vol. 10, May 16, 1867, p. 4; Nov. 21, 1867, pp. 1, 4.

21. *SLR*, vol. 10, June 6, 1867, p. 4; Swett, "History of Shoemaking," p. 25.

22. *SLRec*, Feb. 19, 1872, p. 280. For an earlier advocacy of producing goods for advance orders only, see letter from "G. W. M.", *LR*, Apr. 16, 1870.

23. *SLRec*, Feb. 19, 1872, p. 280; *LR*, Feb. 15, 1873; *SLR*, vol. 14, June 15, 1871, p. 1. Porter and Livesay pointed to the rise of a concentrated urban market for consumer goods created by the national railroad network as a problem as well as an opportunity for manufacturers (*Merchants and Manufacturers*, pp. 154–55).

24. *LR*, Dec. 5, 1869.

25. *SLR*, vol. 15, May 9, 16, 23, 1872, p. 1 for all dates.

26. *LR*, June 5, 1869.

27. *LR*, Feb. 15, 1873.

28. *LR*, Mar. 18, 1868; Annette Mudge Pratt, "E. and A. Mudge and

Co.," *Historical Collections of the Danvers Historical Society* 34 (1946), pp. 2–3; *SLRec*, Jan. 30, 1871, p. 244.

29. See descriptions of Joseph Harris and Sons, *LR*, Mar. 18, 1868; Brown Brothers and Charles D. Pecker, *LR*, June 5, 1869; Keene Brothers, *LR*, Feb. 1, 1873; and Samuel Bubier, *SLR*, vol. 15, May 9, 16, 23, 1872, p. 1 for all dates. For sex segregation in a Toronto shoe factory in 1870, see Kealey, "Artisans Respond," pp. 140–41.

30. The first string team in Lynn was organized by Bancroft and Purinton in 1858, several years before mechanization; *SLR*, vol. 38, Sept. 18, 1884, p. 478. See also the operations of Moses How in Haverhill in chapter 5 and *Daily Evening Voice* (Boston), Mar. 1, 1865. In early 1873 the new Keene Brothers factory seemed to be using both kinds of teams for making operations; *LT*, Mar. 5, 1873. Also see *SLR*, vol. 27, Mar. 27, 1870, p. 482 and *Vind* (Lynn), Feb. 23, 1878. John R. Commons did not regard the factory system to be fully in place until the 1880s when detailed piecework and additional machinery had replaced all team work ("American Shoemakers," p. 75). Brian Palmer cited the use of team shoemaking in Hamilton, Ontario, as a source of resistance to the factory system, in *A Culture in Conflict: Skilled Workers and Industrial Capitalism in Hamilton, Ontario, 1860–1914* (Montreal: McGill-Queen's University Press, 1979), pp. 36–37.

31. *LR*, Aug. 26, 1868. See also advertisements for women lasters, *LT*, Sept. 5, 1868. According to Edith Abbott, women were also used as temporary help to run McKay machines in Haverhill in the absence of male workers during the Civil War; "Women in Industry," p. 349. On female lasters by a Lynn laster, see *BH*, Aug. 19, 1888. Female lasters were possible only in Lynn, where lasters did not work as members of a male team.

32. *SLRec*, Apr. 17, 1871, p. 379; Nov. 13, 1871, p. 116.

33. *LT*, Apr. 2, 1870; *LR*, Nov. 16, 1870; *SLR*, vol. 14, May 11, 1871, p. 4.

34. *SLR*, vol. 15, May 23, 1872, p. 1. The search for an efficient, workable lasting machine continued until the 1890s; see Irwin Yellowitz, "Skilled Workers and Mechanization: The Lasters in the 1890s," *Labor History* 18 (Spring 1977), pp. 197–213.

35. Mudge, "Shoe Trade," in *Proceedings*, ed. Rice, p. 240; MBLS, *Second Annual Report of the Bureau of the Statistics of Labor* (Boston, 1871), p. 238. For skiving, *SLR*, vol. 46, Feb. 28, 1889, p. 556.

36. Alfred D. Chandler, Jr., *The Visible Hand: The Managerial Revolution in American Business* (Cambridge: Belknap Press, 1977), pp. 207–48, especially p. 235.

37. *LT*, Mar. 9, 1872.

38. Dawley argued in *Class and Community* that support for the professional police force, designed to protect property and to control the seasonal work force that swelled the ranks of factory workers, represented the anxieties of manufacturers over social control and class conflict (pp. 122–28).

39. *LT*, Jan. 18, 1868.

40. *LT*, Feb. 8, 15, 29, 1868.

41. *LT*, Feb. 8, 1868.

42. *LT*, Mar. 21, May 9, 1868. By the end of 1868 the fears of the editors of the *Transcript* had dissolved in the general postwar prosperity.

43. *LR*, July 9, 1873.

44. *LR*, Jan. 17, 1872.

45. *LR*, Mar. 4, 11, 18, Apr. 15, 1868, Dec. 4, 1869.

46. The term "floating population" was used in the *LR*, Nov. 16, 1870. The first use of the term "lady" in connection with the seasonal work force of female stitchers appeared in the *LR* on Dec. 23, 1865.

47. *LR*, Nov. 2, 1870.

48. *SLR*, vol. 15, Mar. 28, 1872, p. 1; vol. 18, Sept. 24, 1874, p. 240.

49. *SLR*, vol. 15, Mar. 28, 1872, p. 2.

50. *LR*, Feb. 24, 1872.

51. *LR*, May 2, Oct. 17, 1868; Aug. 30, Oct. 22, 1870; Feb. 24, 1872. Also see *LT*, Aug. 27, 1870.

52. *LR*, Nov. 2, 1870.

53. Testimony of a Lynn shoeworker, MBLS, *Second Annual Report*, p. 247. For parallel development of the urban culture of working-class London and Pittsburgh in the late nineteenth century, see Gareth Stedman Jones, "Working-Class Culture and Working-Class Politics in London, 1870–1900: Notes on the Remaking of a Working Class," *Journal of Social History* 7 (Summer 1974), pp. 460–508; and Francis G. Couvares, "The Triumph of Commerce: Class Culture and Mass Culture in Pittsburgh," in Frisch and Walkowitz, *Working-Class America*, pp. 123–52.

54. "The Queen City!" was published in serial form in thirty-four chapters in the *LRec* from Mar. 16 to July 20, 1872. For the promenade scene, Apr. 20, 1872. The story is set in the context of Crispin activity, 1869–72, and portrays the organization sympathetically as powerful and well intentioned, if some of its members proved to be unworthy and sometimes violent; see especially the issues of June 1 and 8, 1872.

55. *LT*, June 26, 1869.

56. *LG*, Aug. 10, 1872; July 8, 1871. On the Bowery promenade as a cultural form of working-class life in antebellum New York, see Stansell, *City of Women*, pp. 90–101.

57. *LR*, Mar. 19, Nov. 16, 1870. No records of the Woman's Union for Christian Work (also referred to in the press as the Women's Union) have survived other than their published annual reports. For similar activities by middle-class reformers, see Kessler-Harris, *Out to Work*, pp. 86–95.

58. *LR*, Feb. 3, 1872.

59. *LR*, Nov. 16, 1870.

60. Woman's Union Third Annual Report, *LR*, Oct. 23, 1872; Woman's Union Second Annual Report, *LR*, Oct. 28, 1871. Occasionally the Woman's Union filled requests for domestic servants for Lynn families, but during the prosperous years, 1868–71, most women workers preferred stitching.

61. *LT*, Mar. 29, Apr. 5, 12, 1873.

62. *LR*, Oct. 11, 1873; Apr. 11, 1874.

63. For information on divisions within the 1870 female work force in Lynn, see Appendix B. Dublin, in "Women Workers," argued that very significant differences separated the experiences of female shoeworkers from those of female cotton mill hands in the 1830s. Certainly, on the whole Lynn shoeworkers were older, the percentage of boarding migrants was much smaller, and some were married, although Dublin's decision to sample only three working-class wards in 1865 and the custom of homework may have inflated the percentage of married women in the work force. Still the continuities between the experiences and rhetoric of the boarding stitchers of Lynn and the cotton mill hands of Lowell are impressive: most were native-born New Englanders, the migrants had rural families with some property, and as women workers they did not become permanent industrial workers because their work experiences were marked by a high turnover rate. Also see Dublin, "Rural-Urban Migrants," pp. 641–43.

64. See Appendix B. Dublin made no distinction between women who lived as female heads of families or as resident individuals with sisters or dependents and women who as wives and daughters resided in male-headed families; "Women Workers," pp. 10–11.

65. *LR*, Mar. 16, 1872; *LT*, July 5, 1873.

66. MBLS, *Second Annual Report*, pp. 242–49.

67. Ibid., p. 244.

68. Dawley has argued that the factory clock rather than the work season was the essential organizing principle of work for resident shoeworkers (*Class and Community*, p. 129).

69. Dawley described the life of the factory shoeworkers as disciplined and isolated at work as compared to their group experience in the artisan shops (pp. 132–34). This is too sharp a contrast, for even after the cen-

tralization of work and the introduction of some mechanization, male shoeworkers often worked in teams in factories. On teamwork, see Kealey, "Artisans Respond," p. 141.

70. *LG*, June 10, 1871.

71. MBLS, *Second Annual Report*, p. 248.

72. MBLS, *Fourth Annual Report*, p. 306.

73. Dawley discussed the obsession of historians of the Crispin movement with the green hands issue and their failure to identify either the more important questions of wages or the position of most shoeworkers as factory operatives rather than artisans. Using the manuscript federal census of population in 1870, Dawley estimated that more than half of the 3,737 male shoeworkers in Lynn considered themselves Crispins. He regarded the Crispins as workers in transition, as factory workers who had not forgotten preindustrial experience and who were able to utilize the equal rights tradition of the early nineteenth century as inspiration for labor militancy (*Class and Community*, pp. 143–48). Dawley's criticism of John R. Commons's emphasis on the marketplace as the basic dynamic of capitalism called attention to the ideological underpinnings of Commons's work as a scholar and as a progressive reformer, but the marketplace was a real problem for shoeworkers in the nineteenth century. The market in the 1860s and 1870s was shaped by decisions made by capitalists and defended by the ideology of supply and demand as expressed in sympathetic newspapers and in the trade journals. Hall, in "The Knights of St. Crispin," pp. 161–75, also called attention to the overemphasis on the green hands issue by historians such as Don D. Lescohier. In 1958 Hall criticized the failure of historians to examine local strikes and the concerns of the rank and file and advised them to view the labor movement as a movement of people, a social movement (p. 172). Dawley answered this complaint with *Class and Community*, his 1976 study of the shoemakers of Lynn.

74. Frederick Rudolph, "Chinamen in Yankeedom: Anti-Unionism in Massachusetts in 1870," *American Historical Review* 53 (Oct. 1947), pp. 1–29.

75. See a general discussion of Crispinism and the green hands problem in the Lynn *Vind*, Jan. 13, 1877, published by B. B. Scully, an early Crispin member who had experienced both the artisan shop and the factory.

76. *LR*, Jan. 23, 1869; *SLR*, vol. 12, Mar. 18, 1869, p. 4. For other hostile comment, vol. 12, Feb. 18, 1868, p. 4; June 17, 1869, p. 11.

77. *LR*, Dec. 4, 1869.

78. For the English model of arbitration, see Josephine Shaw Lowell, compiler, *Industrial Arbitration and Conciliation* (New York, 1902), pp. 20–27. On July 29, 1872, the *BAd* reconstructed the history of arbi-

tration in Lynn: "Knowing that the settlement of questions between work-men and their employers in England had been by arbitration, and that the principle had been found to work well, and feeling that it ought to have a trial in this country they [the leading firms in Lynn] consented . . . to a like arrangement." No direct evidence has survived to link George Keene to the English model of arbitration, but his expressed sentiments on the need to avoid damaging local competition suggests he probably played an important role in the establishment of arbitration procedures. For a sense of arbitration as a benefit to Lynn and its prosperity, see *LR*, June 27, 1870; *LT*, Sept. 10, 1870; MBLS, *Second Annual Report*, pp. 93–98. No records of the arbitration process have survived, and its activities were kept secret from the press. It appears, however, that the board met once annually to fix wages and did not deal with other disputes. Neither Dawley nor Hall adequately explain why the wage list was adopted in 1870 or rejected in 1872; Dawley, *Class and Community*, p. 186; Hall, "Knights of St. Crispin," p. 161. For post–Civil War labor reform poli-tics, see Dawley, pp. 196–99, and David Montgomery, *Beyond Equality: Labor and the Radical Republicans, 1862–1872* (Urbana: University of Illinois Press, 1981).

79. *LR*, July 28, 31, 1869; *LT*, Aug. 14, 1869; *BJ*, July 29, 1869; *BT*, July 30, 1869. The Daughters of St. Crispin as a name had been in the air since the strike of 1860, used by an anonymous poet in "To the Strikers," which began "Fair Crispin's sons and daughters." *BSt*, Mar. 22, 1860. The *BJ* dubbed the women's procession on March 7 the "Daughters of St. Crispin"; Mar. 8, 1860. The choice of this name for the organization in 1868 linked the group with the 1860 strike but in name only. Philip Foner claimed that the temporary officers of the 1869 convention, Carrie Wilson and Abbie Jacques of Lynn, (whom he erroneously described as the first national officers) were actually veterans of the 1860 strike; see *Women* 1, p. 157. This seems unlikely, for Wilson, who boarded in Lynn in 1870, would have been fifteen years old in 1860, and Jacques, who would have been twenty in 1860, was a native of New York who probably boarded in Lynn like Wilson, but might have been related to one of the two Jacques families in the city. No trace of her was found in the 1860 or 1870 census, but she was listed in the Massachusetts marriage records for Lynn in 1871. Certainly there is no evidence that either ever claimed to have participated in the 1860 events. If Wilson and Jacques were not in Lynn in 1860, other DOSC members might have been, but of Clara Brown and Mary Damon, prominent in the 1860 strike, there is no trace in the activities of the DOSC. Damon still lived in Lynn in the Fifth Ward in 1870, where she kept house for her shoemaker husband and family. Clara Brown married in Lynn in 1870, but was not located in the 1870

census as a stitcher. Andrews and Bliss also drew a direct but erroneous connection between the strikers of 1860 and the Daughters of St. Crispin as an organization; see *History of Women*, p. 108.

80. For DOSC members, there was no issue of green hands, apprenticeships, or foreign labor, and no stitcher could claim to be an artisan.

81. Carole Turbin, "And We Are Nothing but Women: Irish Working Women in Troy," in *Women of America: A History*, ed. Carol Ruth Berkin and Mary Beth Norton (Boston: Houghton Mifflin, 1979), pp. 216–17. For DOSC resolutions on wages in 1870, see below.

82. *LR*, Apr. 21, 1868; *AmW*, May 1, 1869. For a list of the DOSC officers, see *MJ*, May 8, 1869. There were no direct familial connections between the DOSC and the KOSC officers in Stoneham, although Treasurer Maria Osgood, a native of Maine who lived by herself in Stoneham, might have been related to the two Osgoods who were KOSC officers. The diversity of the leadership of the Stoneham lodge in 1869 reflected the diversity of the work force of stitchers in 1870. Of the 313 female stitchers reported in the 1870 census of Stoneham (a number that probably undercounted the seasonal worker) 77 percent were single and 23 percent were married. Fifty-four percent were residents of Stoneham and 46 percent were boarders. Thirteen percent of the total number of stitchers lived in female-headed families or lived alone. In his 1972 article, "Working-Class Women in the Gilded Age," on the Cohoes, New York, cotton mill workers, 1860–80, Daniel Walkowitz concluded that similarly situated female textile workers of Irish immigrant background defended and celebrated a modicum of status and security obtained from steady and relatively skilled work as weavers in the cotton factories. Walkowitz described the female-headed family in Cohoes as disorganized, "scarred," and broken rather than as self-supporting, but female textile workers' sense of satisfaction with their work and status might better be seen as a reflection of their gender expectations as women and as female heads of families rather than as Walkowitz regards it, as a sense of ethnic or community expectations or as "embourgoisement."

83. *LR*, *BT*, July 29, 1869. Foner implied that male shoeworkers had themselves organized the women into a sister organization based on their mutual participation in the 1860 strike: *Women* 1, p. 157.

84. *LR*, July 28, 31, 1869. Not listed in the Lynn census of 1870 as a stitcher, Emma Lane was the wife of a shoeworker and might have stitched shoes at home. Martha Wallbridge was not an officer of Excelsior Lodge in Stoneham, but was listed as a stitcher in the 1870 census.

85. *LT*, July 31, 1869. For perceptions by the Woman's Union for Christian Work that boarding stitchers from country homes represented a different and more refined type of woman worker than the city girls of Lynn, see *LR*, Apr. 11, 1874; Oct. 16, 1875.

86. *AmW*, May 1, 1869. Daniels agreed with the suffragists of New York City that working women should lead their own organizations and saw the female worker, especially those with some skill like the typographers and the shoe stitchers, as representing working women with the potential for independence and equality with men; see Ellen Carol DuBois in *Feminism and Suffrage: The Emergence of an Independent Women's Movement in America, 1848–1869*, (Ithaca: Cornell University Press, 1978), pp. 136–37. Kate Mullaney of the Troy Collar Workers' Union agreed with Daniels that women workers should generate their own leadership; Turbin, "And We Are Nothing But Women," in *Women of America*, ed. Berkin and Norton, pp. 209–10.

87. At its organizing convention in Boston, the Massachusetts Working Women's League chose Emma Lane as its secretary, S. P. Cummings as its treasurer, and Jennie Collins as one of its vice presidents; *Commonwealth*, Oct. 30, 1869. *WAd*, May 8, 1869; *AmW*, May 1, 1869. Daniels, Collins, and the Working Women's Association of Boston were converted to the importance of suffrage for working women in early 1870; *WAd*, Feb. 5, 1870. At the New England Labor Reform Convention in 1870, they successfully supported a resolution for woman suffrage.

88. *LT*, July 31, 1869.

89. The DOSC used the *Lynn Record* and the *Workingmen's Advocate*, while the KOSC used the *Little Giant* and the *American Workman*.

90. *LT*, Oct. 16, 1869. Foner denied that the Working Women's League of Boston had any connections with working women's unions: *Women 1*, p. 153. Dawley wrote that in the 1860s and 1870s, Lynn working women involved in the DOSC were uninterested in women's rights (*Class and Community*, p. 179). Also see Rosalyn Baxandall, Linda Gordon, and Susan Reverby, "Boston Working Women Protest, 1869," *Signs 1* (Spring 1976), pp. 803–8.

91. *LR*, Dec. 25, 1869; Andrews and Bliss, *History of Women*, pp. 108–9; *Baltimore Sun*, Apr. 14, 17, 18, 19, 1871; *LG*, Apr. 22, 1871; and Foner, *Women 1*, p. 158.

92. DuBois, *Feminism and Suffrage*, pp. 126–27; Israel Kugler, "The Trade Union Career of Susan B. Anthony," *Labor History 2* (Winter 1961), pp. 91, 93; Foner, *Women 1*, p. 131.

93. *WAd*, Sept. 4, 1869; Kugler, "Susan B. Anthony," p. 93; DuBois, *Feminism and Suffrage*, pp. 134–35. DuBois's discussion of the role of female printers in the New York Working Women's Association suggests an analogy with the stitchers of Essex County: an elite of relatively skilled and well-paid female industrial workers (pp. 128–32).

94. Kugler, "Susan B. Anthony," p. 94; Foner, *Women 1*, pp. 132–33.

95. Foner labeled the 1868 resolutions "historic"; *Women 1*, p. 133; see also Kugler, "Susan B. Anthony," pp. 93–94.

96. During an earlier strike of typographers' unions against the *New York World* in 1868, the *Rev* had encouraged women to strike-break in order to gain skills in the trade; *Rev*, Mar. 19, 1868, as cited in DuBois, *Feminism and Suffrage*, pp. 132–33. Augusta Lewis had broken into the trade in this way in 1868, and many of the early female typesetters in 1868 were hostile to the men's unions (DuBois, pp. 140–42) and organized their own union in late 1868 in alliance with the suffragists in the New York Working Women's Association. This alliance was broken up by middle-class domination of the association and by Lewis's decision to cooperate with male unionists in strike situations (pp. 152–54). For the disappointing results of this decision, see DuBois, pp. 160–61, and Foner, *Women* 1, pp. 160–62. For a different view of the motives of Anthony and middle-class reformers at the NLU conventions of 1868 and 1869, see Ava Baron, "Women and the Making of the American Working Class: A Study of the Proletarianization of Printers," *Review of Radical Political Economics* 14 (Fall 1982), pp. 31–34.

97. DuBois argued that the typographers' unions admitted women in gratitude for their agreement not to strike-break in 1869 (*Feminism and Suffrage*, pp. 153–54). See Foner for a discussion of less lofty motives by the same male typographers: *Women* 1, pp. 147–48.

98. DuBois, *Feminism and Suffrage*, pp. 147–53; *WAd*, Sept. 4, 1869.

99. *WAd*, Sept. 4, 1869.

100. DuBois argued that Anthony was essentially ignorant of trade union principles; the coalition of feminism and working women foundered on the realities of class, (*Feminism and Suffrage*, pp. 127, 155–56). Foner also argued that Anthony was ignorant of trade unionism (*Women* 1, p. 151), as did Kessler-Harris in *Out to Work*, p. 97. At the 1869 NLU convention, Anthony openly chose radical feminism over trade unionism, a choice she made while conscious of its implications; *WAd*, Sept. 4, 1869.

101. David Montgomery saw the conflict as a classic confrontation between middle-class and working-class prejudices over sex roles and believed that the NLU was well rid of suffragists who could not support trade unionism, (*Beyond Equality*, pp. 397–99). Foner likewise denied the relevance of Walsh's response to Anthony's questioning of the sexual division of labor in the trades as a "typically sexist sentiment that had nothing to do with the issues at hand" (*Women* 1, p. 136). But Walsh clearly recognized the implications of Anthony's proposals and strongly opposed them. He also opposed admitting Chinese or black workers to the trade without the union's permission; *WAd*, Sept. 4, 1869.

102. Kugler and Foner suggested that the death of William Sylvis just prior to the NLU convention was critical to this dispute because with his

support among the trade unionists, Sylvis might have worked out a compromise in 1869: Kugler, "Susan B. Anthony," p. 98; Foner, *Women 1*, p. 137. DuBois argued that the woman suffrage movement and feminism was after 1869 committed to an exclusively middle-class constituency and that as a result women did not make significant gains in the trade union movement until the early twentieth century (*Feminism and Suffrage*, pp. 160–61). Also see Kugler, p. 100.

103. *WAd*, Sept. 4, 1869; *New York World*, Aug. 18, 1869. It is not clear why Emma Lane as First Grand Directeress did not attend the convention in 1869 herself. Had she done so, Anthony would not have had her support.

104. *Rev.*, Aug. 26, 1869.

105. Before the 1869 convention and the death of Sylvis, the editorial policy of the *WAd* had supported women's rights; Foner, *Women 1*, pp. 131–32.

106. *WAd*, Aug. 27, 1870, as cited in *A Documentary History of American Industrial Society 9*, ed. John R. Commons et al. (Cleveland, 1910), pp. 257–67; Andrews and Bliss, *History of Women*, p. 109.

107. *WAd*, May 7, 1870. Willard, writing to the "Ladies Department," argued that women as "the moral head of the family" must have "a voice and a hand in government." Also see Andrews and Bliss, *History of Women*, p. 88.

108. No records or membership lists of the DOSC on the national or local level other than newspaper accounts of its activities have survived, but according to press reports the organization in Essex County was most active in Lynn and Stoneham.

109. Petition for a Hearing Before the Committee on Labor, Feb. 28, 1870, Unpassed Legislation File, 1870, Massachusetts State Archives. On the denial of the KOSC petition, see Montgomery, *Beyond Equality*, p. 369.

110. *BH, BT*, Feb. 28, 1870; *MJ*, Mar. 5, 1870; *LR*, Feb. 17, 1869, on the KOSC. In contrast, the response of sewing women in the Northeast to economic distress was a campaign to petition state legislatures to protect them based on their weakness, vulnerabilities, and disappointed expectations of marriage: Kessler-Harris, *Out to Work*, pp. 77–82.

111. *LRec*, Nov. 29, 1873.

112. Andrews and Bliss, *History of Women*, p. 109. Lane was elected DOSC treasurer in 1870.

113. *WAd*, May 7, 28, 1870. On April 21, 1870, Lane addressed the international convention of the KOSC in Boston although she was no longer First Grand Directeress. *Proceedings of the Third Annual Meeting of the International Grand Lodge of the Order of Knights of St. Crispin,*

Boston, Apr. 19–30, 1870 (Milwaukee, 1870), pp. 31–32. A careful, name-by-name search of the 1870 census of Lynn did not turn up Emma Lane. She had probably relocated to Boston temporarily in her effort to establish a working women's newspaper.

114. The only surviving accounts of the DOSC convention in 1870 are the quotations from the *AmW*, Apr. 30, 1870, in Andrews and Bliss, *History of Women*, p. 109.

115. *Rev*, Mar. 17, 1870, p. 170; Andrews and Bliss, *History of Women*, pp. 89–90. For two different accounts of the reception of Daniels's remarks on suffrage, see the *New York World* and *New York Tribune*, Mar. 11, 1870.

116. *BP*, Apr. 20, 1870. For middle-class suffrage activities in Massachusetts before 1880, see Sharon Hartman Strom, "Leadership and Tactics in the American Woman Suffrage Movement: A New Perspective from Massachusetts," *Journal of American History* 62 (Sept. 1975), pp. 298–99. Kate Mullaney's Collar Workers of Troy, one of the strongest unions for women workers in the nineteenth century, offered no support for prosuffrage women in the DOSC or in the Boston or New York Working Women's Associations. The Troy collar workers represented a successful union of relatively skilled women workers who as a result of the sexual division of labor in local industry enjoyed more organizational power and higher wages than other female workers in that city. Like the stitchers in the shoe industry of Massachusetts, many laundry workers were the sole support of their families. The Troy women were largely of Irish background with strong familial and cultural ties to the community of male trade unionists in Troy and in New York City. These ties to male unionists meant crucial financial support and aid during strikes, representing the collar workers' most valuable and reliable alliance. The most vociferous and intransigent opponents of woman suffrage at the NLU conventions of 1868 and 1869 were the Irish trade unionists of New York City, those very allies who sustained and supported Kate Mullaney and her union. The cultural context of Crispinism and the equal rights tradition in New England exacted no similar price from women shoeworkers, but the issues of suffrage and women's rights continued to divide them. Turbin, pp. 203–19. Also see Carole Turbin, "Reconceptualizing Family," and her "Daughters, Wives, Widows: Family Relations and Women's Labor Organizing in a Mid-19th Century Working Class Community" (Paper, n.d., in the author's possession). On Irish working women, Hasia A. Diner, *Erin's Daughters: Irish Immigrant Women in the Nineteenth Century* (Baltimore: Johns Hopkins University Press, 1983), chap. 4.

117. Cumbler, *A Moral Response*, pp. 1–40. In a 1982 reprint of Cook's lectures of 1871, Cumbler represents Cook's attitudes as the response of Congregational churches in general and the troubled middle class in Lynn to the social challenge of industrialization. When Cook's church burned down on December 27, the lectures were moved to the newly opened Music Hall near the factory district. Cook's concern over the threat of industrialization in Lynn was essentially derivative, as he had acquainted himself with the work and views of the Woman's Union for Christian Work in the fall of 1870.

118. Ibid., p. 53.

119. The version of Cook's lectures that was republished in 1982 rested on Cook's own edition, which was published in Lynn in October 1871. In the hastily prepared 1871 edition, as well as in the 1982 edition, some of the remarks that Cook made extemporaneously to the audience and that were quoted in the local press were omitted (for example, the indignant response of the operatives published in the *LT* on Feb. 4, 1871, and the statements of the proprietors of the workroom, Berry and Beede, in the *LR*, Feb. 15, 1871). Cook quite understandably dropped from the 1871 edition some of the terms he had used on January 22 to describe the character of the female operatives, remarks that once the identity of the women was known, caused him some embarrassment. The 1871 edition conformed to what Cook later found out about the character of the female operatives.

120. Cumbler, *A Moral Response*, pp. 52–53.

121. Cook brought to his perceptions of the moral dangers of the factory system in Lynn the sensitivities of a young man in conflict over his own gender role. His misogynist father disapproved as effeminate his son's extended education and choice of career and warned him against young women as Delilahs who would deprive him of his masculine strength; see letters quoted in Cumbler, *A Moral Response*, pp. 14–15.

122. *LG*, Feb. 4, 1871.

123. *LT*, Feb. 4, 1871; *LR*, Feb. 11, 1871. The remaining six women stitchers did not appear in the 1870 census and probably were members of the floating population.

124. *LT*, Mar. 11, 1871.

125. Ibid.

126. Eisenstein, *Give Us Bread*, pp. 67–73, 86–89.

127. *SLR*, vol. 15, Nov. 23, 1871, p. 3.

128. *LG*, Sept. 2, 1871.

129. "Voice from the Stitchers," in the *LR*, reprinted in the *StA*, Sept. 9, 1871. Anne Philips and Barbara Taylor have argued that skill is often an

ideological category imposed on certain types of work by virtue of the sex and power of the workers who perform it ("Sex and Skill: Notes toward a Feminist Economics," *Feminist Review* 6 (1980), p. 79), in this case a definition of skill by self-supporting, experienced, native-born women.

130. "Voice from the Stitchers," *StA*, Sept. 9, 1871.

131. *LG*, Sept. 2, 1871.

132. *LT*, Sept. 9, 1871. Among the women leaders were Ella A. Little, a twenty-seven-year-old single woman from New Hampshire, located in the Lynn census of 1870 boarding with three other stitchers in the household of a private family. She later became an advocate of woman suffrage; see chapter 7.

133. *LG*, Sept. 2, 1871.

134. *LG*, Nov. 18, 1871.

135. Ibid.

136. *LG*, Dec. 10, 1870; Emma Lane's reply, Dec. 17, 1870. For the 1871 criticism, see *LG*, Sept. 30, 1871; *LR*, Sept. 27, 1871.

137. For letters from "Kate" and Lane, see *LG*, Oct. 14, 1871.

138. *LT*, Jan. 20, 27, 1872.

139. An arithmetical error occurred in the tabulations of the number of women earning eight dollars a week in the *Third Annual Report* of the MBLS in 1872, p. 104. The total number of women shoeworkers earning eight dollars a week is actually 663 rather than 563, which slightly reduces the average weekly wage reported as $10.38.

140. *LR*, July 5, 1871. MBLS, *Third Annual Report*, pp. 436–37. One reason for disunity among the shoeworkers of Stoneham was the failure of the stitchers to cooperate in a strike in early 1871, and the conviction of three of the male strikers as "common railers and brawlers" when they attempted to keep the stitchers from working in the shops; *MJ*, May 21, 1871.

141. *BAd*, July 29, 1872; *LR*, July 31, 1872; *LG*, June 22, 1872; *LT*, Aug. 3, 10, 17, 24, 1872. The *LG* ceased publication after the strike, and the *LRec* became the Lynn newspaper most sympathetic to shoeworkers; see letter, *LRec*, Feb. 22, 1873. The KOSC excluded the Boston press from all its meetings and was subsequently blamed in newspaper accounts for the order system, seasonality in the industry, and the development of country shops; *BT*, *BJ*, July 29, 1872; *BH*, *BG*, July 30, 1872.

142. *LR*, Feb. 1, 1873.

143. *LRec*, Mar. 1, 1873. This would become the Crispin strike strategy in 1875 and 1876.

144. *LRec*, Jan. 25, Feb. 1, 1873. See also the estimates of cuts from 25 to 41 percent in MBLS, *Fourth Annual Report*, as quoted in the *LR*, May 4, 1873.

Chapter Seven: Hard Times and Equal Rights

1. *LR*, Feb. 22, Mar. 26, Apr. 23, May 17, June 25, 1873.

2. *SLR* as quoted in *LR*, Nov. 15, 1873. See also *LR*, Sept. 3, 6, 10, Oct. 23, Dec. 6, 1873.

3. *LR*, Jan. 14, 1874.

4. *LR*, Mar. 28, 1877; *SLR*, Sept. 28, 1882, p. 511.

5. Even before the panic, the *Fourth Annual Report* of the MBLS, pp. 304–6, as quoted in *LR*, May 4, 1873, cited widespread discontent. For the City Mission report, see *LR*, Oct. 1, 1873.

6. *LR*, Oct. 14, 1876; Dec. 15, 1877.

7. *LR*, Jan. 20, 23, 25, Feb. 3, 1875. In 1876 a local KOSC board of arbitration negotiated another general wage scale; *LR*, Jan. 15, 16, 1876. On the patterns of seasonal and cyclical unemployment in Massachusetts, 1870–1920, see Alexander Keyssar, *Out of Work: The First Century of Unemployment in Massachusetts* (Cambridge: Cambridge University Press, 1986), pp. 39–76.

8. "Letter from Howard," *LRec*, Mar. 1, 1873. The skilled hand-loom carpet weavers of Philadelphia were also targeting advance orders as a protest strategy in the 1870s; see Susan Levine, *Labor's True Woman*, pp. 35–36.

9. For the successful use of arbitration by the Crispins, see *LR*, Jan. 27, 1875; Jan. 15, 19, Apr. 12, 1876. Ninety disputes were settled by arbitration in 1876; *LR*, Feb. 21, 1877.

10. *LR*, Feb. 6, 1875. In the first issue of the *Vind*, Editor Scully argued that Crispins must not only advance their own interests by collective action, but avoid injury to their employers' interests; *Vind*, Dec. 23, 1876.

11. *SLR*, Apr. 15, 1875, p. 323; June 21, 1877, p. 797.

12. *LRec*, May 20, 1876.

13. *Vind*, Feb. 23, 1878. The first issue on December 23, 1876, revealed the paper's politics and purposes. For the general struggle to defend the functional autonomy of craftsmen, see David Montgomery, "Workers' Control of Machine Productivity in the Nineteenth Century," *Labor History* 17 (Fall 1976), pp. 485–509.

14. *LR*, Feb. 13, 1875; June 25, 1873; *SLR*, Apr. 5, 1875, p. 337; *Vind*, Nov. 3, 1877, see "Americus" letter. *LRec*, Feb. 5, 1876. The divisions of labor included lining, pressing, closing, baring heels, back staying, staying "lappels," closing on, cording, gumming, stretching round, trimming, closing, foxing, rubbing seams, stitching and cutting buttonholes, sewing on buttons, cording buttonholes, vamping, half-lining, and eyeletting.

15. *SLR*, Aug. 20, 1877, p. 305.

16. *LR*, Jan. 12, 19, 1876.

17. *LR*, Jan. 26, 1876.

18. The use of a remonstrance or formal statement of grievances by the stitchers reflected their Yankee Protestant culture and their educational background, which apparently included British constitutional history.

19. *LRec*, Feb. 5, 12, 1876.

20. *LRec*, Feb. 5, Apr. 15, 29, 1876; *LR*, Apr. 12, 1876. On DOSC social occasions, see *LRec*, Mar. 4, May 6, 1876.

21. *Vind*, Jan. 13, Feb. 3, 1877. This appeal to maintain the sexual division of labor in industry probably applied more to textiles and printing than to the arrangements of boot and shoe production except for lasting.

22. *BG*, Dec. 31, 1877; *BH*, Jan. 15, 18, 1878; *LI*, Dec. 28, 1877.

23. The *LT* supported the smaller manufacturers' position on wage competition; Jan. 5, 12, 19, 1878. In contrast, cf. *LR*, Jan. 2, 23, 29, 1878.

24. *LI*, Jan. 10, 17, 1878. For reminiscences of the 1878 strike, see the interview with shoeworker #6 in *BH*, Aug. 19, 1888.

25. *LI*, Dec. 29, 31, 1877; Jan. 9, 12, 18, Feb. 11, 1878.

26. *LI*, Jan. 14, Feb. 11, 1878; *BH*, Jan. 19, 1878.

27. *LI*, Feb. 14, 20, 23, 1878; *Vind*, Feb. 16, 23, 1878.

28. MBLS, *Tenth Annual Report*, pp. 99–150. Sections of the report on the shoe industry were reprinted in the *SLR*, Mar. 27, 1879, pp. 483–85. Deleted from the reprint was the testimony of advocates of taxes on machines and critics of the wealth of shoe manufacturers and the poverty of shoeworkers.

29. MBLS, *Tenth Annual Report*, p. 122.

30. Ibid., pp. 148–49.

31. *Vind*, Apr. 5, Nov. 1, 1879. Scully was hereby abandoning what Alan Dawley regarded as the radical core of the preindustrial equal rights tradition, which opposed competition. Dawley saw cooperative production rather than arbitration as the best way to avoid the rigors of supply and demand; *Class and Community*, pp. 66, 198.

32. *Cooper's New Monthly*, Apr. 1874, p. 16, lists the last slate of national DOSC officers, including Miss Delia McKay of Stoneham as First Grand Directeress and Mrs. Eliza Rogers of Lynn as Treasurer. Other officers were Miss Mary Weaver (no residence); Miss Katie Stanton, Louisville, Ky.; Miss Maggie Sotspike, Rochester, N.Y.; and Miss Esther Belt, Baltimore, Md. See also the *WAd*, Jan. 9, 21, Feb. 3, 1872, for DOSC activities. No record has survived of the last DOSC convention at Utica, N.Y., in 1872. On the 1878 strike, see *LI*, Jan. 18, 23, 30, 1878; *Vind*, Jan. 5, 26, 1878; *LRec*, Feb. 2, Mar. 9, 23, 30, 1878. For the

DOSC activities as Liberty Lodge and firings, see *LRec*, May 18, Sept. 7, Dec. 28, 1878, Jan. 11, 1879.

33. The circumstances of the life of Americus were deduced from the contents of her nearly fifty letters published in the *LRec* and the *Vind* between 1874 and 1881. Others may have appeared in the *LRec* between March 1879 and April 1880, the issues of which are lost. Her work history and the absence of references to a husband suggest that she was widowed some time in 1875. Her native town may have been Centre Harbor, N.H., where her brother lived. No clue to her identity has survived, although it is likely that most Lynn citizens in the 1870s knew who she was. "Americus" was a typographical error for the pen name that she had originally chosen, "Amicus"; *LRec*, Feb. 17, 1875.

34. *LRec*, Jan. 31, 1874. Emma Lane's last letter to the *LRec* appeared on Nov. 29, 1873.

35. *LRec*, Feb. 14, 28, 1874. For perceptions of class divisions, see a letter from "Galata," *LRec*, Dec. 18, 1875.

36. *LRec*, Mar. 7, 1874.

37. *LRec*, Apr. 4, 1874.

38. *LRec*, May 16, 1874. See also letters from "S.M.E." and "Ye Olden Times," *LRec*, Mar. 7, May 9, 1874.

39. *Vind*, Feb. 24, Mar. 3, 1877.

40. *LRec*, Feb. 12, 1876.

41. *LRec*, June 10, July 13, 1876.

42. *LRec*, Aug. 12, 1876.

43. *Vind*, June 2, 1877.

44. *Vind*, Aug. 4, 1877. See also *Vind*, Dec. 15, 1877; Mar. 28, 30, May 4, June 8, Aug. 3, 1878.

45. *LRec*, letter from "Egg Rock," Nov. 11, 1876; letter from "Americus," Dec. 2, 1876.

46. *LR*, Apr. 11, 1874; Oct. 16, 1875.

47. Although the majority of stitchers were native-born women, 10 percent of the resident daughters in 1870 who lived in male-headed families were Irish-born, as were 13 percent in 1880. Nearly half of all of the fathers of these resident daughters were Irish natives. The growth in the number of Irish immigrant women employed in Lynn between 1870 and 1880 appears slight, and the number of second generation Irish stitchers remained steady between 1870 and 1880.

48. See Appendix B.

49. Massachusetts, *Manufactures and Occupations*, vol. 2 of *Census of Massachusetts, 1875* (Boston, 1877). MBLS, *Sixth Annual Report*, pp. 240–53, has information on the household budgets of forty-three families of shoeworkers in Lynn and reported twelve female wage earners

who were presumably shoeworkers, ten unmarried daughters between the ages of thirteen and seventeen, one married homeworker, and a wife who worked in a factory. For the persistence of homework in Essex County shoe towns, see chapter 8.

50. Letter from "A Stitcher" and editorial, *LRec*, Feb. 1, 1879.

51. *LRec*, Feb. 8, 1879. In the only detailed account of a social occasion sponsored by the DOSC, the names of married stitchers (although some of them might have been widows) dominated the list of participants; *LRec*, May 6, 1876.

52. *LRec*, Feb. 8, 1879.

53. *LRec*, Feb. 15, 1879.

54. Ibid. A perusal of the hundreds of members of the Lynn LPU based on the dues books, 1869–78, Baker Library, Harvard University, yielded the names of only two women. Although the *LI*, Jan. 10, 1878, cited the names of two "girl lasters," their names did not appear in the annual dues book.

55. *LRec*, Feb. 22, 1879.

56. *Vind*, May 19, 1877.

57. *LRec*, Feb. 22, 1879.

58. *LRec*, Mar. 1, 1879.

59. *LRec*, Mar. 8, 1879.

60. Ibid.

61. MBLS, *Sixth Annual Report*, pp. 240–53. For a further analysis of women shoeworkers in the 1880 Lynn census, see Appendix B.

62. *LRec*, Sept. 22, 1877. For similar ideological divisions between native-born American women with a commitment to gender consciousness and equalitarianism and immigrant women with a devotion to class consciousness and to women's traditional role in family life, see Buhle, *Women and American Socialism*. For a discussion of the meaning of womanhood among working-class women and the development of new forms of consciousness in the late nineteenth century, see Eisenstein, *Give Us Bread*.

63. *LRec*, June 26, 1880.

64. *LRec*, July 10, 1880.

65. *LRec*, July 24, 1880.

66. *LRec*, Aug. 14, 1880.

67. *LRec*, Aug. 28, 1880.

68. *LRec*, Sept. 11, 1880.

69. *LRec*, Sept. 25, 1880.

70. *LRec*, Oct. 23, 1880.

71. *LRec*, Oct. 30, 1880.

72. *LRec*, Nov. 13, 1880. Americus wrote one final letter to the *LRec*, Feb. 5, 1881, concerning woman's weaknesses.

73. *LRec*, Jan. 15, 1881. By 1885 some elevators were in general use by employees and visitors to shoe factories; *SLR*, Sept. 17, 1885, p. 474.

74. "Haverhill—Fall of 1880," *SLR*, May 20, 1880; "Haverhill—Spring, 1881," *SLR*, Nov. 4, 1880.

75. *SLR*, May 13, 1880, pp. 759–60; Apr. 21, 1881, p. 654; Aug. 4, 1881, p. 179; Sept. 28, 1882, pp. 511–12.

76. *SLR*, Sept. 28, 1882, pp. 511–12; Mar. 29, 1883, p. 508; Sept. 20, 1883, pp. 469–70.

77. *SLR*, Feb. 23, 1882, pp. 295–96.

Chapter Eight: New England Shoeworkers in the Knights of Labor

1. *SLR*, vol. 34, Sept. 28, 1882, p. 511.

2. Eisenstein, *Give Us Bread*, pp. 3–5.

3. *LRec*, June 12, 1875. For the concept of respectability in working-class life in late nineteenth-century London, see Ellen Ross, " 'Not the Sort that Would Sit on the Doorstep': Respectability in Pre–World War I London Neighborhoods," *International Labor and Working Class History* 27 (Spring 1985), pp. 39–59.

4. *LI*, Sept. 3, 1880.

5. Ibid.

6. This information is based on data from Appendix B.

7. "Letter from Lynn," *SLRev*, Sept. 20, 1888, p. 306. On the Haverhill stitchers, *BSR*, Nov. 28, 1888, p. 61. For generational and cultural divisions within the male work force, see the interviews with shoemakers #2, 4, and 5 in the *BH*, Aug. 19, 1888, p. 18. For another example of the sense of ladyhood as conveying status to women workers in the late nineteenth century, see Cindy S. Aron, "To Barter Their Souls for Gold: Female Clerks in Federal Government Offices, 1862–1890," *The Journal of American History* 67 (Mar. 1981), pp. 835–53. Also see attempts by the Working Girls Club movement, 1884–1914, to elevate the term "working girl" to social respectability, in Joanne Reitano, "Working Girls Unite," *American Quarterly* 36 (1984), pp. 112–34.

8. Andrews and Bliss (*History of Women*, p. 129) give the dates of the organization of all the female assemblies in the Knights. On the Daughters of Labor, *LI*, Dec. 29, 1885; also *LI*, July 22, 23, 1886; *KL* (Lynn), June 25, Oct. 17, Nov. 12, 1885; *SLR*, vol. 40, Oct. 8, 1885, pp. 620–21.

9. *SLR*, vol. 34, Sept. 28, 1882, pp. 511–12; vol. 35, Mar. 29, 1883,

p. 508; Sept. 20, 1883, pp. 469–70; vol. 39, June 11, 1885, p. 1003.

10. See interview with shoemaker #8 in *BH*, Aug. 19, 1888. As a member of the LPU, this laster estimated that "lady members" had dropped from about 100 to twenty, "owing to the almost complete disuse of serge, the material they work on."

11. Howard Mudge Newhall, "A Pair of Shoes," *Harpers' New Monthly Magazine*, Jan. 1885, pp. 280–82.

12. *SLR*, vol. 46, Feb. 28, 1889, pp. 552–58. On the two-needle vamping capability, *BSR*, Nov. 28, 1888, p. 59. On the technical development of the Singer and the Reece buttonhole machines, see McDermott, *History of the Shoe and Leather Industry*, pp. 135–38.

13. "A New Button-Hole and Machine for Making It," *SLR*, vol. 43, Apr. 7, 1887.

14. Commonwealth of Massachusetts, *Census of Massachusetts, 1885*, vol. 2, *Manufacturing, Fisheries and Commerce*, (Boston, 1888), p. 213. On Haverhill, *HG*, Feb. 20, 1895.

15. *BSR*, Oct. 1, 1890, p. 83.

16. Diary of Irena M. Knowlton, (1879–86). I would like to thank Carol Lasser for drawing my attention to the Knowlton diary.

17. *BSR*, Nov. 5, 1890, p. 79.

18. *LI*, July 24, 25, 1884; *KL*, July 18, 1885.

19. *BSR*, Sept. 5, 1888, p. 21.

20. *LI*, July 14, 1884; *LR*, July 18, 1884.

21. *LI*, July 25, 26, Aug. 1, 1884.

22. *LT*, Aug. 1, 1884; see also *LI*, Aug. 1, 2, 1884.

23. *LI*, Aug. 5, 15, 16, 19, 22, 23, 26, 1884. This material contradicts Alan Dawley's assertion that after the demonstration of the political power of the Workingmen's party in 1878, the municipal police were not used against workers in a labor dispute "for a dozen years"; *Class and Community*, pp. 202, 226.

24. *LI*, Nov. 19, 1884.

25. *LI*, Nov. 16, 20, 21, 1884.

26. *LI*, Nov. 26, 1884.

27. *KL*, Nov. 12, 1885.

28. *KL*, Jan. 2, 1886.

29. Ibid.; see Dawley, *Class and Community*, p. 205.

30. *LI*, Dec. 10, 1885. The political system in Lynn between 1878 and 1894 operated as a coalition of middle-class and working-class interests; Dawley, *Class and Community*, p. 215. Given this alliance, there seemed to be little need to enfranchise either middle-class or working-class women. Brian Palmer described the position of the Knights in Hamil-

ton as one of modern chivalry: manly stances taken for moral purity and in defense of the rights of others (p. 182), rather than in the pursuit of equal rights (p. 197).

31. *KL*, July 11, 1885.

32. *KL*, Oct. 3, 1885.

33. *LI*, Dec. 4, 9, 29, 1885; *KL*, Feb. 6, 1886; *SLR*, vol. 40, Dec. 31, 1885, p. 1126; *LSU*, Jan. 2, 1886.

34. *KL*, Dec. 12, 1885.

35. *KL*, Dec. 19, 1885.

36. *L* (Knights of Labor, D.A. 30, Haverhill), Dec. 19, 1885.

37. *KL*, Apr. 10, May 15, 1886; *LI*, Dec. 29, 1885; Mar. 29, 1886. Philip Foner argued that Lynn represented the largest center of women members in the Knights (*Women* 1, p. 189), but the Ladies' Stitching Association was not an assembly but an independent organization. The Yonkers carpet weavers' assembly, which had 2,500 members (Foner, p. 195), was probably the largest. Dawley also misinterpreted the independent character of the Association; *Class and Community*, p. 189. For the Knights of Labor views on true womanhood, see Susan Levine, "Labor's True Woman: Domesticity and Equal Rights in the Knights of Labor," *Journal of American History* 70 (Sept. 1983), pp. 323–39.

38. Andrews and Bliss, *History of Women*, pp. 129–30; Jonathan Garlock, compiler, *Guide to the Local Assemblies of the Knights of Labor*, (Westport, Conn.: Greenwood Press, 1982), pp. 188–89.

39. *L*, Nov. 5, 1884; Jan. 23, 1886. Other legislative goals included an end to convict labor used in manufacturing and an employers' liability law.

40. *L*, Aug. 4, 1884.

41. *L*, Feb. 20, 1885; Mar. 20, 1886; "Haverhill, Mass.," *SLR*, vol. 41, Aug. 13, 1885; *HB*, Jan. 27, 1885; *LI*, Mar. 11, 1886; *L*, Feb. 6, 20, 1886.

42. *SLR*, vol. 40. Sept. 17, 1885, p. 474. See the extended discussion of the country shop system from the manufacturers' point of view in *BSR*, Aug. 29, 1888, pp. 21–25; Sept. 5, 1888, pp. 21–24; Sept. 12, 1888, pp. 21–27.

43. *SLR*, vol. 40, Sept. 17, 1885, p. 474.

44. *SLR*, vol. 41, Nov. 26, 1885, p. 920; vol. 41, Mar. 18, 1886, p. 467; vol. 43, Mar. 3, 1887, p. 407; June 16, 1887, p. 1182.

45. *KL*, Feb. 6, 20, 27, June 5, 1886; *LSU*, Jan. 9, 23, Feb. 6, 1886; *LI*, Mar. 9, 29, 1886. On Philadelphia, see Galster, *Labor Movement*, pp. 54–55.

46. *LI*, Dec. 4, 9, 1885; *LSU*, Jan. 2, 9, 16, 1886.

47. For a view of the politics of the Knights of Labor, which does not, however, address the country shop system or the regional strategy of the Lynn Knights who helped to organize the shoeworkers of Rochester, N.H., see Leon Fink, *Workingmen's Democracy*, pp. 38–65. *HB*, July 3, 1886; Apr. 2, 1887. See also *SLR*, vol. 41, Apr. 8, 1886, p. 603; *LSU*, Jan. 9, 1886. In December 1882 the Lynn lasters had organized their counterparts in Haverhill who worked in the Chick Brothers factory, not as the customary five-man team in Haverhill, but as string teams, which separated the lasters from the makers. The Lynn lasters also organized the lasters in Stoneham a few months later. *SLR*, vol. 35, Apr. 5, 1883, p. 552.

47. *LSU*, Jan. 9, 1886.

48. *LSU*, Jan. 2, 9, Feb. 20, 1886; *KL*, Feb. 27, 1886; *LI*, Mar. 29, 1886. The stitchers were encouraged to appeal their grievances in the interim.

49. *KL*, Mar. 27, 1886; *SLRev*, Nov. 15, 1888, p. 27.

50. *KL*, Feb. 27, June 5, 1886; *LSU*, Feb. 6, 1886; *LI*, Mar. 9, 1886.

51. *KL*, Mar. 6, 1886.

52. *L*, Jan. 23, Feb. 20, 27, 1886.

53. *LSU*, Mar. 27, 1886. See also Feb. 13, 27, Mar. 13, 20, 1886.

54. *L*, Jan. 23, June 26, July 17, 1886; *Worcester Gazette*, July 16, 22, 1886; *BH*, July 21, 1886. The vote was estimated at 5 to 1 against the trade district.

55. *L*, Apr. 10, Mar. 20, 1886. In Hamilton, Ontario, the KOL also successfully bridged the gap of skilled and unskilled workers by organizing into a general body for common ends; see Palmer, *Culture in Conflict*, p. 163. On opposition to the trade district, *LI*, July 22, 23, 1886; *L*, Mar. 20, 1886.

56. *L*, June 26, 1886.

57. *KL*, Mar. 6, 1886.

58. *LSU*, Apr. 3, 1886. For a configuration similar to that in D.A. 30, see the Knights of Labor in Rhode Island, which rested on a coalition of craft unions and textile mill operatives; Paul Buhle, "The Knights of Labor in Rhode Island," *Radical History Review* 27 (Spring 1978), pp. 50–56, 65.

59. *L*, Sept. 18, 1886. Despite his initial opposition to the trade district, Frank Foster resigned over the issue in December 1886, and later became the editor of the *Labor Leader*, of the Massachusetts AFL.

60. *L*, Nov. 27, 1886. On the Richmond convention, see Gerald Grob, *Workers and Utopia* (Chicago: Quadrangle Books, 1961), pp. 115–16.

61. *SLR*, vol. 43, June 16, 1887, p. 1182. Women carpet weavers in the KOL assemblies in Yonkers and Philadelphia controlled their strike

committees and sat on the arbitration committees that negotiated with the manufacturers; see Susan Levine, *Labor's True Woman*, pp. 68–69, 84.

62. *HB*, Mar. 13, 29, 1886. Lizzie Shute, as a popular leader among the Haverhill stitchers, probably led the protest against Barrows; *HB*, Dec. 24, 1885.

63. The lack of local political power and direct participation in the governance of district organizations or on the board of arbitration suggested that for Lynn stitchers, in contrast to those in D.A. 30, equal rights remained elusive. *General Proceedings of the Knights of Labor Convention*, Richmond, Va., Oct. 1886, pp. 14–16.

64. Foner, *Women* 1, pp. 185–87.

65. Andrews and Bliss, *History of Women*, p. 129.

66. Foner, *Women* 1, p. 189; Andrews and Bliss, *History of Women*, p. 124.

67. Knights of Labor, *Proceedings*, Philadelphia, 1884, pp. 721–22.

68. Ibid., p. 722. On Skeffington, see Galster, *Labor Movement*, pp. 48–53. Skeffington's experiences organizing women shoeworkers in Philadelphia made him a staunch advocate of woman suffrage; Andrews and Bliss, *History of Women*, pp. 125–26. The only other female delegate at the Philadelphia convention in 1884, Miss Louisa Eaton, a stitcher who worked in Lynn, took no part in the published debate.

69. Knights of Labor, *Proceedings*, Hamilton, 1885, pp. 152, 167; Foner, *Women* 1, p. 198; Andrews and Bliss, *History of Women*, pp. 126–27.

70. Knights of Labor, *Proceedings*, Cleveland, 1886, pp. 27, 48. Levine's choice of Leonora Barry and Elizabeth Rodgers to exemplify the dual nature of the Knights' concept of true womanhood, equal rights, and domesticity (*Labor's True Woman*, pp. 105, 136–41) shifts the focus of her study away from the carpet weavers who, like the shoeworkers of Massachusetts and Philadelphia, advocated autonomous women's assemblies and who had been the shoeworkers' strong allies in Philadelphia (pp. 70–71). Why the carpet weavers did not attend the Richmond convention is not clear. In Levine's analysis, the Knights permitted women to provide a critique of capitalism based on "hearth and home" values, but encouraged women to regard their work as temporary (like Leonora Barry, a widow who supported herself and her children but who remarried after a short period as an organizer) or supplemental to family income (like Elizabeth Rodgers, who cared for a large family and took in boarders). Levine's concept of "labor feminism" in the Knights involved the equal participation of men and women in political action but did not challenge the domestic sphere as natural for women (pp. 121–26). Paul Buhle disagreed with Levine on the restricted role of women in

the Knights. In Rhode Island the KOL recognized the permanence of women's employment as textile workers and supported both their labor activities and woman suffrage ("Knights of Labor," pp. 58–59).

71. Knights of Labor, *Proceedings*, Richmond, 1886, pp. 163–64, 287–88.

72. Ibid., p. 287; Foner, *Women* 1, pp. 200–201.

73. Andrews and Bliss, *History of Women*, p. 128. Barry's first report in 1887 was signed by Mary Hanafin as president of the Committee on Woman's Work, although she was absent from the convention.

74. Ibid., pp. 115–23, especially p. 116; Wertheimer, *We Were There*, pp. 186–91; Rosalyn Baxandall, Linda Gordon, and Susan Reverby, *America's Working Women: A Documentary History* (New York: Vintage Books, 1976), pp. 120–25; James J. Kenneally, *Women and American Trade Unions* (St. Albans, Vt.: Eden Press, 1978), pp. 11–17. Foner's *Women* 1 provides evidence on the 1886 strike of the Troy collar workers, pp. 207–10, on earlier activities in Chicago, pp. 193–94, and on the Yonkers carpet weavers' strike of 1885, pp. 195–97. Using the correspondence files in the Terence V. Powderly papers, Foner emphasized the positive side of Barry's work as an organizer and lecturer, especially her advocacy of local beneficial and protective associations for women workers; pp. 119, 202–4. These associations seemed, however, to replace the female assemblies.

75. There is nothing in Barry's reports that indicated that as general investigator she had any continued contact with the women delegates to the KOL conventions who had worked to create the Department of Woman's Work.

76. Knights of Labor, "Report of the General Investigator," *Proceedings*, Minneapolis, 1887, p. 1582.

77. Knights of Labor, "Report of the General Investigator of Woman's Work and Wages," *Proceedings*, Philadelphia, 1888, pp. 2, 4–7, 9–10, 12, 14–15. Foner interpreted the figure of 10,000 women members in 1888 as "encouraging"; *Women* 1, p. 205. Hamilton, Ontario, was the site of the first women's KOL assembly in Canada. Led by shoeworker Miss Katie McVicar, Excelsior Assembly #3179 and a second #3040 represented a coalition of female cotton textile and shoe workers and claimed a total membership of about 225. However, when McVicar died in 1886, the assemblies went into decline; Palmer, *Culture in Conflict*, pp. 166–67.

78. Knights of Labor, "Report of the General Investigator," *Proceedings*, Philadelphia, 1888, p. 16. Foner argued that Barry retained her optimism until 1889 (*Women* 1, p. 205), and he regarded the movement for protective legislation as important only after 1904, when it was led by Florence Kelley of the National Consumers' League (p. 304). Kessler-

Harris, *Out to Work*, traced the origin of legislation that sought to protect women as a vulnerable sex to a shift in the attitudes of the woman suffrage movement in the 1880s (pp. 184–85), a group with whom Barry shared the contents of her reports to the General Assemblies and her concerns about women workers.

79. Knights of Labor, "Report of the General Instructor and Director of Woman's Work," *Proceedings*, The Sophia Smith Collection, Smith College, Northhampton, Mass., and the Wisconsin State Historical Society, Madison, 1889, pp. 1, 5.

80. Ibid., pp. 2, 6.

81. On the Brockton convention and the Powderly visit, *BH*, June 7–12, 1887; *BG*, June 13, 1887; *LI*, Mar. 18, July 22, 1887; July 13, 1887. Both of the Knights of Labor newspapers had ceased publication by the summer of 1887.

82. The *BH*, Aug. 19, 1888, published an extensive series of interviews about the country shop system with manufacturers and shoeworkers in Lynn. None were with women workers.

83. Ibid.

84. Ibid.

85. Statement by Allen B. Stevens, Master Workman, KOL National Trade District, *BSR*, Apr. 22, 1891; statements by shoeworkers, *BH*, Aug. 19, 1888.

86. *BH*, Aug. 19, 1888.

87. Hearings, Samuel Crossman vs. Button-hole Makers at Lynn and Beverly, Application #17, State Board of Arbitration, Nov. 17, 1887; *LR*, Nov. 18, 1887. Application #19, J. H. Winchell and Co. and Townshend P. George with J. Merrill Ordway, Nov. 29, 1887, Massachusetts State Board of Arbitration Files; *HG*, Dec. 2, 1887; *SLR*, vol. 44, Dec. 15, 1887, p. 1219.

88. *SLRev*, July 5, 1888, p. 30; *LB*, Apr. 13, 14, 16, 17, 18, 1888; State Board of Arbitration, *Decision in the Matter of the Joint Application of Henry C. Mears, of Lynn, and His Employees* (Boston, 1888). The second hearing was covered by the local press.

89. *BSR*, July 18, 1888, p. 55.

90. *BH*, July 31, 1888.

91. Montgomery, "Workers' Control," pp. 485–509; David Bensman, *The Practice of Solidarity: American Hatfinishers in the Nineteenth Century* (Urbana: University of Illinois Press, 1985), pp. 68–88, 213–14. Paul Buhle's note that the female "burlars" in the Wanshuck textile mills near Providence developed a reputation for resisting encroachments on their autonomy strongly resembled Montgomery's description of workers' control ("Knights of Labor," p. 53).

92. Montgomery, "Workers' Control," p. 500.

93. *LB*, Apr. 17, 1888.

94. *BH*, July 22, 1888, reprinted in *BSR*, Aug. 8, 1888. See also a similar view of the stitchers' lives in "How Girls Work. . . . Shop Girls of Lynn Compared with Other Workwomen," *LB*, Feb. 16, 1886.

95. *BH*, July 22, 1888.

96. *BH*, July 29, 1888. After the interview the *Herald* editor sent another writer to Lynn to check the operatives' stories. The reporter found the manufacturers still insisting that the stitchers were the best paid among women industrial workers; *BH*, July 31, 1888.

97. *SLR*, vol. 44, Nov. 17, 1887, pp. 1019–20. For the debate over the best method of accounting labor costs, see vol. 44, Dec. 8, 1887, pp. 1171–72.

98. Typescript of the testimony of John F. Tobin to the Commission on Industrial Relations, Miscellaneous Documents, Safe of John F. Tobin and Collis Lovely, 1895–1912, BSWU papers.

99. *SLR*, vol. 46, Feb. 28, 1889, pp. 552–58.

100. Frederick Allen, *The Shoe Industry* (Boston: Vocational Bureau of Boston, 1916), pp. 60–61. On the lasters, see Yellowitz, "Skilled Workers," pp. 197–213.

101. *SLR*, vol. 44, Aug. 18, 1887, p. 337; *BSR*, May 29, 1889, p. 63.

102. *HG*, Feb. 26, 1892.

103. For the Brockton convention that formed the national trade district, *BH*, June 7, 1887. On Skeffington, see Galster, *Labor Movement*, pp. 48–51, and Cumbler, *Working Class Community*, pp. 81–82. Powderly came to Lynn in June 1887 to try unsuccessfully to appeal for support over the heads of the local Lynn leaders; *LI*, June 13, 1887.

104. *LI*, Sept. 5, 11, 1889.

105. *HB*, Sept. 17, 1889; *BSR*, Nov. 27, 1889, pp. 73, 75.

106. *BH*, June 10, 1887.

107. *HB*, Feb. 8, 1890.

108. *BSR*, Jan. 15, 1890, p. 69.

109. *HB*, Apr. 20, 1889.

110. *BSR*, Jan. 21, 1891, p. 85. See the opening of the Chick Brothers, W. W. Spaulding, and Perley Stone factories on River Street and the Knipe Brothers factory in the Ward Hill district; *BSR*, Aug. 20, 1890, p. 85; Apr. 8, 1891, p. 97. Although the *BSR* on Aug. 22, 1888, p. 45 noted the presence of an electric light plant in Haverhill, many of these new factories were equipped with the older technologies of steam power and gaslight.

111. *BSR*, Apr. 15, 1891, p. 79; Feb. 17, 1892, p. 89.

112. *BH*, Jan. 11, 1890.

113. *HG*, Jan. 11, 1890.

114. *HG*, Jan. 17, 1892.

115. *HG*, Jan. 14, 18, 1890.

116. *HG*, Jan. 13, 14, 17, 18, Feb. 5, 6, 1890; *LB*, Jan. 14, 1890.

117. *HG*, Jan. 29, 31, Apr. 28, May 1, 6, 1890; *HB*, Feb. 8, May 2, 1890; *LB*, Jan. 3, 1890; see statement by Allen Stevens of Lynn in *BSR*, Apr. 22, 1891, p. 71.

118. *LB*, May 9, 13, 15, 16, 1890; *HG*, May 9, 16, 1890. See also State Board of Arbitration hearings (which the KOL refused to attend), application #90, B. G. Patten Co. of Lynn vs. Cutting and Stitching Departments, Hearing, May 9–15, 1890.

119. Some of the Haverhill cutters stuck by the BSWIU, but by December all cutters were organized by the KOL; *HB*, Apr. 3, 1891; *HG*, Dec. 2, 1891. A BSWIU offer to amalgamate was dismissed by the Knights; *HG*, June 2, 1891. See also *HG*, Mar. 10, 1891; *HB*, Aug. 15, 1890. Many stitchers in Haverhill joined local #4 BSWIU, while the Lynn stitchers stayed in the Lady Stitchers' Assembly.

120. Cumbler emphasized the impact of the local rotation of resident workers on the job during the season and the small size of the shoe shops, which enabled shoeworkers in the Knights of Labor period to contact and communicate readily with each other—activities that were carried over into social contacts in cafes, lunchrooms, and union halls; *Working Class Community*, pp. 56–59.

Chapter Nine: Militancy and Disintegration, 1892–1910

1. *HG*, May 10, 20, 1891; *BG*, Jan. 9, 1895; *LPS*, Jan. 5, 1895.

2. Chick Brothers found that their Jewish workers stubbornly refused to labor on their Sabbath and fired them all in October 1892. *HB*, Dec. 23, 30, 1892; *HG*, Oct. 7, 1893.

3. *BSR*, Feb. 14, 1894, p. 97; Mar. 28, 1894, pp. 99, 101; Aug. 1, 1894, p. 79; Apr. 17, 1895, p. 111; May 8, 1895, p. 115; May 29, 1895, p. 83; June 12, 1895, p. 109; Sept. 18, 1895, p. 95. On business failures, *BSR*, Aug. 9, 1893, p. 71. On the production of medium-grade shoes, *BSR*, Mar. 1, 1893, p. 75; Mar. 15, 1893, p. 75.

4. *BSR*, Oct. 11, 1893, p. 73. On the collapse of demand, *BSR*, Sept. 27, 1893, p. 71; on the Goodyear turn machine, Mar. 29, 1893, p. 103; and Nov. 17, 1897, p. 107.

5. *BSR*, Aug. 14, 1895, p. 93; July 17, 1895, p. 62.

6. *BSR*, Feb. 14, 1894, p. 97; Mar. 28, 1894, pp. 99, 101; Aug. 1, 1894, p. 77.

7. *BSR*, Feb. 8, 1894, p. 85; Jan. 31, 1894, p. 73; Feb. 7, 1894, p. 73; *LI*, Jan. 30, Feb. 1, 1894.

8. Part of this chapter is based on "The Union of Sex and Craft in

the Haverhill Shoe Strike of 1895," *Labor History* 20 (Summer 1979), pp. 352–75. *Census of the Commonwealth of Massachusetts, 1895,* vol. 1 (Boston, 1896), p. 252, cites a total of 8,289 shoeworkers. The 1895 state census examined families by size and sex composition, but warned that family statistics, especially for women, would be distorted by the phenomenon of lodging houses in industrial cities (p. 455). For Haverhill (pp. 394–95), the state census listed 930 females living in lodging houses or rooms. However, many of the 2,500 female shoeworkers in the city lived with private families as boarders and were listed as family members in the state census. No manuscript state census for 1895 has survived. On boarding as an urban phenomenon of middle-class families, see John Modell and Tamara Hareven, "Urbanization and the Malleable Household: An Examination of Boarding and Lodging in American Families," *Journal of Marriage and the Family* 35 (1973), pp. 467–92. On lodging in shoe cities in Massachusetts, see WEIU, *The Boot and Shoe Industry in Massachusetts as a Vocation for Women,* vol. 6 of Bureau of Labor Statistics, *Studies in Economic Relations of Women,* (Washington, 1915), pp. 17–25.

9. *HB,* Dec. 21, 1894; *LPS,* Jan. 19, 1895.

10. *LPS,* Jan. 19, 1895; letter from L. C. Bell, stitcher, Jan. 23, 1895. In one instance, five women rented an apartment, four worked in the shops, and the fifth cooked, cleaned, and laundered for the others.

11. *LPS,* Jan. 5, 7, 10, 21, 1895; *BA,* Jan. 5, 1895; *BG,* Jan. 2, 1895.

12. *HG,* Jan. 4, 1895; *BA,* Dec. 31, 1894. Martin Dodd's study of the disastrous shoe strike in Marlboro in 1898 indicated that the concentration of capital in the nine large factories in town meant that manufacturers could unite effectively against the strikers. The structure of the industry in Haverhill and Lynn featured competition for orders between the numerous smaller shops and large factories. Martin H. Dodd, "Marlboro, Massachusetts and the Shoeworkers' Strike of 1898–1899," *Labor History* 20 (Summer 1979), pp. 376–97. Horace Davis argued that a situation of moderate competition among employers was the most favorable condition for effective unionization in the shoe industry; *Shoes,* p. 205.

13. *LPS,* Dec. 24, 26, 27, 31, 1894; *HB,* Dec. 12, 14, 21, 26, 28, 1894. Foreign-born shoeworkers were featured in the strike parades. Translators were brought into Haverhill from Boston and Concord, N.H., to resolve problems among the various nationalities. Armenian, Italian, and Jewish workers brought their fellow nationals into line, but not without some difficulty; *BrEnt,* Jan. 4, 1895; *LPS,* Dec. 27, 1894; *BP,* Jan. 6, 1895; *BH,* Jan. 25, 31, 1895.

14. *LPS,* Dec. 27, 1894; Jan. 2, 1895. Hannah Duston was a seventeenth-century resident of Haverhill who escaped capture by Indians

and brought back their scalps to bear witness to her deeds. On Hannah Duston, see *Notable American Women, 1607–1950: A Biographical Dictionary*, ed. Edward T. James et al. (Cambridge: Harvard University Press, 1971), vol. 1, pp. 535–36; and Ulrich, *Good Wives*, pp. 167–72.

15. *LPS*, Jan. 2, 1895.

16. The three women had been touring New England in late 1894, speaking on Women and the Labor Movement when the strike began. On Willard, see Ruth Bordin, *Woman and Temperance: The Quest for Power and Liberty, 1873–1900* (Philadelphia: Temple University Press, 1981), pp. 105–8, 112–13. Willard had formed a close friendship with Lady Somerset that resulted in long absences from WCTU activities in the United States in the 1890s. Shortly after her January appearances in Haverhill and in Boston on behalf of the stitchers, she returned to England with Lady Somerset; pp. 140–42. Willard died in 1898, and the commitment of the WCTU to general issues of reform and social injustice died with her; pp. 151–55.

17. Frank Foster, the editor of the Massachusetts AFL paper *LL*, formally welcomed Willard as an ally of labor; *LL*, Jan. 5, 1895. Somerset and Hicks also addressed the crowds and emphasized the importance of organizing women workers. *Lawrence Daily American*, Jan. 2, 1895; *LPS*, Jan. 2, 1895.

18. *LAm*, Jan. 4, 1895.

19. *LPS*, Jan. 2, 1895. Vital Records, Commonwealth of Massachusetts, Death Record of Mary Caldwell Nason, Mar. 1, 1923; *Boston City Directory*, 1898–1923; *HB*, Apr. 23, 1891; Oct. 1, 1892.

20. *LPS*, Jan. 2, 1895.

21. Ibid.

22. Even the editor of the *BSR* condemned the contract shops; Jan. 2, 1895, pp. 66–67.

23. See an interview with an unidentified shoeworker who must have been James Carey, *BH*, Feb. 11, 1895. Carey lived cooperatively with his four sisters who worked in the shoe shops and with other relatives. He supported woman suffrage, raised funds for the stitchers' union, and encouraged the stitchers of Brockton to organize. *LPS*, Jan. 7, 23, 25, 1895; *BG*, Jan. 7, 18, 1895; *BrEnt*, Jan. 28, 1895. Carey declared himself a socialist in 1895; *LPS*, Jan. 23, 1895. On the meaning of socialism in Haverhill as politics and ideology, see John Laslett, *Labor and the Left: A Study of Socialist and Radical Influences in the American Labor Movement, 1881–1924* (New York: Basic Books, 1970), pp. 57–97; and Gary Gerstle, "Socialism in Haverhill, 1895–1900: A New Look" (Paper, 1977, in the author's possession).

24. *BA*, Dec. 31, 1894; Jan. 3, 4, 9, 1895; *BG*, Jan. 9, 1895; *BP*, Jan.

3, 17, 1895; *LI*, Jan. 7, Feb. 2, 11, 1895; *BH*, Jan. 2, 18, 1895; *BJ*, Jan. 2, 1895; *LPS*, Jan. 16, 25, Feb. 2, 1895. Shortly after the strikes at the River Street factories, the strike committee also struck two firms in the central industrial district over the firing of union stitchers; *LPS*, Jan. 5, 1895. *SLR* quoted in the *BA*, Jan. 26, 1895, indicated that the small producers in Haverhill were profiting from the strike. The depression concentrated the local shoe industry into larger units, and this tendency stimulated local opposition to the actions of the large factories by the smaller shop owners. They joined the shoeworkers, who possessed community power as voters and consumers, in much the same pattern as in the Paterson strike in 1877–78; see Herbert Gutman, "Class, Status and Community Power in Nineteenth Century American Industrial Cities—Paterson, New Jersey: A Case Study," in his *Work, Culture and Society in Industrializing America*, (New York: Vintage Press, 1977), pp. 234–60.

25. *LPS*, Jan. 12, 15, 1895; *BP*, Jan. 13, 1895; *BG*, Jan. 12, 14, 1895.

26. *LPS*, Jan. 16, 1895; *BH*, Jan. 17, 1895.

27. Mary Nason was not named in the injunction petition, but during the hearing, the court admitted evidence on her activities as an agent of the strike leadership. *LPS*, Jan. 12, 15, 16, 17, 22, 23, Mar. 4, 1895; *BP*, Jan. 13, 1895; *BG*, Jan. 11, 12, 14, 1895; *BH*, Jan. 17, 25, 1895; *LAm*, Jan. 31, 1895; *LI*, Jan. 18, 1895.

28. Mary Kenney O'Sullivan, typescript autobiography, c. 1930, Schlesinger Library, Radcliffe College, does not mention Nason specifically either in 1892 or in 1895; pp. 85–127, 139–200. Meredith Tax, *The Rising of the Women: Feminist Solidarity and Class Conflict, 1880–1917* (New York: Monthly Review Press, 1980), pp. 56–63. Kenney O'Sullivan remained interested in the new shoeworker federation that emerged from the 1895 strike; she knew its national leadership personally; and despite a pregnancy, she made her way to Marlboro in 1899 during a winter storm to support striking shoeworkers. On feminism and Irish women in the labor movement, see Mary J. Bularzik, "The Bonds of Belonging: Leonora O'Reilly and Social Reform," *Labor History* 24 (Winter 1984), pp. 60–83; and Hasia A. Diner, *Erin's Daughters: Irish Immigrant Women in the Nineteenth Century* (Baltimore: Johns Hopkins University Press, 1983), pp. 70–105.

29. Ames inspected Haverhill factories accompanied by Amy Hicks on January 6; *LPS*, Jan. 7, 1895. *LI*, Jan. 15, 1895; *BG*, Jan. 15, 21, 1895. T. T. Pomeroy was the agent for the BSWIU locals in Haverhill.

30. *LPS*, Jan. 16, 18, 25, 26, Feb. 19, 1895; *LI*, Jan. 26, Feb. 8, 12, 16, Mar. 12, 26, 1895; *BG*, Jan. 15, Feb. 11, 12, 16, 1895; *LAm*, Jan. 4, 1895; *BT*, Jan. 14, 16, 19, 26, 1895; *LL*, Feb. 16, 1895. The report of the Boston delegation was signed by many socially prominent Bostonians,

such as Charles Gordon Ames, Ida Mason, Francis B. Sears, Richard A. Dana, and the young Louis D. Brandeis; *LI*, Mar. 12, 1895. On Brandeis's connections with Lorin Deland, who was a member of the delegation to Haverhill, see Alpheus Thomas Mason, *Brandeis: A Free Man's Life* (New York: Viking Press, 1956), pp. 74–77. In 1902 Josephine Shaw Lowell published a collection of arbitration cases based on English, Belgian, and American experience to advocate the conciliation model to the American labor movement; *Industrial Arbitration and Conciliation* (New York, 1902).

31. *LPS*, Jan. 7, 1895; *BP*, Jan. 8, 1895; *BG*, Jan. 2, 7, 1895; *LAm*, Jan. 5, 1895; *LL*, Jan. 26, 1895.

32. *LPS*, Jan. 5, 17, 23, 24, 1895; *LI*, Jan. 5, 12, 18, 19, 26, Feb. 6, 1895; *BH*, Jan. 18, 1895; *BG*, Jan. 17, 21, 1895.

33. *LPS*, Jan. 27, 1895.

34. *BG*, Jan. 18, 1895. Mary Nason promoted this change and explained to the press during the strike that the use of the word "Lady" had been retained in deference to the aspirations of the younger stitchers. The last reference to "lady stitchers" in Haverhill appeared in the *HG*, Jan. 16, 1895.

35. *BG*, Jan. 18, 1895; *BH*, Jan. 21, 1895; *BAd*, Jan. 4, 1895; *LI*, Jan. 15, 1895. Among these leaders and activists were Margaret C. Barnett, the treasurer of the stitchers' local, a forty-six-year-old single woman who lived with her thirty-six-year-old single sister, who was also a stitcher; Mary Ford, a thirty-eight-year-old, unmarried, native-born daughter of Irish parents; and Mary P. Gardner, a twenty-nine-year-old single native of New Hampshire. All were listed as self-supporting heads of families in the 1900 census of population for Haverhill. In contrast, Leslie Tentler's general study of women industrial workers in major cities at the beginning of the twentieth century concluded that most wage-earning women were economically dependent, young, unmarried members of male-headed families who worked for supplemental income. She argued that working women who supported themselves and lived outside of family life experienced poverty and social isolation; their lives produced personal characteristics of timidity and passivity, and "older women were rarely assertive role models for younger workers." Tentler emphasized the negative qualities of boarding and rooming, in *Wage-Earning Women*, pp. 115–35.

36. *BG*, Jan. 17, 18, 1895; *BrEnt*, Jan. 17, 1895; *BH*, Jan. 21, 1895; *BP*, Jan. 3, 19, 1895; *LPS*, Jan. 25, 26, 28, 1895. On Martha Moore Avery, see Mari Jo Buhle, *Women and American Socialism*, pp. 73–74.

37. *HG*, Jan. 23, 1895.

38. Quote is from *BH*, Jan. 21, 1895. *LPS*, Jan. 10, 1895; *BA*, Jan. 4, 15, 1895; *BG*, Jan. 2, 3, 16, 17, 18, 21, Feb. 6, 8, 9, 1895; *BP*, Jan. 3,

1895. Frank Foster published his poem celebrating the striking Haverhill stitchers, "The Union Girls of Haverhill," in the Jan. 26 issue of *LL*.

39. *LPS*, Jan. 21, 1895; *BH*, Jan. 19, 22, 1895; *BJ*, Jan. 22, 1895; *LI*, Jan. 23, 1895.

40. *BJ*, Jan. 21, 22, 1895.

41. For the militant activities of the young Haverhill stitchers, *BG*, Jan. 13, Mar. 2, 1895.

42. *LPS*, Jan. 4, 12, 1895; *BG*, Jan. 14, Mar. 2, 11, 1895; *LI*, Mar. 8, 1895; *BH*, Mar. 11, 1895; *BP*, Feb. 20, 1895.

43. *BG*, Apr. 11, 1895; *BP*, Apr. 11, 1895. *Proceedings of the First Convention of the Boot and Shoe Workers' Union*, Boston, Apr. 10–13, 1895, pp. 12, 16, 19, 21. The four women delegates from Marlboro represented a KOL stitchers' assembly.

44. *BP*, Apr. 12, 1895; *BG*, Apr. 11, 1895; *HG*, Apr. 10, 12, 15, 1895; *Proceedings*, First Convention, BSWU, 1895, pp. 24–28, 36–37, 39–41, 45–47. In 1897 a woman was elected to the general executive board of the United Garment Workers of America; Andrews and Bliss, *History of Women*, p. 160. Henry F. Bedford's analysis of the 1895 strike and the April convention contained no discussion of the role of women; *Socialism and the Workers in Massachusetts, 1886–1912* (Amherst: University of Massachusetts Press, 1966), pp. 25–32. John Laslett's study of the left and the labor movement focused on the role of the Irish male shoeworkers, while acknowledging but not investigating the important part that Yankee men and women played in the union movement in the industry; *Labor and the Left*, pp. 57–97.

45. *Proceedings*, Second Convention, BSWU, Boston, June 15–20, 1896, p. 111; *BSR*, Mar. 25, 1896, p. 87.

46. BSWU, *Monthly Reports, 1895–1899*, June 1896, p. 4. Also see *Proceedings*, BSWU, 1896, pp. 13–14.

47. *Proceedings*, BSWU, 1896, pp. 1–8, 11–15. Laslett argued that Tobin's shift to more conservative union methods occurred later, in 1899; *Labor and the Left*, pp. 64–71.

48. *Proceedings*, BSWU, 1896, pp. 110–11. Nason voted at the convention with Tobin in support of associating the BSWU with the political activities of socialists; their differences seemed not to be overtly ideological; p. 92.

49. Early in the convention, Tobin appointed Nason to a new committee on organization, in effect preparing for her demotion from the executive committee; *Proceedings*, BSWU, 1896, pp. 65–66, 119; BSWU, *Monthly Reports*, Jan. 1897.

50. BSWU, *Monthly Reports*, Apr., May 1897. Nason's loss was also a loss to socialism in Haverhill and in the BSWU. Mari Jo Buhle found the

Haverhill socialist women's club patronized in 1900 as an auxiliary group and distanced from men's activities; *Women and American Socialism,* pp. 122–23.

51. *Proceedings,* Third Convention, BSWU, Boston, June 21–26, 1897, pp. 25–30, 71, 121. O'Sullivan, "Autobiography," pp. 173–75.

52. *Proceedings,* Fourth Convention, BSWU, Rochester, June 19–23, 1899, p. 4. For BSWU membership, see Davis, *Shoes,* p. 168.

53. *Proceedings,* BSWU, 1899, p. 43. Mary Anderson's autobiography included little on her involvement in the early years of the BSWU: *Women at Work: The Autobiography of Mary Anderson as Told by Mary N. Winslow* (Minneapolis: University of Minnesota Press, 1951). For Tobin's dismissal of women in the BSWU, see Belva Mary Herron, "The Progress of Labor Organization among Women," *University Studies,* vol. 1, no. 10 (May 1905), p. 15.

54. *Proceedings,* Fifth Convention, BSWU, Detroit, June 16–20, 1902, pp. 5–10, 15–16.

55. Ibid., p. 42.

56. See Appendix B.

57. "Social Statistics of Workingwomen," *Massachusetts Labor Bulletin* 18 (May 1901), pp. 29–49.

58. WEIU, *Boot and Shoe Industry,* pp. 59–63.

59. Mrs. John Van Vorst and Marie Van Vorst, *The Woman Who Toils; Being the Experiences of Two Ladies as Factory Girls* (New York, 1903), pp. 3–5, 171–214. The Vorsts distinguished between the needs of self-supporting women for industrial work at good wages and the half-supported girl, whom they proposed to channel into special training schools in industrial arts. On the general topic of factory investigation, see Alan F. Davis, *Spearheads for Reform: The Social Settlements and the Progressive Movement, 1890–1914* (New York, 1967).

60. Vorst and Vorst, p. 5.

61. Ibid., p. 188.

62. Ibid., pp. 188–214.

63. Ibid., p. 214.

64. *BSR,* Dec. 21, 1898, p. 95; May 19, 1897, p. 91; Feb. 23, 1898, pp. 97–99; Jan. 4, 1899, p. 95; Jan. 31, 1900, p. 95; Sept. 12, 1900, p. 99.

65. *BSR,* Jan. 3, 1900, pp. 95–97; Jan. 10, 1900, p. 95.

66. *BSR,* Sept. 19, 1900, p. 107.

67. *BSR,* May 3, 1897, p. 91; Feb. 7, 1900, pp. 95–96; Aug. 11, 1897, p. 95.

68. For the Eaton quote, *BSR,* July 3, 1901, p. 97. Also see Sept. 5, 1900, p. 101; Oct. 24, 1900, p. 111; Nov. 21, 1900, p. 115; Nov. 28,

1900, pp. 113–15; Sept. 11, 1901, p. 97. On the promotion of the union label by Edward Daley of the LPU in the 1890s and his troubles with the Lynn lasters, see Yellowitz, "Skilled Workers," pp. 197–213. On Tobin and the NCF, see Laslett, *Labor and the Left*, p. 79.

69. *BSR*, Sept. 25, 1901, p. 101.

70. *Shoe Workers' Journal*, Sept. 1902; figures cited from the 1900 Census of Manufacture. The report on the shoe industry for 1905 ranked the four top shoe cities by value of product as Brockton, Lynn, St. Louis, and Haverhill; U.S. Bureau of the Census, *Manufactures, 1905*, part 3, *Special Reports on Selected Industries* (Washington, D.C., 1908), p. 239.

71. Thomas L. Norton, *Trade Union Policies in the Massachusetts Shoe Industry* (New York: Columbia University Press, 1932), p. 188; Davis, *Shoes*, pp. 185–86.

72. *HG*, Jan. 23, 1903; *LI*, Jan. 12, 1903.

73. *HG*, Jan. 25, Feb. 1, 4, June 7, July 18, 1902.

74. On opposition from Illinois stitchers to high dues, see Foner, *Women* 1, p. 251; C. L. Baine, "Women in the Shoe Industry," *Life and Labor* 3 (June 1913), pp. 164–67; statement by John Tobin in Herron, "The Progress of Labor Organization," p. 15.

75. *HG*, Dec. 23, 1902.

76. Ibid.; *HG*, Jan. 13, 1903.

77. *HG*, Apr. 2, 1897; *BSR*, May 3, 1897, p. 91; Feb. 14, 1900, pp. 95, 97.

78. *LI*, Jan. 29, 30, 1903.

79. *LI*, Jan. 17, 22, 1903. For Jeanette Hamilton's statement, Jan. 27, 1903.

80. *LI*, Jan. 27, 1903.

81. *LI*, Feb. 10, 1903.

82. *LI*, Jan. 31, Mar. 11, 1903.

83. *LI*, Feb. 18, 1903. Two Nellie Cunninghams were located in the Lynn census of population for 1900. Both were native-born, single lodgers; one would have been twenty-six years old in 1903, the other thirty-three. One of them became the recording secretary of the Lady Stitchers' Assembly; *LI*, June 30, 1903.

84. For Tobin's animosity against an earlier dual union challenge from the Socialist Trades and Labor Alliance, see Laslett, *Labor and the Left*, pp. 67–70. The Central Labor Unions in both Lynn and Haverhill backed off from their support of the unpopular BSWU; *LI*, Jan. 10, 20, 30, 1903; *HG*, Jan. 23, 1903.

85. *LI*, Jan. 10, 12, 21, 22, 1903.

86. *LI*, Jan. 12, 20, 21, 23, 1903; *HG*, Jan. 16, 28, 1903. The superiority of the turned work in Haverhill rested on a craft technique involv-

ing a team of lasters and beaters-out. The "sewed seat" process used by Haverhill workers was superior to the "nailed seat" process used by other turn workmen and was "the most difficult process in shoemaking"; *HG*, Jan. 19, 1903.

87. *LI*, Jan. 1, Feb. 9, 14, 19, Mar. 6, 28, May 5, June 12, 1903. When Gompers came to Lynn, he was hissed at a public meeting of shoeworkers during which many women in the audience walked out; *LI*, May 4, 1903.

88. *LI*, Feb. 7, 9, 11, 19, Mar. 3, 1903.

89. *LI*, Mar. 24, June 26, 1903.

90. *LI*, Jan. 17, 24, Feb. 2, 1903.

91. *LI*, Jan. 27, Feb. 10, 12, 14, 24, 1903; *HG*, Jan. 26, 29, 1903.

92. *LI*, Jan. 27, Feb. 10, 12, 14, 1903.

93. *LI*, Feb. 12, 1903.

94. *BG*, Jan. 25, 1903. Mary P. Gardner, but not Mary Nason, was subsequently included in the injunction issued by the Essex County Superior Court in the 1895 Haverhill strike, but she had not been named in the original injunction petition.

95. *LI*, Jan. 28, 1903.

96. *LI*, Feb. 21, 1903.

97. *LI*, Feb. 12, 17, 20, 27, Mar. 13, 14, 1903.

98. On eggings, *LI*, Feb. 11, 12, 13, 14, 15, 24, Mar. 13, 14, 1903; on the use of asafetida, Feb. 27, 1903.

99. *LI*, Mar. 5, 14, 1903.

100. *LI*, Feb. 24, 1903.

101. *LI*, Feb. 21, 24, Mar. 14, 19, Aug. 13, 1903.

102. *LI*, Feb. 16, 21, 24, Mar. 2, 3, 5, 14, 19, Apr. 18, Aug. 1, 1903. Despite the failure of the Boston stitching shop, Arthur L. Ordway, a Haverhill shoeworker, sought an injunction to prevent the BSWU from spending sick and death benefits to break the strike. The petition was denied; *LI*, Apr. 2, June 12, 1903. In some ways, the Lynn strike of 1903 anticipated the "new unionism" analyzed by David Montgomery in its mass demonstrations of hostility against a union label organization in the AFL; *Workers' Control*, pp. 91–93.

103. *LI*, Apr. 22, May 11, June 12, 19, 23, 26, 30, 1903; *HG*, May 29, 1903.

104. *Shoe Workers' Journal*, Oct. 9, 1903; *LI*, Sept. 26, 28, 29, Oct. 6, 7, 8, 12, 15, 17, 1903. Wetherell's short publication *After the Battle; or, A Lesson from the Lynn Strike by a Fellow Worker* (1903) on the causes of the 1903 strike attributed it to natural laws governing the system of production and consumption (pp. 8–12), which she believed would evolve in time to a higher and more just form. She had been influenced by the Christian socialism of Herbert N. Casson of the Lynn Labor Church.

On Casson see Leslie Wharton, "Herbert N. Casson and the American Labor Church, 1893–1898," *Essex Institute Historical Collections* 117 (Apr. 1981), pp. 119–37.

105. *LI*, Nov. 11, 17, 18, 1903; Feb. 12, 1904.

106. Nancy Schrom Dye, *As Equals and As Sisters: Feminism, Unionism and the Women's Trade Union League of New York*, (Columbia: University of Missouri Press, 1980), pp. 6, 8. On Mary (Mamie) Donovan, see Allen F. Davis, "The Women's Trade Union League: Origins and Organization," *Labor History* 5 (1964), p. 11; and *LI*, Sept. 29, 1903. For the origins of the WTUL and its shift from organizational work to protective legislation, see Foner, *Women* 1, pp. 298–302. In 1903, Mary Kenney O'Sullivan was widowed and became for a short time a labor reporter for the *BG*; Foner, *Women* 1, pp. 298, 311.

107. Rosalyn L. Feldberg, " 'Union Fever': Organizing among Clerical Workers, 1900–1930," *Radical America* 14 (May–June 1980), pp. 60–64. James J. Kenneally regarded the AFL as "victimized" by its limited view of women workers; "Women and Trade Unions, 1870–1920: The Quandary of the Reformer," *Labor History* 14 (Winter 1973), pp. 42–55.

108. The minutes record no participation by Emma Steghagen on this issue. "Minutes of the General Executive Board, Jan. 12, 1904," Actions and Decisions, 1895–1906, BSWU papers.

109. Thomas L. Norton, *Trade Union Policies*, pp. 115–28; Davis, *Shoes*, pp. 181–82; Cumbler, *Working-Class Community*, pp. 81–87. Cumbler saw the strike in 1903 as limited to the community of Lynn and as an expression of local class consciousness. *LPS*, Apr. 29, 1909; *LI*, Jan. 2, 1904; File on History of the Controversy between St. Louis locals, 1903, BSWU papers. For the attempt by the United Shoeworkers' Union to organize nationally, see Laslett, *Labor and the Left*, pp. 84–88.

110. *LI*, Aug. 22, Sept. 7, 12, 13, Nov. 27, 1907; Jan. 30, Feb. 26, 1908; WEIU, *Boot and Shoe Industry*, 1915), p. 100 (BSWU in Lynn in 1911); Leo Wolman, *The Growth of American Trade Unions, 1880–1923* (New York: National Bureau of Economic Research, 1924), p. 139. In 1933 the BSWU was finally forced out of Brockton by dissatisfied shoeworkers; Davis, *Shoes*, pp. 169–178.

111. Alice Kessler-Harris, "Where Are the Organized Women Workers," *Feminist Studies* 3 (Fall 1975), pp. 92–110. Andrews and Bliss's study of women in local trade unions in 1908–9 rated the organization of women shoeworkers as relatively low. Garment workers, textile workers, and bookbinders were significantly better organized; *History of Women*, pp. 136–39. Whether the United Shoeworkers, the SWPU or the Knights of Labor organizations were included in their figures is not clear. Women's involvement in the BSWU was regarded as limited and with little weight in

policy-making. Only the stitchers' local of Brockton remained controlled by women workers; Davis, *Shoes*, pp. 173–74. Although highly critical of localism and "craft jealousy" in Lynn and Haverhill (pp. 164, 166, 188–89), Horace Davis concluded in 1940 that the independent unions in Essex County had since 1895 contributed more to unionism in the shoe industry, and especially to rank and file democracy, than the BSWU.

112. On the scarcity of stitchers, see *BSR*, Feb. 8, 1893, p. 85; Mar. 9, 1898, p. 103; Appendix B.

113. WEIU, *Boot and Shoe Industry*, p. 103; Allen, *Shoe Industry*, pp. 172–75.

114. WEIU, *Boot and Shoe Industry*, p. 94. Protective legislation had a different effect on the textile industry, where the work was less defined through a sexual division of labor. The impact of the fifty-four hour law for women and children in 1912 changed the work schedules of both men and women. The refusal of the textile manufacturers in Lawrence and Lowell to maintain wages produced successful strikes by textile workers led by the Industrial Workers of the World to restore wage cuts; Melvin Dubofsky, *We Shall Be All: A History of the Industrial Workers of the World* (Chicago: Quadrangle, 1969), pp. 227–62; and Mary Mulligan, "Epilogue to Lawrence: The 1912 Strike in Lowell, Massachusetts," in *Surviving Hard Times: The Working People of Lowell*, ed. Mary H. Blewett (Lowell: Lowell Museum, 1982), pp. 79–103. Middle-class women reformers at Hull House successfully lobbied in 1893 for legislation mandating an eight-hour day in the highly seasonal garment-making industry. The legislation did not directly affect shoe production in Chicago, but eliminated work in sweatshops, where women and children predominated as workers, and increased the number of garment workers in factories, where men prevailed; Kathryn Kish Sklar, "Hull House in the 1890s: A Community of Women Reformers," *Signs* 10 (Summer 1985), pp. 658–77.

115. *BSR*, Mar. 18, 1903, p. 103; Thomas Norton, *Trade Union Policies*, pp. 34–40; *BSR*, Oct. 9, 1920, p. 51; Nov. 20, 1920, p. 60.

Bibliography of Primary and Unpublished Sources

Account Books

Adam, Jacob. Account book, Newbury, 1673–93, Baker Library, Harvard University, Cambridge, Massachusetts.

Anonymous. Daybook, Lynn, 1825–27, Old Sturbridge Village, Sturbridge, Massachusetts.

Bacheller, Samuel. Papers, Lynn, 1795–1845, Old Sturbridge Village, Sturbridge, Massachusetts.

Boyce, Jonathan. Account book, Lynn, 1793–1813, Lynn Historical Society, Lynn, Massachusetts.

Breed, Aaron. Account book, Lynn, 1805–17, Lynn Historical Society, Lynn, Massachusetts.

Breed, Amos. Account book, Lynn, 1763–81, Lynn Historical Society, Lynn, Massachusetts.

Brown, James. Account book, Newbury, 1759–89, Haverhill Public Library, Haverhill, Massachusetts.

Brown, Robert. Account book, West Newburyport, 1813–28, Old Sturbridge Village, Sturbridge, Massachusetts.

Buffum, Israel. Account book, Lynn, 1806–47, Lynn Historical Society, Lynn, Massachusetts.

Burrill, John. Ledger, Lynn, 1819–20, Lynn Historical Society, Lynn, Massachusetts.

Chapman, Jeremiah. Accounts, Danvers, 1839–49, Essex Institute, Salem, Massachusetts.

Coburn, James. Account book, Boxford, 1804–21, Old Sturbridge Village, Sturbridge, Massachusetts.

Dole, Stephen. Accounts, Newbury, 1738–90, Old Sturbridge Village, Sturbridge, Massachusetts.

Duren, Samuel R., and Duren Family. Accounts, Woburn and Lexington, 1814–69, Baker Library, Harvard University, Cambridge, Massachusetts.

Eames, Caleb. Account book, Wilmington, 1819–25, Old Sturbridge Village, Sturbridge, Massachusetts.

Fuller, Brown, and Alley. Daybook, Lynn, 1812–13, Lynn Historical Society, Lynn, Massachusetts.

Gage, Bartlett. Accounts, Haverhill, 1829–34, Haverhill Public Library, Haverhill, Massachusetts.

Goodwin, John. Account book, Reading, 1810–34, Collection of Mrs. C. Nelson Bishop, Reading, Massachusetts.

Gould, Andrew. Accounts, Topsfield, 1859–60, Essex Institute, Salem, Massachusetts.

Hutchinson Family. Accounts, Danvers, 1801–60, Essex Institute, Salem, Massachusetts.

Marsh, Deacon David. Accounts, Haverhill, 1721–37, Haverhill Public Library, Haverhill, Massachusetts.

Marsh, David, Jr. Accounts, Haverhill, 1791–1812, Haverhill Public Library, Haverhill, Massachusetts.

Poor, Edward. Accounts, Georgetown, 1828–69, Essex Institute, Salem, Massachusetts.

Porter, Benjamin. Accounts, Danvers, 1765–83, Essex Institute, Salem, Massachusetts.

Porter, Zerubabel. Accounts, Danvers, 1765–1850, Danvers Archival Center, Danvers, Massachusetts.

Preston, John and Charles P. Accounts, Danvers, 1815–45, Essex Institute, Salem, Massachusetts.

Rea, Anna. Accounts, Topsfield, 1814–40, Museum of American Textile History, North Andover, Massachusetts.

Richardson, William. Papers, Stoneham, 1811–39, Baker Library, Harvard University, Cambridge, Massachusetts.

Robinson, Christopher. Ledger, Lynn, 1848–53, Lynn Historical Society, Lynn, Massachusetts.

Tappan, John. Accounts, Bradford, 1827–43, Haverhill Public Library, Haverhill, Massachusetts.

Unidentified shoe manufacturer. Stock book, Lynn, 1830–31, Lynn Historical Society, Lynn, Massachusetts.

Unknown shoemaker. Accounts, environs of Newbury, 1837–38, Essex Institute, Salem, Massachusetts.

Untitled ledger. Lynn, 1790–1824, Lynn Historical Society, Lynn, Massachusetts.

Whittaker, Sarah (Sally). Ledger, Haverhill, 1815–41, Haverhill Public Library, Haverhill, Massachusetts.

Woodman and George. Ledger, Haverhill, 1841–44, Haverhill Public Library, Haverhill, Massachusetts.

Personal Diaries, Reminiscences, and Letters

Appleton, Ann Swett. Letters, 1847–50, Museum of American Textile History, North Andover, Massachusetts.

Barrett, Martha Osbourne. Diaries, Salem, 1848–79, Essex Institute, Salem, Massachusetts.

Knowlton, Irena M. Diaries, Hamilton, 1879–86, Essex Institute, Salem, Massachusetts.

Lye, Joseph P., Jr. Journals, Lynn, 1819–30, Lynn Historical Society, Lynn, Massachusetts.

Lynn Female Anti-Slavery Society. "Minutes," 1836–38, Lynn Historical Society, Lynn, Massachusetts.

Merrill, Isaac W. Diaries, Haverhill, 1828–78, Haverhill Public Library, Haverhill, Massachusetts.

O'Sullivan, Mary Kenney. "Autobiography," Schlesinger Library, Radcliffe College, Cambridge, Massachusetts.

Swett, Philip C. "History of Shoemaking in Haverhill, Massachusetts," Haverhill Public Library, Haverhill.

Trask, Sarah E. Diaries, Beverly, 1849–51, Beverly Historical Society, Beverly, Massachusetts.

Turner, James H. "Memories of Haverhill," Collection of newspaper clippings (1895–1902), Haverhill Public Library, Haverhill, Massachusetts.

Selected Newspapers and Trade Journals

American Workman (Boston). 1869–71.

Awl (Lynn). 1844–45.

Boot and Shoe Recorder (New York). 1888–1920.

Boot and Shoe Workers' Union. *Proceedings of the Annual Conventions.* 1895–1902, Johns Hopkins University, Baltimore, Maryland.

Boot and Shoe Workers' Union. *Shoe Workers' Journal.* 1902–03.

Boot and Shoe Workers' Union. Papers, 1895–1912, Wisconsin State Historical Society, Madison.

Knight of Labor (Lynn). 1885–86.

Knights of Labor. *The General Proceedings of the Knights of Labor Conventions.* 1878–89, Wisconsin State Historical Society, Madison; and Sophia Smith Collection, Smith College, Northampton, Massachusetts.

Knights of St. Crispin. *Proceedings.* 1869–72, Wisconsin State Historical Society, Madison.

Laborer (Haverhill). 1884–87.

Labor Leader (Boston). 1887–97.

Little Giant (Lynn). 1870–72.
Lynn Bee. 1887–91.
Lynn Record. 1872–81.
New England Mechanic (Lynn). 1858–59.
Shoe and Leather Record (Boston). 1870–75, Baker Library, Harvard University, Cambridge, Massachusetts.
Shoe and Leather Reporter (New York). 1860–1900.
Shoe and Leather Review (Chicago). 1888–92.
Vindicator (Lynn). 1876–79.
Workingman's Advocate (Chicago). 1868–71.

Public Documents

Annual Report of the Board of Health of Lynn (Boston, 1850).
Commonwealth of Massachusetts. *Statistical Information Relating to Certain Branches of Industry in Massachusetts for the Year*, 1837, 1845, 1855, 1865, Boston.
Massachusetts Bureau of Labor Statistics, *Annual Reports; Second*, 1870–71; *Third*, 1872; *Fourth*, 1873; *Sixth*, 1875; *Tenth*, 1879; *Sixteenth*, 1885; Boston.
Massachusetts, *Census of the Commonwealth of Massachusetts*, 1865–1915, Boston.
Massachusetts, "Social Statistics of Workingwomen," *Massachusetts Labor Bulletin*, May 1901, pp. 29–49.
Massachusetts, State Board of Arbitration, Applications and Hearings, Massachusetts State Archives, Boston.
McLane Report. See "U.S., Secretary of the Treasury."
U.S., Bureau of the Census, *Manufacturers, 1905*, part 3 of *Special Reports on Selected Industries*, (Washington, D.C., 1908).
U.S., Bureau of the Census, *Report on Manufactures of the United States, 1880*, (Washington, D.C., 1883).
U.S., Census of Manufacture, Manuscripts for Lynn, 1850, 1860, 1870; and for Haverhill, Danvers, Marblehead, 1860, 1870. Washington, D.C.
U.S., Census of Population, Manuscripts for Lynn, 1860, 1870, 1880, 1900, 1910; for Haverhill, 1860, 1900; for Marblehead, 1860; and for Stoneham, 1870. Washington, D.C.
U.S., Immigration Commission, *Boot and Shoe Manufacturing*, part 9 of *Immigrants in Industries* (Washington, D.C., 1911).
U.S., Secretary of the Treasury. *Documents Relating to the Manufacturers in the United States, 1832*, 2 vols. [The McLane Report] 1832. reprint. New York: Burt Franklin, 1969.

Wolman, Leo. "Wages and Hours of Labor in the Boot and Shoe and Hosiery and Knitgoods Industries, 1890–1912," *United States Bureau of Labor Statistics Bulletin*, Aug. 26, 1913, pp. 5–69.

Women's Educational and Industrial Union, *The Boot and Shoe Industry as a Vocation for Women*, vol. 6, U.S. Department of Labor, Bureau of Labor Statistics, *Studies in Economic Relations of Women* (Washington, D.C., 1915).

Unpublished Sources

Cole, Arthur H. "The Boot and Shoe Industry of Haverhill, Massachusetts." Thesis in Economics, Harvard University, 1911.

Gerstle, Gary. "Socialism in Haverhill, 1895–1900: A New Look." Paper, 1977, in the author's possession.

Hall, John Philip. "The Gentle Craft: A Narrative of Yankee Shoemakers." Ph.D. dissertation, Columbia University, 1954.

Mulligan, William H., Jr. "The Family and Technological Change: The Shoemakers of Lynn, Massachusetts, during the Transition from Hand to Machine Production, 1850–1880." Ph.D. dissertation, Clark University, 1982.

"Putnamville and the Early Shoe Manufacturers in Danvers." Lecture based on the Porter Family accounts (1773–1850), Dec. 1905, Danvers Archival Center, Danvers, Massachusetts.

Swett, Philip C. "History of Shoemaking in Haverhill, Massachusetts." Paper, n.d., Haverhill Public Library, Haverhill, Massachusetts.

Thomson, Ross David. "The Origins of Modern Industry in the United States: The Mechanization of Shoe and Sewing Machine Production." Ph.D. dissertation in Economics, Yale University, 1976.

Turbin, Carole. "Daughters, Wives, Widows: Family Relations and Women's Labor Organizing in a Mid-19th Century Working Class Community." Paper, n.d., in the author's possession.

Index

Note on the Author

Mary H. Blewett is professor of history at the University of Lowell in Massachusetts, where she has taught since 1965. Before developing an interest in social history, she wrote her dissertation directed by Richard Kirkendall at the University of Missouri–Columbia on the transition between the Roosevelt and Truman administrations. She won the Berkshire Conference Prize in 1983 for her article "Work, Gender, and the Artisan Tradition in New England Shoemaking, 1780–1860," published in the *Journal of Social History*, to be reprinted in a twenty-fifth anniversary retrospective on the journal. She has been involved in the development of the Lowell National Historical Park, has edited the diary of a Lowell mill girl and a community history on Lowell mill workers since the Civil War, and has written on the impact of the new social history on exhibit interpretation at New England textile museums.

Books in the Series
The Working Class in American History

Worker City, Company Town:
Iron and Cotton-Worker Protest in Troy
and Cohoes, New York, 1855–84
Daniel J. Walkowitz

Life, Work, and Rebellion in the Coal Fields:
The Southern West Virginia Miners, 1880–1922
David Alan Corbin

Women and American Socialism, 1870–1920
Mari Jo Buhle

Lives of Their Own:
Blacks, Italians, and Poles in Pittsburgh, 1900–1960
John Bodnar, Roger Simon, and Michael P. Weber

Working-Class America:
Essays on Labor, Community, and American Society
Edited by Michael H. Frisch and Daniel J. Walkowitz

Eugene V. Debs:
Citizen and Socialist
Nick Salvatore

American Labor and Immigration History; 1877–1920s:
Recent European Research
Edited by Dirk Hoerder

Workingmen's Democracy:
The Knights of Labor and American Politics
Leon Fink

The Electrical Workers:
A History of Labor at General Electric
and Westinghouse, 1923–60
Ronald W. Schatz

The Mechanics of Baltimore:
Workers and Politics in the Age of Revolution, 1763–1812
Charles G. Steffen

The Practice of Solidarity:
American Hat Finishers in the Nineteenth Century
David Bensman

The Labor History Reader
Edited by Daniel J. Leab

Solidarity and Fragmentation:
Working People and Class Consciousness in Detroit, 1875–1900
Richard Oestreicher

Counter Cultures:
Saleswomen, Managers, and Customers
in American Department Stores, 1890–1940
Susan Porter Benson

The New England Working Class and the New Labor History
Edited by Herbert G. Gutman and Donald H. Bell

Labor Leaders in America
Edited by Melvyn Dubofsky and Warren Van Tine

Barons of Labor:
The San Francisco Building Trades
and Union Power in the Progressive Era
Michael Kazin

Gender at Work:
The Dynamics of Job Segregation by Sex during World War II
Ruth Milkman

Once a Cigar Maker:
Men, Women, and Work Culture in American
Cigar Factories, 1900–1919
Patricia A. Cooper

A Generation of Boomers:
The Pattern of Railroad Labor Conflict
in Nineteenth-Century America
Shelton Stromquist

Work and Community in the Jungle:
Chicago's Packinghouse Workers, 1894–1922
James R. Barrett

Workers, Managers, and Welfare Capitalism:
The Shoeworkers and
Tanners of Endicott Johnson, 1890–1950
Gerald Zahavi

Men, Women, and Work:
Class, Gender, and Protest
in the New England Shoe Industry, 1780–1910
Mary Blewett